e·Business

A Canadian Perspective for a Networked World

Second Edition

Gerald Trites
St. Francis Xavier University

J. Efrim Boritz
University of Waterloo

David Pugsley
Cavendish Farms

PEARSON

Prentice
Hall

Toronto

Library and Archives Canada Cataloguing in Publication

Trites, Gerald
E-business : a Canadian perspective for a networked
world / Gerald Trites, J. Efrim Boritz, David Pugsley.—2nd ed.

Includes index.
ISBN 0-13-127179-2

1. Electronic commerce—Management. I. Boritz, Jefim Efrim, 1950– II. Pugsley, David, 1973–
III. Title.

HF5548.32.T748 2006   658'.054678   C2004-906444-4

0-13-127179-2

Vice President, Editorial Director: Michael J. Young
Editor in Chief, Business & Economics: Gary Bennett
Executive Marketing Manager: Cas Shields
Senior Media Editor: Toni Chahley
Production Editor: Jennifer Handel
Copy Editor: Cat Haggert
Proofreader: Tally Morgan
Production Coordinator: Deborah Starks
Manufacturing Coordinator: Susan Johnson
Page Layout: Carolyn E. Sebestyen
Art Director: Julia Hall
Interior and Cover Design: Miguel Acevedo
Cover Image: Getty Images/Taxi/Stephen Simpson

1 2 3 4 5   10 09 08 07 06

Printed and bound in the United States of America.

To Sue, with love

—GDT

To the ever patient Naomi

—JEB

Contents

Preface

Although e-business is a global phenomenon, Canadian businesses face legal and cultural issues that are unique to this country. *E-Business: A Canadian Perspective for a Networked World* is the first text to address e-business in a Canadian context.

E-Business: A Canadian Perspective for a Networked World is not simply a printed textbook. It is a combined textbook/website that reflects a Canadian perspective on the growing and exciting field of e-business. Although only a few years old, e-business has already been accepted by a wide variety of business and educational professionals as one of the most significant events to have taken place in business and in the wider world for several hundred years. Educational institutions are developing new courses, programs, and research efforts in an attempt to embrace this area.

The essential rationale of this combined textbook/website is to provide a dual vehicle for educational delivery—a core textbook and a dynamic website. The two interact with each other to deliver both the core concepts of e-business and recent developments that impact its evolution. The textbook sets out the concepts that guide e-business, and deals fully with the business strategies and models that have emerged. The website extends these core areas to deal with new developments and emerging trends. Linking textbooks to websites is an innovation inspired by the internet revolution that has been adopted by many authors, but this textbook/website has a much more tightly knit and dynamic relationship than is the norm.

There is absolutely no doubt that e-business is quickly changing and evolving. Conventional textbooks alone cannot fill the need to reflect current events in e-business courses. The motivation behind this project is to provide a dynamic tool for teaching e-business.

We have also provided a Canadian perspective, which we believe is important for Canadian students, despite the fact that e-business is often considered as an international or global phenomenon. While e-business is international, at least to the extent that various parts of the world have technologies and infrastructures that can support e-business, there are distinctly Canadian elements and issues that Canadian students need to learn. In addition, students can relate more closely to cases and examples that are Canadian.

Our legal structures and new statutes such as the Personal Information Protection and Electronic Documents Act (PIPEDA) are central to the Canadian experience with e-business. They are influenced by the activities of the Canadian government in establishing infrastructure, such as the Strategis initiatives of Industry Canada and the digitization of Canada Post. E-business in Canada is also influenced by the activities of Canadian business enterprises, such as the very successful BlackBerry, developed by Research In Motion of Waterloo, Ontario; ventures of Rogers Cablesystems and others into Web TV; the movement of the banks into virtual banking; and the Canadian capitalists that experienced the rise and subsequent decline of dot-coms in Canada. Books that are not Canadian simply do not discuss these important aspects of Canadian e-business.

The Combined Text/Website Approach

The textbook is similar to most textbooks in content in that it includes chapters that fully cover the major elements of e-business and case studies. This offers the instructor greater flexibility in crafting course curricula. The book addresses major contemporary trends that have emerged so far, such as integrated enterprise systems, collaborative commerce, mobile wireless systems e-procurement, and customer relationship management. Where it differs from other conventional textbooks is in the extent to which it interfaces with the website.

While the emphasis of the textbook is on the macro issues—those that change less frequently—the emphasis of the website is on the micro issues that are in a constant state of flux. Accordingly, the website presents new case studies, exercises, and problems based on current events. Presentation/discussion materials on new developments are added during the year and tied into the textbook, so that any course can easily encompass them and remain current.

Combined Text/Website Approach

textbook

PART I E-Business Models and Strategy

PART II E-Business Architecture

PART III E-Business Applications

PART IV Conducting E-Business

Online Study Guide

Updates and Additions to the Text

Additional Topics in E-Business

New Developments in E-Business

website

Organization of the Text

The book is divided into four parts comprising 14 chapters, an appendix of cases, and a glossary.

Part I E-Business Models and Strategies

This part places electronic business into an entire business perspective beginning with an introductory chapter (chapter 1) aimed at discussing some of the basics of e-business. It then addresses strategic planning and business models (chapter 2) to ensure that a business mindset is maintained throughout the book.

A new Running Case Study featuring eBay has been included at the end of each part of the text. This case study has been designed to fit this book, with each part related to the major themes in each of the sections. This section includes part 1 of the eBay case with its focus on eBay's e-business strategy, its business model, and its value propositions.

Part II E-Business Architecture

This part reviews the architecture of e-business and explores the impacts on business and management of required technologies such as the internet, intranets, and extranets (chapter 3), enterprise-wide and inter-enterprise systems (chapter 4), security and controls (chapter 5), and billing and payment systems (chapter 6). This section includes part 2 of the eBay case with its focus on eBay's PayPal e-payment system.

Part III E-Business Applications

Starting with supply chain management (chapter 7), this part examines some of the crucial technologies in e-business such as e-procurement, trading exchanges, and auctions (chapter 8), customer relationship management (chapter 9) and business intelligence (chapter 10). It concludes with part 3 of the eBay case, addressing eBay's role in supply chain management.

Part IV Conducting E-Business

This part explores the materials needed to integrate the operation of e-business within the broader business context, including marketing issues (chapter 11), metrics for e-business performance measurement (chapter 12), legal, regulatory, and taxation issues (chapter 13), and small business operations (chapter 14). Part 4 of the running case on eBay, featuring privacy issues, concludes this section.

New to This Edition

In addition to a thorough review and update of the entire text, the following changes have been made to this edition:

- Chapter 1, the introductory chapter, has been reorganized and revised to provide more complete coverage of e-business and to reflect a consistent and comprehensive pedagogy.
- The E-Strategy, New Business Models, Canadian Snapshots, and E-Business in Global Perspective boxes have all been reviewed and updated. Many new ones have been added throughout the book.
- The discussion of strategies and models in chapter 2 has been substantially rewritten and improved to reflect a stronger grounding in contemporary research.
- A new chapter on e-business metrics (chapter 12, "Metrics for Performance Measurement in E-Commerce") has been added to the book.

- A new case on Intel has been added to the book. Other cases have been updated and reorganized: the Sears case from the previous edition's website has been updated and moved into the text, while the cases on Chapters and Starbucks have been updated and moved to the website.

- A new multi-themed Running Case Study on eBay that explores different aspects of e-business following key themes in each part has been added to the text. This case provides a teaching tool that enables the concepts in each of the parts of the book to be highlighted and taught in a linked fashion using actual industry examples.

- New material has been added to reflect the increased importance of PayPal in the area of internet payment systems.

Features of the Text

A special effort has been made with this book to incorporate features that will facilitate learning and enhance an understanding of e-business.

- **E-Business Mind Maps** at the beginning of each chapter provide students with a visual overview of the organization of the text, and show where each chapter fits into the dynamic of e-business as a whole. The mind map illustrates the dynamic relationship between the foundation of e-business (models and strategies), the tools of e-business (architecture), how these tools are used (application), and the environment in which they are used (conducting e-business).

- **Learning Objectives** at the beginning of each chapter summarize the skills and knowledge to be learned in that chapter.

- **Chapter Introductions** provide an overview of the material discussed in each chapter.

- **Key Terms** are boldfaced in the text, defined in the margin of the text, and listed at the end of each chapter. For easy reference, all the key terms and their definitions are collated in a glossary at the end of the text.

- **Weblink Icons** appear in the margin, providing URLs for the companies discussed in the text.

- **E-Strategy Boxes** emphasize the importance of the strategic employment of e-business.

- **New Business Models Boxes** highlight how technology has impacted business models and illustrate how rapid changes in e-business require that business models be flexible and adaptable to remain competitive.

- **Canadian Snapshots Boxes** highlight Canadian businesses to demonstrate how competition and the Canadian marketplace are changing. These boxes demonstrate how e-businesses have developed within the Canadian context and some of the difficulties they have faced.

- **E-Business in Global Perspective Boxes** address global issues and opportunities in e-business. These boxes provide examples of either international companies or companies competing globally, and discuss issues of technology related to the management of e-business.
- **Chapter Summaries** recap the issues discussed in the chapter.

- **Tools for Online Learning Boxes** direct students to our website for self-testing material, updates to the text, streaming CBC videos and accompanying cases, and up-to-date information on new developments in e-business.
- **eBay Running Case Study** addresses particular issues found in eBay that are covered in each of the four parts of the text.
- **Appendix of Cases** includes five decision-based case studies with discussion questions to be used in the classroom or for assignments. These cases provide a mechanism for many of the topics in the text to be applied to current and interesting situations facing e-business managers today. Additional cases are available on the website.

Organization of the Website

While the textbook provides students with a core resource for their studies, the website ensures that the text content is up to date and integrated with the internet for improved learning. The website also provides additional material that complements the text so that instructors and students interested in a particular area may expand the learning experience related to particular topics of interest.

For this new edition, students and instructors will find the following features organized by chapter:

- Learning Objectives
- Self-Test Questions (provide students with immediate feedback)
- Internet Exercises
- Review Questions and Exercises
- Problems for Discussion
- Chapter Summaries
- Weblinks
- Key Terms and Definitions
- CBC Videos and Cases
- Additional Topics in E-Business

Course Design

A major purpose of this text is to facilitate a dynamic course design. The topic is so fast-moving that from the time of course design to delivery there are often significant changes. While the course design can focus on the textbook as a core, the use of the website can vary to reflect current needs.

This text/website is intended primarily for undergraduate courses or first courses in e-business at the Master's level. Essentially, it is for survey courses provided to students who have minimal previous exposure to the subject. There is sufficient material to support a one-semester course.

Potential course designs can include:

1. A chapter-by-chapter, textbook-driven course, with occasional references to the website, lectures, and discussion of problems in class;

2. A topic-driven course, with blended use of the text and the website materials, lectures, and discussion of problems in class;

3. A case-driven seminar course, focusing on particular topics;

4. A web survey that is directed by the organization of the course, but with an emphasis on selected websites.

Accordingly, the text/website can be used to support conventional, lecture-/discussion-based courses as well as seminars using cases and/or web materials.

The authors have found that for undergraduates, a combined lecture- (maximum half-hour) and discussion-based course (with a variety of other tools) provides the best approach for engaging students. Some classes can focus on problems, others on cases, and others on website materials. Of course, combinations of these resources can be used in many classes.

The result is that the resource offers a variety of potential course designs and considerable flexibility in their delivery.

Supplements

The following supplements have been carefully prepared to accompany this new edition:

- *Instructor's Resource CD-ROM:* This resource CD includes the following instructor supplements:

  - **Instructor's Manual:** This manual includes additional background material for cases and exercises as well as a solutions manual.

  - **Test Item File:** This test item file contains over 300 test questions, organized by chapter, with the level of difficulty (i.e., easy, moderate, or difficult) indicated for each question. The test item file has been revised and updated. In addition, the solutions have been carefully reviewed for accuracy.

  - **PowerPoints:** PowerPoint presentations consist of customizable slides for lectures. The slides have been revised and improved both visually and from a content viewpoint.

    Most of these instructor supplements are also available for download from a password-protected section of Pearson Education Canada's online catalogue (vig.pearsoned.ca). Navigate to your book's catalogue page to view a list of available supplements. See your local sales representative for details and access.

- *CBC/Pearson Education Canada Video Library for E-Business:* This video library is a special compilation of video segments from news magazines of the Canadian Broadcasting Corporation. Each video segment has been carefully selected to illustrate topics relevant to e-business. These video segments are accompanied by case studies on the website, and can be viewed online.

Pearson Advantage. For qualified adopters, Pearson Education is proud to introduce the **Pearson Advantage**. The Pearson Advantage is the first integrated Canadian service program committed to meeting the customization, training, and support needs for your course. Our commitments are made in writing and in consultation with faculty. Your local Pearson Education sales representative can provide you with more details on this service program.

Innovative Solutions Team. Pearson's Innovative Solutions Team works with faculty and campus course designers to ensure that Pearson technology products, assessment tools, and online course materials are tailored to meet your specific needs. This highly qualified team is dedicated to helping schools take full advantage of a wide range of educational technology by assisting in the integration of a variety of instructional materials and media formats.

Acknowledgments

We wish to acknowledge the help of many people during the preparation of this work. In particular, we wish to thank our colleagues at the Gerald Schwartz School of Business and Information Systems at St. Francis Xavier University and the Centre for Business, Entrepreneurship and Technology at the University of Waterloo for their advice and support. We also wish to express a hearty thank you to our developmental editor, Toni Chahley, for her cheerful and always helpful prompting and encouragement. We also express our gratitude to the other tremendous Pearson staff who helped us, including James Bosma, Cas Shields, Meaghan Eley, Jen Handel, Cat Haggert, Susan Wallace-Cox, Miguel Acevedo, Deborah Starks, Robin Blair, Laura Canning, Bhavin Desai, and Larry Sulky. We would also like to thank our students who have provided us with a great deal of feedback in our courses and assisted in the development of case studies and supporting materials. Among our students, we owe a particular debt of gratitude to Raghavan Damodaran and Christian Schmuck. We would also like to thank Carla Carnaghan (University of Waterloo), Darren Charters (University of Waterloo), and Elliott Gold (Ridout & Maybee, LLP Toronto) for their reviews and invaluable comments.

Finally, and certainly no less importantly, we wish to thank the people who took the time to review and provide commentary on various chapters:

Devi Ambati (Durham College)

Kimberley Facette (Algonquin College)

Craig Fleisher (University of Windsor)

Kenneth Grant (Ryerson University)

Rebecca Grant (University of Victoria)

Catherine Hajnal (Carleton University)

Peter Mombourquette (Mount Saint Vincent University)

Franklyn Prescod (Ryerson University)

Sheilagh Seaton (Okanagan University College)

Ken Sekhon (Camosun College)

Kit Wilson (Red River College)

Gerald Trites, Gerald Schwartz School of Business and Information Systems, St. Francis Xavier University

J. Efrim Boritz, Centre for Business, Entrepreneurship and Technology, University of Waterloo

David Pugsley
Cavendish Farms

Introduction to E-Business

LEARNING OBJECTIVES

When you complete this chapter you should be able to:

1. Define e-business.

2. Identify and explain the foundations of e-business.

3. Describe how e-business fits into the traditional business environment.

4. Identify and evaluate the major strategies followed by enterprises that adopt e-business.

5. Explain the benefits of e-business.

6. Discuss the challenges facing e-business and how they are being addressed.

Introduction

The reach of the **internet** into so many aspects of our lives is revolutionizing our world. What we have seen so far is only the beginning of a fundamental change that many people have compared to the Industrial Revolution in its scope and potential impact. New types of business have emerged that we wouldn't have thought of only a few years ago. Businesses that have been around for decades have found they need to use the internet to remain competitive. Ultimately, business and a great deal else in society will be changed forever.

During the early years of e-business, the media reported phenomenal success stories about the "new economy." With new dot-com companies opening daily, it seemed that upstart companies could launch directly into global markets through the internet and could raise billions on the stock markets with little or nothing in the way of hard assets. They made billionaires of their owners, many of whom had yet to see their thirtieth birthday. Stories abounded of Amazon.com, eBay, E*TRADE Financial, and Canadian phenomena like Research In Motion. The idea of being able to launch a successful business on the web without needing large amounts of capital to finance hard assets was an appealing one. The cost of entry seemed minimal; the rewards grand.

Reality presented a harsher picture. Amazon lost money until 2003 and even then profits were minimal (see the E-Strategy box). Research In Motion went through a reality check when tech stocks took a nosedive in 2000 and only recovered in 2003, and truly became a Canadian success story in 2004. The financial community and intelligent investors generally confirmed what they really knew all along:

1. A business still needs to make profits to survive and grow, and
2. Many of the traditional business fundamentals continue to make sense in this new electronic world, even though the specific business models are changing and evolving.

Some of the business models of the dot-com companies did not include any plans on how they would make money on a long-term basis. Napster, the original music sharing utility, was a case in point. The company offered the service free of charge to the users, and did not have any other plans, such as advertising, that would generate money to keep it going. Only after Napster had been in operation for some time, and had been challenged in the courts, did it begin to charge fees. It is quite possible that if the courts had not curtailed the company's activities, the original Napster would not have survived for economic reasons.

Increasingly, the mystique of the internet has faded and business is embracing it as a powerful and essential tool for achieving strategic goals and remaining competitive in the new economy.

The glitzy realm of "new economy" businesses represented by the dot-coms is only one part of the world of e-business. While the dot-coms lost some of their lustre they did not lose all of it, because there still are amazing successes happening. Also, large "old economy" companies have been moving heavily into e-business. One example is the adoption by banks of internet banking. Another example is the **trading exchange** Covisint (see the E-Business in Global Perspective box), launched by the automobile industry to streamline its sources of supply and make it more competitive, and since acquired by Compuware Corporation. Such business-to-business (B2B) activity represents by far the biggest part of e-business at this stage in its evolution, although business to consumer (B2C), business to government (B2G) and government to business (G2B) all are showing signs of

E-Strategy

Amazon.Com: Transforming E-Strategy—from Clicks to Bricks

Amazon.com was one of the first companies to sell books on the web. Certainly it was the most widely noticed of the internet start-ups and one that caused traditional bookstores like Barnes & Noble to also open websites to sell their product. Amazon started in 1995 with the idea it would be able to take orders over the web and fill them by ordering from suppliers as demand required. Part of the strategy was to be able to supply books without incurring the infrastructure costs that other businesses had to bear, therefore enabling the company to sell at lower prices.

The reality that emerged was that it took Amazon until 2003 to get out of a loss position and actually report a profit for the year. For a time, Amazon's shares rose despite its losses, but in 2000 the dot-com market corrected itself and Amazon's shares declined considerably. The shares of the company have since begun to recover.

The reason Amazon had trouble making money was that the company had to spend far more on marketing and infrastructure than it had foreseen. The marketing expenditure had been hard to predict because internet marketing was a new field. Infrastructure costs arose because Amazon found that it was having trouble delivering orders on a timely basis and eventually had to make the decision to develop some of its own warehousing and distribution infrastructure to address this issue. Amazon still relied heavily on order by demand, but began buffering this approach with some warehouse buying. Of course, that was completely contrary to the original strategy. To deal with the additional costs, the company had to implement a strategy that would generate higher revenues.

Over the past few years, Amazon has undergone a heavy expansion. The company has moved away from being solely a book seller to include numerous other products, like music, DVDs, and clothes. Much of this expansion was done though partnerships with other reputable companies such as Target or gourmet food company Dean & Deluca. In addition, the company expanded into international markets and entered the Canadian market in partnership with Canada Post. Amazon now offers eBay-style auctions and lets customers list their own items alongside its own. In response to the realities of the marketplace, Amazon transformed a clearly defined strategy of minimizing infrastructure costs to sell books at a lower price, to a strategy that incorporated increased infrastructure costs through warehousing and offered new product lines to pay for this expansion.

Adding new products and catering to new markets was a logical way for Amazon to make effective use of its expanded infrastructure. This evolution in strategy allowed Amazon to add to revenues with minimal incremental cost. It is a classic case of transforming internet business strategy.

Amazon.com
www.amazon.com

Questions

1. What are the challenges arising from Amazon's need to expand into new markets?
2. Has Amazon's fundamental business model changed significantly in its early years? Why or why not?

SOURCE: www.amazon.com.

impressive growth. In addition, there is a wide range of other activities, discussed more fully in chapter 2. These include business to employee (B2E), government to consumer (G2C), government to business (G2B), and numerous variations on this theme.

Another good example of an old "bricks" company moving to the internet is Sears Roebuck, which has been a major retailer for many years, but now has one of the top-rated e-business websites on the internet, grossing over US$18 billion

Sears
www.sears.com

per year. It has been making the transition to the world of e-business—from bricks to clicks—while still retaining its "bricks" presence.

E-Business in Global Perspective

Covisint and the Automotive Industry

Covisint was founded in February 2000 by leading car manufacturers, such as Ford and GM. It is a trading exchange for auto parts on the internet and was expected to process as much as US$750 billion in annual business when it matured. By mid-2000, more than 25 suppliers had signed on to Covisint, including some of the world's biggest auto parts suppliers. The automakers created the trading exchange to solidify their sources of supply and make them more competitive. As a joint venture between the large automakers and their suppliers, Covisint was initially intended to become the preferred method for suppliers to sell their products to the big manufacturers, but has since grown to encompass design and other areas to the point of providing a technological business infrastructure for the industry.

Part of the procurement process on Covisint works on an auctioning basis, where a manufacturer places an order on the exchange and suppliers bid on filling that order at a particular price and time.

The year it began, Covisint came under scrutiny by the U.S.

Federal Trade Commission and the antitrust divisions of the U.S. Department of Justice and the European Commission. These regulators feared that the major auto manufacturers would use the exchange to dictate pricing and purchasing practices suppliers must use, in effect using the exchange as a vehicle for fixing prices. Covisint executives maintained that the exchange would not violate antitrust laws because it is open to other manufacturers.

The regulators were concerned as to whether the exchange would be used to constrict the market by forcing the suppliers to do their business through the exchange as opposed to other means. There were reports that some of the employees of the big automakers indicated this to suppliers, but it is not clear that the companies actually followed this strategy.

Another issue of concern to regulators was whether the exchanges themselves could turn into monopolies. Theoretically, this could happen if buyers and sellers become interested in using only the biggest exchange(s) available. Part of their concern was that the

big buyers or suppliers that own exchanges could have access to information on deals that might give them an unfair trading advantage, but these concerns were subsequently cleared.

Although Covisint has widely been seen as a success, automakers are reluctant to give up their procurement departments and to use only the exchange for their procurement needs. Additionally, suppliers are somewhat hesitant about joining the exchange amid fears of giving up control over prices.

On March 1, 2004, Compuware Corporation completed its acquisition of the assets of Covisint from the automobile companies. Compuware has a large, well-established infrastructure with offices in 53 countries that serve more than 20 000 customers, including 90 percent of the Fortune 500 companies. Compuware wishes to extend the functionality of Covisint services through the use of its 2000 development programmers. Covisint customers often require development and operational support when implementing Covisint services but Covisint has traditionally outsourced this work to various third-parties.

Covisint
www.covisint.com

Questions

1. Why would suppliers register with Covisint? What would be the advantages to them?
2. Will the Compuware acquisition of Covisint make a difference to the success of Covisint?
3. What are the benefits of Covisint to the automobile industry?
4. Did the regulators have legitimate concerns initially? Why or why not?

SOURCE: www.covisint.com.

Small business also continues to enter into e-business activities, sometimes to use the internet for marketing and selling their products to customers and sometimes to take part in B2B activities, such as buying online. The involvement in e-business of small organizations presents a particular set of issues, which form the focus of chapter 12.

The global use of the internet has truly created a networked world, one that is transforming business. Canada is part of this networked world, and Canadian business is going global and using the latest in technology in the process. This book focuses on Canada's unique experience in the world of e-business and the new challenges, both domestic and international, that are being met.

What Is E-Business?

In a very broad and general sense, electronic business has often been defined as any business carried out in electronic form. Therefore, if business transactions are carried out by using **electronic data interchange (EDI)**, this is a form of e-business. If a bank transaction is carried out by electronic transfers between branches, this is a form of e-business. So under this definition, e-business has been in existence for a good many years—certainly years before the internet became an economic force.

ELECTRONIC DATA INTERCHANGE (EDI)
A structured way of creating electronic "forms" that can be transmitted between trading partners to execute business transactions without the need to generate any paper.

The growth of the internet created significant change, opening up new market channels and wider markets and forming the foundation of e-business as we know it. Initially, the use of the internet for selling goods and services was referred to as e-commerce. More recently, the term "e-business" has been used widely to reflect the fact that the effective delivery of e-commerce requires considerable organizational commitment and change. The term "e-business" therefore conveys a much broader meaning. This new meaning is illustrated by Kalakota and Robinson, who have stated, "e-business is the complex fusion of business processes, enterprise applications, and organizational structure necessary to create a high-performance business model."[1]

This definition of e-business connects the idea of business change and structure to the creation of business models that will sustain themselves. Under this definition, e-business relies on the whole business—how it is structured, what technology is being used, and how the business is carried out. Therefore a consideration of e-business extends well beyond the use of the internet, although the internet remains central. It extends into a range of management issues, from strategy to execution to supervision, and incorporates the strategic use of information technology to achieve corporate goals.

We have, however, adopted a definition which, while based on the Kalakota and Robinson definition, places a greater emphasis on the use of technology and particularly the internet. Accordingly, the definition of e-business used in this book is as follows:

> E-business is the strategic use of technology, particularly the internet, to integrate and streamline the business processes, enterprise applications, and organizational structure of a business and create a high-performance business model.

The Foundations of E-Business

E-Business Models

The internet and e-business are causing business model changes (for example, see the New Business Models box, which looks at how e-business has affected the business model of Encyclopædia Britannica). There are several features of internet-based business that have an impact on the business models adopted by businesses, including:

- speed
- convenience
- customization
- redefinition of product value
- media flexibility

Speed Certainly, the use of technology has changed the expectations of people regarding the time it takes to satisfy their needs. We can see this impact on society generally. In the early days of technology, there was a widespread thought that it would free up a great deal of time for people, that they would be able to reduce their workweeks and take long vacations. It hasn't worked out that way, and today we see people living frantic and rushed lives—in great measure a result of their ability to use technology to respond more quickly to people and then get on with the next activity on their list. People expect fast turnaround to their requests, especially where technology is involved.

This means that businesses need to construct their business models so that they can deliver their products or services quickly. It also means that if the competition implements new technology that results in faster delivery, they may well have a competitive advantage.

Convenience One of the reasons people use the internet is for convenience. When they log onto their bank's website, they can check their current balances without going to the bank branch and standing in line for a teller. They can pay their bills without having to write a cheque, stuff an envelope, and go to a mailbox to mail it. It's all about convenience. This fact has had a profound impact on the way in which banks offer their services to the public. Banks have reduced their branches, cut their staff, and set up more ATMs in partnership with retail outlets. Generally, it may be said they have been moving from "bricks to clicks." This has substantially changed their business models—by cutting their infrastructure costs, increasing their technology costs, adding new sources of revenue, and making old sources of revenue obsolete. As they find new ways to add convenience, their mix of old and new changes again, leading to modified business models.

Customization Somewhat related to the idea of convenience is the demand for customized products and services. The use of the internet together with integrated systems makes this possible or, to put it another way, is necessary to make it possible. **Integrated systems** are information systems that are joined together in such a way that they can easily share data between them. One of the leaders in the provision of customized product was Dell Computer Corp., which was the first major vendor to offer computers for purchase through its website. The distinguishing feature of Dell's site was that customers could select from various options for all components of the computer and build a computer that completely fit their needs. Since then, of course, other vendors have followed suit.

The Dell experience clearly demonstrates the impact of customization on business models. As a result of the customization, the company needed a radically different manufacturing and distribution model to enable it to build and deliver the product *after* it had been ordered—a very different activity from filling a retail outlet with inventory or selling to retailers so they could fill their stores with inventory *prior* to the customer buying the product.

INTEGRATED SYSTEMS
Information systems that are joined together in such a way that they can easily share data between them.

Dell Inc.
www.dell.com

New Business Models

Encyclopædia Britannica

Prior to the age of the internet, *Encyclopædia Britannica* was known widely as perhaps the world's premier encyclopedia. It was large (some 20 volumes), expensive, and aggressively sold door-to-door by its salespeople.

When technology began to creep into the encyclopedia business, Britannica's established business models came under pressure. The first technological change that affected it was the invention of the compact disk (CD), a storage medium that could contain billions of bytes. CDs offered a way to package an entire encyclopedia in a very compact format, had the capability to include video and sound, and—very important for a reference book—made it searchable. Another advantage of CD technology was that it was cheap to produce. There was no need for fancy books with expensive bindings.

Microsoft Corp. saw the advantages of this new opportunity

and produced its own encyclopedia in electronic form, *Encarta*, which enjoyed immediate success. *Encarta* was available for approximately US$250, while the *Britannica* print version sold for over US$1500. While *Encarta* arguably lacked the content of *Britannica*, the price difference was great enough to convince many buyers. Seeing the need to respond, Britannica offered a CD version, but it was considerably more expensive than *Encarta* and Britannica couldn't catch up to the market lead that Microsoft had established.

After internet use began to grow, Britannica tried to develop a website where they would sell their product, but this too failed to take off. Then, with their very survival at stake, they implemented a radical revision of their business model. They placed the content of their encyclopedia on a website completely free of charge with the idea

of using the site to attract advertising revenue. In addition, they included links to other websites, the daily news, banner ads, and an online store. With the crash of the dot-com industry, advertising revenues collapsed. To survive, the company was once again forced to change its business model. To compensate for lost revenues, Britannica embraced a two-tiered system. Basic searches are still free, but a premium subscription is required for more comprehensive search results.

The consequence of all this was that Britannica's business model changed from one in which they produced and sold expensive books to another where they gave away their prime product on the internet and made their money on advertising and selling their products through their online store to, finally, one in which they make the product available on a subscription basis. Quite an evolution indeed!

Encyclopædia Britannica
www.britannica.com

Questions

1. What are the advantages of an electronic encyclopedia over a print version?
2. What further evolution might take place in the world of online encylopedias?

Redefinition of Product Value The ability of the internet to convey a variety of information, services, and other features has led to a redefinition of what is meant by a product or service. For example, when Amazon offers books online, they include information about the book, reader reviews, sales ranking, related books, and other information. They also added other services and products to their site in which they determined their customers were likely to have an interest. In other words, they include information with their prime product and the package becomes the product. This has the effect of fundamentally altering their business model, enabling them to charge for some of the additional products and, as was temporarily the case with Britannica, even give away their main product. E-customers have come to expect packages of this type, and such packages must keep up with consumer expectations and needs at all times.

Media Flexibility The incredible capacity of the internet to grow and change and to convey a variety of content (particularly multimedia such as voice, video, and music) means that business is continually challenged to offer new features and services to customers before the customer demands them. This leads to changing product package content and consequently, changing business models.

It should be clear from these points and examples that e-business models constantly change. They not only change when businesses enter into e-business, but also need constant review to keep pace with the fast-moving times. This need for continual change and improvement emphasizes the need for e-business strategy.

E-Business Strategy

The changes in and pressure on business models have been driving numerous strategic initiatives, some of which are unique to e-business and some of which are not. Business models define how a business is going to make money and strategy defines how it plans to achieve the desired business model. We have already seen, as in the case of Amazon, how business models need to change to survive in the current business environment. This need for change leads to a need for new strategies. In the world of e-business, strategy formulation and execution must move fast and in most cases must be tied closely to significant business processes in a way that makes them flexible and responsive. This is known as a flexible business design. More often, the desired flexibility cannot be achieved within a single business organization. The organization must look outside to be able to provide products and services or conduct particular business processes. This has led to a substantial incidence of such strategies as outsourcing, partnerships, joint ventures, liaisons, and mergers. Most recently, it has led to outright collaboration with suppliers, customers, and even competitors.

A major result of all these changes has been the creation of e-business organizations that transcend traditional business organizations—the creation of virtual corporations. A good example of this is the emergence of integrated companies where various businesses integrate their supply chains and collaborate to enable them to remain competitive. Essentially, they join forces within an electronic infrastructure to streamline and even reinvent their businesses. This aptly illustrates the fundamental change being wrought by e-business.

The Structure of E-Business

E-business includes the front-office and back-office information system applications that drive modern business (see figure 1.1). These include the applications that enable information relating to the customers to be captured and used to find better and more efficient ways to serve them—the so-called **customer relationship management (CRM)** applications (discussed in chapter 9)—as well as the applications designed to streamline the acquisition of goods and services—**e-procurement** applications (discussed in chapter 8). E-Business also includes other information system applications that serve to integrate the systems of a business to streamline its value chain. The streamlining of the internal value chain and the external supply chain is a fundamental strategy of e-business that enables businesses to respond quickly to the increasingly stringent demands of e-customers.

In summary, the definition of e-business includes a wide range of business activity—a range that is widening to the point that experts such as Don Tapscott, author of *Paradigm Shift; The Digital Economy;* and *The Naked Corporation*, are saying that ultimately all business will be e-business.[2] The Canadian Snapshots box illustrates how some companies are using e-business. Chapter 2 discusses various e-business models and strategies that companies have adopted.

CUSTOMER RELATIONSHIP MANAGEMENT (CRM)
The set of strategies, technologies, and processes that enable the business to continuously improve offerings to customers.

E-PROCUREMENT
The complete business process of acquiring goods and services through electronic means, from requisition through to fulfillment and payment.

Figure 1.1   Essential Structure of E-Business

E-business encompasses the full range of business activity, from suppliers to customers.

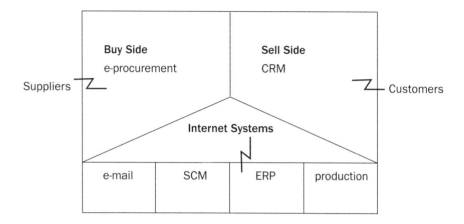

Systems Integration

While the internet is a central enabling technology for the rise of e-business, it is not the only one. To make e-business work, a great deal of activity must take place behind the webpages. The corporate systems need to be organized and integrated in such a way that there is a fast and free flow of information throughout the system regardless of the different technologies, functions, and platforms within the organization. This is called **systems integration**. It is necessary to enable the business to be able to respond to the fast-moving pace of business in the information age and to keep the customers happy. It is also necessary to enable businesses to cope with the growing phenomenon of providing customization of their products for their customers. Increasingly companies offer to customize their products, and the first time the company finds out the form the customization will take is when it gets the order. The company then needs to obtain the materials and process them in time to meet the high expectations of customers. Systems integration is necessary to enable the company to provide this fast turnaround without resorting to increases in inventory.

Several tools are used by companies to enable this integration to take place. Where the internet itself is not used, quite often other networks are used that make use of internet technology. Where such networks are internal to the company, they are referred to as **intranets**. Where they extend outside the company, they are called **extranets**.

The use of this internet technology in intranets and extranets means that these networks have the same look, feel, and functionality as the web. A user often cannot tell when moving from one to the other or to the internet itself. The difference is therefore said to be transparent to the user.

Typically, websites are constructed on separate network servers, called web servers. The data on the web servers include the HTML codes for the actual webpages, as well as the software being used to construct the storefront on the internet. **HTML**, or **HyperText Markup Language**, is a programming language used to create webpages. Of course, the storefront software must be connected with the main system of the company, to enable orders and other requests by customers to be handled by the business. For example, the MySap.com system offered by SAP AG uses an approach of centreing the storefront around an online catalogue.

SYSTEMS INTEGRATION
Process of bringing together various business systems having different technologies, functions, and platforms so they can conduct business processes in such a way that the user does not see that different systems are being used.

INTRANETS
Computer networks within an enterprise that make use of internet technology.

EXTRANETS
Computer networks that make use of internet technology and include users from outside the organization as well as inside.

HYPERTEXT MARKUP LANGUAGE (HTML)
The programming language used to create web pages.

mySAP
www.sap.com/solutions/business-suite.asp

Canadian Snapshots

Research In Motion

Research In Motion Ltd. (RIM) is a high-tech start-up company based in Waterloo, Ontario, and listed on the NASDAQ Stock Exchange and the Toronto Stock Exchange. The company, which started in 1984, specializes in producing handheld wireless products, such as the BlackBerry® wireless e-mail unit, various pagers and wireless personal computer adapters, and radio modems. Its major competition is palmOne, Inc., producer of the popular Zire™, Tungsten™, and Treo™ handheld devices.

Research In Motion has evolved into a leading designer, manufacturer, and marketer of wireless solutions. The company provides platforms and solutions for access to time-sensitive information including e-mail, phone, internet, and intranet-based applications. RIM technology also enables a broad array of third party developers and manufacturers to enhance their products and services with wireless connectivity to data.

RIM is now a world leader in small handheld internet-based technology. Its original product—the BlackBerry—has evolved into a personal digital assistant (PDA) with e-mail and internet browsing capabilities and the ability to send and receive voice calls.

In February, 2004, Sony Ericsson Mobile Communications and Research In Motion announced plans to enable BlackBerry connectivity on Sony Ericsson mobile phones. The agreement allows Sony Ericsson's Symbian OS-based phones to connect to BlackBerry Enterprise Server and BlackBerry Web Client services for enterprise and individual users. The BlackBerry services infrastructure has been adopted by thousands of companies and government organizations around the world. IT departments and consumers are recognizing the productivity benefits that can be gained from wireless access to corporate data and e-mail. The BlackBerry architecture for enterprise customers includes integration capability with corporate information systems, and enhanced security.

RIM's "always on" connectivity and push technology, which automatically delivers e-mails and other data to and from a BlackBerry, has proven to be an efficient and reliable communications platform. Under the agreement with Sony, the BlackBerry services will be able to run on certain Sony Ericsson phones, like the Sony P900, while maintaining the phone's existing functionality. The P900 phone is a multi-faceted device that offers productivity, entertainment, and communications applications as well as full PDA organizer functions and the ability to take colour digital pictures. From RIM's point of view, the agreement provides their end-user customers and carrier partners with additional wireless device choices. while enabling IT departments to leverage their existing BlackBerry infrastructure.

Companies like RIM are leaders in the global wireless market, and are establishing Canada as a major presence in this emerging aspect of e-business.

Research In Motion
www.rim.net

Questions

1. Why would Sony Ericsson have joined with RIM rather than develop their own products to meet the same needs?

2. What is meant by leveraging "their existing BlackBerry infrastructures"?

3. How would wireless devices add to the value of existing information systems from a management and strategic perspective?

SOURCES: www.rim.net; press release, "Sony Ericsson and RIM Announce BlackBerry Connectivity Support in P900 Smartphone," **www.blackberry.net/ news/press/2004/pr-23_02_2004-01.shtml**, October 30, 2004.

EXTENSIBLE MARKUP LANGUAGE (XML)
A tool that is similar to HTML and is compatible, but does not rely on single pre-set tags to identify information.

The online catalogue is linked to the main SAP systems that contain all the product and inventory records and the products that the company wishes to offer for sale at the online store. The data in the main records are located using extensible markup language (XML). **Extensible Markup Language (XML)** is a tool that is similar to HTML and is compatible, but does not rely on single pre-set tags to identify information. Instead, XML provides a mechanism for any document builder to define new XML tags within any XML document.

When the online store is configured, there is the capacity to add graphics to illustrate the products being offered and also the ability to add a shopping cart. Anyone who has shopped online would have seen shopping carts to which products can be added as the user browses through the store. An example can be found on Amazon.com or any number of websites that offer goods for sale. Eventually, the user will make their purchases by going to a check-out screen that allows payment for the goods using credit cards or any other payment system that the store supports. The online catalogue and the shopping cart software would be on the web server along with the webpages.

Using a web server also facilitates security, because it enables firewalls to be strategically located to offer maximum security for both the customer and the company's data. **Firewalls** are separate, highly secure computers, along with related policies and procedures, through which access to the network from the internet is exclusively directed. A common configuration is for a firewall to be set up between the web server and the main system. Some companies also set up firewalls outside the web server as well, leaving only the webpages available to the public. The area of security is explored in chapter 5.

FIREWALL
Separate, highly secure computers, along with related policies and procedures, through which access to the network from the internet is exclusively directed.

Tools for System Integration

While not all e-business is carried out on the internet, it is undeniable that the rise in the use of the internet is the single most important enabler of e-business of any type. Even types of e-business that were carried out before the age of the internet are moving to the internet, or more specifically to the **World Wide Web (WWW)**. The World Wide Web is the user-friendly, graphics-capable component of the internet. A good example of this shift to the internet is EDI, which started on private networks called VANs (for value added networks), but has been moving to the web because of the economies that are possible when using standardized, internet-based systems as opposed to proprietary, private networks. Chapter 3 discusses the workings of the internet and the World Wide Web.

WORLD WIDE WEB (WWW)
The user-friendly, graphics-capable component of the internet.

Businesses achieve the systems integration they need by using intranets to tie together their systems internally, and by using extranets to tie their systems to those of their customers and suppliers. They also use tools like enterprise resource planning (ERP), supply chain management (SCM), customer relationship management (CRM) and e-procurement to achieve this integration both externally and internally. All of these tools are essential to e-business and are explored fully in chapters 4, 7, 8, and 9. The purpose here is to set out how they fit into a broad perspective on e-business.

ERP systems are large software systems that a business uses to automate its activities across their full range. Consisting of the software sold by several major vendors—including SAP, Oracle, and PeopleSoft—an ERP implementation represents a major initiative for any business. Implementation of an ERP system often requires significant changes in business processes to accommodate the software, sometimes to the point of re-inventing the business. On the plus side, ERP systems offer the ability to share a common pool of data across an entire enterprise and to run their applications using a very common format. They also offer management the opportunity to have immediate access to the latest information about the organization's activities and performance.

The implementation of ERP systems predated the development of e-commerce, and many installations were prompted by the Y2K crisis that was being predicted in the late 1990s as a result of computer systems having to be changed to accommodate the years beginning with the numerals 20-, rather than just 19-. The "crisis" turned out to have been overblown, but the event created a strong focus on the software systems used by businesses. The incredible boom in e-business and the related need to integrate systems has led to a continuance of interest in ERP systems, and in many companies they are viewed as essential to delivering on e-business needs.

Customer relationship management systems also are very large information systems and present many of the issues and difficulties as ERP systems. However, CRM systems are viewed as essential to enable the organization to deliver on their customer needs on a timely basis. They accomplish this by accumulating information about customers and then using that information to offer them a product that is tailored to their needs. The idea of CRM is to be able to acquire new customers, enhance the profitability of all customers, and retain the profitable ones. CRM does not always involve integrating systems with customers, but some of the more advanced systems do. The use of CRM systems, because they involved obtaining and analyzing information about customers, is closely linked to e-marketing from a strategic point of view. E-marketing is covered in chapter 11.

E-procurement systems are of two main types—buy-side and sell-side systems. **Buy-side** procurement systems essentially involve systems within a business that fully automate purchases by staff and involve electronic contact with outside suppliers, often through the internet or an extranet. **Sell-side** procurement systems, on the other hand, involve systems that are essentially trading communities, or exchanges that link directly to the systems of both suppliers and customers. Many sell-side systems are fully integrated with the systems of their participants. Trading exchanges are an important aspect of contemporary e-business. These topics are dealt with in chapter 8.

The use of large integrated information systems like ERP and CRM led to the availability of large quantities of data within enterprises. The question then arose as to how to make most effective use of these data. Clearly, there was a need to find ways to organize and analyze the data so the best use could be made of them, particularly for strategic purposes. The tool that arose to meet this need was **business intelligence (BI)**, which is the subject of chapter 10. Business intelligence is a powerful application, or set of applications, that allows businesses to capture, analyze, interpret, and report on data across an enterprise, thus creating valuable information for the enterprise.

The Domains of E-Business

Business-to-Consumer (B2C)

E-business that involves interaction between businesses and consumers is referred to as business-to-consumer (B2C) e-business. In the B2C arena, companies are offering a growing range of goods and services on the internet directly to consumers, often bypassing their traditional distributors. Besides the books that are offered on Amazon.com, early initiatives in B2C involved the sale of investments, through such sites as E*TRADE Financial and Schwab.com. These sites are particularly interesting in that the former is an internet upstart and the latter is an old-economy entrant into e-business, but both have been successful in their efforts.

A notable example of consumer-oriented e-business is banks, who have formed their business strategies around aggressive e-business strategies. Banks have been involved in e-business for many years, particularly when they began to install **automated teller machines (ATMs)** during the 1970s. An ATM is a user-friendly, kiosk-based computer that enables bank customers to carry out their own banking transactions. The process of moving customer service to an automated format,

---

BUY-SIDE
The purchasing end of the supply chain, which consists of suppliers and the processes that connect with them.

SELL-SIDE
The selling end of the supply chain, which consists of customers and the processes that connect with them.

BUSINESS INTELLIGENCE (BI)
A powerful application, or set of applications, that allows businesses to capture, analyze, interpret, and report on data across an enterprise, thus creating valuable information for the enterprise.

Charles Schwab
www.schwab.com

AUTOMATED TELLER MACHINES (ATMS)
User-friendly, kiosk-based computers that enable bank customers to carry out their own banking transactions.

Figure 1.2   Cost of Banking Transactions (US Dollars)

The cost of banking transactions drops dramatically when the internet is used for processing them.

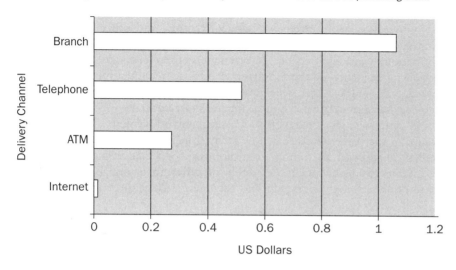

where the customer actually performs the input activity for the bank, proved to be a lucrative strategy. The banks did not have to pay to have this input performed; the customers actually paid them for the "privilege"! The banks installed more ATMs, reduced their staffing, closed branches, and made more money. Then, during the 1990s, the banks moved their e-business to the internet by introducing internet banking. After some shaky starts, with concerns about security and sometimes using doubtful technology, all of the banks now offer substantial internet banking services to their customers. People can log on to the bank website and view their account balances and recent transactions, make transfers of funds, pay bills, and request other services. Internet banking has been very successful and offers even greater cost savings to the banks (see figure 1.2) than do ATMs.

B2C has been growing and changing the business environment. E-tailing, or electronic retailing, will continue to be an expanding phenomenon as the use of the internet expands to greater numbers of people.

Business-to-Business (B2B)

In the business-to-business (B2B) arena, activity has centred on the streamlining of the supply chain by establishing shared systems between suppliers and customers using the internet or related technology. The **supply chain** is the set of processes that encompasses purchases of raw materials or resources through to final delivery of a product or service to the end consumer. Activity in the B2B world has focused on the buy-side, which deals with the procurement activity of a business, and the sell-side, which relates to relationships with customers and the consequent marketing and selling activity. In a sense, of course, the two are simply opposite sides of the same coin.

SUPPLY CHAIN
The set of processes that encompasses purchases of raw materials or resources through to final delivery of a product or service to the end consumer.

Government to Business (G2B) and Business to Government (B2G)

Many governments of the world make their services available to their constituencies over the internet. Canadian government departments have also been using electronic filing methods. Notable among these is the Canada Revenue Agency

(CRA), which has very successfully implemented a system for taxpayers to file income tax returns electronically on the internet, as have the U.S. Internal Revenue Service and U.K. Inland Revenue among many others. Statistics Canada has been developing a system of electronic filing of reports, and other departments, for example the National Energy Board, have implemented systems for e-filing of information. Canadian federal government departments are operating under the general guidance of the Government On-Line (GOL) initiative (see www. gol-ged.gc.ca/index_e.asp), which was started in 2000. Similarly, the United States established a comprehensive e-government strategy on Feb 27, 2002, which is now in process of implementation. Governments implement electronic services because of the cost savings that flow from reducing the volume of paper to be handled. In addition, they know from various surveys that businesses and individuals often prefer to be able to deal with the government online. This domain of e-business is growing very rapidly and becoming much more important.

The Benefits of E-Business

It is important to consider why the tremendous growth in e-business over the past few years has taken place. Clearly, there has been a strong interest in the internet, as well as considerable hype, but for it to be adopted by businesses, there must be solid business justification for its use. Put simply, the benefits of using the internet must be greater than the costs, such that it will result in a satisfactory contribution to profits.

These business reasons generally involve the quest for improved profitability, but more specifically include:

- increasing sales
- reducing costs
- improving customer service
- minimizing competitive pressure
- expanding market reach
- addressing user concerns

Increasing Sales

The internet offers the possibility of increasing sales through various means. It represents a new sales channel, one that can be used to support and augment the more traditional channels, like stores, mail-order catalogues, and field sales personnel. This new sales channel also may reach new people, particularly those who use the internet most frequently and are comfortable buying online. Finally, the internet offers the possibility of reaching new geographical areas around the globe, many of which would not have been economically accessible before the advent of the internet.

Reducing Costs

One of the clear advantages of e-business is the lower cost of executing transactions, as illustrated so well by the banking business. This lower cost comes from the ability of e-business to move the input process from the staff to the customers and outside users, as well as from the reduced necessity to produce, handle, and store paper documents.

Another example can be found in airline travel. Under the old reservation systems, the customer would call or visit the airline or a travel agent and state his or her requests to an employee, who would then enter those requests into the computer system and generate confirmations and tickets. Now all the major airlines have internet reservation systems, which enable the customer to log in and type all their requests into forms provided on the site. The system confirms the availability of the flights and the specific requests such as seating or special meals, then generates tickets that can be mailed from a central point or electronic tickets that are faxed or e-mailed to the customer. Some of the airlines now no longer require any kind of ticket, just a picture ID to confirm the identity of the person who is listed on their system as having paid for a seat. All of the input has been carried out by the customer and no airline employee involvement has been required other than perhaps (and more rarely) taking a printed ticket off a printer and inserting it into an envelope for mailing. Reduced need for customer service personnel leads to considerable cost savings. In the case of the electronic ticket sent by e-mail, the customer is even printing the ticket, which leads directly into one of the other reasons why internet commerce is cheaper—infrastructure.

Under older traditional systems, businesses owned the hardware and software, and rented or purchased much of the communications capability. The internet offers a communications platform that is largely cost-free to all users. Certainly, there are internet-related costs, such as fees customers pay to internet service providers (ISPs), and there is still a need for businesses to establish additional internet-related infrastructure, such as new servers and firewalls to ensure security. However, the cost of these additional items, though sometimes considerable, is small in comparison to the cost that would be incurred if a communications infrastructure comparable to the internet had to be acquired by the business. **Internet service providers (ISPs)** are companies that offer internet access and related services to individuals and businesses for a fee. Connections are offered through telephone lines, cable, satellite, or wireless connections

The use of the internet and its applications for e-business involves many different processes carried out in the business. As technology is applied, it is necessary to rationalize and improve these processes to make efficient use of the technological and human resources required. Consequently, e-business offers an opportunity to achieve economies in the improvement of business processes, and this is one of the techniques used by businesses entering into e-business to reduce costs. It is important to note, however, that the cost reductions derived from business process change come after the change has been executed and is running smoothly; the cost of conversion can be very high, particularly because of the issues around the adaptability of the people involved.

Another cost reduction measure inherent in e-business involves the costs of procurement from suppliers. Automation of these procurement activities should result in cost savings. In addition, when procurement activities are more closely tied into the processes of the suppliers, it often means improved supplier relations and the resulting opportunity to obtain better prices.

INTERNET SERVICE PROVIDERS (ISPs)
Companies that offer internet access and related services to individuals and businesses for a fee. Connections are offered through telephone lines, cable, satellite, or wireless connections.

Improving Customer Service

A company's website is an important vehicle for customers and prospective customers to obtain information about the company, its products, and its people.

Some examples of additional services to customers offered through the web include:

- instructions for finding the business, including directions or maps to store locations, bank branches, etc.

- webpages detailing the specific services offered by a firm and providing contact information for the persons in charge of each area
- reader surveys offered by news sites like globeandmail.com and CNN.com, where users can quickly vote on an issue and read the real-time results of the vote
- product demonstrations, for example websites devoted to automobiles that provide details and working demos of particular models

Competitive Pressure

Finally, many companies find they simply must use the internet for competitive reasons. Part of this reason relates to image—if the competitors are doing it, then people will ask why the company isn't. It also relates to simple economics. If the competition is obtaining financial benefits such as increased sales and reduced costs from using the web, then they will eventually obtain a competitive advantage, and it will be necessary for their competitors to use the web to survive.

Increased Market Reach

The worldwide use of the internet has played a major role in increasing business' interest in using it. One of the major implications is that it allows a business to reach a far wider market than it previously could. The internet offers business the opportunity to reach people all around the world. Therefore, if companies wish to do business in a new country, or wish to establish direct, cost-effective communications links with existing business partners in other areas of the globe, they can do so through the internet.

Some businesses have used the internet to establish a global market for their products. Of course, there are limitations to this global internet reach. For one thing, there are significant parts of the globe that do not have any internet access, or where access is extremely limited. Much of the underdeveloped world falls into this category because they do not have the communications infrastructure necessary to support the internet. As shown in table 1.1, the penetration of the internet in these countries is significant, and as shown in figure 1.3, the number of internet users has been growing consistently and considerably since 1995. There seems little doubt that this trend will continue into the foreseeable future around the globe.

The Challenges of E-Business
Privacy and Security

As more commercial transactions have taken place over the internet there have been concerns about the lack of security and privacy. Initially, it was widely acknowledged that there was little or no security available on the internet and that it was an environment rife with hackers, viruses, and other threats to data and system integrity. As a result of this lack of security, people were reluctant to allow any of their private information to be transmitted over the internet and were especially reluctant to provide information such as credit card numbers.

This latter point relates to another perceived shortcoming with regard to the internet—the lack of a satisfactory payment system. Since the internet is an electronic medium, hard cash cannot be used to pay for goods or services purchased online. Various other methods have been tried, and for a time, the most common method was the use of credit cards through forms that were filled out offline and faxed to the vendor. Now, the use of credit cards directly is the most common means of payment on the web.

Table 1.1   The World Internet Population, 2003

Worldwide distribution of internet users.

Country	% Internet Penetration	# Internet Users
Sweden	75.8%	6 726 808
Hong Kong	67.0%	4 571 936
Australia	64.2%	12 823 869
Netherlands	63.7%	10 351 064
United States	63.2%	184 447 987
Denmark	62.7%	3 375 850
Iceland	59.5%	175 000
Switzerland	58.6%	4 319 289
United Kingdom	58.2%	34 387 246
South Korea	56.1%	26 270 000
Singapore	54.6%	2 308 296
New Zealand	54.5%	2 063 831
Germany	53.9%	44 139 071
Canada	**53.1%**	**16 841 811**
Finland	50.8%	2 650 000

SOURCE: Internet World Usage Stats, **www.internetworldstats.com**.

Security and Payment Systems

Since those early days of the commercial use of the internet, considerable progress has been made in addressing these issues. Security over the internet, at least on commercial sites, has vastly improved in recent years. Many commercial sites have installed firewalls, which are highly secure computers added to a corporate network, through which access to the network from the internet is exclusively directed (see figure 1.4 for the basic structure of a firewall). To augment security, they also have made increased use of **encryption** (the use of a mathematical formula—an algorithm—that is applied to electronic data to render it illegible to anyone without the decoding key) to prevent unauthorized persons from reading data.

ENCRYPTION
The use of a mathematical formula (an algorithm) that is applied to electronic data to render it illegible to anyone without the decoding key.

While they have not been overcome, these barriers to the spread of commerce on the internet have at least substantially improved in recent years. Nevertheless, the most recent surveys indicate that one of the most prevalent concerns of internet users in conducting business online is the provision of their credit card information and privacy concerns generally. The press has reported numerous instances of identity theft, under which the perpetrators find enough information (such as SIN numbers, address and telephone information, employment, etc.) about another person—the victim—that they can reconstruct their economic identity, and then use that identity to gain credit and actually purchase items and services. The victims eventually find out when their credit rating deteriorates, or they begin receiving telephone calls from creditors demanding payment. The issue of online privacy is being addressed through legislation around the world (see chapter 13 for further discussion).

Many of the privacy concerns of internet users are addressed in Canadian privacy legislation, notably the Personal Information Protection and Electronic Documents Act (PIPEDA). The Act was introduced in 2000 and came into effect on January 1, 2004. For the first time, it created an enforceable right to privacy for individuals with respect to the collection, use, and disclosure of their personal information by the private sector in the course of commercial activities. As a result of this act, the Office of the Federal Privacy Commissioner has been established to

Figure 1.3   The World Internet Population, 1995–2002

The number of internet users has grown considerably since 1995.

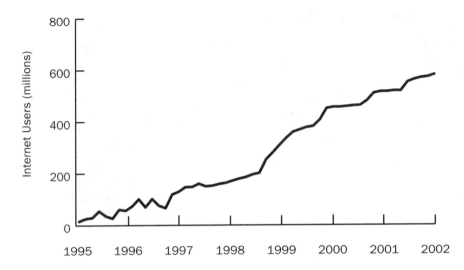

SOURCE: Nua.com, **www.nua.ie/surveys/how_many_online/world.html**, November 1, 2004.

administer it and act as something of a watchdog on matters concerning privacy of information. In addition, most provinces have established similar legislation, as has the United States, the European Union, and numerous other countries.

Again, while the new legislation does not deal with all the issues that are important to e-commerce participants, it does address many of them and provides a framework for at least some of the future legislation that will surely follow.

Regarding the topic of payment systems, considerable progress has been made through the banks offering internet services, which include the ability to pay bills online. Although internet banking has become routine for many Canadians, true online payment systems are non-existent or in their pilot phase. For example, many companies, such as telephone companies, notify their customers by e-mail when their bill is ready and offer customers the ability to read the bill on their website. In some instances, it can then be paid online, or else can be paid through internet banking or conventional means. However, these systems have not achieved the degree of success that the online banking systems have, and credit cards are still the number one payment method in cyberspace. Although payment systems, such as PayPal, have gained popularity, a universally accepted online transaction system is still not available. **PayPal** is a payment system, owned by eBay, that allows money transfers over the internet in a variety of currencies. Merchants as well as individual users can use the system.

PAYPAL
Payment system, owned by eBay, that allows money transfers over the internet in a variety of currencies.

Figure 1.4   Basic Firewall Architecture

A firewall is placed between the internet and the networks to enable outside access to the networks to be controlled.

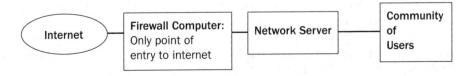

Other more advanced technologies, not yet used widely for commercial purposes, are beginning to be implemented, principally by credit card companies. An important example is the wireless PayPass card by MasterCard, which will be discussed more fully in chapter 6. Essentially, PayPass is a wireless smart card, which offers the capability to buy something in a store simply by waving the card at a receiver at the cash register. A **smart card** is not much bigger than a credit card, and contains a computer chip that is used to store or process information.

SMART CARD
A card, not much bigger than a credit card, that contains a computer chip that is used to store or process information.

Chapter Summary

In a very broad sense, electronic business is normally defined as any business carried out in electronic form. More recently, the term "e-business" has been used to refer to the process of carrying out business using the internet as a strategic tool. In this text, e-business is defined as the strategic use of technology, particularly the internet, to integrate and streamline the business processes, enterprise applications, and organizational structure of a business to create a high-performance business model.

The rise in the use of the internet is the single most important enabler of e-business of any type. Even types of e-business that were carried out before the age of the internet are moving to the internet.

The internet and e-business are changing business models. This means that businesses need to construct their business models such that they can deliver quickly to meet expectations. People use the internet for convenience and also expect a customized product.

Business models have changed substantially, by cutting infrastructure costs, increasing their technology costs, adding new sources of revenue, and making old sources of revenue obsolete. Changing product package content also contributes to changing business models. The changes in and pressure on business models have been driving numerous strategic initiatives, some of which are unique to e-business and others which are not. As illustrated so well by the example of Britannica, business models and strategies have been undergoing an evolution and no doubt will continue to evolve in the future.

There are numerous domains of e-business, principally business-to-consumer and business-to-business. In B2C, companies are offering a wider range of goods on the internet. The internet also ushered in the idea of online auctioning and other bidding-related retail systems. Perhaps more importantly, the auctioning idea has extended into business-to-business procurement systems and trading exchanges where auctioning is perceived as a way in which suppliers can be made more competitive and responsive to their customers.

Activity in the B2B world has focused on the buy-side, which deals with the procurement activity of a business, and the sell-side, which relates to relationships with customers and the consequent marketing and selling activity. E-business also includes the front- and back-office information system applications that form the engine for modern business. The streamlining of the internal value chain and the external supply chain is a fundamental strategy of e-business that enables the business to respond quickly to the increasingly stringent demands of e-customers.

Businesses achieve the integration they need in their systems by using intranets to tie their systems together internally, and by using extranets to tie their systems to those of their customers and suppliers. ERP systems are used in a business to automate its activities across their full range and achieve the required integration.

Buy-side procurement systems essentially involve systems within a business that fully automate purchases by staff and involve electronic contact with outside suppliers, often through the internet or an extranet. Sell-side procurement systems, on the other hand, involve systems that are essentially trading communities, which link directly to the systems of both suppliers and customers.

There are numerous benefits of e-business, including increasing sales, reducing costs, improving customer service, minimizing competitive pressure and expanding market reach. However, there are challenges as well, which largely have revolved around privacy and security and their consequent role in the ability to make payments on the internet. There has been considerable progress in meeting these challenges, through better security techniques and payment systems.

Key Terms

automated teller machines (ATMs)   *(p. 12)*
business intelligence (BI)   *(p. 12)*
buy-side   *(p. 12)*
customer relationship management (CRM)   *(p. 8)*
electronic data interchange (EDI)   *(p. 5)*
encryption   *(p. 17)*
e-procurement   *(p. 8)*
Extensible Markup Language   *(p. 10)*
extranets   *(p. 9)*
firewall   *(p. 11)*
HyperText Markup Language (HTML)   *(p. 9)*

integrated systems   *(p. 6)*
internet   *(p. 2)*
internet service providers (ISPs)   *(p. 15)*
intranets   *(p. 9)*
PayPal   *(p. 18)*
sell-side   *(p. 12)*
smart card   *(p. 19)*
supply chain   *(p. 13)*
systems integration   *(p. 9)*
trading exchange   *(p. 2)*
World Wide Web   *(p. 11)*

Tools for Online Learning

To help you master the material in this chapter and stay up to date with new developments in e-business, visit **www.pearsoned.ca/trites**. Resources include:

- **Review Questions and Exercises**

- **Problems for Discussion**

- **Recommended Readings**

- **Updates to Case Studies and Textual Material**

- **Streaming CBC Videos with Cases**

Endnotes

1. Ravi Kalakota and Marcia Robinson, *E-Business 2.0: Roadmap for Success* (Reading, MA: Addison Wesley, 2000).

2. Don Tapscott and David Ticoll, The Naked Corporation (Toronto: Viking Canada, 2003).

— CHAPTER 2

Internet Business Models and Strategies

LEARNING OBJECTIVES

When you complete this chapter you should be able to:

1. Describe the key elements of an internet business model.

2. Explain similarities and differences between B2C and B2B models.

3. Explain the similarities and differences between models based on "bricks," "bricks and clicks," "clicks and bricks," and "clicks."

4. Describe key revenue-generating approaches used by internet business models.

5. Define and explain the importance of e-business strategy.

6. Describe the relationship between internet business models and strategy.

7. Identify key areas addressed by a strategic plan.

Introduction

Broadly, a **business model** may be defined as the manner in which a business organizes itself so as to achieve its objectives, which normally involve the generation of profits. Although there are various views about what components should make up a business model, we will consider the following eight components of a business model:[1]

1. *External forces.* Political, economic, social, and technological factors, pressures, and forces from outside the entity that create opportunities for the entity or threaten its business objectives.
2. *Markets/formats.* The domains in which the entity may choose to operate, and the design and location of the facilities.
3. *Customers.* The individuals and organizations that purchase the entity's output.
4. *Core business processes.* The processes that develop, produce, market, and distribute an entity's products and services.
5. *Core products and services.* The commodities that the entity brings to the market.
6. *Alliances.* The relationships established by an entity to attain business objectives, expand business opportunities and reduce or transfer business risk.
7. *Strategic management process.* The process by which the entity's mission is developed, its business objectives are defined, business risks that threaten attainment of the business objectives are identified, business risk management processes are established, and progress toward meeting business objectives is monitored.
8. *Resource management processes.* The processes by which resources are acquired, developed, and allocated to the core business activities.

A major aspect of e-business strategy is how the business plans to use the internet for these purposes to create an internet business model. An **internet business model** is developed using the internet as a tool to implement a business model. An e-business **strategy** is the sum of all the choices that a business makes within these eight categories and how it fits them together to offer a unique value to its customers that differentiates its e-business model from those of its competitors. In other words, the term "business model" denotes a general description of how a business structures its activities to earn profits, while the term "strategy" focuses on the specific choices in that set of activities that are aimed at giving the entity a unique position in its industry and, thereby, a competitive advantage. Once all the choices are made, however, there is little distinction between an entity's business model and its business strategy and these terms become interchangeable.

Traditional business models have usually revolved around a central product or service. The idea was that a business would acquire or make goods, and sell them for amounts in excess of cost. Often, a business would add services or accessories to augment its profits or customer satisfaction, but the central feature of the traditional business model was the sale of a product or service at an amount in excess of its cost. This model fits the traditional industrial environment very well. Manufacturing organizations, such as Ford Motor Company, exploited this model by adopting a mass production model that enabled them to reduce unit costs and selling prices and still generate profits. Much traditional business literature has been devoted to the idea of maximizing revenues, minimizing costs, and generating competitive advantage.

During the last few decades of the twentieth century, there was an increase in the number of organizations that sold services rather than goods. These organizations, which include various types of professional firms (such as accountants and consultants) and, increasingly, technology-related service firms, have followed a model similar to that of traditional manufacturers. They focused their efforts on a service or related package of services, hired people with the skills to provide these services, and sold their time and skills to their clients at a price in excess of the cost they had to pay. As the environment has changed, the nature and scope of the services companies have offered has changed, but they have continued to follow the same basic business model of selling something in excess of its cost. This chapter discusses business models and strategies that are being used to exploit the advantages of doing business on the internet.

External Forces

As mentioned earlier, an internet business model involves the use of the internet as a strategic tool for generating profits and achieving other business objectives. The internet is a technological factor that creates the business opportunities described in this chapter. During the tech boom (also called the tech bubble) from August 1995 to March 2000, numerous media reports and articles by influential business executives suggested that the internet "changes everything" so that "old economy" business models no longer apply. This view gained widespread acceptance as companies like Amazon.com and E*TRADE Financial raised huge amounts of capital in the stock market without having ever made a profit. Some business writers pointed to the success of these ventures in raising capital and announced that the old rules didn't apply anymore.

When the tech bubble burst, the dramatic declines in the share prices of dot-com stocks acted as a reality check and renewed the realization that a business still needs to make money in the long term. While this does not seem like a radical insight, the exuberance about the possibilities arising from the innovative use of the internet had blinded many investors to this simple reality. Although the tech bust represented a setback for many internet-based businesses and the failure of many dot-com startups, e-business continues to represent a rich mine of opportunities and numerous internet-based business models have developed in recent years.

According to Michael E. Porter: "The essence of strategy is choosing to perform activities differently than rivals do . . . Competitive strategy is about being different. It means deliberately choosing a different set of activities to deliver a unique mix of value."[2] Porter cautions against a strategy based on price competition. The internet is a very competitive environment that leads to relentless price reductions to the point where most entities will find it difficult to earn a profit. This leaves room for a very small number of players with very cost-effective operations in any particular sector or domain. Instead, Porter recommends competing on quality, features, and service.

The New Business Models box illustrates a situation where a new business model was introduced for the music industry, based on this type of differentiation.

Markets/Customers

The literature uses broad classifications such as business to consumer (B2C) and business to business (B2B) to discuss categories of markets and customers. For example, Amazon.ca operates in the business to consumer (B2C) domain. Other widely used B2C models involve the provision of services such as auctions (eBay), travel reservations (Expedia), and financial services (President's Choice Financial).

Expedia
www.expedia.ca

President's Choice Financial
www.pcfinancial.ca

New Business Models

Digital Distribution of Music: An Evolving Business Model

During the late 1990s, Napster turned the music industry on its head by facilitating the transfer of free music between people connected to the web. The industry at first directed its efforts to legal battles with Napster over copyright issues, and won. But soon, new file sharing services were launched that were more difficult to combat. It was clear that the rules of the game had changed and the industry needed to find new ways to deal with the distribution of music over the internet that would be economically viable for the industry and for the artists.

In October 2002, Roxio responded to the industry climate, bought Napster's assets and a year later launched a legal version of Napster 2.0. Napster 2.0 now requires customers to use proprietary software to access its online music selection and pay for the music they download. With over 500 000 songs to choose from, customers pay US$0.99 per song,

and US$9.95 for a full album. Napster also offers a subscription service that enables users to listen to an unlimited number of songs streamed over the internet for US$9.95 per month.

While Napster boasts of a brand recognition ratio of 92.5 percent, first mover advantage goes to iTunes.com, launched by Apple Inc. in April of 2003. Like Napster, iTunes requires customers to use proprietary software to access its online music store. The number of music offerings on iTunes is comparable at 400 000 songs, and the prices for downloading are the same as those at Napster. In addition to downloadable songs, iTunes also offers downloadable audio books and currently has 5000 books online.

Both companies offer their own brand of mobile digital audio players. The Napster product was created in partnership with Samsung and works exclusively with PCs. The iPod, Apple's mobile

digital audio player, works exclusively with iTunes, and is both Mac and PC compatible. According to market studies, the iPod ranks first in market share at 31 percent.

Some analysts believe that consumers will be put off by the need to pay for these services, preferring instead to exchange unlimited songs over the internet for free. Peer-to-peer software such as Gnutella and LimeWire enables users to share an unlimited quantity and variety of songs at no cost. Copyright laws dealing with this issue vary. While music labels have attempted to discourage illegal sharing of music through several high profile lawsuits against downloaders, their ability to continue may be hampered if the courts do not grant them the right to obtain information on user identities from internet service providers. As a result, many observers feel the market for this type of service is still vague and uncertain.

Napster
www.napster.com

iTunes
www.apple.com/itunes

Questions

1. How do the business models of Napster 2.0 and Apple respond to the realities of purchasing music in the age of the internet?

2. Given the current legal climate surrounding music downloads are Napster 2.0 and Apple likely to succeed?

SOURCES: S. Jobs, *iTunes for Windows Introduction*, **www.apple.com/quicktime/**; **http://ptech.wsj.com/solution.html**, accessed October 23, 2003; J. Graham, "Meet the New Napster—and the Rest of the Pack," *USA Today*, **www.usatoday.com/tech/ techreviews/products/2003-10-13-download-options_x.htm**, accessed October 13, 2003; Roxio, **www.napster.com**, accessed October 17, 2003; D. Fester, "Q&A: Choosing a Digital Music Service for Windows Users," *PressPass*, **www.microsoft.com/presspass/features/ 2003/oct03/10-15musicservices.asp**, accessed October 22, 2003.

While the business press devotes a great deal of attention to B2C models, business to business (B2B) models actually represent a much higher proportion of e-business activity conducted in the economy and often involve multi-year, large volume, high value contracts between business partners. For example, Ariba Inc.,

Ariba Inc.
www.ariba.com

recently merged with FreeMarkets, arranges reverse auctions where pre-qualified suppliers bid on contracts offered by a buyer. In contrast to a regular auction, where a seller offers goods to many buyers who compete by bidding up the sale price of the goods being auctioned, a **reverse auction** has one buyer offering a supply contract to many sellers who compete by bidding down the supply price for the contract. Other examples of B2B models involve the sale of computers (Dell Inc.), office supplies (STAPLES Business Depot) and job listings (Workopolis).

In addition to B2C and B2B models used for conducting e-commerce activities on the internet, there is a category of business to employee (B2E) internet models that are used by many entities to support their e-business activity; for example, through websites that enable employees to register for benefits, monitor the status of their benefits, and update personal information as necessary; or, websites that provide employees with training and procedural guidance.

Finally, it is important to recognize that governments can utilize internet business models to enhance the delivery of services to citizens and to secure services from business entities. Canada is considered one of the leaders in the use of the internet by various levels of government for the delivery of services to citizens. The objective of the federal government's G2C initiative is to provide easy and seamless access to services that may involve more than one government department or other levels of government, while protecting the confidentiality of information and users' rights to privacy.[3] Some examples of government to consumer (G2C) e-business activities include online tax filings (Canada Revenue Agency), driver's license renewal kiosks and information dissemination over the web (provincial and federal governments). Examples of government to business (G2B) activities include tax filings (Canada Revenue Agency) and the open bidding system on government contracts (Contracts Canada). The federal "Government On-Line" program has its own website at www.gol-ged.gc.ca.

While labels such as B2C and B2B can help focus discussion, they can be misleading. Figure 2.1 illustrates a common internet business scenario, where a business can be involved in B2C (business to consumer), B2B (business to business), and B2E (business to employee) domains at the same time. A consumer purchases goods or services over the internet from a business (B2C) that also sells its goods or services to another business (B2B). The two companies operate internal intranets for their employees and other insiders (B2E) and connect with each other through an extranet, which is an expanded portion of their respective intranets or a restricted portion of the internet.

Core Business Processes

Most businesses today have some degree of internet presence. The "bricks versus clicks" label is used to distinguish the degree to which core business processes depend on the internet. Figure 2.2 illustrates the continuum of internet business models based on the bricks versus clicks dichotomy. The "clicks" label is applied to business models that are solely or predominantly based on the internet (these are also called "pure plays"), whereas the "bricks" label is applied to business models that are solely or predominantly based on provision of goods and services through physical outlets such as stores or branch offices.

Pure play e-businesses are completely focused on the internet, with physical sites devoted solely to housing the management and operations personnel and e-business technology infrastructure. Some examples of pure play internet business models are Hotmail, Yahoo!, eBay, E*TRADE Financial, and Destina.ca. Pure plays typically deal solely with electronic goods and services rather than physical

REVERSE AUCTION
A reverse auction has one buyer offering a supply contract to many sellers, who compete by bidding down the supply price for the contract.

STAPLES Business Depot
www.staples.ca

Workopolis
www.workopolis.com

Canada Revenue Agency
www.cra-arc.gc.ca

Government of Canada
www.canada.gc.ca

Contracts Canada
www.contractscanada.gc.ca

Government On-Line
www.gol-ged.gc.ca

Hotmail
www.hotmail.com

Destina.ca Inc.
www.destina.ca

Figure 2.1   Types of E-Business Relationships and Interactions

An e-business can be involved in a variety of relationships and interactions with customers, suppliers, and other entities.

goods or services. Unless the goods or services being provided are digital, it is very difficult to implement a pure-play model. As discussed in chapter 1, Amazon originally attempted to implement a pure-play model whereby it would hold no inventory but would simply broker sales on behalf of book publishers, distributors, and specialty bookstores. However, Amazon found that to provide satisfactory customer service it had to have warehouses to stock the high-demand physical products (books, DVDs, electronics) that it had to distribute in timely fashion or risk losing business to competitors.

On the other end of the continuum are business models that are almost entirely focused on delivering goods or services through physical sites, with websites used primarily to display brochures, flyers, and coupons to attract customers to the physical sales or service sites. Some examples of such business models are McDonald's, Shoppers Drug Mart, and Canadian Tire.

Between these two extremes lies a continuum of e-business models with varying degrees of reliance on the internet for the conduct of business activities. A step up from the "bricks" model is the use of a web storefront to create an alternative channel for some or all of the entity's products or services, as if the e-commerce website was simply a special type of store or branch. Examples of this approach include Indigo Books and Music, Inc., Sears, Future Shop, and Royal Bank of Canada.

Another step up from the web storefront is the use of internet-based sales channels for users to order goods and services, supported by a physical distribution network. Examples of such business models are Netflix, Inc., Amazon, 1-800-Flowers, Grocery Gateway, and President's Choice Financial.

Some analysts have observed a growing convergence between pure play e-businesses and traditional offline businesses. This has led some soothsayers to predict the disappearance of the "e" in e-business due to the adoption of e-business

McDonald's
www.mcdonalds.ca

Shoppers Drug Mart
www.shoppersdrugmart.ca

Canadian Tire
www.canadiantire.ca.

Indigo Books and Music, Inc.
www.chapters.indigo.ca

Sears
www.sears.ca

Future Shop
www.futureshop.ca

Royal Bank of Canada
www.royalbank.com

Netflix Inc.
www.netflix.com

1-800-FLOWERS.COM, Inc.
www.1800flowers.com

Grocery Gateway, Inc.
www.grocerygateway.com

Figure 2.2   Continuum of Internet Business Models

Internet business models range from "bricks" to "clicks" with many variations between these two end-points, even within the same product or service sector.

Focused on physical sites with "e" capability mainly used for brochures, flyers and coupons to attract customers to physical sites; e.g., bakkaphoenixbooks.com

Predominantly physical sites with a Internet store as an alternative channel for some or all of the entity's products or services; e.g., barnesandnoble.com

Internet based ordering; supported by a network of physical distribution or service sites; e.g, amazon.com

Completely focused on the Internet with physical sites solely devoted to housing management and e-commerce operations; e.g., apple.com/itunes/store/books

bricks   clicks

models by all businesses. Others predict that customers will use websites primarily to research their purchases, but will continue to make their purchases in a physical store, limiting the growth of some e-business models; however, statistics on online shopping behaviour contradict this view and, on the contrary, show a continuing expansion of e-commerce activity.[4] Even during the sharp pullback in technology spending after the tech bust, e-commerce spending and revenues continued to grow very significantly.[5]

Indeed, some of the most exciting developments in business today stem from innovations that are made economically feasible and compelling by the networking aspects of the internet: stores that never close, elimination of geographic barriers in the supply and demand chain, pervasive use of auctions to replace fixed prices, continuously-gathered customer feedback to rate products and services, seamless delivery of digital goods and services, and many other such innovations.

Some B2B processes appear to be similar to B2C processes; however, often the B2B models are more complex than their B2C counterparts from both a revenue and a cost perspective. Revenues are often generated under some form of long term agreement that defines the terms of business between the supplier and the customer. The process of negotiating, establishing, and maintaining these arrangements adds complexity and cost to the business model, but once in place, results in a long term relationship rather than the unpredictable, one-off nature of much B2C commerce. For example, STAPLES Business Depot and Dell have specific webpages devoted to their major business customers that are similar to those used by retail customers, except that they are customized for each major business customer, listing pre-negotiated items for sale at pre-negotiated prices. To arrange its reverse auctions, Ariba Inc. employs specialist industry consultants who help buyers create the supply specifications, pre-qualify suppliers, set up the auctions, and manage the auction processes, supported by proprietary software developed for this purpose.

As mentioned earlier, B2B business dealings often involve long term arrangements that are documented in legal contracts containing specific performance requirements by the parties to the relationship, often including financial penalties for failing to comply with the terms of the agreement. Many of the contractual arrangements with "downstream partners" (companies closer to the point of sale) implicitly require the B2B entity to manage its "upstream partners" (companies closer to the point of production) to facilitate its fulfillment of its obligations to its downstream partners. As a result, entities involved in B2B commerce must invest a great deal of attention and effort to managing their B2B relationships and create and maintain trust in those relationships.

Core Products and Services/Revenue Models

The literature discusses the following 11 e-business revenue models:[6]

1. Merchant Model—Sales of non-digital and digital products (per unit or volume price)
2. Direct Sales by Manufacturer Model—non-digital and digital products (per unit or volume price)
3. Manufacturer Service Model (indirect revenue)
4. Subscription Model (includes free trial model)
5. Utility Model (service fee)
6. Infomediary Model (service fee)
7. Licensing Model (licensing fee)
8. Advertising Model (fee per ad displayed)
9. Affiliate Model (commission on sales generated)
10. Community Model (advertising-type fees)
11. Brokerage Model (transaction fee per transaction and/or percentage of order value)

From this list of models, it is possible to identify the following five subsets: direct sales of products and services (categories 1 and 2), sales of intellectual property/information (categories 4, 5, 6, and 7), intermediation (category 11), advertising (categories 8, 9, and 10), and non-revenue (3 and not-for-profit sites). A noteworthy reference source on these models is a website maintained by Michael Rappa (http://digitalenterprise.org/models/models.html). This section provides examples of these revenue models and illustrative products and services.

1. Merchant Model Wholesalers or retailers of goods and services (online retailers are often referred to as "e-tailers") exemplify the merchant model. If the business sells and distributes only over the web, it is a pure-play e-tailer (e.g., Apple iTunes Music Store). If it also has a traditional bricks-and-mortar presence, it is referred to as a "bricks and clicks" or "clicks and mortar" operation, or a "surf-and-turf" site. Such sites are often based on an online catalogue. A good example of a bricks-and-clicks retail operation is Sears. Its very successful entry into web retailing was made easier by its long history of selling through a catalogue.

2. Direct Sales by Manufacturer Model Product manufacturers can use the web to sell their products directly to customers. As discussed earlier, there are several variations of this model, depending on to whom the manufacturer sells. If it sells to end consumers, then this effectively opens a new distribution channel, which streamlines the distribution process by bypassing wholesalers and distributors. However, this situation can also create **channel conflict**, a situation in which various sales channels for a single organization operate in competition with each other. Distributors may not approve of this system and may even rebel, as was the case with Levi's when it started selling jeans directly to customers online. Still, by using the web to sell to customers, manufacturers can better track buying habits and preferences—thus creating a considerable advantage. Nike has been able to satisfy its distributors as well as maintain a direct sale website. One of its features enables customers to custom build their own shoes. Perhaps the most widely cited example of the effective use of the manufacturer direct sales model is Dell.

If the web is used by a manufacturer to sell to other manufacturers, wholesalers and distributors, then it takes on the form of a B2B site rather than a B2C operation. Sometimes the two kinds of sites are combined, where the site is avail-

iTunes
www.itunes.com

Sears
www.sears.ca

CHANNEL CONFLICT
The situation in which various sales channels for a single organization operate in competition with each other.

Nike
www.niketown.com

able to consumers but there is a login for large business customers, government entities, wholesalers, or distributors where they can obtain special pricing or other special services, as with Dell.ca. Either way, the use of the web has the potential for greater efficiency than the traditional means of distribution.

3. Manufacturer Service Model Product manufacturers that use the web to provide customer service for their products employ the manufacturer service model. By using the web for this purpose, a company can help support its sales growth and reduce the cost of maintaining extensive technical support personnel. An often-cited example of the effective use of the web for customer service is Cisco Systems.

Cisco Systems
www.cisco.com

4. Subscription Model Some businesses have users subscribe to their site, paying a monthly or annual fee, in order to view some or all of the content or obtain other services. This model has seen uneven success because of the general reluctance of web users to pay for content. For example, some businesses that tried to have users pay for their content, including Encyclopædia Britannica Inc. and Pantellic (Nova Scotia-based owner of the online photo site PhotoPoint.com), suffered a substantial drop in visitors as a result. Pantellic subsequently went out of business. However, some sites have been successful with the subscription model. For example, America Online, Inc. provides access to the internet and to its extensive online content for a monthly fee. Netflix provides DVDs to subscribers by mail. Newspapers offer some of their content for free and require subscriptions to view the full content. The website of Halifax's *The ChronicleHerald* provides an example of this approach. Some print publications like *Business Week* allow their subscribers to access their online editions at no additional cost. Subscription models often use free trial subscriptions to persuade customers to sign up for a full subscription.

America Online, Inc.
www.aol.com

The ChronicleHerald
www.herald.ns.ca

Business Week
www.businessweek.com

5. Utility Model The utility model is a user "pay as you go" site. It offers specific services "on demand" for a fee. Usually it is necessary to open an account to make use of the services and to facilitate the charges. The utility model offers an advantage over subscription sites in that the user only has to pay for the content he or she specifically wants. For example, CompuServe provides local internet dial-up access numbers in major cities around the world to enable users to avoid long distance charges when they are abroad. Access time is metered and charged to a credit card number. The development of good micropayment systems (discussed in chapter 6) would be a boost to sites implementing the utility model, as they could charge small amounts for small services.

CompuServe Interactive Services, Inc.
www.compuserve.com

6. Infomediary Model Sites that build on the economic value of information about people's purchasing habits are referred to as "infomediaries." These sites offer something free to users, and in exchange, ask them to fill out information about themselves and their buying habits. Sometimes they require a registration process for users to enter the site. The data collected this way are then sold to other businesses who are charged a service fee for having their e-commerce activity monitored and analyzed by the infomediary service provider. An example of an infomediary is BizRate.com. BizRate.com provides an online merchant rating service that merchants subscribe to. Online shoppers fill out a short survey each time they shop at a BizRate.com member site. BizRate.com uses the survey to assign ratings to the online merchants on various dimensions that are then displayed on those sites. BizRate.com also provides detailed analyses to its clients to help them improve their ratings.

BizRate.com
www.bizrate.com

7. Licensing Model Licensing models are often applied to long-lived intellectual property such as software. Licensing revenues are often based on a formula that takes into account the number of locations and users. The customer pays a one-time licensing fee to be able to use or resell the software. Software that is used to

BANNER ADS
Small icons containing advertising messages that, when clicked, take the user to the site of the advertiser.

CLICK-THROUGH COUNTS
The number of times that users have clicked on a banner ad to take them to the website to which it refers.

enable e-commerce such as that sold by Ariba, Commerce One, i2 Technologies, and BroadVision are examples. Such software is part of the infrastructure of an e-business, along with hardware, facilities, networks, and support personnel.

8. Advertising Model From an economic point of view, advertising on the web works similarly to the way it works in traditional media such as radio and television. Content is provided on the website (either free or at a bargain discount) that is intended to attract people, and advertisements are placed on the site for a fee paid by the advertiser. Quite often, the site makes its profits from the advertising revenue rather than from the content itself. On the web, the advertising model has been prevalent, as users have become accustomed to receiving free content. The advertising messages on the web often take the form of **banner ads,** which are small icons containing advertising messages that, when clicked, take the user to the site of the advertiser. Sometimes the fees payable on these banner ads are dependent on the **click-through count** on the banner ad. Click-through counts are the number of times that users have clicked on a banner ad to take them to the website to which it refers, and are counted automatically by software on the website. Since a single user could click on the banner ad several times, click-through counts do not necessarily result in an accurate count of individual users who use the ad. Click-through counts and other metrics used by advertisers are discussed in more detail in chapter 12.

The advertising model is only viable when there is a sufficiently large volume of user traffic on the site. Therefore, the strategies followed by advertising sites tend to focus on volume generation by offering diversified content and a wide array of services, like e-mail, chat, news, and message boards. Generalized portal sites like Yahoo! and AltaVista exemplify this approach. In contrast to these sites, Google provides one main service, a highly rated search engine that has attracted a large volume of traffic and with it, significant advertising revenue.

Yahoo! also provides an example of a personalized portal—one that allows the user to customize the interface to show items of particular personal interest. This service is offered through the My Yahoo! service. Numerous other generic sites offer this capability to develop user loyalty while maintaining a high volume of traffic. There is also a value-added element to personalized portals through improved access to information that may be more relevant to the user.

The idea behind a personalized portal is that users will use it as their own entry point onto the internet. Whereas ordinary portals attempt to do this as well, personalized portals seek to lure the user into using the site regularly because they allow the user to structure the site to cater to his or her particular interests.

Some portals target a defined user base, such as sports enthusiasts, investors, or homebuyers. Such specialized portals still seek large volume, but since they can't count on volumes as large as those of general portals, they often charge a premium for their advertising. The premium is supported by the claim that users with a particular interest are on the site, and since their interests are known, product advertising can be targeted to them. As users become more sophisticated in using the web, specialized portals are likely to grow in number.

Other sites use the "incentive marketing" approach, which involves paying visitors for viewing some content or filling out forms or entering contests. Payment takes the form of some kind of point scheme similar to frequent-flyer programs offered by the airlines. An early entrant to this kind of site was Cybergold, which offered an "earn and spend community" by bringing together advertisers interested in incentive-based marketing. Cybergold was subsequently bought by MyPoints.com, Inc. Advertising methods and e-marketing are discussed in more detail in chapter 11.

9. Affiliate Model A good example of an affiliate model is a banner ad exchange. Affiliate programs can be joined through affiliate manager sites, such as Affiliates World, which offer a point of contact for all those interested in exchanging banners. Sometimes, the arrangement includes payment of commissions to the sites hosting banner ads when sales are made to customers using them to enter the site. For example, Example Inc. might enter into a banner arrangement with Amazon under which an Amazon banner ad is placed on the Example website. Amazon tracks the entry points of people entering their site, and therefore knows which visitors have entered their site through the banner ad on Example.com. Amazon also can track when those people buy goods, and how much they spend. They can then pay a commission to Example.com for the sales.

Affiliates World
www.affilates-world.com

For Amazon, this is a way of building sales. For Example Inc., it is a way of generating some revenue from Amazon with no risk and very little cost. Amazon was a pioneer with this type of model and was granted a broad-ranging patent on the process that some observers feel may inhibit the activities of others in the field.

10. Community Model Community sites depend on user loyalty and community identification for their viability. The sites are usually built with volunteer labour and feature a variety of content from the community, usually provided free of charge, although sometimes the site charges to host the content. The challenge for these sites is to provide adequate functionality and keep them current, given their reliance on volunteers. They can present an opportunity for businesses to advertise and to provide a convenient access point to their own site. A successful community site can function as a portal to local businesses, almost as a virtual shopping mall. Funding for these sites is sometimes solicited as donations from community members. An example of such a site is the WorldGenWeb Project.

The WorldGenWeb Project
www.worldgenweb.org

11. Brokerage Model Brokers are often referred to as market-makers because they bring buyers and sellers together and facilitate transactions between them. Brokers generate revenues through a variety of transaction fees and commission charges for the transactions they enable or facilitate. There are a large number of brokerage sites and they take on a variety of specific forms, the major ones being:[7]

- classifieds
- virtual malls
- market exchanges
- buy/sell fulfillment sites
- auction brokers
- reverse auctions
- transaction brokers
- metamediaries
- search agents

As the discussion below will illustrate, there are many types of **brokerage sites**, but it is clear that one feature they have in common is the fact they bring together buyers and sellers to facilitate business transactions on the web. Chapter 8 discusses in more detail how some forms of brokerage sites operate on the internet.

BROKERAGE SITES
Sites that bring together buyers and sellers to facilitate business transactions on the web.

Classifieds These are simply sites that provide advertisements similar to the classified ads one finds in newspapers. The broker charges for the listings, regardless of whether a transaction ultimately takes place. An example of this kind of site is workopolis.com, which lists job advertisements for jobs across Canada. Employment agencies also use this site to find jobs for people or people for jobs.

Edistributor.com is a variation on this theme. It hosts catalogues for a large number of product manufacturers for the benefit of volume and retail buyers.

Virtual Malls As the name indicates, a virtual mall is a site that hosts a number of online merchants. The mall charges fees for set-up, listings, and transactions. Yahoo! provides a good example, which also illustrates the combination of a mall with a popular portal site, assisting businesses to attract a large volume of visitors to the site.

Market Exchanges Market exchanges are a part of the business model often referred to as trading exchanges, which have been one of the fastest growing types of B2B business. Figure 2.3 illustrates a typical market exchange. In market exchanges, pricing of transactions can be determined by simple offers, negotiations, or auctions. A good example of a market exchange is ChemConnect Inc., which is now the biggest online exchange for chemical trading. Trading exchanges are more fully discussed in chapter 8.

Buy/Sell Fulfillment Sites A buy/sell fulfillment site takes customer orders to buy or sell a product or service. This is a very widely used model, ranging from online financial brokerages, like E*TRADE Canada, where customers place, buy, and sell orders for transacting financial instruments, to online auto brokers such as CarsDirect.com, Inc., to online travel agencies. In this kind of site, the broker charges a transaction fee, but often a lower fee than can be obtained offline because the cost of executing transactions on the internet is lower, enabling the savings to be passed on to the customer. E*TRADE Canada provides a good example of this pricing practice, where the price of executing trades is much lower than it would be if carried out by a traditional broker. Another example is Hotels.com, which lists discounted hotel rooms, charging a listing fee to the hotels and a transaction fee to the customer at the time of the reservation (and payment).

Auction Brokers An auction broker is a site, like eBay.com, that conducts auctions for sellers who list their products on the site. The broker charges the seller a fee, which is typically scaled to the value of the transaction. Normally the seller establishes a minimum bid and then accepts the highest offer. Specific offering and bidding rules will vary according to the site. Auctions are very effective ways of maximizing revenues, although they require a sufficient number of participants to compete for a given item at a given place and time. Because the internet enables

Figure 2.3   Structure of a Market Exchange

A market exchange provides a vehicle for suppliers to connect with buyers. The exchange provides the tools for buyers to list supply requirements, for sellers to register their supply offers, a price setting mechanism such as an auction for buyers and sellers to negotiate a price, and a fulfillment process for the resulting transactions.

Companion Website

to accompany

E-Business: A Canadian Perspective for a Networked World

Second Edition

www.pearsoned.ca/trites

As a student purchasing an access code for this Companion Website, you are entitled to a prepaid subscription to premium services on our web-based learning environment. You will have unlimited online access to the Review Questions and Exercises, Problems for Discussion, Recommended Readings, Case Studies, textual material, streaming CBC Videos, Practice Quizzes, and many other Web resources.

What do you do with this access code?

1. Locate the site:
Launch your Web browser and type **www.pearsoned.ca/trites** into the location area.

2. Use your Pearson Education Canada access code:
The first time you access the site, you will be required to register using this access code. Type in the access code on this page (one word per box) and follow the steps indicated. During registration, you will choose a personal User ID and Password for logging onto the site. Your access code can be used only once to establish your subscription, which is non-transferable. Once your registration has been confirmed, you will need to enter only your personal User ID and Password each time you enter the site.

This code is valid for 8 months of access to this website.

Warning: Once you enter your access code, registration processing may take up to 3 minutes to complete. If you do not wait for confirmation before proceeding, the access code will become invalid.

3. Log onto the site:
Once your registration is confirmed, follow the link to the website to log on with your newly established User ID and Password.

CSTE-AHEAD-BOTHA-TYPED-SAINT-HEARD

This access code is only valid with the purchase of a new book.
For help using this access code, please email us at

online.support@pearsoned.com

Printed in Canada

remote participants to interact online in an **asynchronous** manner (activities are not conducted in real time but involve delays, such as sending email messages for others to pick up and respond to at a later time), many physical barriers to holding auctions are eliminated and auction models are becoming widespread on the internet. Chapter 8 discusses in more detail how various types of B2C and B2B auction sites operate on the internet.

Reverse Auctions Whereas a standard auction involves a seller auctioning goods off to a group of buyers, a reverse auction has sellers competing to fill a buyer's order. A notable example of a reverse auction broker site is Priceline.com with its patented "name your own price" model that was first applied to airplane ticket purchases. Guru.com is a site devoted to matching professionals who wish to sell their services with buyers who have projects that need to be completed. Guru.com uses a reverse auction whereby the freelancers bid on the contracts posted by the buyers—lowest bid wins.

Transaction Brokers A transaction broker facilitates the completion of a transaction by enabling payment. Credit card companies are transaction brokers. They receive a fee from the merchant for facilitating payments for customer purchases. PayPal is an example of a third-party transaction broker that operates on the internet to facilitate settlements for purchases for a small fee per transaction. PayPal provides a plug in "shopping cart" that sellers can easily add to their websites. Buyers purchase items by depositing funds into the seller's PayPal account. The seller then retrieves the funds from its PayPal account.

Metamediaries These are intermediaries that gather and coordinate the products and services offered by other intermediaries that specialize in specific areas. A good example is Edmunds.com, Inc., which links numerous automobile sellers, service providers, and automobile buyers; organizing information from numerous disparate sources for a unified view of a group of products and related services such as specific car models, accessories, financing, and insurance.

Search Agents A search agent is a site that uses an intelligent software agent or "bot" to search the internet for the best price for a good or service wanted by a buyer. Examples of this type of site are RoboShopper and MySimon.

As the previous discussion makes clear, there are many approaches to offering goods and services over the internet. While some analysts have challenged the validity of some of the models discussed in this section, all of them are in use today and the ultimate proof of their validity will be their degree of acceptance in the marketplace. As most businesses begin to take advantage of the internet for at least some of their activities, they are implementing these models, sometime creating new variations of them. As they gain experience and observe their e-business models' strengths and weaknesses, businesses will often combine them with other models, seeking to create a unique value proposition for their customers; for example, news sites that offer both subscription and utility services, as well as infomediary and licensing opportunities.

Alliances

The literature on e-business models emphasizes the importance of various types of relationships, emphasizing the networking benefits of partnerships, alliances, and other collaborative relationships that can help companies leverage their resources and competencies to create competitive advantage.[8] However, this view is not shared by all. Michael E. Porter believes that some entities have forfeited their pro-

ASYNCHRONOUS
A term for activities that are not conducted in real time but involve delays.

Priceline.com Incorporated
www.priceline.com

Guru
www.guru.com

PayPal
www.paypal.com

Edmunds.com, Inc.
www.edmunds.com

RoboShopper
www.roboshopper.com

MySimon
www.mysimon.com

Canadian Snapshots

Old and New Dogs with New E-Tricks

The Canadian Imperial Bank of Commerce (CIBC) has been engaged in web banking through its website for several years. During 2000, CIBC and Sympatico-Lycos Inc. (SLI) joined forces to create Amicus Bank, a no-fee web bank that they would operate in conjunction with each other. Their idea represents a common view that the web can bring about fundamental changes in the banking industry.

David Marshall, CIBC's vice-chairman of electronic banking, said, "What we are seeing now is the start of the next 10 years in banking. Companies not traditionally in banking services have figured out there's not a great mystique about banking, so there really is no practical barrier to offering financial services."

The CIBC-SLI deal was viewed by analysts as a template for online companies trying to boost their revenue. Until that time, such companies had been prevented from entering retail banking, which involves taking customer deposits, by a lack of trust from both the public and the banking regulators. The partnership between CIBC and SLI was designed to overcome that obstacle by having the backing of the established firm, CIBC, and by offering chequing and savings accounts and other services to the internet provider's customers. Sympatico has a monthly online audience of some seven million visitors. This provides an extensive target market of potential customers for an online, no-fee, high-interest banking

service. Both partners had somewhat different goals for this venture. Sympatico hoped to supplement its ad revenue by selling additional services to its audience. It also planned to use the banking venture to bridge into other financial services, like brokerage, mortgages, and automobile sales financing. CIBC, on the other hand, wanted to extend its banking services to new customers by linking with partners that had a household brand name and that were leaders in their industry. It already had partnerships with Loblaw Companies Ltd. in Canada, and Winn-Dixie Stores Inc. and Safeway Inc. in the United States, along with mutual fund giant Investors Group Inc. According to a company spokesperson, the venture would avoid the high marketing costs of creating brand awareness and the high costs of building a branch network and could thereby pass the savings on to customers by offering no-fee banking and low rates on products such as savings accounts, GICs, loans and mortgages.

Other banks also expanded into online banking, among them, Canada's largest bank, the Royal Bank of Canada, which bought a 20-percent stake in AOL Canada Inc. in 1999 and has a marketing agreement with AOL. In contrast with the CIBC-SLI approach, the Royal Bank promoted the online banking services under its own name, rather than a separate brand.

By mid-2000, Amicus had 600 000 customers in North

America and was hoping to have 800 000 customers by year-end, since the low-cost service offered by Amicus could not be matched by traditional banks with their expensive infrastructures, including branches. Also, the Amicus customers had access to CIBC's extensive network of automated banking machines.

However, by late 2002 CIBC shut down the U.S. operations of Amicus and scaled back e-banking operations in Canada, laying off about 1100 employees, most of them in the United States, and incurring a pre-tax loss of $375 million. In Canada, CIBC also shut down bizSmart, a no-fee internet, telephone, and kiosk banking program for small business that was located in about 60 Business Depot stores.

Although Winn-Dixie's Marketplace Bank had grown to 185 outlets and Safeway's Safeway Select had grown to 161 outlets, the market reach of these outlets was not sufficient to make the units profitable. Weaker demand for online banking services in the U.S. relative to Canada appeared to be the main reason for Amicus' downfall. Apparently, the market for internet-based services didn't grow as fast in the United States as had been anticipated, based on the success of President's Choice Financial in Canada. It seems that, unlike Canadians, Americans still preferred paper cheques and branches to telephone and internet banking.

Canadian Imperial Bank of Commerce (CIBC)
www.cibc.com

Questions

1. How does the strategy for Amicus fit with the corporate strategy of CIBC? How does it fit with the corporate strategies of its partners?

2. Given the ups and downs that Amicus has experienced to date, do you think its strategy can still work? Explain.

SOURCES: www.computerworld.com; J. Middlemiss, "Amicus Retreats from the U.S.," *International News* (January 7, 2003), **www.banktech.com/story/internationalNews/ BNK20030107S0006**, accessed March 4, 2004.

prietary advantages by engaging in misguided partnerships and outsourcing relationships that rob them of their distinctiveness.[9] The Canadian Snapshots box describes a situation where several entities sought to achieve a strategic purpose by collaborating in the implementation of an internet business model.

Resource Management

The final component of an e-business model is resource management. As noted in the introduction, resource management refers to the processes by which resources are acquired, developed, and allocated to the core business activities. In an internet-based business model, as in most business models, a key resource is capital. Capital can be raised from friends, family, venture capitalists, banks, and equity markets, depending on the entity's stage of development. That capital is then used to acquire or develop other resources such as technology and people that will implement the business model. In many cases, the entity will outsource some of the its activities to firms with specialized competencies in areas such as web hosting or IT infrastructure provisioning and will need to have processes to identify alternative suppliers, select the most appropriate supplier, and enter into a contract for the required services that protects the entity's interests. When the entity develops its own technology or business process, it will need to have sound project management processes in place to prioritize projects, staff them, and effectively manage project activities. To effectively align the resource management activities with the entity's strategic objectives will require a performance measurement system that utilizes metrics linked to strategic objectives to guide and motivate entity personnel to take actions that are congruent with the entity's strategy. Subsequent sections of this book will deal with these issues extensively.

Internet Business Models and Business Strategy

While it is clear that there are many business models being used to deliver value through the use of the internet, these models are not all mutually exclusive. They can be combined in numerous ways to achieve business goals. For example, an e-tailer may make use of the simple merchant model, but also may use the site to advertise its bricks-and-mortar business. It may enter into banner exchanges and make money through banner ad commissions, or it may enter into other affiliate programs, virtual malls, and market exchanges.

The specific model or combination of models that a business uses helps to define its internet or e-business strategy. The e-business strategy will determine the value proposition that differentiates the entity's e-business offerings from those of its competitors, a distinctive value chain tailored to its value proposition and choices of how various elements of the e-business will fit together and with other aspects of the business. Will the site be used as a stand-alone initiative? Or will it be used to complement the existing business or even to launch a new type of business? The business models described earlier in this chapter provide a menu for the business strategist to consider when addressing these questions.

The E-Business in Global Perspective box on the following page illustrates a situation where various models are combined to achieve a strategic purpose. Although this case involves several different organizations trying to work together, the same approach can apply to a single organization. In any event, the thrust of a great deal of contemporary e-business involves several different organizations working together in collaboration to achieve a common strategic aim or goal.

E-Business in Global Perspective

E-Models at ChinaECNet

ChinaECNet is a web portal founded in 2000 as a joint venture between U.S.-based Avnet Inc. and China's Ministry of Information Industries. It is China's leading digital media network dedicated to the electronics manufacturing industry. It comprises an online platform with over 108 000 registered members and *GEC Magazine* (*Global Electronic Components Magazine*) with a circulation of 36 000. Its membership mainly comprises electronic engineers and purchasing professionals.

Phoenix-based Avnet, Inc. is an authorized B2B distributor for the products of more than 250 of the world's leading technology manufacturers. Its two operating groups, Avnet Electronics Marketing and Avnet Technology Solutions, market, inventory, distribute, and add value to electronic components, embedded systems, and enterprise computing products for customers in 68 countries. Avnet also delivers supply-chain and design-chain services and value-added services such as device programming, systems integration, and systems configuration. Through the joint venture with the Ministry of Information Industries, Avnet's goal was to sell parts and integrate its own supply chain business into the Chinese internet.

ChinaECNet provides the Chinese engineering and manufacturing communities with direct, web-enabled procurement services for electronic components and product information. The portal enables small- and mid-sized domestic Chinese suppliers and manufacturers to easily enter into electronic business. Its Online Procurement Platform serves the component information needs of over 2000 Chinese OEMs (original equipment manufacturers). On a regular basis, over 230 OEMs purchase components through this platform.

With a connection to Avnet's SAP system, Chinese customers can instantly access over 200 000 different types of components for pricing and delivery information. They can also fulfill their orders online.

In addition to the Online Procurement Platform, ChinaECNet provides material procurement and an inventory management platform for many major Chinese OEMs. On a secure platform that is only accessible by the OEMs themselves, Chinese OEMs can review worldwide inventory, lead-time, and pricing. They can also use this web-enabled platform to manage their orders, inventory, and shipments.

ChinaECNet also hosts a public component exchange platform that lists both buy and sell information. Currently, there are over 200 000 listings with buyers and sellers worldwide. Transactions resulting from these listings take place independently of ChinaECNet. Another feature of the website is the Data Sheet Center, which currently contains cross linkages to over 700 000 component data sheets available for users to access and download, helping to speed up Chinese engineers' development process and facilitate purchasing professionals' purchasing decisions. These services provide a variety of benefits that would normally be available only to large or electronically sophisticated companies. They include, for example, the ability to link to foreign supply chain management (SCM) networks, giving companies, through the internet, many of the automated supply functions of more complex SCM systems.

Another benefit offered by ChinaECNet is that registrants can operate without the extensive government regulations that have been blamed for bogging down Chinese foreign business. For example, it has been the Chinese practice that most foreign vendors must use a Chinese agent through which to sell to Chinese customers, and foreign vendors are also banned from accepting Chinese currency as payment. ChinaECNet, however, can electronically send invoices directly to customers, who can pay in Chinese currency by bank transfer.

ChinaECNet
www.chinaecnet.com/eng

Questions

1. Discuss the business model being followed by Avnet Inc., ChinaECNet, and the Chinese manufacturers using the portal.
2. How do these business models work together to result in competitive advantages for all participants?

SOURCES: www.computerworld.com; www.avnet.com, accessed November 6, 2004; www.chinaecnet.com/eng/about/us.asp, accessed November 6, 2004.

The previous discussion has identified a number of revenue models for e-business. However, as noted at the beginning of this chapter, a business model includes other components in addition to the approach a company will take to generate revenue. It also includes a set of related business operations and outlines the model's cost structure, required investments in tangible and intangible assets, and other factors. To achieve profitability, an internet business model must not only generate revenue, but do so utilizing effective business processes that are executed and managed by competent, motivated personnel, and supported by an appropriate technology infrastructure as will be discussed in parts 2 and 3 of this book.

Fitting the E-Business Strategy Into the Corporate Strategy

For many businesses, the procedural aspects of corporate strategic planning are a well-established feature of management. Strategic plans are developed periodically, sometimes every year, sometimes every few years with annual updates. They require employees from across the organization to be involved in determining goals, strategies, and work activities.

As illustrated in figure 2.4, most strategic planning exercises involve a process of developing a broad vision, considering the constraints and assumptions that constrict or guide that vision, and defining strategic objectives for the business that come as close as possible to the vision. The strategic objectives must give recognition to the constraints, which might be based on resource restrictions, environmental constraints like legal and regulatory stipulations, and other matters. Each year, the process of strategic planning will normally involve reviewing the previous year's plans and updating those plans to reflect new trends and events or even a changed vision. Then a plan is drafted, reviewed, and analyzed by the various stakeholders and a second draft prepared. Finally, the plan is approved and action begins.

The process illustrated in figure 2.4 should result in a strategic plan that addresses five key areas:[10]

1. Arenas where the entity will be active, including the product categories, market segments, geographic areas, core technologies to be employed, and value creation stages.

2. Vehicles for moving towards goal achievement such as internal development, joint ventures, licensing or franchising, and acquisitions.

3. Differentiators that represent competitive advantages such as image, customization, price, styling, and product reliability.

4. Staging the speed and sequence of moves such as the speed of expansion and the sequence of initiatives.

5. Economic logic for obtaining returns on investment, such as being the lowest cost producer due to scale advantages or scope and replication advantages, or obtaining premium prices for outstanding service or proprietary product features.

Of course, the strategies and objectives in this kind of a plan are those that relate to the success of the business as a whole. The e-business strategy must fit into the corporate plan. See the E-Strategy box for an example of how an e-business strategy can support the overall corporate strategy of a business.

How the e-business strategy fits into the corporate plan depends on the extent to which the business is involved in e-business. If it is a pure-play situation,

Figure 2.4 The Strategic Planning Process

The strategic planning for e-business must fit with the strategic planning for the enterprise as a whole.

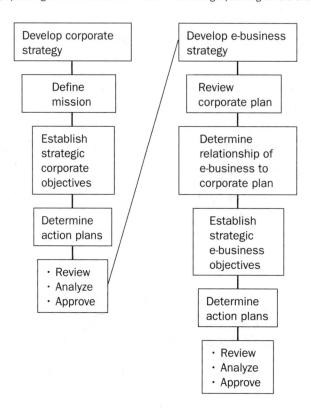

where the only business is e-business, then the corporate strategic plan will be one and the same as the e-business plan. At the other end of the spectrum, where the e-business is a small part of the overall business, there may be a separate e-business strategic plan prepared. If this is the case, then there needs to be a process under which the objectives of the e-business plan are compared to the corporate objectives for consistency of purpose and aligned with them.

This means that e-business planning must be done in conjunction with, or in a manner consistent with, the entity's IT strategy and its overall corporate strategy. E-business planning involves the following activities:

- Defining how e-business can help the entity achieve its overall objectives. This step involves analyzing the entity's overall vision and mission; analyzing the industry, the company and its competition; and identifying areas where e-business can contribute to the entity's success, considering issues such as whether to be a leader or follower, the geographic scope of the e-business, the technologies to be utilized, and the value creation opportunities created by those technologies. An approach to industry analysis that is widely used is the Porter Five Forces analysis, which considers 1) the barriers to entry in the industry, 2) the threats posed by substitute products or services, 3) the bargaining power of suppliers, 4) the bargaining power of buyers, and 5) the rivalry among existing competitors as the basis for a company's strategy.[11]

- Assessing gaps between the entity's current IT resources and performance capabilities and its desired strategic objectives. This step involves analyses such as SWOT (Strengths, Weaknesses, Opportunities, and Threats) to identify technology, competency, and resource limitations as well as opportunities.

E-Strategy

Building an E-Business at Siemens AG

Siemens AG is a major international company that decided to use e-business to support its need to reduce inventory cycle times and streamline its supply chain. Its medical manufacturing arm, the Medical Solutions Operating Group (MED), makes medical technology systems such as ultrasound imaging and digital echocardiography systems. It began revamping its e-business strategy in December 1998 in response to the corporate vision. In step with corporate goals, the group launched a "High Speed Logistics" project with a specific aim of increasing group-wide inventory turnover by at least 25 percent within a two-year time frame.

The group began by rerouting inventory from MED's major component suppliers, which included Hewlett-Packard, Infineon Technologies, and Intel. Previously, MED would take delivery of components from these suppliers, route them to their own storage facilities, and then send the parts to the production line. Under the High Speed Logistics project, however, the components are sent directly by the suppliers to the production line for assembly, eliminating the need for factory storage. There were also other savings. Notably, the number of freight forwarders was reduced from three to one, and the group began to use its own factory experts to install its systems, rather than third-party contractors. One of the main challenges the project team had to overcome was motivating team members. There was a high level of complexity to the supply chain solutions, making them difficult for the team to understand. Teams were motivated by explaining the goals and how they would be achieved.

After two years, the delivery process was trimmed from 15 days to 5, inventory turnover increased by 53 percent, and the delivery cycle was shortened by 86 percent. After the success of this program, MED began another project that focused on moving suppliers and customers to its intranet site, where orders could be placed and suppliers could see component requirements. The company's internal intranet became a focal point for suppliers and customers, greatly simplifying the ordering process. Prior to this initiative, orders were given and taken by EDI, phone, and fax, which caused typing errors and language issues. The use of the intranet enhanced the accuracy of the orders, made billing and invoicing faster, and provided greater transparency to help speed up order fulfillment and further reduce inventory levels.

Siemens AG
www.siemens.com

Questions

1. Discuss how the e-business initiatives of MED served the larger purposes of Siemens as a whole.
2. Do you think MED handled the issue of team motivation as well as they could have?

SOURCE: www.Informationweek.com.

- Formulating strategies to fill gaps. Strategies can be 1) competitive—competing head-to-head on price, cost, quality, and service; or attempting to outflank competitors by attacking them indirectly; 2) defensive—blocking competitors with patents and other barriers; or, 3) cooperative—relying on alliances, partnerships, and joint ventures. Developing these strategies creates an e-business model to achieve the entity's strategic objectives. This model will specify the value propositions offered to customers, how revenues are generated (i.e., what products and services are provided and how), what resources are required, and what costs are incurred to support core e-business activities.
- Performing a risk assessment aimed at identifying weaknesses in the e-business model and compensating for them.

- Defining the IT policies, infrastructure, applications, business processes, information architecture, and information flows designed to serve the e-business model and compensate for any weaknesses and risks identified in the risk assessment phase.
- Defining a tactical plan that includes the sequence of anticipated acquisition or development and implementation steps, resource requirements (human, technological, operational, and financial), and project management requirements.
- Measuring e-business performance, as discussed in chapter 12.

It should be clear that the process of strategic planning for e-business presents numerous challenges of coordination and communication in an organization. Not only do the various types of planning—corporate, IT, and e-business—need to be consistent, but the various stakeholders in the organization need to be involved and their individual perspectives and objectives reconciled. When the business is an established one, the challenges are compounded in that they likely have had strategic plans for some years before the advent of e-business, and the introduction of the e-business must therefore take place in the context of established hierarchies and organizational structures, which will often be resistant to change. On the other hand, when the business is a new internet startup, the whole organization depends on the e-business, and the importance of finding viable business models and developing successful strategies is not only more critical but must be built from the ground up.

Many if not most of the new dot-coms failed because they were not successful in finding business models and strategies that would work to make them economically viable. The problems that many businesses have experienced in venturing from their traditional spheres of activity to e-business, although they have had a lower profile, can often be traced to the same general failures. Even when a business finds a successful strategy, there is no assurance that it will continue to work for very long. The world of e-business and technology is changing so quickly that constant review and re-assessment of the strategic plans must be carried out, and the business must remain flexible in its approach to be able to adapt to the inevitable changes that will take place.

Chapter Summary

Broadly, a business model may be defined as the manner in which a business organizes itself so as to achieve its objectives, which normally involve the generation of profits. Most often, business models are defined in terms of how a business plans to generate revenues, the costs it must incur to generate the revenues, the investments that its stakeholders must make to fund the business development and operations until they generate positive net cash flows, and other critical success factors that enable it to make money on a long-term basis. A major aspect of strategy for e-business is how the business plans to use the internet for these purposes.

An internet business model involves the use of the internet as a tool for implementing a business model. Numerous internet-based business models have developed in recent years, including B2C and B2B variants, pure play as well as bricks-and-clicks approaches and numerous traditional as well as innovative revenue-generating and cost-containment activities.

The specific model or combination of models that a business uses helps to define its internet or e-business strategy. The models provide a menu for the business strategist to consider when addressing strategic questions.

For many businesses, the procedural aspects of corporate strategic planning are a well-established feature of management. Corporate plans are developed and e-business plans must fit into the corporate plan. The manner in which the e-business strategy fits into the corporate plan depends on the extent to which the business is involved in e-business. If it is a pure-play situation, where the only business is e-business, then the corporate strategic plan will be the same as the e-business plan. Where the e-business is a small part of the overall business, there may be a separate e-business strategic plan prepared. Because e-business includes elements of IT, an IT plan must be prepared or incorporated into the e-business plan. All of these plans must be consistent and coordinated with each other. The process of strategic planning for e-business presents numerous challenges of coordination and communication in an organization.

Key Terms

asynchronous *(p. 33)*

banner ads *(p. 30)*

brokerage sites *(p. 31)*

business model *(p. 22)*

channel conflict *(p. 28)*

click-through counts *(p. 30)*

internet business model *(p. 22)*

reverse auction *(p. 25)*

strategy *(p. 22)*

Tools for Online Learning

To help you master the material in this chapter and stay up to date with new developments in e-business, visit www.pearsoned.ca/trites. Resources include:

- **Review Questions and Exercises**

- **Problems for Discussion**

- **Recommended Readings**

- **Updates to Case Studies and Textual Material**

- **Streaming CBC Videos with Cases**

Endnotes

1. T. Bell, F. Marrs, I. Solomon, and H. Thomas, *Auditing Organizations Through a Strategic-Systems Lens: The KPMG Business Measurement Process* (KPMG Peat Marwick, LLP., 1997).

2. Michael E. Porter, "What Is Strategy?" *HBR OnPoint* (November–December 1996).

3. "Information Technology: Government On-Line." *Report of the Auditor General of Canada to the House of Commons* (November 2003), Chapter 1, p. 6

4. C. Ranganathan, et al., "Managing the Transition to Bricks and Clicks," *Communications of the ACM* 46, no. 12 (December 2003): 308–316. Pattarawan Prasarnphanich, Mark L. Gillenson, "The Hybrid Clicks and Bricks Business Model," *Communications of the ACM* 46, no. 12 (December 2003): 178–185.

5. T.J. Mullaney, H. Green, M. Arndt, R.D. Hof, and L. Himelstein, "The E-Biz Surprise," *Business Week* (May 12, 2003): 60–68.

6. Michael Rappa, *Business Models on the Web,* www.digitalenterprise.org/models/models.html, accessed March 9, 2004.

7. Michael Rappa, *Business Models on the Web,* www.digitalenterprise.org/models/models.html, accessed March 9, 2004.

8. Don Tapscott, "Rethinking Strategy in a Networked World (or Why Michael Porter Is Wrong About the Internet)," *Strategy+Business* (Third Quarter, 2001): 1–8.

9. Michael E. Porter, "Strategy and the Internet," *Harvard Business Review* (March 2001): 63–78.

10. Donald C. Hambrick and James W. Fredrickson, "Are You Sure You Have a Strategy?" *The Academy of Management Executive* 15, no. 4 (November 2001): 48–59.

11. Michael E. Porter, "Strategy and the Internet," *Harvard Business Review* (March 2001): 63–78.

E-Business Models and Strategy

Overview

When Sir Tim Berners-Lee, the father of the World Wide Web, invented the web a little over 10 years ago at the CERN research lab in Switzerland, he could not possibly have imagined the impact of his invention on our daily lives. During the "gold rush" times of the dot-com revolution, a few visionaries saw potential in the new technology and founded companies in their university dorm rooms, basements, or garages. Giants like Yahoo! and Amazon started this way. Although some of the early pioneers broke new ground by effectively using the internet as a new sales channel, many of the new ventures had business models that were not well thought out, or not considered at all. When Jeff Bezos founded Amazon, he didn't really develop a fundamentally new business model. Instead, he took the traditional catalogue mail-order business model and adapted it to the internet. In the early years of the web, most e-commerce sites consisted of a website where products were simply listed, similar to traditional mail-order catalogues. Progressive e-commerce ventures allowed for online ordering, but in many cases one still needed to call the company to order the goods. This period in internet time became known as the brochureware phase. Many online retailers today still follow this rather traditional approach.

eBay, the online auction company, was different. Instead of selling goods and services itself, it acted as an intermediary between buyers and sellers. The company, which today is the largest online trading exchange in the world, has created a completely new business model of a type that is only possible on the internet. Almost everyone in the world has heard of eBay. According to the company's mission statement, eBay aims "to provide a global trading platform where practically anyone can trade practically anything." Although the company originally started as an online flea market, it has grown rapidly over the past ten years and is now used not only by individual buyers and sellers around the world, but also by many companies and even governments as a way to efficiently buy and sell goods and, to some extent, services.

To be fair, eBay founder Pierre Omidyar probably did not intend to develop a revolutionary new e-commerce model when he launched eBay as a hobby in his living room back in September 1995. Rumour has it that Omidyar, whose day job was to conduct developer relations at General Magic, launched eBay as a trading exchange for his girlfriend, who collected Pez dispensers. Word about eBay spread quickly around the internet and people soon began to use it as a trading platform for a wide range of goods and services. The venture quickly outgrew Omidyar's living room as it gained popularity with internet users around the world.

Pierre Omidyar has since given up his position at the helm of eBay. He is now a full-time philanthropist, but continues to serve as the chairman of the board of directors at eBay. The company realized that the time had come to evolve from its "startup leadership" to a more "managed leadership". In March 1998, Meg Whitman was hired as the new president and CEO. Although she did not have a background in technology, she did have substantial management experience through positions at Bain & Company (a global management consulting firm), the Walt Disney Company, and FTD Inc. Under her leadership, the company continued to grow rapidly and, in 1999, eBay went public. The company is now listed on the NASDAQ stock market.

Sotheby's Meets the Flea Market

On an average day, millions of items are listed on eBay. People from around the globe use the eBay platform to buy and sell items in countless different categories. Virtually everything is traded on eBay, including books, antiques, collectibles, electronics, home furnishings, sporting goods and memorabilia, and movies and DVDs, to name just a few of the categories. Almost every item imaginable can be found on eBay. Expensive items such as cars and real estate are also traded. Even airplanes and other unusual items have been sold (and, of course, bought) on eBay. The company, which calls itself a community, has tens of millions of registered members from around the world. In addition to its main website, ebay.com, the company also operates localized sites in over 20 countries including Canada, Australia, Germany, Japan, the United Kingdom, and India. eBay is also present in the Latin American and Chinese markets through its investments in Mercadolibre and EachNet.

Traditionally, auctions were the best way to sell something while obtaining the best selling price possible. Although the process was efficient, it was also cumbersome. Auctions were usually conducted by auction companies, that sold items on behalf of the owners in return for a commission. Items had to be physically transported to the auction houses and potential buyers had to physically gather at the auction house. This made auctions a very complicated form of trading and they were typically only used for trading certain kinds of goods. eBay's business model, which combines the traditional auction method with the global internet, has brought auctions into everyone's home and office.

eBay became so successful because it combined the traditional price-finding technique of auctions with the approachability of a yard sale. In a sense, eBay has created a sophisticated global flea market. Users register on the eBay website and list an item they would like to sell. If, for example, Tony in Toronto wants to sell the ugly old painting from his basement, he can simply list it on eBay. He creates an account, lists his painting, and specifies a starting bid price. Over the next few days, his painting is listed on the eBay website. Interested buyers can submit their bids for the painting, just like they would in a traditional auction. At the end of the auction period, Heather from Halifax has won the auction for the beautiful antique painting, which would look great in her living room. She sends Tony a cheque, and he ships the painting. After the transaction is completed, Heather can "rate" Tony on the eBay website. Her review becomes part of Tony's eBay profile and can be seen by other potential future buyers. This feature is very useful in creating trust in the eBay community. A positive rating can have a substantial impact on the sales prospects of a seller and it can give the buyer confidence that he can trust the seller. A bad rating, on the other hand, can severely hurt a seller's chances of selling an item at a decent price. The rating system is an important aspect of eBay, since buyers and sellers don't know each other and are often several thousand miles apart. Since eBay would not work without trust, it is important that buyers have a way of finding out about other buyers' previous experiences with a seller.

eBay also offers a variety of additional transaction options. In addition to its auctions, the company offers a "buy it now" option, where goods can be purchased immediately at a fixed price. The "Half Zone" is also a special section on the eBay site where members can buy books, movies, music, and video games at a fixed price. In addition, eBay operates a special section called eBay Motors, which is dedicated to buying and selling vehicles.

eBay's Revenue Model

Since eBay never takes ownership or possession of any of the items sold on its trading platform, the company earns its money with a two-tiered fee structure. First, it charges an "insertion fee" for each listing. A second transaction fee, or "final value fee," is charged after an auction has ended. Those fees are always paid by the seller. The "insertion fee" ranges from US$0.30 for an initial asking price up to US$0.99 to US$4.80 for an initial asking price of over US$500. The "final value fee" is typically 5.25 percent of the final sale price for all auctions under US$25. As the sale price increases, the fee gradually decreases.

Exchanging Payments at eBay

One weak spot of eBay has always been the exchange of money between the buyer and the seller after an auction has ended. In a traditional e-commerce setting, customers typically pay for their purchases with a credit card, which (in most cases) also provides reasonable protection against fraud. In the early years of the internet, the web lacked a satisfactory payment scheme to allow people to exchange payments with each other, while offering reasonable assurances of trust and security. The only two options were, in many cases, cheques and money orders—which had to be obtained and sent offline and were obviously not the best solution for either the buyer or the seller. This payments dilemma proved to be especially difficult for eBay, since it depended heavily on its members' ability to exchange payments. To address this problem, eBay acquired PayPal, an online payment system that lets users exchange payments directly over the internet.

Reasons for eBay's Success

The success of eBay over the past decade is truly astonishing. No one would have expected that an online trading site for Pez dispensers would, within the short time span of ten years, become a global auctioning powerhouse. There are several reasons why eBay has enjoyed such success, but mainly, it was the right idea at the right time. Before the arrival of the web, no one could have imagined the possibility of linking individuals around the country and around the world together to enable them to trade directly with each other.

Peer-to-peer has been a buzz word in the technology industry for the past several years. The term, popularized by the music sharing service, Napster, refers to a network without any dedicated central control over communication within the network. Although eBay does have a "central point" in its network, it can be argued that eBay turned commerce into a peer-to-peer network—every participant can trade with everyone else, and everyone can be a buyer as well as a seller. This truly is a new concept compared to the "old" mail-order type business models.

Another important factor in eBay's success is its small exposure to risk compared to other trading companies. Since the company only acts as an intermediary, it does not have to worry about storing inventory or shipping orders to a customer. During more difficult economic times, eBay will most likely earn lower commissions and fees, but it will never be faced with having to write off parts of its inventory. This essentially minimizes the risk for the company and makes eBay's business model very scalable.

A third reason for the company's success lies in the combination of auctions with the internet. Collectibles have long since stopped being the primary market for eBay. Instead, many businesses and even governments have found in eBay an efficient platform and a viable alternative to their old ways of doing business. Even some large companies now offer their products or surplus production on eBay. In addition, eBay has proved very useful in determining the right price for a product. It has become practice in many companies to use eBay as a price-finding tool. By simply offering a new product on eBay, a seller can quickly determine how much buyers are willing to pay for an item. Using eBay to find out this information has often proven to be more accurate than many marketing estimates—without the need for lengthy and expensive market analysis studies.

The Competition

This combination of success factors has made eBay one of the prime dot-com companies, one that has largely been unmatched. Although there are now over 1500 auction websites on the internet, not one has posed a serious challenge for eBay. Some of eBay's larger dot-com rivals, however, have been trying to get into the auction business. Search engine giant Yahoo!, for example, has also begun to offer auctions. In addition, Yahoo! has made it possible for smaller businesses to offer their goods as part of the Yahoo! shopping portal mentioned in chapter 2. Although this is not a direct competition to eBay's auction business, it nevertheless tries to aggregate smaller sellers under the Yahoo! umbrella.

Another, more serious, competitor is online retailer Amazon. The company, which started as an online bookstore, has become an e-commerce powerhouse. Amazon now offers, either directly or through partners, a full assortment of goods. In addition to its traditional "e-tailing" business, Amazon has also begun to offer used goods through several different sales channels. Amazon.com Auctions offers eBay-style auctions. Shops let individuals and small businesses set up a presence in Amazon's online mall, similar to Yahoo's shopping mall. A third offering by Amazon is called Amazon Marketplace. Marketplace lets Amazon customers and other businesses list their new and used products alongside those of Amazon. If, for example, a customer wants to buy a Nokia mobile phone on the Amazon website, he or she would be offered a new phone by Amazon, as well as (potentially) cheaper offers on Amazon Marketplace. Before Marketplace, a customer may have compared the Amazon offer to an offer from eBay. By allowing competition with itself on its own site, Amazon has made a strategic move to keep customers away from eBay.

Potential Threats

As powerful and stable as eBay is at the moment, there is also a substantial potential for threats. All of the reasons for eBay's success which were described earlier could also lead to problems for the company. The scalable infrastructure is easy to replicate. Theoretically, one computer in an entrepreneur's living room, connected to the internet, is enough to create a competitor. Other larger companies may also be interested in a piece of the pie. The offerings of Yahoo! and Amazon are good examples of this trend. By becoming too large, eBay could also be trying to be too many things to too many people. More specialized sites may be better able to cater to certain market segments.

eBay's success has been remarkable, but they can't take anything for granted, as the internet continues to pervade business and there are new entries into the world of e-business every day.

Questions for Discussion

1. If eBay were just starting up today, would its success be as remarkable? Explain.
2. How would eBay's business model and strategy be classified under the discussions in the textbook on Business Models and Strategy? Explain.
3. Why have there been no strong competitors for eBay? Is this likely to last? Explain.
4. If you were developing a strategic plan for eBay for the following year, what would be the main elements of the plan?

CHAPTER 3

Evolution and Applications of the Internet

LEARNING OBJECTIVES

When you complete this chapter you should be able to:

1. Describe the internet, its history, and its overall significance.

2. Describe how the internet is appropriate for e-business.

3. Identify the components of the internet.

4. Identify the relationship between the internet, extranets, and intranets.

5. Describe situations in which the internet, extranets, and intranets are used for e-business.

6. Explain what a virtual private network is and how it can facilitate e-business transactions.

Introduction

Everyone knows what the internet is—or do they? It is the world's largest communications network, connecting millions of computers from more than 100 countries. In fact, the internet is a network of loosely connected networks whose size and number of users are growing rapidly. The internet works over virtually any type of connection, ranging from dedicated fibre-optic cables to coaxial cables to telephone lines to satellite connections to wireless frequencies. The internet links people and organizations large and small in every corner of the world. Some of the main features of internet technology that make it attractive to business are that it is a global standard; it is easy to implement on almost any technology platform; it is reliable; and it is fast.

More technically, the internet connects uniquely numbered computing devices that relay information from point to point using the **Internet Protocol (IP)**, or IP with other protocols layered on top of IP. The IP is a set of rules for sending and receiving messages at the internet address level. The IP was created to provide a mechanism for routing a data packet to its destination. The most common protocol used in addition to IP is the **Transmission Control Protocol (TCP)**. TCP uses a set of rules to exchange messages with other internet points at the data packet level. The TCP ensures reliable, flow-controlled data packet delivery. IP provides the addressing system that enables computers to be logically connected so they can send messages to each other, while TCP provides the mechanism for subdividing the information being sent into small packets (that is, data packets) and sending and correctly re-assembling those packets of information at their destination. From these basic but robust components has sprung the globe-spanning network of networks that has become the key enabler of the e-business models and strategies that are the subject of this book.

Due to its universality, the internet reduces barriers to competition created by space, time, and information asymmetries. It defeats distances and borders by enabling people with similar interests who are separated by great distances to interact in online communities, enabling buyers and sellers from far flung regions of the world to interact online in electronic marketplaces, and enabling co-workers to share knowledge and collaborate in a way that would otherwise not be possible. It overcomes time zones by enabling buyers and sellers to interact asynchronously around the clock, and it creates level playing fields for buyers and sellers by providing almost unlimited access to information.

In addition, while the internet has the capacity to bring together vast networks of users, a key feature that distinguishes it from other mass media such as radio, television, and newspapers is that it permits interactive communications between sender and receiver and personalization of communications and marketing to suit individual tastes and preferences. Finally, because the internet provides a common and reliable communications platform for other information services, there is virtually no limit on the software applications that can be layered upon it to enhance the basic communications capabilities of TCP/IP. For example, business technology applications can be added to support management, investor relations, treasury and finance, human resource management, research and development, IT services, procurement of goods and services, inbound and outbound logistics, operations management, marketing and sales, and after sales support. All of these applications will be discussed in subsequent chapters of this book.[1]

As impressive as this network is, the popular conception is that the internet just grew, with no particular planning or control. The fact is, however, that the internet is not just a random network that grew up by accident. There is a very

INTERNET PROTOCOL (IP)
A protocol that uses a set of rules to send and receive messages at the internet address level.

TRANSMISSION CONTROL PROTOCOL (TCP)
A protocol that uses a set of rules to exchange messages with other internet points at the data packet level.

definite structure to it that is not widely known, together with specific organizations that manage it. To have an understanding of e-business it is useful to know what the internet is, how it is structured, and who the major players are in its operation and governance.

In this chapter we will review the history of the internet and its components and learn about how they enable e-business models and strategies.

History of the Internet

In 1968, the U.S. Defense Advanced Research Projects Agency (DARPA) formed a network intended for sharing research and development work among corporate, academic, and government researchers. As this was during the Cold War, one of the specifications was that the network should be designed to withstand a nuclear attack. On this new network, called ARPANET, each computer had a unique address, and any computer could communicate with any other computer by specifying its unique address. At about the same time, DARPA began the development of **packet switching**, a method of transmitting data by breaking it up into small segments or packets and sending the packets individually in a stream. The packets are not necessarily sent together, but rather are disassembled, transmitted separately, and then reassembled when they arrive at their destination. After successfully trying out packet switching on media such as radio, the possibility arose of using these packet switching methods as a protocol for transmitting data between computer systems. Previously this would have been very difficult, as different computers used differing technologies. The introduction of a standard protocol made it possible to transmit data between many different types of computers, as long as they had the protocol installed on their computers. A **protocol** is a special set of rules that the sending and receiving points in a telecommunication connection use when they communicate. Protocols exist at several levels, including hardware and software. Both end points must recognize and observe a protocol to be able to understand the contents of transmissions. Protocols are often described in an industry or international standard.

The new protocol could also be used by entire networks, and if two or more networks had the protocol installed, then those networks could be linked together and share data between themselves. Since each computer, also referred to as a node on the network, had its own unique address, every computer could still be accessed on this network. Thus, the ARPANET became a system of linked networks.

A set of protocols was developed based on the Transmission Control Protocol and the Internet Protocol (IP). Together, these protocols are referred to as the TCP/IP protocol.

As the research program grew, it became necessary to form a committee to guide the work. As a result, the Internet Configuration Control Board (ICCB) was formed, which in 1983 was renamed as the Internet Architecture Board (IAB). In that same year, the TCP/IP protocol was declared by the U.S. Defense Communications Agency to be the standard protocol for the ARPANET.

As knowledge of and the role of the internet expanded, it gained growing support from several U.S. government organizations. A coordinating committee was formed that became known as the Federal Networking Council (FNC). It liaises with the Office of Science and Technology Policy, which is headed up by the President's Science Advisor, and is responsible for setting science and technology policy affecting the internet.

PACKET SWITCHING
A method of transmitting data by breaking it up into small segments or packets and sending the packets individually in a stream. The packets are not necessarily sent together, but rather are disassembled, transmitted separately, and then reassembled when they arrive at their destination.

PROTOCOL
A special set of rules that the sending and receiving points in a telecommunication connection use when they communicate. Protocols exist at several levels, including hardware and software. Both end points must recognize and observe a protocol to be able to understand the contents of transmissions. Protocols are often described in an industry or international standard.

The Canadian Internet

In Canada, the internet began in earnest in 1990 when CA*net was created with support from the National Research Council. The purpose of CA*net was to provide internet connectivity between universities and research organizations in Canada through a unified high-speed network. CA*net linked over 20 regional networks across Canada, most of them provincially oriented, such as ONET in Ontario, BCNET in British Columbia, and ARNET in Alberta. For several years, CA*net was the only internet backbone in Canada. An **internet backbone** is an organized and managed communications system, often based on fibre-optic cables, that forms the central connection for a section of the internet. In partnership with Bell Advanced Communications it operated until March 31, 1997, when it was superseded by CA*net II.

In 1995, Canada entered the world of asynchronous transfer mode (ATM) networks, which transmit data faster than previous networks, with the introduction of the National Test Network (NTN) in partnership with Bell Advanced Communications, AT&T Canada, and Teleglobe Canada. An **asynchronous transfer mode (ATM)** is a switching technology that organizes digital data into 53-byte cell units and transmits them using digital signalling technology. A cell is processed asynchronously relative to other related cells; in other words, not necessarily in a pre-specified sequence. NTN was one of the first national ATM networks in the world, although access was initially limited to specific researchers and labs located at universities and other research facilities across the country. In 1997, NTN was upgraded to form the basis of CA*net II by linking it with international organizations using the Internet Protocol.

The core capacity of CA*net II was 155 Megabits per second (Mbps). Data transmission speed is measured in **Megabits per second (Mbps)**, which means a million bits per second, and states the number of data bits that are transmitted per second on a particular medium. Bell Advanced Communications and AT&T Canada jointly provided the underlying ATM networks, while Teleglobe provided a connection to Europe.

CA*net II connected to individual universities, government labs, and research institutes through Regional Advanced Networks (RANs), which operated in every province. Approved organizations could access CA*net II directly through any of the 15 Gigabit points-of-presence operated by Regional Advanced Networks and the three participating carriers. A **point of presence (POP)** is an access point to the internet that has a unique IP address. An internet service provider (ISP), which is an organization that sells access to the internet, has at least one point-of-presence on the internet. In 1998, the federal government began working with CANARIE Inc. (a Canadian not-for-profit corporation supported by its members, partners, and the federal government) to build a national R&D internet network, CA*net 3, based on fibre optic technology. **Fibre optics** transmit information as light impulses along a glass or plastic wire or fibre. Fibre optic media carry more data than conventional copper media and are less subject to electromagnetic interference. Most telephone company long-distance lines are now fibre optic.

Exponential growth in network traffic, expected growth in new high bandwidth applications, and planned extreme high bandwidth grid projects required that a new network be built to support leading-edge research in Canada. To this end, in 2002 the Government of Canada committed $110 million to CANARIE for the design, deployment, and operation of CA*net 4. Through a series of point-to-point optical wavelengths, most of which are provisioned at OC-192 (10 Gbps) speeds, CA*net 4 yields a total initial network capacity of between four and eight times that of CA*net 3.

INTERNET BACKBONE
An organized and managed communications system, often based on fibre-optic cables, that forms the central connection for a section of the internet.

ASYNCHRONOUS TRANSFER MODE (ATM)
A switching technology that organizes digital data into 53-byte cell units and transmits them using digital signalling technology. A cell is processed asynchronously relative to other related cells; in other words, not necessarily in a pre-specified sequence.

MEGABITS PER SECOND (Mbps)
A measure of speed for data transmission. Megabits means a million bits per second, and states the number of data bits that are transmitted per second on a particular medium. Gigabits means a billion bits. Terabits means a trillion bits.

POINT OF PRESENCE (POP)
An access point to the internet that has a unique IP address.

FIBRE OPTICS
The transmission of information as light impulses along a glass or plastic wire or fibre.

International Developments

An international Coordinating Committee for Intercontinental Research Networks (CCIRN) was formed to include the FNC of the United States, CANARIE of Canada, and its counterparts in Europe. Co-chaired by the executive directors of the FNC and the European Association of Research Networks (RARE), the CCIRN provides a forum for co-operative planning among the principal North American and European research networking bodies.

The Internet Architecture Board (IAB) remains the coordinating committee for internet design, engineering, and management. Today, the IAB is an independent committee of researchers and professionals with an interest in the technical strength and growth of the internet. The IAB meets quarterly to review the condition of the internet, approve any proposed changes or additions to the TCP/IP protocol, set technical development priorities, and discuss policy matters that may need the attention of the internet sponsors.

The IAB has two extremely important continuing task forces:

- the Internet Engineering Task Force (IETF), and
- the Internet Research Task Force (IRTF).

The Internet Engineering Task Force The IAB established the internet Engineering Task Force (IETF) to help coordinate the operation, management, and evolution of the internet. There was a recognition that the internet had grown to widely geographically dispersed networks and, perhaps more importantly, had moved from experimental to commercial deployment. Of course, since that time, the commercial applications on the internet have grown exponentially, and the importance of the IETF to e-business has also expanded tremendously.

The IETF has responsibility for specifying the short- and mid-term internet protocols and architecture and recommending standards for IAB approval, providing a forum for the exchange of information within the internet community, identifying relevant operational and technical problem areas, and convening working groups to explore solutions.

The IETF is a large open community of network designers, operators, vendors, and researchers concerned with the internet and its protocols. The work of the IETF is performed by a large number of working groups. The working groups tend to have a narrow focus, such as particular security issues or encryption standards, and are normally disbanded when their project is completed.

The Internet Research Task Force The Internet Research Task Force (IRTF) was formed to promote research in networking and the development of new technology. Since the distinction between research and engineering is not always clear, there is sometimes an overlap between the activities of the IETF and the IRTF. The IRTF is generally more concerned with understanding than with products or standard protocols. The IRTF is a community of network researchers, generally with an internet focus, and is organized into a number of research groups, focusing on subjects such as the development of privacy-enhanced electronic mail software.

Internet Technologies

The internet, as we have seen, is a collection of interlinked networks. In a real sense, the internet can be viewed as a very large client-server network, and is often discussed in those terms. A client-server network can be analyzed in terms of clients connecting to servers as illustrated in figure 3.1. The figure shows a series

Figure 3.1   Client-Server Network

A client-server network can be analyzed in terms of clients and servers.

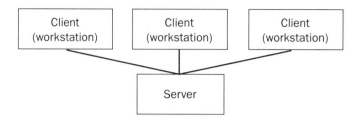

of three **clients**, which are the computers with which users gain access to and operate applications on the network. The **server** is a large central computer that forms the nucleus of a network, and contains the network operating system, as well as case-specific network-based applications. The server is a passive computer that awaits processing requests from the clients.

Figure 3.2 expands the diagram in figure 3.1 to specify some of the major characteristics of the World Wide Web as a client-server network. Users use their computers (called clients) to communicate with a special set of servers on the internet, known as **web servers**, with the help of web browser software running on the client computers. A web server is a server attached to a network that is dedicated to specific applications that must be run on the World Wide Web, or used by web users, or interfaced very closely with the web. Servers are owned by the company where the user works or by an internet service provider (ISP) that the user has signed a contract with, such as Sympatico or Interlink. The ISP then connects to the regional network, or else directly to an internet backbone, such as CA*net, and through that to a web server at the website targeted for communication. The website is identified by a **uniform resource locator (URL)**, which is the address of a resource on the World Wide Web. The URL contains the name of the required protocol followed by a colon (normally http:), an identification that a web server is the target (such as //www), and a domain name that identifies a specific web server followed by a slash (e.g., gm.com/), and perhaps a specific file name (such as index.html) to make http://www.gm.com/index.html. Increasingly, the letters www are no longer required as web servers are assumed

CLIENT
A computer that is used by a network user to gain access to and operate applications on the network.

SERVER
A large central computer that forms the nucleus of a network, and contains the network operating system, as well as case-specific network-based applications.

WEB SERVER
A server attached to a network; it is dedicated to specific applications that must be run on the World Wide Web, or used by web users, or interfaced very closely with the web.

UNIFORM RESOURCE LOCATOR (URL)
The address of a resource on the World Wide Web.

Figure 3.2   Overview of the World Wide Web Network

This figure specifies some of the major characteristics of the World Wide Web as a client-server network.

Canadian Snapshots

Internet Services at Telus

Telus Corp., the giant telephone and telecommunications company based in British Columbia and Alberta, bought Toronto internet services company Daedalian eSolutions Inc. for approximately $29 million in 2001. It was the fourth in a series of such purchases. At its 2001 annual meeting, Telus said that it planned to spend $800 000 or more on ventures outside Western Canada as well as another $1.4 billion on wireless services and internet protocols.

Daedalian was founded in 1984 and has more than 200 employees. Revenues in fiscal 2000 were about $22 million. According to an analyst, Telus paid less than what other telephone companies are paying for such a company.

Telus said that Daedalian's employees had necessary skills related to web design and consulting, in addition to their skills in running an ISP. The company's clients included the Bank of Montreal, the City of Toronto, and several Ontario government ministries. Daedalian provided customized internet applications, e-commerce solutions, systems integration and development, hosting, data warehousing, and managed business services. Earlier, Telus had announced the purchase of Williams Communication Canada, Inc., of Markham, Ontario, a data and voice equipment service provider. And in January 2001, Telus bought the data network and facilities management business of NorthWest Digital in Calgary.

Telus's strategy is to implement data and internet-related services. Telus adopted this strategy because it feels there is very little margin to be earned in voice communications, but a lot of margin in data communications and related services, so it is placing its expansion strategy squarely on the internet. Telus has concluded that the internet is an extremely important market in which to establish a presence. Another reason that Telus was interested in Daedalian was its Ontario location, which Telus felt would be useful. Analysts feel that Telus's incursion into the Ontario market by buying an Ontario ISP is significant because it gives Telus access to the Ontario internet services market. Daedalian became part of the e-business division of Telus Client Solutions, which is focused on e-business enablement.

Telus
www.telus.com

Questions

1. How would you describe the strategy that Telus is following in the internet services market?
2. Does it make sense that Telus would expand into Ontario?
3. Why does it matter where Daedalian is located?

SOURCE: Globetechnology.com, **www.globetechnology.com**.

General Motors
www.gm.com

unless otherwise specified. Index pages are often assumed as well. If a user logs into the World Wide Web, for example, and wishes to shop for a General Motors car from home, he or she would connect and log into the web server of a local ISP. Then the user would enter the URL of General Motors (which is www.gm.com). A signal would go from the user's computer's browser to the ISP's router and then would be forwarded through the best path to GM's primary web server. Since TCP/IP is being used, the various packets in the message will take different routes through the networks, but will all arrive at the same server at the other end and be reassembled according to the instructions embedded in the packets.

However, what a person sees after logging onto the internet is typically only a part of the internet—the World Wide Web. When the internet was first implemented, it had several specialized applications, including Gopher, Veronica, and FTP. These were simply sets of functionalities for certain specific purposes. For example, Gopher and Veronica were used to find and retrieve certain kinds of information, and FTP was used for transporting large files or data sets. None of these functions were user-friendly, and this created serious limitations on the usefulness of the internet for non-technical people. User interfaces were character-based rather than graphical or icon-based, and required the knowledge of various commands that users had to enter in command lines to make the system work.

In 1993, however, a new tool emerged in the form of a user-friendly, graphics-capable interface that enables users to connect to and navigate websites on the internet. It was known as Mosaic. This new interface software, which became known as a **web browser**, led directly to the emergence and popularity of the World Wide Web on the internet. Mosaic evolved to become Netscape Navigator, one of the most significant pieces of software that helped make possible the internet as we know it. Navigator (or Netscape Communicator, which includes Navigator) was once the most popular web browser, with over 90 percent market share. It is now estimated that Microsoft's Internet Explorer enjoys 90 percent of the browser market. The WWW still provides a bridge to the older technologies that remain on the internet, such as FTP, to facilitate file transfers and other functions by clicking on icons rather than entering the old commands.

WEB BROWSER
Software with a user-friendly, graphics-capable interface that enables users to connect to and navigate websites on the internet.

Other Technologies

So far we have outlined two of the most important technology applications used on the internet—the TCP/IP protocol and web browsers. Other technologies are also critical to the internet, including HTML, HTTP, XML and CGI.

HyperText Markup Language (HTML) HyperText Markup Language (HTML) is a set of codes that must be inserted in a file for it to be displayed on the World Wide Web. It essentially amounts to a specialized type of programming language that tells the web browser how to display the words and images in the file on a webpage. Files coded with HTML are called hypertext files. Figure 3.3 shows the HTML source code for the main entry webpage of the website for the University of Waterloo's Centre for Information Systems Assurance. **Source code** is the format in which a program is written that can be read by humans and that is then converted into a different format that the computer can recognize. In the source code in figure 3.3 can be seen the metatags that are used to identify the contents of the page. **Metatags** are identifiers within HTML that identify the content of the website. In this case, the metatags are near the top of the figure, and can be identified by the word "meta" that begins the code inside the angle brackets. Metatags are used by search engines to identify web pages. Accordingly, the words included within metatags on a website are very important, since they will help web users to find the site when they enter a search request on a search engine. Other lines in the source code reproduced in figure 3.3 show the content that appears on the actual page that the web users will see.

HYPERTEXT MARKUP LANGUAGE (HTML)
Code that must be inserted in a file for it to be displayed on the World Wide Web.

SOURCE CODE
The format in which a program is written that can be read by humans and that is then converted into a different format that the computer can recognize.

METATAGS
Identifiers within HTML code that identify the content of the website.

HyperText Transfer Protocol (HTTP) HyperText Transfer Protocol (HTTP) is a set of rules used in exchanging hypertext files (such as text, graphics, sound, and video) for display on the World Wide Web. It is by far the most common protocol used for reading webpages on the web. As will be discussed in Chapter 5, several security protocols have been developed for use with HTTP to ensure the security of files and messages that need to be exchanged during e-commerce.

HYPERTEXT TRANSFER PROTOCOL (HTTP)
A set of rules used in exchanging hypertext files (such as text, graphics, sound, and video) for display on the World Wide Web.

Figure 3.3 A Website's Source Code

This shows a sample of the source code for the entry website of the University of Waterloo's Centre for Information Systems Assurance.

```
<?xml version="1.0" encoding="iso-8859-1"?>
<!DOCTYPE html PUBLIC "-//W3C//DTD XHTML 1.0
Transitional//EN" "http://www.w3.org/TR/xhtml1/DTD/xhtml1-
transitional.dtd">
    <html ><!- InstanceBegin template="/Templates/uwcisa.dwt"
codeOutsideHTMLIsLocked="false" ->
    <head>
    <!- InstanceBeginEditable name="doctitle" ->
    <title>UWCISA</title>
    <!- InstanceEndEditable ->
    <meta http-equiv="Content-Type" content="text/html;
charset=iso-8859-1" />
    <meta http-equiv="content-type"
content="text/html;charset=iso-8859-1">
    <meta name="description" content="The key objectives of the
Centre are to stimulate relevant research, support the devel-
opment/delivery of educational materials, communicate about
important ISA issues and Centre activities and promote inter-
action among ISA educators and practitioners.">
    <meta name="KeyWords" content="UWCISA, CISA, Centre for
Information Systems Assurance, Information Systems Assurance,
Information Systems Audit and Control, Accounting,
Accountancy, University, Waterloo, education, auditing,
finance, taxation, CA, accountant, accountants, ">
    <PARA />
    <!- InstanceBeginEditable name="head" ->
    <!- InstanceEndEditable ->
    <PARA />
    <style type="text/css">
    td img {display: block;}h2 {
    font-family: Arial, Helvetica, sans-serif;
    color: #006699;
    }
    p {
    font-family: Arial, Helvetica, sans-serif;
    }
    h3 {
    font-family: Arial, Helvetica, sans-serif;
    color: #006699;
    }
    </style>
```

SOURCE: Reprinted with permission from University of Waterloo Centre for Information Systems Assurance.

Extensible Markup Language (XML) Extensible Markup Language (XML) is similar to HTML in that they both contain symbols to describe the contents of a page or file. While HTML describes the content only in terms of how it is to be displayed and interacted with, XML describes the content in terms of what data is being included. For example, "phonenum". This provides more flexibility in execution of the file; for example, the phone number could be stored, displayed, or dialed. The data described can be in a separate server; thus XML can be used to gather information from across the internet.

Common Gateway Interface (CGI) Common Gateway Interface (CGI) is a method used by a web server to pass a user's request that has come over the internet to an application program and receive data from the application program that can be sent back to the user. This is necessary since web servers can only handle HTTP requests for HTML files, and require other servers to process other requests. It is a standard internet-based method and therefore can be recognized by web servers around the world.

All of these technologies are needed to be able to use the World Wide Web for business purposes. The web is a vehicle for communication, and tools such as CGI, and other programming aids beyond the scope of this book, such as ASP, JSP, PHP, and ColdFusion, are becoming important tools to allow interaction between users and the web servers. Although the web worked for some years without XML, XML is becoming an essential part of the web because of its power, flexibility, and its multiple-language support.

Another technology that is not a part of the core set of technologies, but that has become important to the display of web pages, is Java. **Java** is a programming language that was originally invented by Sun Microsystems for the purpose of enhancing web pages. It is the program that is used, for example, to create many of the little animated icons one sees moving about on web pages. Since its inception, its use has grown markedly beyond webpages to include many business and e-business applications. Various other technologies are used on the web for similar purposes, such as Flash and Shockwave, but while important for modern webpages, they are not considered core technologies.

COMMON GATEWAY INTERFACE (CGI)
A method used by a web server to pass a user's request that has come over the internet to an application program and receive data from the application program that can be sent back to the user.

JAVA
A programming language that was originally invented for the purpose of enhancing webpages and is used to create animations and moveable, interactive icons.

Intranets and Extranets

Intranets

An intranet is a network that is internal to an organization and uses internet technologies. Since these technologies include the use of browsers, the network appears to users to be the same as the internet. Since it uses the same protocols as the internet, such as TCP/IP, it can interact seamlessly with the internet. Intranets have all of the advantages of the internet, including ease of use, compatibility with other systems, and simplicity.

Intranets play an important role in the e-business strategies of many organizations. Initially, they were used to convey information to employees that once was printed—documents like procedure manuals, personnel manuals, policy statements, and major announcements. Essentially they were used to save printing costs and to speed up the dissemination of information.

In the next step of their evolution, they began to be used for applications that employees could use to input information into corporate applications. For example, they have been used to input time reports on assignments in process and make changes to personnel information such as addresses and telephone numbers. Essentially, applications like this on intranets transfer the input process to the employees, empower the employees to maintain their own records, and support those who are travelling by giving them remote access to the intranets. The latter use is an example of how intranets support and facilitate e-business, as they enable employees to work from outside their offices, or in client's offices, and input timely information for management and others with whom they must collaborate. The E-Strategy box provides an example of how Shell has found intranets useful as a strategy for dealing with a particular specialized need of their business.

E-Strategy

Handling Waste at Shell

When a company like Shell Oil Co. moves hazardous chemicals, the chemicals must be accompanied by a safety sheet. The purpose of safety sheets is to make available information about the health hazards and flammability of a particular substance to anyone who handles the products. For Shell, the preparation of these sheets has always been costly. To address this cost factor, the company rolled out an intranet application for creating and distributing "material safety data sheets" to employees and perhaps customers. With the intranet, the safety sheets can be easily distributed online.

Users and analysts say intranets are gaining popularity in the chemicals industry as an efficient and inexpensive way to manage many safety sheets. Other companies are likely to follow Shell's lead. One consultant said that companies can save as much as 25 percent of the cost by distributing safety sheets on an intranet.

Besides the savings in printing and handling paper, there are savings in computing costs. If Shell had used a mainframe system for this purpose, it would require accounts for each user who needs access, which would have to be paid for whether they were used or not. With the intranet, access can be provided to anyone with a web browser, so departments can be charged based on actual usage rather than the number of accounts. Also they have many different technologies in the company, and web technology can run on many different PC operating systems.

Shell is such a diverse group, with numerous subsidiaries having their own computing standards, that it couldn't even launch a client/server system. If it had used the existing set of technologies for tracking safety sheets, it would have been required to develop mul-

tiple versions of the client application and then redistribute them every time the application changed. The intranet application, on the other hand, can be updated once in a central database and accessed through web browsers, which run on many operating systems.

The U.S. Occupational Safety and Health Administration's (OSHA) Hazard Communication Standard requires widespread access to the distribution of the safety sheets. Shell has obtained OSHA approval that electronic access satisfies the requirement as long as PCs are readily available to workers.

Shell spent between US$3 million and US$4 million to develop and deploy the intranet application. Eventually, it hopes to recover some of the costs by selling the software to other companies, and is already recognizing significant savings through the use of this application in its various locations all over the world.

Shell
www.shell.com

Questions

1. How did the use of web technologies make this application possible?
2. What issues would management have had to deal with to make this application viable?

SOURCE: www.computerworld.com.

Extranets

Extranets are networks that are available to users outside of a company and may use web technology. In the case outlined in the E-Strategy box, if Shell is successful in opening the application up to customers, then the intranet that was available only to employees will become an extranet because it will also be available to customers.

Extranets have all the advantages of intranets but extend those advantages to outside parties—most often, suppliers and customers. Accordingly, a prime purpose of the use of intranets and extranets is to automate and streamline the supply chain. For suppliers, extranets are used to enable companies to place purchase orders online and for the suppliers to fill those orders. On an extranet, companies can place their catalogues online, and their customers can place orders online. All of the documentation can be in electronic form, and if the applications are sophisticated enough, all of the transactions can be executed online.

An extranet can also be an excellent way to deal with inquiries about availability, delivery times, and other customer concerns and to provide promotional information to the customers. For suppliers, extranets have been extended to implementing joint applications such as vendor-managed inventory (VMI) applications, in which the suppliers manage the company's inventory levels by monitoring quantities on hand and automatically replenishing the stock when needed. Applications like this are critical to contemporary e-business. They reduce costs, improve the timing of business transactions, and foster key business relationships. These are the reasons why extranets have proven to be powerful and popular business tools adopted by a growing range of companies. The E-Business in Global Perspective box, which provides the example of Hyundai Motors using an extranet to build parts sales, illustrates how e-business can help the overall business to succeed.

Hyundai Motors
www.hyundaiusa.com

E-Business in Global Perspective

Scrapping Paper at Hyundai

Hyundai Motors America has built an extranet to link car dealers, auto parts distributors, and independent repair shops to boost the sales of parts by, they hope, as much as 10 percent. Parts sales have been declining. The extranet, which runs on the World Wide Web, is also intended to help Hyundai build a database of information on the independent repair shops as well as customers. The extranet was formally launched on April 6, 2001.

Before the launch of the extranet, repair shops seeking information on the 35 000 parts Hyundai sells had to use either paper catalogues and microfiche documents or call the Hyundai office in New Jersey. Because of

the time-consuming nature of this process, repair shops often tended simply to go with third-party products that were cheaper but not always of the same quality.

By using the extranet, repair shops and other registered users will be able to order vehicle parts from an online electronic catalogue that will then be fulfilled by participating dealers. Hyundai figures that the extranet will be much faster than catalogues or microfiche and can also be used to provide certain information, such as the status of an order, that is needed for everyday operations.

Dealers and distributors must pay US$50 monthly to participate in the extranet, but the payback is

that they can use it to order parts wholesale, check parts inventories, and monitor order and account status information. By launch time, more than 40 percent of Hyundai's 470 dealers in the United States had signed up on the extranet.

The extranet project is part of an overall Hyundai strategy to make its parts more readily available to consumers. Hyundai also initiated a separate supply-chain project in which it is building small warehouses for auto parts at 50 of its largest dealerships to replace three large centres in California, Chicago, and New Jersey. With this approach, the parts will be closer to the customers, and all of the inventories will be available through the extranet.

Hyundai Motors America
www.hyundaiusa.com

Questions

1. How will the extranet help to solve the problem of declining parts sales for Hyundai?
2. How does the use of web technology inherent in an extranet help to achieve this objective?

SOURCE: www.computerworld.com

Virtual Private Networks

Many extranets and intranets actually run on the internet in order to save the cost of acquiring broadband network capability, dedicated telephone lines, and the other paraphernalia that is necessary to set up a conventional network. The major distinguishing feature of an intranet or an extranet from a normal website in this circumstance is the existence of a login requiring a user ID and a password to obtain access. Clearly, having a network on the internet exposes it to the well-known security shortcomings of the internet. A good hacker can find the intranet or extranet by surfing the internet and only has to crack the ID and password to gain access—a comparatively easier job than if the network is set within the bounds of the corporate networks.

VIRTUAL PRIVATE NETWORK (VPN)
A secure and encrypted connection between two points across the internet.

A **virtual private network (VPN)** is one answer to these concerns that has been adopted by many companies. A VPN is a secure and encrypted connection between two points across the internet. VPNs transfer information by encrypting the data in IP packets and sending the packets over the internet by a process called **tunnelling**. Tunnelling is a process under which data packets are transmitted over the internet by including an additional header that establishes its route through the internet. This adds some assurance and security to the transmission process because it is known where the data are and where they are going at all times. The route to be followed by the data is called a tunnel. Most VPNs are built and run by internet service providers and have been used to replace remote access and international proprietary networks.

TUNNELLING
A process under which data packets are transmitted over the internet by including an additional header that establishes its route through the internet.

By using the internet, VPNs reduce networking costs and staffing requirements, somewhat akin to outsourcing, but with better cost reductions. Using VPNs for international networks is quicker than waiting until links can be established by the carriers.

When a user sends data through a VPN, it goes from that user's PC to a firewall, which encrypts the data and sends it over an access line to the company's internet service provider. The data is then carried through tunnels across the internet to the recipient's internet provider. From that point, the data travels over an access line, through another firewall where it is decrypted and sent to the recipient's PC.

How VPNs Facilitate E-Business Transactions

VPNs are driven by a need for wide-ranging networks that have the advantages of the internet in terms of cost and availability, but without the disadvantages of the internet in terms of security. By providing a secure environment, VPNs address the internet's limitations and, as a consequence, add considerable flexibility to a company's network options. In other words, they make the internet a more viable business system.

VPNs are used as a framework in which to develop extranets as well as intranets. Extranets range outside a company and, therefore, tend to serve the need for wide area networks. Intranets, on the other hand, are internal to a company. However, in large companies, the network must cover a large geographical area, and may well be global in scope.

Chapter Summary

The internet is the world's largest network, connecting millions of computers from more than 100 countries. The size of the network and the number of users are growing rapidly. It began as a military project in 1968 when the U.S. Defense Advanced Research Projects Agency (DARPA) formed a network intended for sharing research and development work among corporate, academic, and government researchers. They formed a new network called ARPANET and a protocol to make it work—TCP/IP.

In Canada, the internet began in 1990 when CA*net was created. The purpose of CA*net was to provide internet connectivity between universities and research organizations in Canada. In 1997, CA*net II was formed by linking with international organizations using the Internet Protocol. Then, in 1998, the federal government began working with CANARIE to build a national research and development internet network, CA*net 3, based on fibre optic technology. CANARIE is now working on an enhanced version, known as CA*net 4.

The Internet Architecture Board (IAB) is the coordinating committee for internet design, engineering, and management. The IAB established the Internet Engineering Task Force (IETF) to help coordinate the operation, management, and evolution of the internet. The IETF is a large open community of network designers, operators, vendors, and researchers concerned with the internet and its protocols. The Internet Research Task Force (IRTF) was formed by the IAB to promote research in networking and the development of new technology.

The World Wide Web (WWW) is a special set of servers on the internet, known as web servers, that is equipped to communicate with web browsers.

The main technologies used on the internet are TCP/IP, Common Gateway Interface (CGI), HyperText Markup Language (HTML), HyperText Transfer Protocol (HTTP), and Extensible Markup Language (XML).

An intranet is a network that is internal to an organization and uses internet technologies. Since these technologies include the use of browsers, the network appears to users to be the same as the internet. Since it uses the same protocols as the internet, it can interact seamlessly with the internet.

Extranets are networks that are available to users outside of a company and use internet technology. On an extranet, companies can place their catalogues online, and their customers can place orders online. Applications like this are critical to contemporary e-business. They reduce costs, improve the timing of business transactions, and foster key business relationships.

Many extranets and intranets actually run on the internet, in order to save the cost of acquiring broadband network capability, dedicated telephone lines, and the other paraphernalia that are necessary to set up a conventional network. Clearly, having a network on the internet exposes it to the security shortcomings of the internet. A virtual private network (VPN) is one solution that has been adopted by many companies. A VPN is a secure and encrypted connection between two points across the internet. It can transfer information by encrypting the data in IP packets and sending the packets over the internet by a process called tunnelling. Most VPNs are built and run by internet service providers and have been used to replace remote access and international proprietary networks.

Key Terms

asynchronous transfer mode (ATM) *(p. 51)*
client *(p. 53)*
Common Gateway Interface (CGI) *(p. 57)*
Extensible Markup Language (XML) *(p. 56)*
fibre optics *(p. 51)*
HyperText Markup Language (HTML) *(p. 55)*
HyperText Transfer Protocol (HTTP) *(p. 55)*
internet backbone *(p. 51)*
Internet Protocol (IP) *(p. 49)*
Java *(p. 57)*
Megabits per second (Mbps) *(p. 51)*
metatags *(p. 55)*

packet switching *(p. 50)*
point-of-presence (POP) *(p. 51)*
protocol *(p. 50)*
server *(p. 53)*
source code *(p. 55)*
Transmission Control Protocol (TCP) *(p. 49)*
tunnelling *(p. 60)*
Uniform Resource Locator (URL) *(p. 53)*
virtual private network (VPN) *(p. 60)*
web browser *(p. 54)*
web server *(p. 53)*

Tools for Online Learning

To help you master the material in this chapter and stay up to date with new developments in e-business, visit **www.pearsoned.ca/trites**. Resources include:

- **Review Questions and Exercises**

- **Problems for Discussion**

- **Recommended Readings**

- **Updates to Case Studies and Textual Material**

- **Streaming CBC Videos with Cases**

Endnotes

1. Michael E. Porter, "Strategy and the Internet," *Harvard Business Review* (March 2001): 63–78.

CHAPTER 4

Enterprise-Wide and Inter-Enterprise Systems

LEARNING OBJECTIVES

When you complete this chapter, you should be able to:

1. Describe what is meant by enterprise-wide systems.

2. Describe how enterprise-wide systems fit with e-business strategy.

3. Identify the key features of enterprise systems.

4. Describe how inter-enterprise systems are created.

5. Evaluate the structures for setting up enterprise and inter-enterprise systems.

6. Explain how enterprise and inter-enterprise systems are crucial to e-business.

Introduction

Enterprise-wide systems are any information systems that are deployed throughout an enterprise. They are intended to make information available to all personnel in the enterprise who need it, regardless of where they are located. They are based on the concept that the personnel should have confidence that the information they have is as accurate and up to date as what others in the enterprise are receiving and, therefore, everyone is "on the same page."

Enterprise-wide systems became widely used as business enterprises continued to spread out around the globe and management decisions were pushed down in the organizations so that local managers had more autonomy to make decisions, but still needed to be up to date on activities in the rest of the organization. Such systems take many forms, including enterprise resource planning (ERP) systems (described below), supply chain management (SCM) systems, and customer relationship management (CRM) systems (described in chapters 7 and 9 respectively)

There are different ways of creating enterprise-wide systems. Some companies link systems by using middleware and extensible markup language (XML), and the linked set of systems can be referred to as an enterprise-wide system. **Middleware** is software installed to link different systems together to make them work together. Middleware is often used to enable an ERP system to pass data back and forth between it and a legacy system. A **legacy system** is an old, usually outdated application that has not yet been replaced or upgraded. ERP systems are discussed in the following sections. The advent of e-business spurred the development of enterprise-wide systems since they are needed to enable an enterprise to fully integrate its data and systems to the supply chain to respond quickly to customer needs.

ERP Systems

Enterprise resource planning (ERP) systems have all the characteristics of enterprise-wide systems, but what sets them apart is that they are created as enterprise systems, and all the functionality needed in a typical large enterprise is built into the same set of software. They are specifically designed to enable personnel throughout an organization to view the same set of data rather than requiring it to be moved across applications. In this way, ERP systems overcome the traditional functional "silos" that have historically inhibited the free flow of information in enterprises. Accordingly, ERP systems are large, have a comprehensive set of functionality, and utilize centralized databases to hold the data of an organization so that all personnel are, in fact, reading the same data.

Many organizations saw the turn of the millennium as a strong incentive to implement ERP systems. The reason for this was the Y2K bug. **Y2K** is a term referring to the year 2000 and was a common abbreviation to categorize the computer glitches that were widely predicted to take place when the calendar turned to the year 2000. Organizations around the world were faced with a wide mixture of incompatible legacy systems that, in many cases, were not Y2K-ready. Faced with this looming deadline, many organizations tried to make the best out of the situation and replaced their outdated and often incompatible systems with new, off-the-shelf ERP systems. Since ERP implementations are massive undertakings that often don't leave one stone in an organization unturned, a positive side effect was that organizations were often able to initiate business processes reengineering (BPR) through best practices built into the software. **Business process reengi-**

neering (BPR) involves fundamentally rethinking and radically redesigning existing business processes to add value or prepare for new technologies.

The largest vendors of ERP systems are Oracle, PeopleSoft, and SAP. In addition, Microsoft is aggressively targeting small and mid-sized businesses with its Navision and Great Plains product lines. Because of the importance of systems integration in e-business and the important role that can be played by ERP systems in that integration, all of these vendors are positioning their products as e-business solutions.

A typical ERP system has numerous modules. The breadth of the applications is immediately apparent—they cover the entire range of business applications, including areas like financial accounting, sales and distribution, materials management, and human resources.

Financial accounting modules include all the bookkeeping requirements for a company. These modules collect all the transactions of the company and assemble them into the financial statements and other reports regarding profitability and financial position. As with all modules, the financial accounting reports can be used on a "drill down" basis, where the overall financial results can be presented in a report, and then the user can access progressively detailed reports according to division, geographic area, and even particular stores by clicking on selected numbers in the report. In this way, detailed information about the company can be made available throughout the organization.

Sales and distribution modules capture and record data about individual sales and then pass the necessary information to the shipping area of the company. The data on sales and shipments is then passed along to the financial accounting module for inclusion in the bookkeeping records and the financial reports.

Materials management modules are used to manage all the materials that go into the production of the final product. For example, if automobiles were being built, this module would keep track of the inventories of the individual components, such as engines, seats, fenders, and headlights. Detailed specifications and costs of these components would also be kept in this module. Again, this module would integrate with the financial accounting module.

Human resources modules, of course, include the payroll system as well as all the records the company must maintain about the personnel in the organization. As with all modules, the data in this module can integrate with other modules as needed.

The scope of the modules is one of the defining characteristics of ERP systems. Another defining characteristic is the fact that the system works across an entire organization, whereas companies that do not employ ERP systems often have a variety of different systems in place, some based on functionality (i.e., financial reporting software), some to cover the different geographical areas, and some to support the different business units of a company. Finally, the sheer size of an ERP system is another defining characteristic, and one of the characteristics that leads to many of the implementation and management issues usually associated with ERP systems.

Characteristics of ERP Systems

Client-Server Systems A significant characteristic of ERP systems is that they are client-server systems built on relational database systems. A **client-server system** is a network configuration that evolved from networks built around central computers (servers) to provide computing power to the users on their own desktop computers (clients). A **relational database system** is a logical database model that

BUSINESS PROCESS REENGINEERING (BPR)
Fundamental rethinking and radical redesign of existing business processes to add value or prepare for new technologies.

CLIENT-SERVER SYSTEM
A network configuration that evolved from networks built around central computers (servers) to provide computing power to the users on their own desktop computers (clients).

RELATIONAL DATABASE SYSTEM
A logical database model that relates data in different tables within the database by sharing a common data element (or field) between them. The common data element can serve as a reference point in the tables to other data elements in a data record.

relates data in different tables within the database by sharing a common data element (or field) between them. The common data element can serve as a reference point in the tables to other data elements in a data record.

There are various forms of client-server systems, the differences primarily defined by strategic objectives. There are three basic elements to any information system—data, processing (applications), and output (display). The strategic forms of client-server systems are derived from the idea that these three system elements can be distributed between the client and the server in several ways. The processing element, for example, can be distributed to the clients, giving rise to a form of client-server system called a distributed processing system. Systems that simply have servers and clients are referred to as two-tier client-server systems. When the applications are distributed to servers dedicated to applications (i.e., when the processing is done), the system is referred to as a three-tier client-server system. If the data itself is distributed to the clients, the resulting system is known as a distributed data client-server system. Most ERP systems are configured as three-tier client-server systems, which means they have applications servers available in the organization. A system like this makes the applications more manageable, making it possible to place them closer to the user groups who are responsible for using them. This is illustrated in figure 4.1.

Client-server systems dominated the 1980s and '90s, so ERP systems thrived using this model. More recently, however, there has been a strong movement to extend this model to create what has become known as web-enabled applications. As an example, SAP has invested a great deal in a system called MySAP, which is a highly web-enabled system that extends the capabilities of ERP to the internet. Its leading competitor, Oracle Corp., also introduced a new version of its basic software that was web-enabled as well, and then introduced an integrated suite called Oracle E-Business Suite. Of course, web-enablement is crucial to the effective use of ERP systems in e-business since it makes the integration of the ERP systems with the internet much more effective and seamless.

The integration of the web into the ERP products is having an impact on the basic architecture of ERP system, to the point that some vendors are touting their products as having moved from a client-server system to a network-computing architecture. Oracle, for example, in announcing version 11i of Oracle Applications, made that statement, arguing that a client-server model is too rigid. They pointed out that in a network-computing model such as the internet, the

Oracle Corporation
www.oracle.com

Figure 4.1   Three-Tier Client-Server System

This graphic shows the basic structure of a three-tier client-server system, with the clients in the top row, the application servers in the middle row, and the network server in the bottom row.

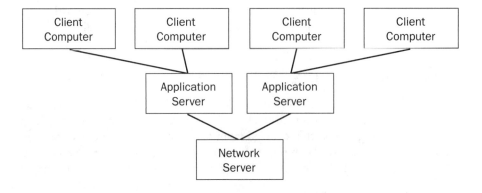

architecture of the network is fluid, placing the data, processing, and output where it makes sense. In fact, in many ERP systems, the initial configuration of the software can reflect this flexibility. It does become much more difficult, however, to change the system after the initial configuration.

Relational Databases The fact that ERP systems are built on relational database systems is an important feature of ERP systems, since they provide a vehicle through which the data in the organization can be held and managed. All ERP systems use a relational database for this purpose, with some providing more flexibility than others as to exactly which database can be used. A very common database used for these purposes is Oracle, which of course underlies the Oracle Applications ERP system. Oracle also is one of the most common database systems used for SAP. Others are Microsoft's relational database (SQL Server) and IBM's DB2.

Database systems consist of files that contain fields of information. For example, a database containing sales information would have fields for customer number, customer name, address, product number, and product name, among other information. Databases consist of several different files like this, all linked in various ways. Relational databases are linked by identifying a common field between two or more individual files in the database, where the applications can go to look for information related to that field. This field that is common to both files is known as a "relational" field. In the example above, both files might have a field to record a customer number—a common relational field—in which case, this field can be used as the relational field. Complete systems contain many files and many relational fields.

Package Software *Package software*, as a characteristic of ERP systems, means that it is software that is bought off the shelf in a form that is installed and then operated. This characteristic differentiates package software from that developed in-house. While the program code for packaged software is not normally changed, the program itself does need to be customized as much as possible to the specific company adopting it. Such customization must be carried out by using the functionality contained within the software as provided. Because of the size and complexity of ERP systems, the customization process is in itself a large and complex project.

Business Process Reengineering Business process reengineering is one of the characteristics of ERP systems in the broad sense because all of them require extensive BPR to fit them into the business, or more correctly, to fit the business to the software. By definition, BPR means that the business processes being carried out by the organization must be substantially changed to accommodate the processes that are built into the software. These changes can involve changing the steps carried out during the processes, changing who does them, combining them, or replacing them. The BPR element of ERP implementations is one of the most difficult aspects of such projects.

Implementing ERP

Several notable news stories have emerged in recent years about specific failures with regard to ERP implementation projects. A widely publicized story concerns Hershey Foods and a major implementation in 1999 that ran into trouble.[1]

In late 1999, Hershey Foods announced that problems in the final phase of its ERP implementation project had resulted in delays in filling its orders to the extent that it was taking them more than twice as long to fill orders than previously. Their announcement was made during their busiest season, when back-to-school and Halloween orders were flooding in. Retailers scrambled to find other suppli-

Hershey Food Corporation
www.hersheys.com

ers, and Hershey lost out significantly, particularly with the lucrative Halloween trade. To make matters worse, there were reports that many of those customers stayed with the other suppliers they had found for the Christmas season as well.

The impact of all this on Hershey's financial statements was substantial. Their reports showed that in the third quarter of 1999, sales were down about US$60 million from the same period in 1998, and net income fell by US$20 million. For the fourth quarter, sales were down US$42 million and earnings were down US$11 million from the fourth quarter of 1998.

In a statement released with the third-quarter results, Hershey CEO Kenneth L. Wolfe said, "our third-quarter sales and earnings declined primarily as a result of problems encountered since the July start-up of new business processes in the areas of customer service, warehousing, and order fulfillment. These problems resulted in lost sales and significantly increased freight and warehousing costs."

Hershey's implementation plan involved replacing about 80 percent of its legacy systems with a system that included SAP R/3 combined with other software from Manugistics and Siebel Systems. The implementation team was formed in early 1997, with a view to going live by the spring of 1999. It was a tight deadline, with little room for error. As with many ERP implementations at the time, they were driven to complete in time for the Y2K deadline. They also had a strong interest in preparing themselves for the emerging world of e-business—the world of the twenty-first century.

As always with major projects, some things went wrong, and the pressure wrought because of the tight deadlines skyrocketed. The timetable slipped and the last phase of the implementation, which included the critical functions of warehouse management, transportation management, and the order-to-cash process, was moved to the third quarter. This happened to be the company's heaviest shipping season. They couldn't keep up and orders couldn't be filled in time, customers were unhappy, and lower earnings followed.

Hershey, SAP, and the press had lots of possible reasons and excuses for this outcome. Lack of adequate training was frequently cited. Also, some pointed to a lack of distribution capacity, although it's hard to see how this factor could be attributed to the implementation process. One author put forward the view that Hershey's computer network just couldn't handle the new system, and that Hershey didn't check it out well in advance—a classic systems sizing issue. **Systems sizing** is the process of assessing the volume and processing requirements that will be placed on a new information system and thereby determining the size of system required, including hardware and software. Hershey wouldn't have been the first company to run into this oversight. It's not unusual for an enterprise to implement a complicated system only to find the infrastructure can't handle it. This is especially true of an ERP system, which is huge, causes a heavy traffic flow, and requires lots of capacity for data transmission and storage. With a big-budget implementation, it makes sense to do everything possible to eliminate the risks, and one of the first places to look is to check the platform on which the system is intended to run.

There were no reports from Hershey as to whether they checked their network before starting the implementation project, so it's not known whether this was the problem or not. Some reporters thought it might have been, pointing out that with a full probe of the network, modelling it and profiling the applications that would run on it, Hershey could have checked the impact of the R/3, Manugistics, and Siebel systems on its network. By doing this, they could have seen the loads those applications were going to put on the network, and would have been able to identify problem areas. Put another way, thorough testing of the

SYSTEMS SIZING
The process of assessing the volume and processing requirements that will be placed on a new information system and thereby determining the size of system required, including hardware and software.

system, including stress testing, might have done the job. **Stress testing** is a process consisting of high-volume entry, processing, and output of test data designed to determine whether the system has the capacity to handle the volumes that will be required of it.

Another issue was training. Some informed people felt that this was the main problem—that Hershey underestimated the amount of training required and so the people running the system couldn't cope. Even with modern high-tech systems, the people running it are critical to the process. An enterprise must make sure the people have the skill sets needed to operate and support the new system, and that proper processes are in place for supporting the users (see the E-Business in Global Perspective box for an example).

STRESS TESTING
A process of high-volume entry, processing, and output of test data designed to determine whether the system has the capacity to handle the volumes that will be required of it.

E-Business in Global Perspective

Global ERP at Millipore

Millipore Corp., a manufacturer of water-filtration devices, decided to go with a new upgrade being offered by Oracle for its premier ERP system, Oracle 11*i*. The company operates internationally, and the new system is intended to enable a company to install a single global ERP system. For Millipore, this would extend the advantages of ERP to its full global operations.

Preliminary to implementation, the company moved its European ERP system from their own ERP server to one at company headquarters in Bedford, Massachusetts, leaving only its Japanese division on a separate system. Millipore executives said putting everything on the U.S. server would reduce data centre costs, in addition to giving users a unified view of the company's business. The project team knew they needed to be careful, however, because their users would be very

unforgiving if response times suffered, even a little bit.

While centralizing the servers, the company also began a six-month project to create a common accounting structure for Millipore's business units, as well as an overhaul of the company's network infrastructure.

The new system also required a database upgrade, changes in the order management module, and a change to Oracle's graphical user interface (GUI). The database upgrade needed to be tested heavily to determine how well the centralized system would be able to handle end-user workloads. A whole 12-person team, working with Oracle development personnel, had to be assigned just to test and debug the new order management module.

The switch to Oracle's GUI required strengthening the company networks by installing new

switches to double or even triple its wide-area bandwidth. However, Millipore didn't have a good understanding of the bandwidth requirements of the new GUI—just that it would definitely require a much higher capacity. They needed to initiate performance testing for this aspect of the initiative.

They had a tight deadline, with testing scheduled for the summer and "going live" scheduled for October. They ran into a setback when Oracle announced a delay in the release of the new upgrade. That was when Millipore decided to go ahead more cautiously. They wanted to be very sure the new upgrade would work well in all environments. In some of the less technologically developed areas of the world, they could run into problems, but they didn't have the option of skipping those areas in the implementation. It was all or nothing.

Millipore Corp.
www.millipore.com

Questions

1. What issues would Millipore have had to consider when it did the risk benefit analysis for this project?
2. What would be the implications of the delay in the project?
3. Do you think they made the right decision to move ahead cautiously?

SOURCE: Craig Stedman, "Move to Single Global ERP System No Easy Task," Computerworld.com (January 14, 2000) **www.computerworld.com/news/2000/story/ 0,11280,40734,00.html**, accessed December 3, 2004.

Integrating ERP

ERP systems that are implemented across an organization offer the most direct way of integrating systems. If, for example, all the modules of SAP are implemented, then the modules will automatically be able to "talk to" each other. The major issue that arises in this situation is that the enterprise's business processes and the processes built into the overall ERP system are not likely to match requiring more business process change to implement the ERP system. With large systems in particular, the business processes must be changed to fit the software, rather than changing the software to fit the existing processes. On the positive side, the interface with users is standard across the modules, minimizing the training required for personnel who change their jobs within the company. (Table 4.1 provides an outline of the steps for ERP integration, as provided by Oracle Corporation.)

Another way to integrate an ERP system is to implement a number of systems in an organization by choosing the best fit for particular functionality—a "best-of-breed" approach. This enhances the possibility of attaining a good fit between the business processes and the software, requiring less business process

E-Strategy

Best of Breed at Dell

When Dell Computer Co. decided to implement enterprise-wide systems, it chose the ERP software of Glovia International for inventory control, warehouse management, and materials management as part of its strategy. Dell had also chosen i2 Technologies' supply chain management system and Oracle's order management system to implement what is known as a best-of-breed strategy. The concept of a best-of-breed strategy is to choose specific functionality from a variety of software packages instead of relying on one all-encompassing product. Then the packages need to

be knit together by using middleware and other linkages.

The company had tried to implement SAP's R/3 ERP system in 1994 for manufacturing applications, but had felt it to be "too monolithic" to be able to keep up with their changing business needs. After trying to implement the system over the following two years, they finally cut back the effort in 1996, using SAP only for human resources. They had tried to customize the product to match their business model, but found they couldn't keep up with the very rapid changes in this area.

Dell management pointed out that the Glovia software was scalable on Dell hardware, but also flexible enough to integrate with the other software they had chosen to run. In addition, they felt Glovia had the capability to break into smaller pieces for implementation. This was before SAP modularized its software to offer the same capability.

Dell undertook a global implementation of Glovia in 2000, with approximately 3000 Dell employees in the United States, Ireland, and Malaysia slated to use the software.

Dell
www.dell.com

Questions

1. Based on what you know of Dell, evaluate their best-of-breed strategy against a single-vendor strategy.
2. What are the risks of a best-of-breed strategy?
3. Which strategy—best-of-breed or single-vendor—is likely to remain valid for the long term?

SOURCE: Informationweek.com. May 11, 1998.

Table 4.1   Steps in ERP Implementation

These steps are recommended by Oracle Corporation in its methodology for implementation of an ERP system.

Phase 1: Definition

1. Set up and organize the project team.
2. Conduct project team orientation.
3. Plan the implementation project.
4. Identify and document the overall business and system requirements.
5. Define the future business model of the organization.
6. Describe the application and information technology architectures.
7. Develop a training plan for team members.

Phase 2: Operations Analysis

8. Collect the business process information and requirements.
9. Fit the required business processes to the standard built-in ERP processes.
10. Develop the business requirements scenarios and the gap analysis.
11. Refine the applications and technology architectures.
12. Prototype business processes.
13. Begin consideration of the feasibility of the business process design.

Phase 3: Solution Design

14. Develop detailed documentation of business procedures.
15. Consider and set specific application configuration options for customization.
16. Design any custom extensions, interfaces, and data conversions.
17. Determine process and organizational changes required to enable implementation.

Phase 4: Build

18. Code and test the customization carried out, including all enhancements, conversions, and interfaces (development team).
19. Create and execute performance, integration, and business system tests.

Phase 5: Transition

20. Conduct data conversion.
21. Conduct final training for the users and support staff.
22. Conduct a production readiness check.

Phase 6: Production

23. Cutover to production.
24. Fine-tune the system to make sure it is actually running as it was intended.
25. Begin the process of regular maintenance.
26. Turn over the system to the continuing management of the organization.
27. Begin ongoing support by the continuing IS personnel.

SOURCE: "Using Oracle Applications" (Boss Corporation, Indianapolis, 2000). Reprinted with permission of NetLedger Inc. All rights reserved.

change. However, more time must be spent during implementation on the interfaces between the systems, and sometimes these interfaces don't work as well as the users would like. The E-Strategy box outlines a best-of-breed approach that was used at Dell Computer. The essential point is that good integration is absolutely essential for e-business purposes.

Middleware

The term middleware is used to designate any software that is used to link applications together. It differs from the idea of importing and exporting information between applications, because middleware involves the creation of a direct linkage through which data can flow uninterrupted. For example, accounting applications, such as Simply Accounting by ACCPAC, have functions in their menus that specifically allow data and reports to be imported from and exported to spreadsheets for further analysis. This process is not middleware because it requires the import and export functions to be executed. The use of middleware between applications like accounting software and spreadsheets is seamless (i.e., it is not seen by the user). The data moves as though it were still in the same application.

Middleware is used in enterprise systems because it is important that data move freely and easily across the enterprise. While the large systems like ERP and CRM systems are large enough to minimize the use of middleware, they do not eliminate that need. The process of using middleware to knit applications together across an enterprise is known as **enterprise application integration (EAI)**. EAI is the process of planning, implementing, and managing the ability of applications in an enterprise to share information efficiently, often involving legacy systems and ERP systems.

Examples of middleware include Microsoft Message Queue Server (MSMQ). This software is designed to enable application programs to communicate with other application programs through a built-in messaging system that asynchronously sends and receives messages. Database systems, such as Sybase, DB2, and Oracle, are also used as middleware by providing a direct linkage to specific data and a repository of data that is in transit. Data often resides on networks, midrange, and mainframe systems, and database systems can provide direct, read/write access to integrate that data into an application. Such linkages are used in e-business to build data warehouses, automate sales forces, and integrate Internet-based applications.

ENTERPRISE APPLICATION INTEGRATION (EAI)
The process of planning, implementing, and managing the ability of applications in an enterprise to share information efficiently, often involving legacy systems and ERP systems.

Extensible Markup Language (XML)

In chapter 3, Extensible Markup Language (XML) was defined as a very powerful tool that is similar to HTML and is compatible with it, but does not rely on single preset tags to identify information. Instead, XML provides a mechanism for any document builder to define new XML tags within any XML document. This means that in addition to being a markup language, XML is a meta-language that can define new tags. Data can be tagged within a system using XML and then found quickly by an XML-enabled browser.

As with HTML, tags can be identified in XML by words that are bracketed by "<" and ">". Tags within such brackets can also be definitional. A major difference between HTML and XML, however, is that HTML specifies exactly what each tag means, while XML uses the tags only to identify the data, and leaves it up to the application reading the data to find that data. For example, an XML document might be a report that shows the total sales of a company. The XML tag might read for that part of the report where the number is intended to appear. The XML tag will be sent to another application and that application will read the tag and go to the data fields for total sales and insert the number in the document. Of course, in order to do this, the application needs to be "XML enabled," which means it contains the software code that enables it to read and interpret the tags.

XML is used for the integration of systems from the internet back into the basic information systems of the company, the CRM and ERP systems, the accounting systems, and any other components of the supply chain. The internet application sends an XML request (tag) back to the source data within the applications, which then sends that specific data back to the internet. The whole process should be very fast and seamless. In effect, XML is a process for drawing structured data from a variety of sources and placing it into a text file for a user.

XML is not just a single technology, but rather has been referred to as a family of technologies. It is built on specifications that represent agreements within the information systems (IS) community. The core specification is XML 1.0, which defines what "tags" and "attributes" are, but there are several other parts of XML. For example, there is XLink, which describes a standard way to add hyperlinks to an XML file, as well as XPointer and XFragments, which are syntaxes for pointing to parts of an XML document. The details of the XML protocol are quite complex, but such detail is not needed to gain an understanding of its applicability for e-business.

Collaborative and Inter-Enterprise Systems

Collaborative systems and inter-enterprise systems are becoming increasingly common as electronic business becomes more sophisticated and companies become more interlinked. **Collaborative systems** are information systems that work between enterprises to enable them to work together on common business initiatives and ventures. Inter-enterprise systems arise because of the growth in collaborative e-business between enterprises and their customers, suppliers, personnel, and competitors.

COLLABORATIVE SYSTEMS
Information systems that work between enterprises to enable them to work together on common business initiatives and ventures.

Collaboration with Customers

An early form of collaboration with customers arose out of the customization of products and the involvement of the customers in the customization process. Levi Strauss & Co. was an early innovator in this area. Through their website, they offered customers the option to create their own jeans by inputting their own measurements and then ordering them over the web. By having the ability to create a pair of jeans that fit their measurements in the way they wanted, customers were essentially collaborating in the design of those jeans. The collaborative system in this case was the internet. There had to be a way for the input measurements to reach the sales order system within the company, and that would also be part of the collaborative system. This, of course, would require integration of these two parts of the system.

Another example is Cisco Systems, one of the world's leading suppliers of technical network equipment like routers, hubs, and switches. They have initiated several applications that use the web as a vehicle for collaboration with customers. For example, their customers can sign into a website with interactive chat rooms and whiteboard tools that allow customers to interact with Cisco representatives to discuss technical problems. The whiteboard tools are used to exchange drawings to explore possible solutions to the issues. This was a successful initiative and was later expanded to include the capability for customers to simultaneously interact with company representatives using the telephone and the web. The truly collaborative element comes in when customers click on a "help" button to request an immediate telephone call from a Cisco representative and establish a link between their respective web browsers. As the customer and the representative speak on the telephone, they can navigate the web together using their linked browsers, sharing electronic documents and completing shared forms on the web-

Cisco Systems
www.cisco.com

site. This linked browser system is a good example of a collaborative system based on the use of the internet.

Collaboration with Suppliers

Ford Motor Company
www.ford.com

Several automobile manufacturers are involved in collaboration with their suppliers, to the point that some are saying that the car manufacturers could eventually be out of the car manufacturing business, acting instead as coordinators of the activities carried out by their suppliers. Ford Motor Co. provides a good example of using collaborative techniques for product design. Before the advent of collaboration, Ford would send drawings of new products to their suppliers, who in turn would add in their component and send it back to Ford, who would then pass it along to other suppliers involved in that particular product. Through a process of revision and circulation among suppliers, the ultimate product would evolve. Naturally, this process took a considerable amount of time, even though the drawings were transmitted electronically, because it was a linear process, with each participant revising the drawings in succession.

To improve on this process, Ford adopted a system they called "digital mockup," which operates on a website and enables all of the suppliers to work on the design at the same time. This meant the process changed from a sequential one to an interactive, fully collaborative activity. As with the other examples, the internet is the prime enabler for this collaborative system. Ford has had success with this type of system, and uses a very similar system for its "World Car" design, under which collaborators from around the world work together on the system to design new cars. Collaborative systems of this type are spreading not only throughout the automobile industry, but other industries as well.

Collaboration with Personnel

For several years, Lotus Notes has been used in businesses for purposes of collaborative work on projects. The advantage of Lotus Notes is that it is designed for collaboration by enabling personnel on a project to file their papers in a central location and have them fully accessible by other team members, regardless of their location. It was ideal for consulting assignments for large companies, because consultants in Toronto, Halifax, and Vancouver, for example, could work using Lotus Notes, which would maintain their files on a central server, say in Toronto, and enable all of the consultants to view, review, comment on, and even change that documentation. In this way, the working paper files for the entire consulting job could be assembled in a central location on a coordinated basis and thus eliminate duplication and minimize inconsistencies as the job proceeds, rather than just at the review stage. This system can be used between companies as well as within companies.

Collaboration with Competitors

Trading exchanges provide an excellent example of collaboration between competitors, such as the Covisint exchange of the automobile industry described in chapter 1. Over 2000 exchanges were formed during the dot-com boom, in virtually all industries. One of the objectives of this approach was to go public with the exchange company, thereby raising capital for the trading exchange on the stock market. Since the initial bubble in the stock market with dot-coms, however, this aspect of exchanges has largely ended. In addition, many of the trading exchanges have gone out of business. Even Covisint had to change its business model and ownership to survive. However, numerous exchanges still exist, and provide a good example of collaborative commerce.

Canadian Snapshots

Big Changes at Sobeys

During 2000, Sobeys Inc., one of Canada's largest food retailers, was immersed in an implementation of the SAP ERP system. In December of that year, the company experienced a five-day database crash that left them scrambling to fill the shelves in their stores just before the busy Christmas season.

Shortly before that, on November 25, the company had announced the appointment of a new President and CEO, Bill McEwan, who moved in from the position of President and Chief Executive Officer of the Atlantic Region of the Great Atlantic and Pacific Tea Company, Inc. (A&P). Prior to joining A&P he was Vice President, Market Development, Coca-Cola Beverages Ltd.

On January 24, 2001, Sobeys announced they were abandoning SAP's distribution product but planned to retain SAP's payroll and financial systems. "We do have a meeting set up with [SAP]," said Stewart Mahoney, vice-president of treasury and investor relations for Empire Company Limited, parent company of Sobeys. Empire holds 65 per cent of Sobeys. "We will be having thorough discussions on the phase-out... of that (distribution) system." He said that the decision

was precipitated by the crash of the database system in November. He also announced that a new Information Officer would be joining the company shortly.

The company also announced that they would record an after-tax special charge of $49 900 000, or 82 cents per share ($89 100 000 or $1.47 per share pre-tax), due to dropping the SAP distribution system. The next day, Sobeys stock dropped by 16 percent. It finished the day at $20.35, down $3.25, or about 14 percent.

SAP, of course, announced their disappointment, referring to the recent shuffling in the Sobeys management structure as possibly being behind any technological trouble. "When companies change executive management, this sometimes results in changes in a company's information technology strategy," SAP's release said. SAP said they had a strong team at the company and said they had worked on the problems with the IBM database, which had been at the middle of the problem.

Mr. McEwan said the SAP software couldn't deal with his firm's large transaction volume and that they had plans for a new system that would provide "better functionality in half the time." He added

that "We have come to the conclusion that what appeared to be growing pains with the implementation of these enterprise-wide systems are in fact systemic problems of a more serious nature. We have determined that there is insufficient core functionality in the SAP software component of our enterprise-wide systems to effectively deal with the extremely high number of transactions in our retail operating environment."

Industry analysts said that retail companies represent some of the most difficult businesses for the implementation of enterprise-wide solutions, given the large numbers of transactions and the wide range of products. It requires careful training of the staff, which some reports stated might have been lacking at Sobeys. Sobeys disagreed with this.

At the time of announcing its decision to discontinue further development and implementation of the SAP enterprise-wide software and systems initiative, SAP had to be phased out of operation in Sobeys Atlantic Division and 30 corporate Sobeys stores in Ontario. The operations of Sobeys Quebec, Sobeys West, Serca Food Service and the remaining 379 stores in Ontario had not been converted to SAP.

Sobeys Inc.
www.sobeys.com

Questions

1. **What factors would management have had to consider in making this important decision?**

2. **What is typical and not typical about this decision?**

SOURCE: Ivan Smith, *History of Nova Scotia*, Chapter 76, **www.littletechshoppe.com/ ns1625/nshist76.html**, accessed November 11, 2004.

Managing Inter-Enterprise Systems

Most of the collaborative systems described in the preceding sections are at least partially based on the internet. Indeed, the internet has been the prime enabler for virtually all such collaboration in recent years. As collaboration increases in intensity and scope, and as it becomes more complex, the systems will also grow and become more difficult to manage. The management of the systems is being approached in different ways—by outsourcing, by placing the systems management in the hands of a separate entity (such as an exchange), by establishing a management agreement with one or more of the participants in the collaboration, and by having each of the participants manage the part of the system that simply falls within their own system. The approach depends in part on who is the owner of the system and who is designated as the system manager, which is a matter that can be covered in any agreements entered into to govern the collaboration.

New Business Models

ERP Goes Open Source?

Everyone knows that ERP software costs thousands and even millions of dollars. So far this has been true, but this is about to change if several open source initiatives have their way. Until recently, Linux was the only open source system that has really made inroads into the commercial world. Everyone can use it for free and modify the code as they wish. Linux, as an operating system, is different because it has many enthusiastic contributors who donate their spare time to improve it. While it is difficult to imagine an enthusiastic open-source programmer who will use his evenings to code human-resources software for the benefit of an international corporation, open source may be coming to ERP software.

Companies like IBM and HP have poured extensive resources into open source projects such as Linux. Although their "contribution" is for the common-good, they can still profit from selling value-added services such as customization and consulting services. So far, this business model has proven to be quite successful. So why not try the same with ERP?

There are currently two main projects in this area: the GNU Enterprise project (GNUe) and Compiere. GNUe, which is still in its early stages, eventually wants to evolve into a full-fledged ERP system. The other project, Compiere, is already available and targets mostly small and mid-sized businesses. In the case of Compiere, the software is developed by ComPiere Inc., which offers commercial support. On its website, Compiere is described as a "fully integrated business solution for small–medium enterprises," and has already been deployed in various companies around the world. So far, Compiere seems to be ahead, but it will certainly be interesting to see how GNUe develops.

GNUe
www.gnuenterprise.org

Compiere
www.compiere.org

Questions

1. Do you think it is possible for open source ERP projects to enjoy the same success as open source projects such as Linux? Why or why not?
2. Will open source ERP be able to compete with the likes of SAP and Oracle?
3. What are the advantages and disadvantages of open source ERP for the different stakeholders?
4. Frequently, consultants are used for an ERP implementation. How could consultants benefit from open source ERP?

SOURCES: www.gnuenterprise.org, www.compiere.org, accessed July 15, 2000.

When a collaborative system is adopted, specific processes need to be changed, as some will be reallocated between the partners, or by the new entity. As a result, job descriptions change and the need for personnel changes, because of the efficiencies achieved, often involving the need for staff reductions and cutbacks.

Chapter Summary

Enterprise-wide systems are information systems that are deployed throughout an enterprise to draw together their data and make it available to anyone who needs it. Such systems may be single systems like enterprise resource planning (ERP) or customer relationship management (CRM) systems, but also can be smaller systems linked together using middleware, Extensible Markup Language (XML), or other tools. E-business spurred the development of enterprise-wide systems since they are necessary to enable an enterprise to fully integrate its supply chain to respond quickly to customer needs.

Enterprise resource systems have all the characteristics of enterprise-wide systems. They have different modules, like financial accounting and sales and distribution, that cover the full range of business activity. Implementing ERP systems is a major activity, involving considerable risk. Implementations usually require considerable process change and reengineering. With the large systems in particular, the business processes must be changed to fit the software rather than changing the software to fit the existing processes. ERP systems that are implemented across an organization offer the most direct way of integrating systems.

Middleware is used in enterprise systems because it is important that data move freely and easily across the enterprise. While the large systems like ERP and CRM systems are large enough to minimize the use of middleware, they do not eliminate that need. The process of using middleware to knit applications together across an enterprise is known as enterprise application integration (EAI).

XML is used for the integration of systems from the internet back into the basic information systems of the company, the CRM and ERP systems, the accounting systems, and any other components of the supply chain. The internet application sends an XML request back to the source data within the applications, which then sends that specific data back to the internet application.

Different types of collaborative systems exist within companies and between companies that are collaborating. The most common collaborative system is based on the internet. A linked internet browser that is connected to an application system is a good example. Another example is a trading exchange's system that is linked to the systems of the participants through the internet. In such a case, the collaborative system consists of the exchange system, the internet linkages, and those parts of the participants' systems that are linked to the rest of the system.

Key Terms

business process reengineering (BPR) *(p. 65)*	middleware *(p. 64)*
client-server systems *(p. 65)*	relational database systems *(p. 65)*
collaborative systems *(p. 73)*	stress testing *(p. 69)*
enterprise application integration (EAI) *(p. 72)*	systems sizing *(p. 68)*
enterprise-wide systems *(p. 64)*	Y2K *(p. 64)*
legacy system *(p. 64)*	

Tools for Online Learning

To help you master the material in this chapter and stay up to date with new developments in e-business, visit **www.pearsoned.ca/trites**. Resources include:

- Review Questions and Exercises

- Problems for Discussion

- Recommended Readings

- Updates to Case Studies and Textual Material

- Streaming CBC Videos with Cases

Endnotes

1. The Hershey Foods story is reproduced with permission from G. Trites, *Enterprise Resource Planning—The Engine of e-Business* (Toronto: Canadian Institute of Chartered Accountants, 2000).

CHAPTER 5

Security and Controls

When you complete this chapter you should be able to:

1. Identify the security risks of internet-based business.

2. Describe generally how e-business is made secure.

3. Identify the major components of security systems for e-business.

4. Identify and evaluate the major security strategies.

5. Explain the major issues in implementing good security.

6. Describe the significant types of security tools available.

Introduction

Every information system is subject to the risk of error, fraud, malicious acts, or disasters. **Risk** is the probability of an event occurring that leads to undesirable consequences such as lost revenues, excessive costs, misappropriation or destruction of assets, unreliable information, erroneous decisions, unauthorized disclosure of confidential or private information, competitive disadvantage, disruption of business activity or legal or statutory sanctions. An **error** is an unintentional act or omission that leads to undesirable consequences. Errors include accidents, unintentional improper use of system features, flaws in system design, development or implementation and errors in system maintenance. According to the National Computer Security Association, over half of the security risks faced by companies are attributable to carelessness, errors, or omissions, rather than to malicious intent. **Fraud** is an intentional act that relies on deception to misappropriate assets or obtain other benefits. **Malicious acts** intentionally lead to the destruction of facilities, hardware, software, or data. Malicious acts include hacker attacks, viruses, sabotage, vandalism and terrorism. **Disasters** are acts of nature such as floods, storms, tornados, earthquakes, or fires; power failures; or other events that can lead to destruction of assets and disruption of business activities. Every company faces these risks to some extent and has to assess the degree of risk that can be tolerated and design appropriate countermeasures if the risks it faces are greater than its tolerable level of risk.

What Are the Key Risks Faced by E-Businesses?

E-business risks arise from threats that are either not prevented from occurring or are not promptly detected and corrected if they occur. Risks of errors or omissions are created or magnified in e-business because it constantly creates new services, business models, processes, technology, fulfilment processes, and sourcing.

New services. Internal risks associated with new services include lack of standards, regulations and rules, and support systems. External risks associated with new services are natural hazards, legal issues, and environmental issues.

New business models. The internet has facilitated the introduction of new business models that face unique risks not faced by traditional offline business models. These include revenue leakage, poor image, and inability to foster trust and confidence on the part of business partners.

New processes. E-business enables businesses to integrate with their customers and suppliers in a manner that was not possible before (e.g., real-time information processing associated with just-in-time manufacturing). Such arrangements are often accompanied by strict product specifications and product deliveries, with penalties for non-compliance written into their contracts. If the company develops a reputation for failing to meet such contractual obligations, then this can also impair its ability to obtain additional business.

New technology. E-businesses use leading edge technology that may have issues associated with scalability, security, and availability. In addition, such systems may not be able to integrate with existing systems.

New fulfillment processes. The online fulfillment process has brought expectations of "instant" deliveries resulting in real-time procurement requirements. Such expectations give businesses less room for error within their supply chains.

Outsourcing IT activities. It is common for e-business entities to outsource various aspects of their IT activities to outside service providers, ranging from website hosting to fulfillment to the entire IT infrastructure. In many cases, outsourcing of parts of e-business systems splits the responsibilities for controls, with the attendant risks of non-performance and insufficient monitoring by the outsourcing service provider. If not properly defined and monitored, such outsourcing arrangements can lead to a loss of control over the entity's e-business activities.

In addition to the business risks caused by e-business innovations, entities face the risks of abuses attributable to malicious attacks perpetrated by employees and parties external to the entity, such as fraudsters, hackers, and vandals.[1] The most common abuses involving malicious acts that have been reported by various surveys are (in order of frequency of occurrence):

- infection by malicious pieces of code (virus, Trojan, worm)
- installation or use of unauthorized software
- use of official computers for illegal or illicit activities (pornography, e-mail, harassment)
- installation of unauthorized hardware
- use of official computers for personal profit (gambling, spam, managing personal e-commerce websites, online investing)
- physical theft, sabotage, or intentional destruction of equipment, especially laptop theft
- denial of service attacks (deliberate attacks to disable an entity's communications systems, preventing it from providing services)
- website, web server attacks
- abuse of insecure passwords
- electronic theft, sabotage, or intentional destruction or disclosure of proprietary data or information
- financial fraud

As mentioned previously, more than half of the damage suffered by entities experiencing security breaches is attributable to carelessness, errors, or omissions. Thus, an entity's security program must address its users' security awareness, procedural guidance and training, compliance incentives, and compliance monitoring. However, although it is important not to overlook the threats posed by acts of nature and human errors and omissions, it is equally important not to underestimate the risks that intentional malicious acts pose to e-businesses. It is also noteworthy that annual CSI/FBI surveys indicate that a major source of such threats are individuals inside the corporation or organization, such as disgruntled employees, followed by external hackers.[2] Foreign corporations and foreign governments are consistently reported threat sources, albeit at a much lower frequency.

Studies of the impact of hacker attacks and system outages on stock prices of e-business entities indicate that security breaches involving access to confidential data and website outages are associated with significant stock price declines.[3] These findings indicate that stakeholders are sensitive to e-business risks and reinforce the importance of measures to address **threats** that might result in risks. A threat is a condition or force that increases the risk of error, fraud, malicious acts, or disaster. It is important to recognize that there is always a risk that one or more events can happen that will lead to undesirable consequences. Not all risks can be prevented; for example, nobody can prevent an earthquake from happening. The

THREATS
Conditions or forces that increase the risk of error, fraud, malicious acts, or disaster.

only thing that can be done is to take steps to ensure that the consequential losses will be minimized. For example, **viruses**—computer programs that are inserted into computer systems on an unauthorized basis, unknown to the system owner or user, and with an intent to take some action on that computer that can be mischievous or malicious—will continue to be developed, and even with virus protection software installed it is likely that at some time a virus will succeed in penetrating the protective barrier provided by the anti-virus software. By having backups of its software and data, a company can minimize the consequences of a virus attack.

Controls

The entry of a company into electronic business raises some unique challenges, and business has adopted various security strategies to deal with them (see the New Business Models box). These challenges centre heavily around the use of the internet as a vehicle of communication with customers and business partners, as well as being an integral part of the IT platform.

Preventive, detective, and corrective measures to reduce the risk of error, fraud, malicious acts, or disaster to an acceptable level are known as **controls**. There are two broad categories of controls—general and applications controls. Within each of these broad categories there are several types of controls. Following is an overview of controls generally, then an examination of those controls that are particularly important to e-business.

All controls are guided by strategy, policy, and implementation procedures. Indeed, strategy and policy are essential parts of a security system, as they involve institutionalizing the degree of risk that is acceptable and the knowledge and culture among personnel that is necessary to implement security procedures and make them effective.

General Controls

General controls are not unique to a particular application or applications and include several categories:

- security management
- general access controls
- system acquisition or development controls
- system maintenance and change controls
- operations controls
- business continuity controls

Security Management The policies and procedures that management adopts and implements to guide the security program of the enterprise fall under the security management category. These policies are approved by top management, often as a result of a strategic security plan, and are then monitored by a security committee. Security personnel, such as security officers to manage the access controls, are appointed, and policy manuals are distributed to appropriate personnel to ensure that all are aware of the policies and procedures.

General Access Controls There are two kinds of access to a computer system— physical access and logical access. **Physical access controls** are measures taken by an enterprise to safeguard the physical safety of a resource by restricting access to

New Business Models

Outsourcing Security at First American Bank

In recent years, outsourcing has been a strategy in almost every area of business activity, including IT. Many security people feel, however, that security is something that should not be outsourced, especially at the largest and more conservative companies. But in the past few years, the option of outsourcing IT security—through an enterprise known as a managed security service provider (MSSP)—has grown in popularity and respectability. Companies have been handing over key parts of their security structures to MSSPs, including firewalls, anti-virus software, virtual private networks, and intrusion detection.

Some of them, like First American Bank, are relatively small companies that have big security concerns. At that bank, a vice president got a call at 2 a.m. from a technical analyst at the Unisys security command centre. The analyst detected suspicious activity but hadn't been able to isolate and identify the source of the trouble.

He said that if the problem wasn't solved soon, the network would have to be shut down as a security precaution. The VP gave the go-ahead to shut down the network.

A short while later, the security analyst determined that a malicious attack hadn't occurred after all; instead the problem was network interference, caused by local telephone lines. The network was brought up again and the VP went back to sleep. The analyst, or others like him, continued to monitor the bank's network on a 24/7 basis. The VP's attitude was "Better safe than sorry."

Security is extremely important to a bank, as its lack could raise questions about its trustworthiness and lead to a flight of customers. First American had entered into internet banking and didn't fully understand all the security risks posed by the internet. For these reasons and also because they did not have sufficient staff resources to mount a sophisticated security system internally, the bank

decided to go with the e-@ction Security Solution offered by Unisys.

When they were asked to provide the service, Unisys did a three-day security assessment, which included an inventory of the bank's IT systems, discussions of their growth plans, and a thorough evaluation of their existing security systems. After the assessment was completed, the bank compared the cost of the Unisys service with that of developing an in-house, round-the-clock network-monitoring operation such as that of the e-@ction Security Solution, and Unisys got the contract.

MSSPs, like most services, don't promise absolutely 100 percent reliability, so companies using their services might also buy hacker insurance. But companies are buying into MSSPs more frequently, for reasons similar to those of First American, and because they can't keep up with all the latest security threats and be in a position to respond to them.

Unisys
www.unisys.com

Questions

1. **If First American had not gone with the Unisys service, what issues would they have had to address?**
2. **What are the risks to First American of adopting an MSSP?**
3. **Discuss the matters First American would have had to consider in making the decision to adopt the Unisys service.**

SOURCES: George V. Hulme, "Companies are outsourcing IT security to cut costs of around-the-clock surveillance. But some doubt the risk is worth the savings," **Informationweek.com**, accessed July 16, 2001.

it. These controls include many security features like fences, surveillance equipment, alarms, and security guards. They also include locks on computer consoles, server rooms, and gates. Any measures designed to protect the physical security of the system fall under this category.

LOGICAL ACCESS CONTROLS
Controls that are included in software to permit access by authorized personnel in accordance with the privileges granted to them and to prevent access by unauthorized personnel.

BIOMETRICS
Access controls that rely on physical characteristics such as signatures, fingerprints, palmprints, voice recognition and retina scans to authenticate the identity of a user before permitting access.

Logical access controls are controls that are included in software to permit access by authorized personnel in accordance with the privileges granted to them and to prevent access by unauthorized personnel. They involve the use of user IDs, passwords, biometrics, and the granting of permissions and rights by the security software. **Biometrics** are access controls that rely on physical characteristics such as signatures, fingerprints, palmprints, voice recognition, and retina scans to authenticate the identity of a user before permitting access. Logical access controls can be established at various software levels. If they are established at the applications level, then they are considered applications controls. If they are established at the operating system or the database level, they are considered general controls. To look at it another way, if the access controls affect more than one application, they should likely be considered to be general controls. Figure 5.1 illustrates the basic levels of software at which security can be implemented.

Firewalls One of the most important elements of control over the security threats posed by the internet is the use of firewalls. In reality, they are not walls at all, but rather computers or routers added to a network system with very high security capability. Firewall computers must be installed at the only point of entry between the internal network and the internet. If they are not the only access point, they cannot be effective, because hackers and other intruders will be able to enter the system through the least secure point. The Canadian Snapshots box highlights some of the issues surrounding the use of firewalls and other security devices.

Firewalls must be a part of the overall security policy of the company, and must also be accompanied by specific policies that determine how the firewall is configured, who has access to it, and how the firewall actually works. Normally, a company involved in e-business will make use of two firewalls, as shown in figure 5.2. The reason for this is that when a network is connected to the internet, it must have a **web server** that can be accessed by way of the internet. Of course, this exposure to the internet can add unnecessary exposure to the network if it is not controlled. Control is achieved by having a firewall placed between the web server and the internet, referred to as the "Outside Firewall" in figure 5.2, and an inside firewall placed between the web server and the internal network itself.

By using these two firewalls, protection can be gained by configuring the firewalls to play a role appropriate to their placement. The outside firewall is set to accept transactions that only call upon the web server, and it restricts the types of transactions to those that the web server is authorized to handle. The inside

Figure 5.1   Security Software Structure
Basic layers at which security is established.

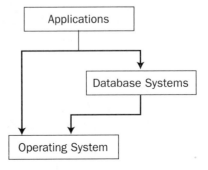

Canadian Snapshots

Hackers at AlphaShield

AlphaShield Inc. of Burnaby, British Columbia, formerly known as Saafnet, has developed products that are based on the observation that high-speed internet access, through connections such as cable modems and digital subscriber lines (DSL), is always open, making home computer users increasingly vulnerable to hacker attacks.

The company has developed a hardware device that is placed between a computer and its modem and intermittently disconnects the computer. Users do not notice the disconnections and can surf the web as usual, but the disconnections do prevent virtual thieves from having enough time to enter and tamper with the system.

The device works by creating a gate that only opens when the user clicks on the mouse button or otherwise activates a command to get information. From the user's viewpoint, it is seamless, but from the hackers' viewpoint, they are locked out of the system because they only have periods of a few seconds while the gate is open—long enough to activate a command—to try to hack into the system.

AlphaShield was so convinced that their product would work flawlessly that the company planned a contest in 2001 where anyone who could determine the IP address of the web server hosting the website would be awarded a prize of US$1 million. The contest was to run for five days, with participants invited to go to Saafnet's website and get an internet protocol address of the computer. Anyone who brought back a piece of code or password that Saafnet preregistered on that computer would be the winner of the grand prize. There has been no word since from AlphaShield, but some groups have reported that AlphaShield's appliances are prone to a flaw that could allow a cracker to inject packets into an established session. This would compromise the security the device would offer.

Hacking contests have also been held before by other organizations. RSA Security Inc.'s 56-bit encryption code was broken during a contest held over the internet in 1996. In September 2000, Secure Digital Music Initiative (SDMI), an industry group, invited hackers to crack into several encryption methods that protect the copying of digital music files. Later that year, Argus Systems Group called on people to try to penetrate software that secures a web server, over a one-week time period.

Some experts feel that these contests can be misleading and do not prove the product is secure. They say there is no way of knowing whether anyone really tried to break the security of the system or how effective any attempts were. Many people feel there is no such thing as a computer that is 100 percent secure, other than unplugging the computer from any data lines—what is referred to as an "air gap." In a world of wireless computers, even an air gap may not be fully secure.

AlphaShield Inc.
www.alphashield.com

Questions

1. **Do you think that hacker contests are a good idea?**
2. **What other precautions can homeowners with high-speed internet access take?**
3. **How serious are the threats against home systems that are exposed to hacker attacks over the internet?**

SOURCE: John Leyden, "'$1M Hacking Challenge' Product Is Flawed," *The Register* (January 30, 2003) **www.theregister.co.uk/2003/01/30/1m_hacking_challenge_product/**, accessed November 26, 2004.

firewall is set to process only those requests to network data that, again, are authorized. For example, the inside server might be set to accept requests to display information on company products, but to reject requests to gain access to payroll information. There are many ways that firewalls can be configured, but all are done with the same objective—to enforce the security and data access policies of the enterprise.

Figure 5.2   Platform Structure for E-Business Security System

The relationship of a network system to its firewalls.

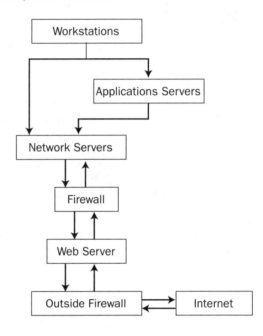

Intrusion Detection Systems An entity should be equipped with monitoring devices and processes for real-time monitoring of security threats to alert appropriate personnel of the occurrence of unusual activity, allowing them to act in a rapid manner. Unusual activity should be detected and transmitted to the appropriate person (e.g., security administrator).

An **intrusion detection system (IDS)**, shown in figure 5.3, monitors devices and processes for security threats and can alert security personnel of the occurrence of unusual activity as it occurs. The IDS generates alerts based on a "threat score" determined from an analysis of user activity. A passive IDS performs various network related surveillance activities including monitoring, logging, and flagging anomalous behaviour. An active IDS can log users off the network or close off access through the firewall.

The difference between a firewall and an IDS is that an IDS has an extensive database of attack signatures or patterns, which allows it to detect intrusions dynamically. In contrast, firewalls either permit or block connections based on a comparatively small number of criteria and do not track related activity patterns.

A potential problem with some IDSs is that they generate a large volume of false-positives, thereby tying up resources and making it difficult to attend to the real attacks. A poorly tuned, active IDS can undermine productivity and service delivery by preventing customer access. Thus, IDSs must be continuously monitored and updated. Configuring the IDS alert threshold involves a delicate balance between ensuring that all threats are detected and false positives are minimized.

System Acquisition or Development Controls When new applications systems are acquired from system vendors or developed in-house, it is very important that the systems that emerge from the process be those that management approved. This means that through the acquisition or development process there must be good control to ensure that errors or omissions are not introduced during the programming, testing, or implementation phases.

INTRUSION DETECTION SYSTEM (IDS)

A system that monitors devices and processes for security threats and can alert security personnel of the occurrence of unusual activity as it occurs.

Figure 5.3   Intrusion Detection, Incident Analysis, and Incident Response

An intrusion detection system analyses, logs, and reports threats to security personnel who respond to them as required.

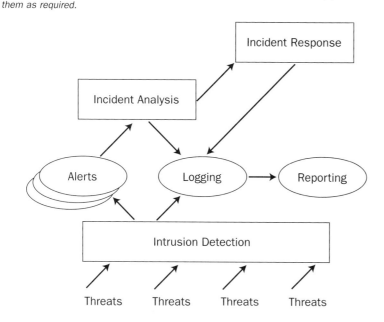

Control during the acquisition or development process is normally accomplished by setting up different directories or sometimes even separate systems on which to carry out the installation, programming, testing, and implementation phases. Figure 5.4 illustrates this process. Programs are written in the development area. They are then tested in the testing area by the programmer and others. The prime control over these different areas is that access is restricted to those who need it. The development area is accessible only by the programmers, and testing is accessible only by those doing the testing. Once they are felt to be ready, and the users and management have signed off on them, the new programs are "promoted" to the production area. This is the area where the programs actually run live and use the data of the enterprise to execute procedures and create reports. The process of following this established approach and obtaining appropriate approvals is crucial to ensuring that the programs that are actually placed into production in the enterprise are the proper ones.

System Maintenance and Change Controls After the programs are developed and implemented, they are continuously subjected to changes to implement corrections or enhancements. This process, usually referred to as system maintenance, must be subjected to controls similar to development controls, since the same risks and threats exist.

Operations Controls Control over the operations of a computer system include the operation of servers, scheduling of jobs, and maintenance of system infrastructure. Operations controls are often in the hands of technical support people in the organization. Often, these people have particular parts of the operations assigned to them. Operations controls include such activities as review of system logs, monitoring system activity, and review of exception reports on system activity.

Business Continuity Controls Systems must always be available to organizations, and especially when they are involved in e-commerce, downtime can be costly and

Figure 5.4   Directories for Systems Development
Systems development activities progress through three directories.

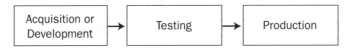

even disastrous. Therefore, steps must be taken to be able to recover data and programs on a timely basis in the event of system interruptions or disaster. This means the enterprise must have a business continuity plan that maps out the steps to be followed in the event of a system failure or disaster. A **business continuity plan** ensures that a business can *continue* in operation after a disaster or other event occurs that could otherwise disable the computer systems for a lengthy period of time. The steps must be detailed and the plan must be carefully tested. Normally, testing is done in as much detail as possible, and all the steps must be documented in detail. Of course, the testing should be repeated periodically and documentation kept up to date.

Part of the business continuity plan is a disaster recovery plan. A **disaster recovery plan** is a detailed plan of action that enables an information system to be *recovered* after a disaster has made it inoperable. An effective disaster recovery plan normally addresses at least the following points:

- the nature of potential disasters that might pose a risk (power failures, floods, fires, storms, terrorists, etc.)
- the roles and responsibilities of information systems personnel and users in an emergency
- detailed scripts for all personnel involved in the operation
- a contact list, including home phone numbers, of IS personnel and external service providers
- critical processing priorities (to guide the order in which systems will be restored)
- procedures to be followed for testing, review, and update of the plan itself
- the backup hardware to be used, and its location and access requirements
- the location and availability of backups of systems software, application programs, data files, database, and documentation
- the off-site storage locations and access requirements of all backups, including a copy of the plan itself
- power requirements and contingency plans if power is down
- communications requirements and contingency plans if communications are down
- detailed procedures for rebuilding the system on the backup computers, including estimated time for completion

Applications Controls

All applications that a business uses consist of three basic areas—input, processing, and output. Thus, applications controls must be established for each of these areas. In addition, a category that has assumed increased importance is that of communications controls. Input controls include those that validate the input, such as check digits and input masks. **Check digit** controls perform a calculation on a set of digits such as an employee ID number and then add the result of that calculation to the number. This enables the integrity of the set of digits to be checked whenever required. **Input masks** establish formats for input areas in a

BUSINESS CONTINUITY PLAN
A plan that ensures that a business can continue in operation after a disaster or other event occurs that could otherwise disable the computer systems for a lengthy period of time.

DISASTER RECOVERY PLAN
A detailed plan of action that enables an information system to be recovered after a disaster has made it inoperable.

CHECK DIGITS
Controls that perform a calculation on a set of digits such as an employee ID number and then add the result of that calculation to the number.

INPUT MASKS
Established formats for input areas in a screen that allow certain numbers of characters and/or digits to be entered.

screen that allow certain numbers of characters and/or digits to be entered. Processing controls include those discussed previously under system acquisition/development and maintenance controls, which help to ensure that only properly tested and approved processes are used in applications. Other processing controls include log monitoring to ensure that all processing steps were completed, process status checking to ensure that all program steps were executed without error or interruption, and reconciliations of input and output control totals to ensure that the programs processed completely and accurately all the information submitted for processing. **Control totals** are values based on counts of records, monetary values, or hashes that are used to reconcile inputs and outputs and thereby control completeness and accuracy of processing. A **hash** is a total based on a field that is not expected to change (e.g., total of all employee number fields in a file) and is therefore useful for ensuring that no unauthorized additions, changes, or deletions have occurred in a file of records containing that field.**Time stamping**, the process of adding a tag containing the time that a record is created, modified, or moved, is used to control the timeliness of data processing and the currency of information. Output controls include controls over the distribution of reports, including access to online reports. If reports are in paper form, then output controls determine the printer that is used, where it is located, and who has access to it. Such controls also include procedures to have the output picked up by authorized personnel for distribution. If the reports are online, access controls are established to determine who can view the reports.

Control Over Communications Communications controls are particularly important in e-commerce to ensure that commitments made over the internet are not repudiated due to the inability to establish the authenticity of the sender and/or receiver or the integrity of the message in transit. A major communications control is encryption (see figure 5.5 on the next page), which is discussed further in the sections that follow. Encryption is one of the most important control tools used in e-business to protect the confidentiality of information. **Message digests** are control totals (similar to check digits) that are used to control completeness, accuracy, and validity of transmissions. A message digest calculates a unique number from the content of a message that can then be added to the message and checked by recalculating the number to ensure that the message has not been tampered with. **Digital signatures,** encrypted message digests that can only be decrypted by a key that authenticates the sender's identity, combine encryption and message digests to ensure the authenticity of transmitted messages.

Encryption Encryption techniques are fundamental to control over the communications process, a process that is central to e-business. Encryption is the conversion of data into a form called a cipher, which is very difficult to read without possession of a "key." The encryption conversion is achieved by applying an algorithm, or formula, to the data bits that comprise the data, converting it into the cipher. The key is a set of data that can be applied to the cipher to decipher it, that is, convert it back to the original data. Application of the key is referred to as the decryption process.

Encryption is used in various aspects of e-business, including e-mail, transmissions to execute banking transactions on the internet, and other sensitive transmissions. The major web browsers—Netscape Navigator and Microsoft Explorer—include encryption capability, and strong encryption is available for these products as well.

There are various strengths available in encryption, measured by the length of the key. The most common standard is the 56-bit encryption key, which is supplied as a standard feature of the two web browsers. There are over 72 quadrillion

CONTROL TOTALS
Amounts based on counts of records, monetary values, or hashes that are used to reconcile inputs and outputs and thereby control completeness and accuracy of processing.

HASH
A total based on a field that is not expected to change (e.g., total of all employee number fields in a file) and is therefore useful for ensuring that no unauthorized additions, changes, or deletions have occurred in a file of records containing that field.

TIME STAMPING
The process of adding a tag containing the time that a record is created, modified or moved.

MESSAGE DIGEST
A unique number calculated from the content of a message that can then be added to the message and checked by recalculating the number to ensure that the message has not been tampered with.

DIGITAL SIGNATURE
An encrypted message digest that can only be decrypted by a key that authenticates the sender's identity.

(72 057 594 037 927 936) possible keys in the 56-bit DES system. The 56-bit encryption was broken in 1997 by a team led by Rock Verser, a freelance computer consultant. Verser had formed the "team" by sending out messages on the internet asking people to download some keys and run them against a test program. He had 14 000 members on his team, and they tried about 18 quadrillion keys before finding the right one.

Despite the fact the 56-bit encryption code was cracked, the Verser episode illustrated the magnitude of effort that is required to decrypt a message using even the 56-bit encryption technology. It is still used because most people do not have the capability to go through such a process. However, the fact that it has been done has led to the use of the 128-bit technology for more sensitive transmissions. For the standard browsers, 128-bit encryption can be downloaded from the websites of the browsers' manufacturers and added to the browsers to make them capable of high-encryption transmissions. For internet banking, the banks in Canada require their customers to install the 128-bit encryption technology for their browsers before they can obtain access to internet banking. Links are provided on the banks' login web pages to simplify this process.

Encryption works by using a key that is generated by the person who initiates a transaction and then providing a key to the recipient that will enable the transmission to be decrypted. This can be done on a symmetric basis or an asymmetric basis. When it is done on a symmetric basis, the sender of the message simply provides the recipient with the same key used for encryption.

The asymmetric approach, illustrated in figure 5.5, is carried out by using a system of private and public keys, which are created together in pairs. A **private key** is a set of data used to encrypt and decrypt data transmissions that is known only to the person who generated it. A **public key** is a set of data used to encrypt and decrypt data transmissions that is made known to outsiders, and can be obtained by the recipient of the message. In a typical transmission, Ann might send a message to Bill that she wants to keep secret. She encrypts it with her private key and when Bill receives it, he decrypts it using her public key. Only her public key will decrypt a message encrypted using her private key.

Since the public key works on the message, Bill knows that Ann sent the message, which establishes the property of authentication of the user. **Authentication** confirms that a particular person or server is, in fact, the person or server that is identified in a transaction. In addition, since the public key worked in the decryption, Ann cannot deny she sent the message, establishing the property of **non-repudiation**.

On the other hand, if Ann wants to make sure that only Bill can open the message, she will encrypt it with Bill's public key. Only his private key can open

PRIVATE KEY
A set of data used to encrypt and decrypt data transmissions that is known to only one person.

PUBLIC KEY
A set of data used to encrypt and decrypt data transmissions that can be shared with anyone.

AUTHENTICATION
The property that confirms that a particular person or server is, in fact, the person or server that is identified in a transaction.

NON-REPUDIATION
A property that confirms that a particular person did indeed send a message and cannot deny that fact.

Figure 5.5   The Asymmetric Encryption Process

Sample method of encryption.

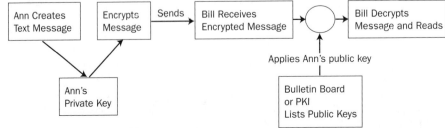

the message and, of course, only he has that key. In practice, a combination of symmetric and asymmetric encryption is used, usually by using the **Secure Sockets Layer (SSL) protocol**. The SSL protocol is a security protocol associated with TCP/IP that establishes a secure communications channel between web clients and servers. The **Secure HyperText Transfer Protocol (S-HTTP)** provides security for transmissions involving webpages. Note that S-HTTP is different from HTTPS, which is related to SSL (see the E-Business in Global Perspective box). Secure protocols such as SSL and S-HTTP are commonly used by banks and other e-commerce sites to encrypt transmissions between a user and a web server. Without a secure protocol, much e-commerce activity would not be feasible.

Under the SSL protocol, a system of server authentication is used by making use of server-related digital certificates administered by certificate authorities (CAs) and digital signatures. **Digital certificates** are electronic documents that

SECURE SOCKETS LAYER (SSL) PROTOCOL
A security protocol associated with TCP/IP that establishes a secure communications channel between web clients and servers.

SECURE HYPERTEXT TRANSFER PROTOCOL (S-HTTP)
A security protocol for use with HTTP that provides security for transmissions of messages between clients and web servers.

DIGITAL CERTIFICATES
Electronic documents that contain the identity of a person or server and the related public key.

E-Business in Global Perspective

S-HTTP at Terisa

In April 1995, a coalition consisting of America Online Inc., CompuServe Interactive Services Inc., IBM, and Netscape Communications Corp. took equity investments in Terisa, a California company that had developed a commercial version of S-HTTP. An interesting aspect of this investment was the involvement of Netscape, since they had been promoting their SSL protocol.

Both SSL and S-HTTP are part of the Open Systems Interconnection protocol, albeit at different levels, and are quite complementary to each other, rather than competitive. SSL works at the network level to secure TCP/IP sessions, while S-HTTP works at the message level for HTTP-based web servers and clients. In addi-

tion, S-HTTP can authenticate a user, whereas SSL can only authenticate the server. S-HTTP is better suited for online banking transactions. There had been a good deal of competition between the two protocols, which had been confusing the marketplace and slowing improvements in security, which were widely known to be needed to enable the growth of e-business.

Other security industry participants expressed less than full enthusiasm for the coalition. They said they would rather see activity like this coming through the standards bodies rather than private industry. Their concern was that an integrated S-HTTP/SSL would become a proprietary product rather than being an open system, available to the public, which

S-HTTP was. Many people agree that security protocols need to be openly agreed upon so that recognized security specifications can be built into systems in a form that will be recognized by, and therefore usable in, a variety of platforms and systems.

In response to these concerns, Terisa worked with the Internet Engineering Task Force and the World Wide Web Consortium standards bodies to create a common security standard. In 1997, Spyrus acquired Terisa and provided a complementary package of software and hardware solutions that would make security in popular web servers and other equipment affordable.

Spyrus
www.spyrus.com

Questions

1. What would be the advantage of combining SSL and S-HTTP?
2. Why do security protocols need to be "open"?
3. What role should the standard-setting organizations, such as the Internet Engineering Task Force (IETF), play in security protocols?

SOURCE: Computerworld.com, accessed April 17, 1995; Tim Clark, "Security companies merge," Cnet News.com, accessed May 16, 1997.

CERTIFICATE AUTHORITIES (CAS)
Organizations that issue digital certificates and sign them with digital signatures to establish the authenticity of the certificates.

contain the identity of a person or server and the related public key. **Certificate authorities (CAs)** are organizations that issue digital certificates and sign them with digital signatures to establish the authenticity of the certificates. Using SSL involves a series of negotiations when a browser contacts a web server. First, the browser obtains the server certificate and examines the digital signature on it. The digital signature would have been placed on the certificate by the certificate authority using the CA's own private key. The browser checks that this is a CA that it trusts and then decrypts the signature with the CA's public key, thereby establishing the authenticity of the certificate authority. Access to the public key is accomplished by accessing the CA's online database. The browser and the server then agree on a master key for the session, which is used to encrypt and decrypt all transmissions for that session. The master key is generated by the browser and then sent to the server by encrypting it with the server's public key. Since it can only be opened by the server for which it is intended, the identity of the master key is secure. From that point on, the encryption process for that session is carried out on a symmetric basis.

S-HTTP is an extension of HTTP that enables individual messages to be encrypted. This is in contrast with SSL, which encrypts all the transmissions for a session. The S-HTTP protocol was designed for transaction confidentiality, authenticity/integrity, and non-repudiation of origin (i.e., it can authenticate the user, whereas SSL can only authenticate the server), thus it is particularly desirable for e-commerce and online banking transactions that may arise spontaneously while a user is browsing a website. According to its developers, the protocol emphasizes maximum flexibility in choice of key management mechanisms, security policies, and cryptographic algorithms by supporting option negotiation between parties for each transaction. Thus, S-HTTP does not require the user to have a public key or a public key certificate. Option negotiation is used to enable clients and servers to agree on how a message should be encrypted, with numerous options being available.

Public Key Infrastructure (PKI) The importance of digital signatures for business, and the essential role that public and private keys play in them, means that there is a need for a great many keys. Since the public keys must be accessible by anyone, they need to be stored in a database that is accessible to the public. In addition, there is a need for a reliable system for managing the keys—one that is secure and backed by a reputable organization. This is where a public key infrastructure (PKI) is used.

PUBLIC KEY INFRASTRUCTURE (PKI)
A system that stores and delivers keys and certificates as needed and also provides privacy, security, integrity, authentication, and non-repudiation support for various e-business applications and transactions.

A **public key infrastructure (PKI)** is a system that stores and delivers keys and certificates as needed and also provides privacy, security, integrity, authentication, and non-repudiation support for various technological and e-business applications and transactions (see figure 5.6). A PKI system will manage the generation and distribution of public/private key pairs and publish the public keys accompanied by certificates that confirm the identity of the key owner. All of this is included in open bulletin boards accessible by the public or all people who need to know the information. The latter qualification is needed to recognize that some PKIs are set up by particular companies, and only make the databases available to the corporate personnel and their business partners rather than the general public.

A PKI structures its data—the keys and certificate authorities—in a logical fashion for orderly management and accessibility. A user's public key and identification are placed together in a certificate. The user's certificate authority then digitally signs each certificate to provide the necessary authentication, which can be verified by using the CA's public key to verify the CA's signature on the certificate. With this system, any user can get any other user's public key from a bulletin

Figure 5.6   Flow Chart for PKI Systems

This chart shows the parties and procedures involved in the use of a PKI system.

board to verify its authenticity.

In summary, PKIs integrate digital certificates, public-key cryptography, and certificate authorities into a total, enterprise-wide network security architecture. A typical PKI for an enterprise encompasses the issuance of digital certificates to individual users and servers, end-user software, integration with corporate certificate directories, tools for managing certificates, and related services and support.

VPNs and Security In chapter 3 we looked at virtual private networks (VPNs), noting that they include (a) the use of firewalls, (b) tunnelling through the internet, and (c) the use of encryption.

Firewalls are, of course, a prime tool for adding security to a network. They are usually deployed as part of a VPN system if they are not already in place. The concept of tunnelling means that messages are directed through predetermined paths on the internet. This has security implications, since the path through which the messages are directed can be made secure to minimize the opportunities for unauthorized persons to intercept those messages through sniffing techniques. **Sniffing** is the use of electronic devices attached to transmission lines that can detect and capture data transmissions on those lines. Newer models of sniffing devices can work on wireless transmissions as well.

As previously discussed, encryption is one of the key techniques for protecting information residing on, or transmitted through, the internet. VPNs are set up by installing VPN software, which always includes the ability to encrypt messages being sent and to decrypt them when received. This means that even if messages are intercepted through sniffing, they cannot be understood by an unauthorized person.

SNIFFING

The use of electronic devices attached to transmission lines that can detect and capture data transmissions on those lines. Newer models of sniffing devices can work on wireless transmissions as well.

Security Policies

It is clear that an essential element of good security is a set of security policies that establish the acceptable transactions that can be carried out through internet connections. These policies should be centrally defined and must be consistent with, or part of, the overall corporate security policies. The security policies are the starting point for the security framework within an organization. Policies link management's objectives and the operational procedures implemented to achieve them. Policies are formal statements of organizational and managerial intent, standards define minimum performance requirements, and guidelines provide behavioural direction. The core policies should describe the function of the security program, outline oversight, establish roles and responsibilities, identify laws and regulations requiring compliance, and outline a framework for asset classification, asset management, change management, and exception management. The policies, standards, and guidelines should be approved and should be periodically updated in response to changes in the environment, technology, and business requirements identified through systematic monitoring of these factors.

Prior to developing security policies, the company should conduct a risk assessment to determine where the risks are. This will enable the security policies to address the risks that actually exist. The security policies should be comprehensive, and view security from a comprehensive end-to-end perspective, and not just as a series of components (i.e., firewalls, passwords, etc). Security policies should be integrated into the overall policies governing the entity's e-commerce activity.

Business objectives should be the foundation for security aims and initiatives. Some common security goals include:

- compliance with service level agreements, defined external and internal commitments, and any other contracts
- compliance with laws and regulations
- protecting data confidentiality
- making certain that unauthorized persons or systems cannot inadvertently or intentionally alter data without being detected
- ensuring that the information accessed is genuine
- making the data accessible and usable
- logging transactions and data exchanges
- verifying the identity of a person engaged in a business transaction

Determining the right level of security is a difficult balance, as too little security opens the company to attacks, while too much security slows system performance and can impact employee morale, as well as customer satisfaction. All those that will be affected by the security policy should be invited to collaborate in its development. Such a process can increase employee buy-in to the policy. Care should be taken to ensure that the security policy is suitable for the entity's business partners.

When the policies are developed, they should be documented and approved by the board of directors for distribution to staff. The major components of a security policy are outlined below.

1. Security Administration

This part of the policy covers the duties of the persons responsible for security administration, including the person in charge of security and the administrators of the various networks, operating systems, databases, and applications. It also establishes to whom the person in charge of security reports. Increasingly, that person is reporting to higher levels of executives, and often has responsibilities for privacy as well as security.

For controls to be enforced and meaningful to employees, upper management must play an active role. Senior management should establish that security has high visibility in the arenas of corporate governance and business processes. The latter may require management to realign lines of communications, authority, and responsibilities. The entity must ensure that there are resources available to implement the security program defined by policy. If the security function is in-house, it must have a budget sufficient to employ knowledgeable IT staff with tools and authority to ensure a secure IT infrastructure. If there are no resources available in-house then outsourcing should be considered. The vendor selected should be reputable and trustworthy.

Whether in-house or outsourced security is used, it will require a budget sufficient for the type of security program required. The amount to be expended must be aligned with the severity of risks faced and the organization's capacity to respond. In this regard, the security budget needs to be linked to the overall corporate mission of generating value for the owners and employees of the organization.

Effective budgeting for security is complicated by the fact that the amount of spending is not a guarantee of the level of security achieved. Also, effective spending on security can lead to invisible outcomes, in the sense that security incidents are prevented, hence invisible. This, in turn, can lead to the perception that the spending is pointless and can be cut back. Security is largely a fixed cost that does not depend on the volume of data. Some security measures are inexpensive and merely require attention to detail. A by-product of security measures is a potential increase in the overall efficiency and effectiveness of the business.

2. Standard Operating Procedures

Security standards adopted by the security group should be based on an accepted standard such as ITCG, COBIT, SysTrust, ISO 17799, etc. Standards represent agreed-upon performance requirements against which operating procedures can be assessed. At present, there are several competing standards that cover similar grounds but are organized differently and have varying levels of acceptance by different professional groups and jurisdictions. Once an organization adopts one of these standards, it will need to translate them into operating procedures that fit its circumstances so that they will become part of the daily duties performed by the organization's personnel (e.g., new passwords, access log review, etc.). Because exceptions are bound to arise, the standards should explicitly establish procedures to be used for exceptions to standard operating procedures.

3. Information Management

Many companies include in their security policy an information management policy that describes the importance of the corporate information and identifies the "owner" or custodian of the information. This policy includes details such as all applications and data used in the organization, a description of the level of security required for each application or data set, and identification of appropriate business managers as custodians of the applications and data.

4. Privilege Management

As an entity's use of e-business expands, its user base can include employees, customers, suppliers, and business partners. To effectively manage such a diversity of users requires centralized control of user privileges by the security management unit. The most basic privilege in a computerized business system is access. However, very quickly an entity will find that it must distinguish what types of access to permit to what types of assets, to whom and under what circumstances—who can do what, to what, and when. Thus, entities must identify who can gain physical access to system facilities and resources and under what circumstances, and who can read and write to various files and which software functions they can use under what circumstances. To implement effective access controls will require the establishment of user registration and authorization, identification and authentication, and the establishment of user privileges and permissions based on the **principle of least privilege**—granting the minimum privileges required by individuals to complete the tasks they are responsible for, and no more. While this principle may seem obvious, low adherence to this principle is a major cause of system vulnerabilities. Many software systems are configured for maximum privilege by default. Also, many organizations are not prepared for the administrative and user management issues that arise when the principle of least privilege is enforced as the underlying basis for access control.

PRINCIPLE OF LEAST PRIVILEGE
Granting the minimum privileges required by individuals to complete the tasks they are responsible for, and no more.

5. Physical Security

Procedures to be followed with regard to safeguarding the physical safety of the hardware, software, and communications infrastructure are normally covered in the security policy. This would include control over servers, the related network/telecommunications equipment, workstations, and access to the premises. With the increasing use of mobile devices such as laptops and personal digital assistants and their capacity to store vast amounts of information, it is important to consider security measures for such devices in the security policy.

6. Logical Access Control

The policy with regard to logical access control would focus on the user IDs and password system adopted in the company. It would also include the policy guiding the assignment of access rights to specific user IDs, such as which screens, programs, and data a user can access and what actions they can perform on them (such as read, write to, change, or execute). The policy is often broken down into those related to control over personal computers, controls over access to networks, and any other unique components of the system to which personnel might be granted access, such as intranets, database systems, and the internet. The security policy should also address controls over giving access to temporary personnel (e.g., contract workers, consultants, customers, etc.).

7. End-User Computing Policy

The end-user portion of the security policy sets out the responsibilities of users who use corporate computers and systems. This is important for reminding users of their responsibilities for the security of the system and defining those responsibilities. The policy would include items such as reminders that users must comply with corporate security policies and procedures, take care of corporate equipment, and only use the company's computer resources and information for authorized business purposes.

The end-user policy also normally sets out responsibilities for backing up data, protecting against viruses, keeping passwords secret, and taking other precautions for protecting the privacy of corporate data. The end-user policy also normally identifies the software brands that will be supported by the company.

A major issue with regard to end users is that they often have access to powerful programs and tools that can be used to construct ad-hoc information systems. Sometimes such ad-hoc systems can become, unofficially, a critical part of the overall information system and, therefore, need to be safeguarded. To provide proper control over such "unofficial" systems, the security policy needs to define the controls that apply to ad hoc systems and the levels of system that might require different levels of control.

8. Software Acquisition, Development, Maintenance, and Change

It is important in most organizations to take precautions to ensure that any applications are developed or modified using techniques that provide for data integrity and appropriate audit trails. A security policy on software development and maintenance would define a procedure for setting up and managing the various directories that are used in the process, such as development, testing, and production. It would include the process for review and approval, who owns the programs, and the required documentation and access rights to various parts of the system that are used in development and maintenance.

9. Personnel Management

Highly qualified IT personnel are necessary to enable an enterprise to operate and manage the system, but there is a risk to having them in that they have the skills to circumvent established controls. Therefore, a security policy must deal with the area of personnel management, including training and education. This would include matters such as distribution of duties, confidentiality agreements, passwords, and control over equipment.

10. Security Monitoring

The security policy should provide for a compliance verification and auditing program to ensure that the procedures established to implement the policy are followed. Monitoring of systems activity is crucial in establishing a secure system, as it helps the security personnel identify inappropriate activities both on the part of staff and on the part of unauthorized intruders. Security personnel should consider the use of automated tools for this purpose. The security policy should establish how monitoring will take place, who will carry it out, and reporting procedures on events that occur, such as usage anomalies and security violations. The security policy should also provide for a regular, ongoing vulnerability assessment and management program.

Security compliance procedures (e.g., audit, monitoring, etc.) need to be balanced with employee productivity and satisfaction. Overly intrusive measures can be viewed as an invasion of the employee's personal space. Compliance procedures should be complemented with information sessions that make security an integral part of the corporate culture. A memorandum must be issued to users to advise them that monitoring is being done, the type and frequency of monitoring, and the implications of breaching security.

11. Disaster Recovery, Contingency Planning, and Insurance

The basic existence and general nature of the disaster recovery plan should be outlined in the security policy, which should also stress the importance of the plan,

E-Strategy

Insurance at Counterpane

Counterpane Internet Security Inc., a California company involved in the managed security services market, offers to purchase up to US$100 million in insurance coverage for its clients to protect against loss of revenue and information assets caused by internet and e-commerce security breaches. The insurance is backed by Lloyd's of London.

Other insurance companies have offered policies that are designed to compensate for security-related losses under loss-of- business or act-of-vandalism clauses, but they usually carry very high premiums and it is difficult to collect the benefits. Counterpane's product, which they call "Internet Asset and Income Protection Insurance," specifically provides insurance for losses resulting from a breach of security or technology failure related to damage to information assets such as data, customer lists, credit-card numbers, and other digital information. Claims can also be made for related business interruption losses. Premiums are comparable to other forms of business insurance.

Lloyd's security insurance covers the cost of repairing and replacing data or software following the destruction or corruption of electronic devices from an attack. It also covers lost revenue following a service interruption or service impairment caused by malicious hackers.

The concept for the insurance coverage is that the insured company must demonstrate that it has met the requirements of the insurable risk model that is prescribed and accepted by Counterpane. Assistance in a security crisis and any subsequent negotiations, even including payment of a ransom demand, is also part of the package.

Until this package was developed, there did not exist an acceptable model of risk control assurance from security companies that insurance companies could use to write policies against. One of the benefits of this service, besides the insurance coverage, is the incentive it provides for companies to maintain acceptable levels of control over their systems.

The insurance plan is only one of the services that Counterpane offers in its managed security business. They provide managed, around-the-clock incident response services that are designed to help companies formulate responses to security-related incidents. They offer security experts for their clients' staff and their boards, in an overall approach to security. Their experts undertake continuous monitoring for flaws in security technologies to help companies make the most of their security products. The alternative for most companies would be to hire a security manager to watch the system logs and report on the activities.

Counterpane locates its security experts in two security centres, where they monitor customer networks through encrypted tunnels. They collect audit information from clients' existing security products, including servers, firewalls, and intrusion detection products. The service operates on a 24/7 basis.

The security experts use a system called "Socrates" to manage the network information they gather with data on known attacks to prioritize events, pinpoint attacks, and filter out false alarms. Socrates can be configured to monitor specific network systems and maintains its own separate logs to help prevent intruders from erasing logs to mask incursions. If an attack occurs, Counterpane reacts with pre-set procedures to deal with it.

Counterpane Internet Security
www.counterpane.com

Questions

1. Why does the concept of insurance fit with security strategy?
2. To what extent is the use of Counterpane an outsourcing exercise?
3. What would management need to do in including Counterpane in its security strategy? What would be their responsibilities and duties?

SOURCE: "Counterpane Internet Security website, **www.counterpane.com**, accessed May 25, 2004.

who is responsible for it, and generally how it is administered. One of the essential elements of disaster recovery and contingency planning is the provision for backup of systems. The security policy should therefore contain detailed guidance as to the backup procedures in force within the company for all systems including communications. An important element of a contingency plan is insurance. The security policy should define the risks that should be insured. The E-Strategy box explores insurance in more detail.

12. Periodic Updates of Security Policy

Security policies should be periodically reviewed and updated to take into account technological changes, business changes, and the entity's experience with security incidents, vulnerability, assessments and compliance enforcement.

Chapter Summary

Every information system is subject to risk of error or fraud. Preventive and corrective measures to deal with the threats to a system, and therefore minimize the risk borne by the system, are known as controls. All controls are guided by strategy, policy, and implementation procedures, which involve institutionalizing the degree of risk that is acceptable, and the knowledge and culture among personnel that is necessary to implement security procedures and make them effective.

There are two kinds of controls—general and applications controls. General controls include security management, general access controls, software development controls, operations controls, and business continuity controls. Applications controls include input, processing, output, and communication controls. All controls must be approached in a holistic fashion. This means that the e-business controls must be completely integrated with and consistent with the controls over the enterprise's information systems generally.

The entry of a company into electronic business raises some unique challenges, and business has adopted various security strategies to deal with them. Some of the most important elements of control over the security threats posed by the internet is the use of firewalls, intrusion detection systems, and encryption. All threats must be covered by good security policies that establish the acceptable transactions that can be carried out through the internet connections.

Encryption techniques are fundamental to control over the communications process, a process that is central to e-business. The major web browsers—Netscape Navigator and Microsoft Explorer—include encryption capability, and stronger encryption is available for these products as well. Most encryption is carried out by using pairs of private/public keys to encrypt and decrypt messages and other data transmissions.

The secure socket layer (SSL) protocol makes use of these keys along with the certificates issued by certificate authorities. Under the SSL protocol, a system of server authentication makes use of server certificates administered by certificate authorities and digital signatures. Access to the public key is accomplished by accessing the CA's online database. The master key is generated by the browser and then sent to the server by encrypting it with the server's public key.

A public key infrastructure (PKI) is a system that stores and delivers keys and certificates as needed, and also provides privacy, security, integrity, authentication, and non-repudiation support for various technological and e-business applications and transactions. A PKI system will manage the generation and distribution of public/

private key pairs and publish the public keys accompanied by certificates that confirm the identity of the key owner.

Comprehensive security policies should be developed that view security from an end-to-end perspective and that are integrated into the overall policies governing the entity's e-commerce activity. Prior to developing security policies, the company should conduct a risk assessment to enable the security policies to address the risks that actually exist. Security policies should be periodically reviewed and updated to take into account technological changes, business changes, and the entity's experience with security incidents, vulnerability assessments, and compliance enforcement.

Key Terms

authentication *(p. 90)*
biometrics *(p. 84)*
business continuity plan *(p. 88)*
certificate authorities (CAs) *(p. 92)*
check digits *(p. 88)*
control totals *(p. 89)*
controls *(p. 82)*
digital certificates *(p. 91)*
digital signature *(p. 89)*
disaster recovery plan *(p.88)*
disasters *(p. 80)*
error *(p. 80)*
fraud *(p. 80)*
general controls *(p. 82)*
hash *(p. 89)*
input masks *(p. 88)*
intrusion detection system *(p. 86)*

logical access controls *(p. 84)*
malicious acts *(p. 80)*
message digest *(p. 89)*
non-repudiation *(p. 90)*
physical access controls *(p. 82)*
principle of least privilege *(p. 96)*
private key *(p. 90)*
public key *(p. 90)*
public key infrastructure (PKI) *(p. 92)*
risk *(p. 80)*
Secure Hypertext Transfer Protocol (S-HTTP) *(p. 91)*
Secure Sockets Layer (SSL) protocol *(p. 91)*
sniffing *(p. 93)*
threats *(p. 81)*
time stamping *(p. 89)*
viruses *(p. 82)*

Tools for Online Learning

To help you master the material in this chapter and stay up to date with new developments in e-business, visit www.pearsoned.ca/trites. Resources include:

- **Review Questions and Exercises**

- **Problems for Discussion**

- **Recommended Readings**

- **Updates to Case Studies and Textual Material**

- **Streaming CBC Videos with Cases**

Endnotes

1. A. Briney, "Security Focused: Survey 2000," *Information Security* 5, no. 1 (September 2000): 40.

2. Computer Security Institute, *2003 Computer Crime and Security Survey* (San Francisco: Computer Security Institute, May, 2003).

3. K. Campbell, L.A. Gordon, M.P. Loeb, and L. Zhou, "The Economic Cost of Publicly Announced Information Security Breaches: Empirical Evidence from the Stock Market," *Journal of Computer Security* 11 (2003): 431–448; M. Ettredge and V.J. Richardson, "Assessing the Risk in E-Commerce" (proceedings of the 35th Hawaii International Conference on System Sciences, IEEE Computer Society, 2003); J.H. Anthony, W. Choi, and S. Grabski, "Market Reaction to E-Commerce Impairments and Website Outages" (manuscript, Michigan State University).

Billing and Payment Systems

LEARNING OBJECTIVES

When you complete this chapter you should be able to:

1. Describe the characteristics of payment systems that have been used on the internet.

2. Describe how billing and payment techniques relate to corporate strategy.

3. Identify and describe the emerging billing and payment systems.

4. Describe the advantages and disadvantages of these systems.

5. Evaluate the suitability of billing and payment methods for various e-business scenarios.

6. Indicate the trends most likely to prevail in the future.

Introduction

Ever since enterprises began to offer goods and services for sale on the web, there has been a need for some kind of system to enable sales to be completed by paying over the web. The ability to complete sales in this way is viewed as being good for business. Moreover, it is much less expensive to carry out transactions, including payments, on the web as compared to other methods. In figure 1.2 (see page 13), for example, it was shown that the cost of conducting a transaction through a bank branch costs over US$1, while conducting that same transaction over the internet costs only 1 or 2 cents. This is a remarkable fact that clearly shows why so many businesses are interested in moving transactions to the internet.

Another reason related to business-to-consumer (B2C) commerce is that if customers can pay online, there is a greater chance that they will buy, as opposed to situations where they must go offline to pay. For business-to-business (B2B) commerce, there is also an incentive to have online billing and payment for economic reasons, as there is a tendency for numerous transactions to be carried out with the same regular customers. The savings in serving these customers can be dramatic; and on the other side of the coin, the savings for the customers in procurement costs can be significant.

Even more than ten years after the "break-through" of the internet, however, online payments, especially in the B2C sector, are still a problematic issue. The decades-old credit card system remains the main payment method for goods and services online. Unfortunately, the shortcomings of credit cards in the real world have become even more severe in cyberspace—credit card fraud on the internet is widespread. So far, however, credit cards have been the only (almost) universally accepted payment method on the internet with reasonable transaction costs. There have been numerous attempts to develop online payment systems in the past, but almost all of them have failed. Some of the more visible of them have included DigiCash, Mondex, NetCash, NetCheck, First Virtual, Intell-A-Check, and NetCard. Another payment system is described in the E-Business in Global Perspective box. Even PayPal, the most successful and innovative online payment system so far, has yet to reach a critical mass and truly universal acceptance. Online payments, initiatives to make credit card use on the internet more secure, and the PayPal system will be discussed in more detail later in the chapter.

The problems have centred on the difficulty of developing a system that is secure, convenient, and accepted by enough people to make it economically viable. The need for security is clear: if there is too great a chance their money will be lost in a transaction, either through fraud or error, consumers will not use the system, and if they do, legal issues will arise for the businesses using those systems. Such a system must also be convenient. People using the web do not have the time and inclination to enter into significant time commitments just to purchase something online. In fact, several companies have noted the unwillingness of consumers to even enter information in a registration screen. Finally, a system must gain acceptance by the customers, the financial institutions, and the vendors in order to be viable. It is far too expensive to initiate a system that is not used.

Characteristics of Traditional Payment Systems

Electronic Data Interchange (EDI)

Electronic data interchange (EDI) is a way to conduct transactions, including payment transactions, in electronic form. It is based on the use of widely accepted

E-Business in Global Perspective

900 Dialer—Online Payment System or Invitation for Fraud?

If a person wants to buy something over the internet, and doesn't have a credit card or a debit card or doesn't want to use them, there's a problem. What do they use to pay for the purchase? 1-900 premium numbers have been around for many years. Although they are commonly known for their use as payment for various kinds of (so-called adult) entertainment, they are also used for much better purposes, such as charitable donations. To donate, a person simply calls the 900 number and the donation is added to the following month's phone bill. Although this can be convenient, it can also be fairly risky. A child, who sees a 900 number on TV for a $50 donation to a charity, could easily cause her parents several hundred dollars in charges.

These 900 numbers can also be used to process payments over the internet. One possibility is that a visitor to a website is given a 900 number to call. When the number is called, a confirmation code is given, which has to be entered into the website. Another possibility is an automated "dialer." When accessing a website that requires payment, the visitor permits a small "dialer application" to be installed on his or her computer. This dialer then disconnects the regular internet connection and connects to the 900 number of the website to pay for the charges.

In the early stages of the internet, dialers were seen as a real alterative for online payments. In recent years, however, less-than-reputable business people and even criminals have used dialers to defraud internet users. Dialers that were installed with the consent of the user often charged more than they initially stated or called the 900 number repeatedly. In other cases, dialers were installed on the systems of unsuspecting users through viruses, file-sharing net-

works, and loopholes in internet browsers. Unless a computer is connected though a DSL or a cable connection and all regular modems are disconnected, the risk of dialers is immense. Even if the telephone company blocks 900 telephone numbers, dialers may still be able to connect to an expensive number in a different country. There have been numerous reports in newspapers about internet users that have been cheated out of thousands of dollars. It is often difficult for victims to dispute the charges as the telephone companies are obligated to collect them and the people responsible are in many cases in different countries. In some European countries, dialers have become such a serious problem that legislation has been introduced to give internet users more protection. Given the bad name of dialers, they no longer appear to be a viable online payment alternative for reputable businesses.

TIBS
www.tibsystems.com

Questions

1. Should Canada follow the European approach and outlaw dialers?
2. Do you think asking customers to manually call a 900 number is a feasible alternative? Why or why not?

---

standards for formatting data in EDI transmissions. Persons using EDI must be signatories to an EDI agreement and must have their information systems configured to be able to recognize and process the transactions.

EDI has been used for many years as a means of settling payments, especially in the B2B world. Traditionally, EDI systems have made use of **value added networks (VANs)** as a platform for operating them. Value added networks are privately owned networks that are rented to users, along with a package of related services, to operate their EDI systems by providing an environment within which they can work and by connecting them to their customers and suppliers. Generally, EDI has been costly and, in its "traditional" form, has been used most often by very large companies. Since the internet became more widely used for conducting business transactions, EDI has moved from the VANs to the web. The web is a much more cost-effective platform for EDI transactions than the VANs, because access to it is much less expensive, and the technology is widely recognized and used, making it easier to communicate with various other organizations. The use of the internet for replacing or augmenting existing VANs for EDI transactions is a logical step in streamlining payment systems for B2B commerce.

Normally, organizations using web-based EDI set up a web browser interface that links with the corporate systems. For payment purposes, the links would be with the cash systems to enable the payments to be processed through the corporate bank accounts. Such linkages would not be direct, because of security issues. The conversion of EDI systems from VANs to the internet involves many security issues because of the difficulties of securing the internet and the involvement of cash. In addition, it involves integration of the systems within the company, with the internet, and with the other parties to the system over the internet.

Cash

The issue of introducing electronic payments systems for both B2B and B2C purposes leads to the question of what characteristics are required of payment systems in general for them to be effective. It is instructive to consider the characteristics of that most traditional method of payment—cash.

Cash is portable, because it can be carried easily with a person. In addition, it is widely acceptable by stores, other companies, and other people. This means cash can be carried easily from store to store, and customers can be reasonably confident that it will be accepted by the stores for payment of goods. In addition, there is normally no need to identify oneself in order to gain acceptance of the cash. Therefore, cash has the characteristics of portability, acceptance, and anonymity. Finally, the cash provides for an instant transfer of value from the buyer to the vendor.

Portability While traditional cash cannot be transported on the web, the transportability feature is relatively easy to achieve in the case of electronic cash, as it only requires that the payment be capable of being transported over electronic media. The means of achieving acceptance have proven to be much more elusive.

Acceptance The acceptability of cash at one time was based on its value relative to gold. There was a commitment of the government that any bank note could be turned over to the government of Canada for gold, equal in value to the denomination of the bank note. During the 1970s, this approach was abandoned and no such commitment of the government has existed since then. The acceptance of the dollar now rests on the strength of the economy, the stability of the currency, and the extent to which it is used. Since Canada generally has a strong economy and a stable government, acceptability has not been a problem in recent years.

Anonymity The anonymity provided by cash is of particular interest in web-based transactions, since there is a widespread concern about the privacy of personal information on the web. Any system that is set up to protect the privacy of information will be advantageous for this reason.

Instant Transfer of Value The idea that cash provides an instant transfer of value is an important one. This is not necessarily the case for other methods of payment. If a credit card is used for payment, for example, the vendor must send the signed voucher to the sponsoring or financial institution for payment in cash. The vouchers themselves cannot be used to purchase something. The transfer of value, therefore, takes some time, the actual length of which varies according to the type of card and the method used to process payments. Cash has none of these problems; it can be used immediately by the vendor for purchases.

DigiCash

Of the various online payment systems that have been invented and tested so far, one called eCash, developed by DigiCash, is the closest to approximating the attributes of cash. The product did not gain acceptance, and the company itself went bankrupt, but their attempt is interesting and revealing for those interested in the challenges of developing an online cash payment system.

eCash was built on the basis of public key cryptography—involving the use of a private key to sign messages and a public key to verify the signatures. For example, if Laura wants to send a private message to George, she encrypts it with her private key, and when he receives it, he applies her public key to verify that it was sent by her. With this approach, George is able to authenticate Laura as the sender. Because the message was unencrypted with her public key, it means it could only have been encrypted with her private key, because her public key is the only key that will unencrypt a message encrypted with her private key. Her public and private keys are key pairs. No other keys will act with them. Since it can be demonstrated that her private key was used, and that she is the only person with access to that key, she cannot argue she didn't send it, so the eCash system has the feature of non-repudiation. This encryption system can be used for any business documents. Under the eCash approach, Laura would generate a note and sign it with her private key—a digital signature. The bank would verify the signature with its own private key and charge her account. It would send to Laura the signed note and a digitally signed withdrawal receipt for Laura's records.

Laura would then send the signed note to George to pay for some goods. George would receive the note, use the public key of the bank to check the bank's digital signature, and then send the note to the bank, which would credit George's account and return an electronic deposit slip to him. George would then send the merchandise to Laura along with a receipt. With this system, eCash would fulfill most of the characteristics of the old-fashioned cash. Although it would not be portable, it would be easily transferable by electronic means. It would also provide an instant transfer of value, as the cash would be deposited in the vendor's account when the transaction takes place. However, it did not succeed, and other methods have since come forward.

Digital Cheques

Cheques have been used for many decades for settling business transactions and have many of the attributes of cash. They differ from cash largely in that they are not anonymous and carry a greater risk to the vendor accepting them in that they might not be honoured by the bank. For this reason, cheques are most useful for dealing with long-term, regular customers. Several attempts to emulate cheques in the digital environment have been made. One of the digital cheque products was called NetCheck.

NetCheck, like DigiCash, makes use of cryptography to provide the signatures and endorsements that are used in processing paper-based cheques. Except for the fact that NetChecks are electronic, they operate exactly the same as paper-based cheques, can be used with existing chequing accounts, and contain all the same information, although they do provide for the inclusion of additional information. Like DigiCash, however, NetCheck did not gain enough acceptance to enable them to be used widely in daily commercial activity. Electronic cheques are being developed by others, and the idea may still lead to viable products.

One significant electronic project is sponsored by the Financial Services Technology Consortium (FSTC), which has done some important work on electronic cheques in their project that led to the development of eCheck (discussed below).

The FSTC (see the New Business Models box) is a U.S.-based, not-for-profit organization comprised of banks, industry partners, financial services providers, technology companies, academic institutions, and government agencies. It carries out research and development of technology-based solutions to meet financial services industry needs, particularly emphasizing payment systems, electronic commerce, and information delivery. In addition to its eCheck project, FSTC has undertaken numerous other projects intended to make electronic payments more viable or to address issues related to them. These have included, for example, a project called Paperless Automated Check Exchange and Settlement (PACES) and another referred to as Bank Internet Payment System (BIPS). PACES is a process for settling cheques within the banking system by using

New Business Models

Standards at the FSTC

The Financial Services Technology Consortium (FSTC) has 17 bank representatives and about 75 other financial technology players as members. The group is charged with creating the standards that will direct electronic payments in the future.

Standards are one of the most important issues facing global e-business. Standards are what make it possible for different groups, and people in different parts of the world, to do business. Standards make it possible for the participants in business transactions to understand what the others are doing—to communicate with them. For standards to work, they must gain acceptance by the people doing business—by the market. An organization such as the FSTC can promulgate the standards, but without this acceptance, they will not serve a useful role.

However, the FSTC does have acceptance, and there is a pressing need for their standards.

One of the areas concerning the FSTC is the role of banks in the payment system for transactions on the internet. They want to make sure that the banks play a dominant role because of their established expertise with payment systems and their financial credibility. Because of the growth of business on the web and the variety of methods available, almost half of all online credit-card payments are processed by non-banking organizations. Several of the founding members of the FSTC are major banks, such as the Bank of America, Citibank, and JP Morgan Chase. Through the standards they create, the FSTC hopes to make the position of the banks more competitive.

The FSTC initiates a project by signing up interested members, who then ante up enough money to fund it. Entry into their cheque-imaging project, for example, was US$250 000, which could either be paid in cash or in kind by means of a gift of equipment or the time of a knowledgeable person.

More recently, the growing popularity of wireless devices has caused the FSTC to increase its focus on wireless transaction standards. One of the main projects of the FSTC, at present, is the Secure Mobile Financial Transactions Initiative. The objective of this project is to develop standards for a secure infrastructure for mobile financial services. More information about past and current projects of the FSTC can be found at the organization's website, located at www.fstc.org.

Financial Services Technology Consortium (FSTC)
www.fstc.org

Questions

1. Discuss how the initiatives of the FSTC could benefit e-business.
2. Visit the website of the FSTC and read about current projects. What other projects do you think would be useful for the FSTC to carry out?

electronic images of the cheques captured at the first bank where they are presented. BIPS is a facility offered by banks under which their customers can make payments on the internet by logging onto a special interface set up by the bank. The FSTC issues white papers and reports on their projects, which are very influential. Their white papers are available on the internet.

eCheck

The eCheck website (www.echeck.org) says that these digital cheques:

- contain the same information as paper cheques
- are based on the same rich legal framework as paper cheques
- can be linked with unlimited information and exchanged directly between parties
- can be used in any and all remote transactions where paper cheques are used today
- enhance the functions and features provided by bank chequing accounts
- expand on the usefulness of paper cheques by providing value-added information

In fact, eChecks work in exactly the same way as paper cheques do, except for the electronic base. An electronic cheque writer creates (writes) an eCheck and electronically sends (gives) the eCheck to the payee. The payee deposits the eCheck by electronically conveying it to the bank, and then receives credit, and the payee's bank clears the eCheck to the paying bank. The paying bank validates the eCheck by checking the digital signature and then charges the cheque writer's bank account for the eCheck. eChecks are based on the Financial Services Markup Language (FSML), a variation of HTML. They include digital signatures, digital certificates, and other encryption-based features.

An electronic cheque under the FSTC approach would be created by a smart card "chequebook" that would include a digital signature for the cheque along with all the information that would be included on a normal cheque. The cheque would then be delivered by means of an electronic transmission and clear through an electronic clearinghouse.

The fact that the cheque originates from a smart card provides a degree of security because the smart card is not connected to the computer system and, in addition, has its own password system. Of course, the digital signature adds considerable security because it is based on public key encryption, enabling any authorized party to the transaction to authenticate the cheque.

Somewhat related to the electronic cheque project is another project underway by the FSTC on cheque imaging. This is a process involving the creation of a digitized image of a cheque by the payee's bank at the time of deposit. The bank then sends the digital image, not the original cheque, through the payment clearing system. The purpose of the project is to speed up the payment process and reduce the opportunity for fraud. From a business perspective, cheque imaging has appeal because it substantially reduces the costs of processing cheques.

One of the big problems with this system is that images are well known for their large file size. When they are transmitted, therefore, they require a very wide bandwidth, to the point that it would strain existing bandwidth normally available in most parts of the world. Another issue is that the legal system has not recognized imaged cheques, adding some uncertainty to their use for consummating business transactions.

Finally, the FSTC has a project underway called the "electronic commerce" project, which is focused on creating an infrastructure to process web based transactions through the existing bank payment systems. The first phase of the project involved creating communications links from the internet to automated clearing-houses and money transfer systems. One of the challenges of this project is to find ways to attach the payment systems to the internet without compromising their security.

Mondex

A well-known payment method that has received support from financial institutions is the Mondex electronic cash system. Mondex, distributed as part of the Mastercard franchise, utilizes a smart card, which is a plastic card that looks like a credit card but contains a microchip that is used like a purse to store information about cash transactions and cash on hand. The card also contains some security features, designed to protect transactions between it and another Mondex card. It also contains security that restricts access to the information on the card. Mondex is easily transportable over digital connections, telephone lines, and the internet, since it is electronic.

Mondex
www.mastercardonline.com

The idea is that the card would be "loaded" by the owner at a bank or at a Mondex-compatible ATM machine and then used at retail and other locations to buy goods, rather like a debit card, except that it is paying out the money stored in its own memory rather than having to log into the buyer's bank account. In this way, Mondex can act as an electronic substitute for cash.

Mondex can be applied in two broad areas, unlike eCash. While eCash can be transported over communications media, it was never designed to be carried by a person like real cash. Mondex, however, can be used in both arenas—the card can be carried around by a person and the signals can be sent over the internet. This additional flexibility brings it closer to the functionality of real cash.

Its acceptability depends on its acceptance by the financial institutions, which in Canada has largely been accomplished, at least in principle. Although they have been slow to implement Mondex, most of the banks still say that it will be launched. There have been field tests in several cities in Canada, including Guelph, Sherbrooke, and Toronto. In addition, Mondex's acceptability for use by people in the streets and in stores depends on the extent to which the stores themselves have adopted the card readers that are necessary to make the system work. In this respect, its progress has been extremely slow. Visa also has a similar product, called Visa Cash.

Credit Cards

When commerce over the web began, the payment mechanism often took place offline. Typically, a website would provide a page that people could download, print, and fax to the company. In addition, many people would review websites for research and comparison purposes and then go to the store to buy the goods. While this is still common, it was much more common when web-based commerce began. Slowly, the idea of providing the capability of people to input their credit card information into the website itself and consummate the transaction online became more common. The issue that companies had to deal with, however, was that the security provided on the website needed to be significantly increased. Where credit cards are used for payment, numerous systems offer customers the opportunity to register by entering information about themselves, including their credit card information, in a personal profile that is kept in a secure area by the vendor. Then when the customer enters the site to buy products, that customer needs only to log into the personal profile and does not need to enter all the additional information many times over. The vendor has an interest in setting up the personal profile to make it easier for the customer to buy, and the customer has an interest in doing this to save the time required to input information every time. An additional advantage of this system is that the credit card information is only entered and transmitted once per vendor, reducing the risk of detection by unauthorized parties during transmission.

The need for increased security was related to the needs of both the company and the customer. From the customer's point of view, the security is needed to ensure that their credit card information is not made available to other people who might make illegal use of it. In addition, for reasons of personal privacy, customers normally do not want any information about themselves to be passed along to others without their knowledge and permission. From the company's point of view, there is a need to provide good security to safeguard their customers' interests—and to avoid the possibility of litigation being brought against the company if web customers' reasonable expectations of security are not met.

As a consequence, most websites that accept credit cards have adopted measures such as encryption. Normally, when a user enters into the secure parts of websites, a warning will appear on the browser screen that indicates that he or she is entering a secure area. In the case of Microsoft's Internet Explorer, a small lock on the lower corner of the screen will move into a locked position. When the user moves out of the secure area, a warning to this effect will also appear, although there is an option in the browsers to turn off these warnings at the discretion of the user. In addition to encryption, many online businesses have also submitted themselves to an independent trust audit as an additional assurance for customers.

In the late 1990s, credit card fraud increasingly became a problem. Although most sites used encryption to ensure the privacy and integrity of the credit card information during transit across the internet, most credit card fraud was committed by using stolen card numbers. In most cases, only a name, credit card number, and expiry date were necessary to order goods and services online and have them shipped virtually anywhere in the world. Since it is not difficult to obtain someone's credit card number, it should not come as a surprise that fraud was rampant. Some e-tailers even reported that the majority of incoming orders were fraudulent. To curb this growing problem, several initiatives were undertaken. On the technology side, the industry put high hopes into new electronic encryption and authentication initiatives such as **secure electronic transaction (SET) protocol**, a method of securing credit card transactions with encryption and authentication technology. Unfortunately, many of these initiatives hoped that consumer's cards would soon be converted to smart cards and, additionally, that smart card readers would become widespread in consumer devices such as personal computers. Unfortunately, smart cards were not as successful as originally hoped and even today, most bankcards are not equipped with smart card capabilities.

Nevertheless, credit cards on the internet have become safer to use. Many online merchants, for example, will only ship to the billing address of the credit card holder. In addition, credit card companies have developed new systems to verify the legitimacy of a credit card user without the need for additional hardware (see E-Strategy box).

SECURE ELECTRONIC TRANSACTION (SET) PROTOCOL
A method of securing credit card transactions using encryption and authentication technology.

Emerging Billing and Payment Systems

So far, we have discussed payment systems. With the growth of web commerce, there has been a great deal of interest among businesspeople in developing efficient and effective systems for billing and payment over the web—in other words, sys-

E-Strategy

Verified by Visa

Many consumers are afraid to give out their credit card numbers over the internet. The most common fear is that the credit card number will fall into the wrong hands during transit across the internet. To alleviate this fear, online merchants have invested heavily in state-of-the-art encryption technologies. Most consumers feel safe when they see the reassuring 128-bit encryption lock on the bottom of their computer screen. Unfortunately, this is a false sense of security. The same consumers who are so worried about online security often do not hesitate for one second to entrust their credit card to an unknown waiter in a restaurant, who often has more

than enough time to write down the card number and expiry date. In many cases, this information is sufficient to go for a nice online shopping tour, even for a criminal with only limited technical abilities. Although many e-tailers reacted to this abuse by limiting shipments to the billing address of the credit card holders, fraud remained a big problem. Vendors are reluctant to install additional hardware, such as smart card readers, so credit card companies had to come up with new ideas to make online shopping more secure. VISA's answer to the problem is called "Verified by VISA." To participate, cardholders simply have to visit the VISA website and pick a password which is then

associated with their account. To make an online purchase, a customer proceeds to the online checkout as usual and submits her credit card number. The customer is then prompted to enter her VISA password to approve the transaction. As an added layer of protection for the customer, this online password is directly transmitted to VISA for verification, not to the online merchant. Although many initiatives to make online transactions more secure have failed to garner widespread support, Verified by VISA seems to be on the right track. In the United States, companies such as 1-800-flowers.com, Jet Blue Airways, and Walmart.com have joined the program.

VISA
www.visa.com

Questions

1. Discuss the implications of "Verified by VISA". How does it affect consumers as well as merchants?
2. Do you think the system could be used in the bricks-and-mortar world? How?

tems that incorporate online billing as well as payment. The cost-effectiveness of web-based transactions has been a major factor in sustaining this interest, as has the opportunity to develop an additional channel of business. As a result, the billing and payments systems in place have evolved considerably and continue to evolve. The principal billing and payment systems in current use include those established by Canada Post and the banks. In addition, PayPal has emerged as a powerful new payment system, and with the growing usage of mobile phones and other wireless devices, mobile-payment (m-payment) schemes are beginning to develop.

Canada Post

The billing and payment system referred to as epost was developed by Canada Post Corporation and the Bank of Montreal. The epost system is an electronic mailbox that people can use for several mail functions, including the ability to receive and pay bills through the epost website. An individual must register with the site and select the bills they wish to receive online from those available through epost. Then the bills will be received electronically and can be paid online by using a credit card or electronic funds transfer through a bank's payment system.

Canada Post's epost
www.epost.ca

As far as possible epost emulates traditional mail in an electronic environment. It makes use of high security and provides an electronic post office box free of charge. All pieces of mail are stamped with an electronic postmark to guarantee they have not been opened or tampered with. The security environment includes firewalls and 128-bit SSL encryption technology. To date, epost has not achieved much market penetration.

The Banks

On their websites, the banks have provided systems for billing and payment that are among the most popular of this type of service. For several years, the banks have offered their customers the capability to log into their online banking pages at their websites. Online banking has offered customers the ability to use their debit card number, together with a password, to log in and view their bank account balances and transactions. They also have the capability to transfer funds from one account to another and pay bills. Ultimately, it will likely be possible for people to deposit and withdraw funds from their home computer, but this will depend on the introduction and integration of smart-card technology, such as that of Mondex, by using card readers that plug into the user's computer.

A relatively new addition to the online offerings of the banks is that of e-mail payment. In Canada, five of the major banks have adopted the *Interac* Email Money Transfer service developed by Acxsys Corporation. After logging in and navigating to the appropriate webpage, a customer enters the name and e-mail address of the intended recipient. Then the system requires that the customer enter a question to which only the recipient would know the answer. The send button is then clicked. The recipient receives an e-mail instructing him or her to go to a website to answer the question and transfer the money immediately to his or her bank account. If the recipient doesn't have online banking privileges, or if their bank isn't part of the *Interac* service, the funds are deposited to their account after a period of a few business days. The system works very quickly and efficiently. These e-mail payment systems show considerable promise because of their convenience and ease of use.

In recent years, banks have expanded their online banking to include electronic billing. While online bill payments have been possible for quite a while, it has been used in relation to bills mailed through the old "snail-mail" system. Customers would receive their bills—say from American Express—and then go to the online banking function on their bank's website and pay it online. To make this payment, they would need to select American Express from the list of participating organizations as one of the organizations they would be paying to, and then make the payment. Once the selection is made, it would remain in their profile and would not have to be selected from the main list again.

With the addition of electronic billing to their online banking functions, the participating organizations can elect to have the bills sent electronically rather than by regular mail. This means that bills can be transmitted faster and more cheaply, and paid online just as the mailed bills would have been paid. This system is gaining support from many organizations and has a great deal of potential for the future.

M-Payments

Few areas in e-business have been filled with more hype than mobile payments. Since the mid-'90s, consumers were promised that cash and plastic cards were going

Acxsys Corporation
www.certapay.com

to be a thing of the past. At various times, it has been said that almost every version of mobile technology could be used for payments: mobile phones, PDAs, wireless smart cards. One company even foresaw that microchips embedded in our clothes would soon make payments, as we know them, obsolete. Most of the promised payment technologies, however, never made it past their field test phase, and socks and pants still refuse to pay our bills. It is interesting to note that some of the promised technologies actually did succeed—PDAs and mobile phones are widespread. Unfortunately, they have not yet succeeded as payment devices. A major reason why m-payments have so far failed to reach critical mass is a lack of standards—standards that would convince people that a particular technology will reach critical mass in usage. Until consumers see that a payment system has the potential to reach critical mass, they will refuse to embrace it. Similarly, merchants are reluctant to invest in a payment infrastructure if there is a danger of buying into the wrong system. After all, what good does a state-of-the-art wireless smart card reader do if the customer doesn't own a cell phone that can make use of it? For m-payment technology to succeed, global standards are required and need to be backed up by reputable organizations, similar to the way that credit cards have developed.

The following section gives a brief overview of two different wireless payment technologies. There are many more technologies out there, and new ones are constantly being developed. The following two, however, seem to be the most promising at the moment. Although none of them have yet reached a "critical mass," some of them have been quite successful when implemented for a specific purpose or within a particular region.

Mobile Phones Since most people today already own a mobile phone, it is an obvious candidate for m-payments. There are two main advantages of mobile phones: First, mobile operators usually have the necessary billing information for customers and a billing infrastructure in place. Second, most people carry their mobiles with them almost all of the time. The big advantage is therefore that consumers don't need any additional devices. On the merchant side, systems can be employed under which very limited additional hardware is required and in some cases, existing transaction technology can be used. One problem with mobile phones is that there are still no standards when it comes to processing payments. European operators who tried mobile phones as payment devices failed to agree on interoperability standards when conducting their field tests. As a result of this, mobile phones are still not really a viable payment alternative. Nevertheless, some interesting uses have been developed. One example is a new system to pay parking fees in Austria. The system, developed by Siemens, allows drivers to send a text message with their license plate number and the requested parking time to traffic authorities. The fee is automatically charged to the driver's mobile phone bill. An advantage of the system is that frequent trips to the parking meter to pay for additional time are no longer necessary. Ten minutes before the parking time expires, a reminder text message is sent. The driver can then add more parking time simply by sending another text message to the system. The fee is added to the mobile phone invoice of the driver. Another interesting application is a soft drink vending machine that accepts wireless payments. The concept is simple and not tied to any specific mobile system. A customer simply dials a 900-toll number printed on the machine. As soon as the number is called, the machine will dispense the drink and the charge will be added to the phone bill. This could also be used for online payments as the user only has to use his or her mobile phone and does not need to disconnect from the internet. In addition, there would be no danger of accidentally installing an unwanted dialer. As discussed earlier in the chapter, the use of 900 numbers in a payment system is controversial and could leave the door open for fraud. Nevertheless, it may be a viable m-payment alternative in the short-run until more standardized systems have been established.

Wireless Smart Cards The most widespread and perhaps the most promising m-payment systems are wireless smart cards based on **radio frequency identification (RFID)** technology. RFID technology uses radio waves to transfer data between a reader device and an item such as a smart card.

The technology is simple and cheap to deploy. It works by adding a sophisticated wireless chip to a smart card, which can be read by a corresponding reader device. There are several reasons why RFID technology may be the most attractive and promising alternative for m-payments. First, the transmitter chips are cheap and can be mass-produced. Second, the technology does not require a power source such as a battery. Third, the system can be made to be secure, although this is an ongoing issue. Data that is sent between the chip and the reader can be and usually is encrypted and the content of the chip can only be read if the reader device is in close proximity. The fourth, and probably most important point, is that the technology has proven itself in the field and is already in use. The best-known application for RFID is probably the Exxon Mobile Speedpass system. Customers who register for the system are issued a key chain with a built-in RFID transmitter. To buy gasoline, a customer only has to wave the key chain in front of the pump to authorize the transaction. The charge is then automatically added to the customer's credit card. A significant security problem with this system is that if the wand is lost, the finder can easily use it at a pump, because there is no password or access code attached to the wand.

Mastercard is currently testing its own RFID system, called Paypass, in the Orlando, Florida area. Customers are given a regular Mastercard credit card, which also contains a RFID chip. At participating locations, a customer need only wave his or her card in front of the card reader to approve the transaction. The Paypass program is very promising, because it is backed by Mastercard. Since the cards have a normal magnetic strip, the cards are also "backwards compatible" to the existing credit card infrastructure.

PayPal

Credit cards have become the de-facto standard for payments on the internet. The problem with credit card transactions, however, is that they are usually quite expensive and only accepted by professional online merchants. For small transactions between individual users, PayPal has become a good alternative to sending a cheque through snail mail. PayPal, which is owned by eBay, is the world's largest online payment service, with over 40 million member accounts. To send money, a user must simply open an account with PayPal. After a deposit is made with PayPal, sending money is easy. Simply specify the email address of the recipient and the transfer is completed. If the recipient is not a PayPal member yet, he or she will receive an email with instructions on how to open an account and receive the payment. PayPal can also be used to request money and, for a fee, to accept credit card payments. Since PayPal is owned by eBay, it is not surprising that the system is heavily tied in with the eBay auction platform to facilitate payments between eBay members. Because of the success of eBay, PayPal has also been very successful.

Chapter Summary

Payment systems have traditionally included cash, cheques, and credit cards. Attempts have been made to emulate all of these in digital form for use on the internet. Early attempts to develop digital cash and cheques have failed to gain acceptance by financial institutions and users.

Credit cards continue to be a prime method of payment, but concerns about their security and safety remain. However, the Financial Services Technology Consortium has been seeking ways to improve on the use of electronic payment systems. Public/private key encryption techniques are a prime way to provide security. The secure electronic transaction (SET) protocol uses public/private key technology, encryption, and digital certificates to enable the cardholders to check that online parties are valid merchants qualified to accept their particular credit card, and also allows merchants to validate that the prospective customer has a valid card. Where credit cards are used for payment, numerous systems offer the customer an opportunity to register by entering information about themselves, including their credit-card information, in a personal profile that is kept in a secure area by the vendor.

Mondex has received some limited support from financial institutions, but has developed very slowly. Mondex is a smart card system that is used like a purse to store information about cash transactions and cash on hand. It also contains security features that restrict access to the information on the card.

With the growth of e-commerce, there has been a great deal of interest among businesspeople in developing efficient and effective methods of billing and payment systems over the web. As a result, the billing and payments systems in place have evolved considerably and continue to do so. The principal billing and payment systems in current use include those established by Canada Post, the banks, and the vendors themselves.

Canada Post's epost system is an electronic mailbox that people can use for several mail functions, including receiving and paying bills. Banks have also provided systems for billing and payment that are among the most popular of this type of service. For several years, banks have allowed customers to log into their online banking pages in their websites. In some cases, vendors themselves have also offered online billing and payment systems on their sites. Most of these systems are similar to those of epost and the banks, offering the ability to transmit and receive bills electronically, view them on the company website and then pay them online using a variety of payment methods.

Some newer payment systems show considerable promise. These include the use of mobile telephones and PDAs to execute payment transactions. They also include newer online payment systems such as PayPal, which has been one of the more successful new systems. Finally, the new e-mail payment systems offered by the banks may well catch the interest of people and become widely used.

Key Terms

radio frequency identification (RFID) *(p. 114)*   value added networks *(p. 104)*
secure electronic transaction (SET) protocol *(p. 110)*

Tools for Online Learning

To help you master the material in this chapter and stay up to date with new developments in e-business, visit **www.pearsoned.ca/trites**. Resources include:

- **Review Questions and Exercises**
- **Problems for Discussion**
- **Recommended Readings**
- **Updates to Case Studies and Textual Material**
- **Streaming CBC Videos with Cases**

E-Business Architecture

Overview

In the early days of the web, a website with some basic information about the company and an e-mail address was enough to establish an internet presence. This has since changed and global e-businesses like eBay now require a well-structured (e-business) architecture and stable infrastructure. "E-business architecture" refers to the IT infrastructure of a company, but covers a wider spectrum of issues, including everything a company needs to conduct its business and to remain in business. For a pure-play e-business like eBay, its architecture starts with its IT infrastructure. This includes all of the technology needed for the company to conduct its day-to-day operations, such as servers, data storage systems, and networking technologies. For a company such as eBay, IT infrastructure is clearly a major enabler to remain competitive. After all, a bricks-and-mortar auction house can still hold auctions without electricity. eBay, of course, would be shut down completely without power. Although the specific technology infrastructure of eBay is well beyond the scope of this case, it does deserve some attention as it is a good example of the growing pains of a company.

When Pierre Omidyar first developed eBay in his living room in 1995, the system was quickly written in the C++ programming language. eBay calls this original system eBay Version 1. As the company grew, eBay's systems grew along with the company. Although the system was continually expanded and eventually became eBay Version 2, it was nevertheless still based on the original Version 1 written on Pierre Omidyar's personal computer. As the system continued to grow, it became increasingly difficult to maintain and adapt a system that was originally intended for only a few users when the number of users expanded to millions. eBay also became more and more concerned about outages, which began to occur at increasingly frequent intervals as the site grew. One outage lasted almost three days. Not only did lengthy outages erode customer and investor confidence in eBay as a company, they also translated directly into lost revenues. In 2000, eBay decided that it needed to change its entire technology infrastructure to be able to continue growing and to remain competitive. For Version 3 of the eBay system, the company established the following architectural principles and objectives:

- performance, scalability, and availability
- business continuance

- functionality, with the specific need to absorb business changes
- security, including authorization/authentication protocols and data integrity
- open-standard components for vendor product interdependence

This list shows that eBay tried to move from an undefined and unstructured system that evolved during the early years of the company to a more structured and defined e-business architecture. In 2001, eBay decided to use a very scalable infrastructure solution based on the Java Platform.

Another component of e-business architecture is the billing and payment systems. As mentioned in the eBay case in part I, eBay knew it needed a good payments system, and in July, 2002, acquired PayPal. In a "normal" e-business such as priceline.com, billing customers and processing payments is very important for obvious reasons. After all, payments from customers keep the company going. In eBay's case, however, billing and payment systems take on an especially important role. eBay not only needs to bill and process fees for itself (listing and auction fees), but it also needs a way to facilitate the exchange of payments between its members. Although members can exchange funds through "old fashioned" means such as mailing a cheque back and forth, it was in eBay's own best interest to offer its members a payment system that let them transfer money in a quick and secure fashion. Additionally, controlling the flow of funds between its members also provides eBay with an additional source of revenue. Although PayPal is now part of eBay, it continues to operate independently under its founder. Considering the importance of PayPal to eBay, it worthwhile to take a closer look at this payment system.

PayPal Overview

PayPal was founded in November 1999 by Max Levhin and Peter Thiel. As already mentioned in the first eBay case, the internet was growing at a rapid rate in the early years of the web, but lacked a real payment system that facilitated payments between individual users on the internet. PayPal was founded with the intention of providing a fast and secure way to conduct transactions over the World Wide Web. The venture became an instant success. Within its first year of operations, the company had attracted over one million customers and had secured 100 million dollars in equity financing. The success of PayPal quickly inspired competitors to start their own internet payment systems, most notably American banking giant Citibank. None of its competitors, however, managed to replicate PayPal's success. In February 2002, the company went public. It didn't take long for eBay to notice the success of PayPal. After all, the payment system was a perfect fit for the auction house. Many of its members already used the service to pay for their eBay purchases. In July 2002, eBay purchased PayPal for US$1.3 billion. The transaction made sense for eBay: PayPal could be tightly integrated with the eBay auction site, and transaction fees could provide an additional source of revenue for the company. Since acquiring PayPal, eBay has linked the PayPal payment services into the auction process. Every auction and every "Buy it now" listing now offers the ability to pay for the purchase by using the PayPal service. This integration has been a win-win situation for both companies. eBay members have an additional payment choice, and PayPal has gained a large number of customers. Over 61 percent of PayPal's revenues now stem from payments processed as a result of an eBay auction. Of course, this also means additional fee revenues for eBay/PayPal.

PayPal Services

What makes PayPal so appealing to many internet users around the world is the fact that all it takes to receive money is an e-mail address. The service lets its users send money securely, cost-effectively, and conveniently to virtually any person or business with an e-mail account. To send money, a credit-card or a chequing account is required. The process is quite simple. To transfer $50 to pay for an eBay purchase, a buyer creates a PayPal account and specifies the e-mail address of the recipient. The $50 is then charged to the credit card of the sender. After confirming receipt of the money, PayPal automatically contacts the recipient of the payment. If the recipient is already a known PayPal customer, the money is instantly transferred into his or her PayPal account. If not, PayPal asks the recipient to supply his or her bank information for an electronic transfer of funds. Alternatively, PayPal can also send a cheque to the recipient of the money. In addition to sending payments, PayPal customers can also send a "money request," which is somewhat like a traditional invoice. After receiving the request, the recipient can use the PayPal service to send a payment.

PayPal offers three levels of service. Its basic level, the Personal Account, lets users send and receive money for free. Charges do, however, apply for all credit card transactions. The second account type is called Premier Account. The Premier service offers additional services such as lower fees and no limit for receiving credit card payments, special online tools, and an ATM debit card for direct access to funds received via PayPal. The company also offers a Business Account, which offers better reporting capabilities as well as access to multiple logins.

PayPal originally offered payments only in U.S. dollars. More recently, however, it has also introduced payments in other major currencies. Other features that have been added to the service include the ability to download transaction histories and to use mobile devices such as Blackberries and mobile phones to access PayPal accounts. PayPal's main source of revenue is transaction fees. Fees are charged for all credit card transactions. In addition, the service also charges a fee for all funds received with a Premier or Business account. Fees also apply to withdrawals from international banks as well as for currency conversions.

Security at PayPal

As discussed earlier, a sound e-business architecture is vital to the success and the survival of any e-business. PayPal is a case in point. Similarly to its corporate parent eBay, the security and a reliable infrastructure are vital to its continuing and uninterrupted operation. Since the company processes financial transactions and handles very sensitive information, issues like security, fraud protection, and data security are paramount to the success of the company. After all, the success of the service depends on the trust and confidence of its users. Compromised user data could prove disastrous as the PayPal service stores very sensitive financial information about its customers. To protect itself, PayPal relies heavily on encryption technologies. All sensitive data that are exchanged between PayPal's servers and the web browsers of users are encrypted using 128-bit SSL encryption. PayPal's servers are protected both electronically and physically. The systems are housed in secure facilities. They are located behind firewalls to protect them against hacker attacks. Of course, even the most sophisticated security and protection schemes don't help against fraudulent users. A classic example of fraud at PayPal is the use of stolen credit cards. Some criminals try to use the PayPal service to send money to themselves with a stolen credit card. These types of fraud can never be completely eliminated, but they can be reduced through the use of technology. PayPal has developed a fraud detection system called Igor. The system is a sophisticated data mining solution that continually scans PayPal's various databases and cross-references them to detect potential cases of fraud. If, for example, many accounts have been created within a short period of time under a single address, the system "flags" the accounts and alerts a member of PayPal's anti-fraud team.

Customer Relationships—PayPal Style

PayPal's databases contain a wealth of information about its millions of customers. This information includes very sensitive information such as name, address, phone number, e-mail address, and other contact information. Most importantly, PayPal stores bank account and/or credit card data for many of its customers. This data is a burden on the company, as it needs to be protected at all costs. But it is also a very valuable asset. As discussed earlier, this data can be used, or "data-mined," to detect potential cases of fraud. All of PayPal's data is aggregated in its customer relationship management (CRM) system. In addition to regular customer data, the CRM system can be used to store and analyze additional information such as click-stream data and log-file data. The potential of this collection of data is enormous. For example, it can be used to analyze whether a customer is eligible for a PayPal debit card. The marketing potential of this information is also substantial. If, for example, the system identifies a very attractive customer with a large transaction volume, the PayPal could offer the customer a Premier Account at a preferential rate. Its affiliation with eBay also provides both companies with additional opportunities. PayPal's and eBay's databases could be cross-referenced and analyzed, for example, to gain additional knowledge about customers.

Conclusion

Both PayPal and eBay are good examples of how important e-business architecture is to the success and survival of a business. For a large company such as eBay/PayPal, managing this architecture can be a daunting task. The importance of this task, however, cannot be underestimated. After all, a crash and a lengthy outage of the eBay auction system could have disastrous consequences that could even threaten the survival of the company.

Questions for Discussion

1. Why is the PayPal system a good example of e-business infrastructure for eBay?
2. What are the risks that PayPal presents for the potential of fraud?
3. What are the benefits of PayPal to eBay and do the benefits exceed the risks? Why or why not?
4. How could the customer information accumulated by PayPal be used to advance the strategic initiatives of eBay?

Part 3
E-Business Applications

— CHAPTER **7**

Supply Chain Management

LEARNING OBJECTIVES

When you complete this chapter you should be able to:

1. Describe the process and components of supply chain management (SCM).

2. Identify and describe the forces affecting SCM.

3. Explain how e-businesses can use technology in SCM.

4. Contrast the traditional supply chain with the internet-enabled supply chain.

5. Outline how business-process reengineering can be carried out and why it is necessary as part of implementing SCM.

6. Describe partnership strategies and implementation concerns for SCM.

7. Describe order fulfillment/delivery issues related to SCM.

8. Describe the issues that reverse logistics raise in internet-enabled supply chains.

Introduction

Supply chain management (SCM) has become an increasingly important component of corporate strategy over the past several years. Driven by the need for companies to reduce costs and prices while improving customer service and product quality, SCM is also recognized as an essential aspect of e-business implementation. Dell Computer Corporation is an excellent example of a company that has been able to maximize the efficiency of its supply chain to allow for reduction of costs, reduced inventories, increased speed of delivery, and customized (made-to-order) products for its customers over the web or by direct telephone order. (See the New Business Models box for a discussion of Dell's make-to-order approach.) SCM is a business technique involving strategic decisions enabled through the application of technologies. Throughout this chapter, both the strategic and technological aspects of SCM will be discussed.

New Business Models

Innovations in Supply Chain Management at Dell Computer Corporation

Dell Computer is widely recognized as a leader in the sale of customized computers through the web. Users can log in (**www.dell.com**), design the computer they want, and order it online. Dell's job is to source the components, assemble, and ship the computer in the very short timeline that online customers have come to expect. A key to Dell's ability to achieve this performance is its use of SCM. Dell is one of the world's leading companies in supply chain management. Its make-to-order approach to e-business was recognized early as an industry-changing concept that involved numerous changes to the supply chain. The initial goal at Dell was to reduce inventories, increase efficiency, reduce obsolescence, and facilitate the delivery of custom products to customers. To achieve this goal, Dell began to "substitute information for inventory." By 1998 Dell had reduced its inventory levels to approximately seven days but was not satisfied. Compared to many traditional industries and other competitors,

seven days was a risky inventory level that could result in stockouts and poor customer service.

Supply-Side Streamlining

Dell decided that it was necessary to increase the level of information sharing with key suppliers to better facilitate planning. Customized web pages for top suppliers were created that allowed access to Dell's forecasts, sales data, customer information, defect rates, and other product-related information. In addition, Dell began to require its suppliers to share the same types of detailed information, to allow for improved planning at their point in the supply chain. Through effective communication, high-technology solutions, and sound planning, Dell has reduced inventories for many items to a level measured in only hours rather than days—creating a true just-in-time inventory system.

After establishing strong links with suppliers, Dell also extended its communications through a supplier portal called Valuechain.Dell.com, allowing for more complete exchange of infor-

mation between suppliers and the company. In late 2000, Dell extended the portal with a web-based supply chain initiative (coined DSI2) aimed at improving forecasting further up the supply chain. The goal was to share information with second- and third-tier suppliers and increase the effectiveness of the complete supply chain (see figure 7.1).

Customer Focus

Dell has also worked to implement SCM on the customer portion of its supply chain. To improve sales and customer service, Dell created "Premier Pages" for many of its business customers (80 percent of its business), which aimed to reduce the complexity of ordering. The Premier Pages were established in conjunction with customers such as Ford Motor Co. and held information on pre-approved product configurations and established pricing—effectively taking several steps out of the traditional purchase order process. Ford estimates that this initiative alone saved US$2 million in procurement

Figure 7.1 Dell's Supply Chain Configuration

Dell's supply chain involves information sharing by its members.

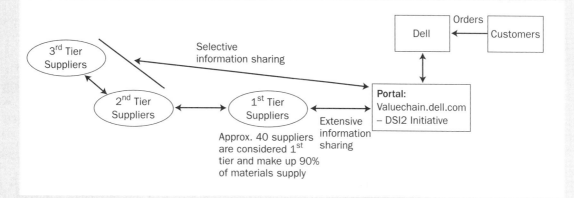

costs and is very satisfied with its relationship with Dell.

Service Enhancement

After achieving great success in the core of its supply chain, Dell decided to apply similar management concepts to its customer service and support divisions. Again focusing on the customer, Dell set goals to provide high-quality service, on time, and at reasonable prices, as a means of bolstering commitment to the brand. To improve its service area, Dell decided to partner with UPS SonicAir® for parts inventory management and distribution to ensure its important same-day and next-day services. Through effective partnership and supply chain strategies, Dell has achieved a 95 per-

cent service level for parts availability and on-time delivery. Considering that Dell handles approximately 60 000 calls per day, this is an impressive accomplishment.

Calls are screened first at the high-tech call centre where the staff connect through the internet to the customer's machine to identify any problems. Each product is embedded with diagnostic equipment so that Dell is able to analyze many functions remotely as well as access product information and configuration to ensure parts availability. Unless the call is handled remotely, the service request is logged and Dell's service processes take effect.

Dell uses EDI and web technologies to relay service requests immediately to both SonicAir and a

technician to facilitate planning on a tight schedule. At that point SonicAir's logistics system ensures that required parts are moved to the appropriate location and confirms the schedule with Dell. Technicians are scheduled to work at either a repair depot or the customer's location, and arrival of the parts and technician is coordinated. Reducing downtime and providing high-quality after-sales service again scores high marks with Dell's customers.

Dell exhibits leading-edge management strategies for the supply chain and e-business in general—combining strategic planning, technological innovation, and strong implementation.

Dell
www.dell.com

Questions

1. Dell has enjoyed success in its strategy for several years. Why are others having difficulty in copying it?
2. What other industries do you think would benefit from Dell's supply chain model?
3. Should Dell get into bricks-and-mortar retail operations to expand its potential market to those who don't buy online?

SOURCES: Ann Saccomano, "Dell Computer Builds Service," *Traffic World* 259, no. 4 (1999): 26–27; "Dell Aims Web-Based SCM Program at Forecasts," *Electronic Buyers' News* (August, 2000); Tom Stein and Jeff Sweat, "Killer Supply Chains," *Informationweek* (November 1998).

The supply chain is the set of processes that encompasses raw materials or resource purchases through to final delivery of a product or service to the end consumer. Therefore, the supply chain includes sourcing, transportation, manufacturing, distributing, wholesaling, retailing, and final delivery of goods. The chain is not necessarily a linear or simple process: some authors have suggested that "supply web" is a more appropriate term to describe the complex interrelationships involved in the supply chain.

Supply chain management (SCM) is the process of coordinating and optimizing the flow of all products or services, information, and finances among all players of the supply chain, from raw material provider to the end consumer. SCM includes functions such as forecasting the demand for various types of materials, ordering from suppliers in economic order quantities, inbound logistics, warehousing, manufacturing, outbound logistics, sales, and delivery to the end consumer. Therefore, we can say that the supply chain includes upstream, internal, and downstream components, all of which need to be effectively managed.

A number of terms are used in practice that are interchangeable with or closely related to supply chain management, such as *value chain management, integrated logistics, integrated purchasing strategies,* and *supply chain synchronization.* Keep in mind that many business terms are adapted to suit specific industry and company preferences. Logistics is the term you may commonly hear used and is now considered to be nearly interchangeable with SCM. Traditionally, **logistics** is the process of planning, implementing, and controlling the efficient and effective flow and storage of goods, services, and related information from point of origin to point of consumption. In essence, the supply chain integrates a number of very important topics in e-business. For instance, B2B e-commerce is an essential component of managing the buy-side (and often the sell-side) of the supply chain. B2C e-commerce is an essential component of managing the sell-side of the supply chain for organizations that deal directly with the end consumer. B2B has been affected substantially by SCM, as well as e-procurement and trading exchanges, which are discussed in more detail in chapter 8. Both B2B and B2C have been shifting to the customer focus of business through customer relationship management (CRM), which is the topic of chapter 9. In this chapter, SCM is discussed from an inter-organizational perspective to allow the reader to fully understand its importance to success in e-business.

The Traditional Supply Chain

In the traditional supply chain model (see figure 7.2), suppliers produced goods in the most efficient manner for their business (typically large batches), and sent large orders to customers (either retailers or wholesalers). This system was referred to as the **push system**, where vendors supply product downstream until the end consumer chooses whether or not to purchase what has been made. The suppliers produce goods based upon their efficiencies and push them to customers rather than relying on demand to determine production. The system was most effective in the early days of manufacturing, as a means of driving unit costs down and bringing prices within the reach of most people. The best example of this is the mass production techniques used by Henry Ford. The system worked best for highly standardized products in markets where there was very high demand. The movement of large orders was considered to be a cost-effective method of production that required inventory to be held at various stages of the supply chain. The manufacturer would hold raw materials as well as finished goods, while downstream members of the supply chain would each hold inventories of their own.

SUPPLY CHAIN MANAGEMENT (SCM)
The process of coordinating and optimizing the flow of all products or services, information, and finances among all players of the supply chain.

LOGISTICS
The process of planning, implementing, and controlling the efficient and effective flow and storage of goods, services, and related information from point of origin to point of consumption.

PUSH SYSTEM
A supply chain model in which suppliers produce goods based upon their efficiencies and push them to customers rather than relying on demand to determine production.

Creating large batches of product was considered efficient for each individual company, but supply chains became burdened with excess inventories. As buyers became more discriminating, and markets more narrowly defined, the traditional push system became full of inefficiencies that increased production costs, storage costs, cycle times, obsolescence, and consumer wait times.

Early attempts to improve the efficiency of the supply chain made use of electronic data interchange (EDI) for communication between supply chain firms. Despite the efforts to improve communications, many firms were unable to drastically improve performance due to difficulties in setting standards for the EDI format across many supply chain members. In addition, the data being transferred was often based on data that came from legacy systems (lacking timeliness and often accuracy).

Common attempts at supply chain management have focused on reducing inventories and achieving some levels of efficiency within the value chain. However, simply reducing inventory levels along the chain is not enough in today's business environment.

Forces Affecting Supply Chain Management

The rapid pace of change in the business world today has affected SCM in a number of ways. Some of the major forces of change include:

- globalization
- mass customization
- price sensitivity
- customer focus and time to market
- just-in-time inventory and inventory reduction
- enterprise resource planning
- outsourcing

Globalization

While companies continue to expand their global presence, challenges to the efficiency of the supply chain become more complex. For example, establishing a reliable transportation and delivery system in a foreign country is complicated by domestic policies, tariffs, and customs regulations. When customers are waiting for delivery, the supply chain needs to perform: slow delivery from a foreign supplier could result in a lost sale, future lost business, and negative publicity. (A further analysis of the impact of globalization on e-businesses is provided in chapter 13.)

Figure 7.2   The Traditional Supply Chain

The traditional supply chain was focused on efficiency of production gained through batch manufacturing that often resulted in excess inventories throughout the supply chain.

Supplier	Manufacturing	Distributor	Retailer	Consumer
Inventories	· Raw Materials · Work in Progress · Finished goods	Goods in Transit	Finished Goods	

Mass Customization

The advent of e-business has shifted power from companies to consumers (in some respects at least), resulting in consumers asking for products or services that are tailored to their specific needs. The internet and computer technology have played a major role in enabling businesses to meet the needs of consumers more easily by simplifying the process of customization, data capture, and information sharing with partners in the supply chain. For example, Dell allows customers to customize their computer system for any component from internal RAM to external colours, while providing a very rapid turnaround time. To support this service successfully, Dell must be able to quickly establish production plans, purchase required components, and arrange shipping of its products. This form of customization is very popular with customers and is likely to reach into other products as well in the near future.

Price Sensitivity

The internet provides individuals with the ability to easily compare prices and gather product information. This shift has resulted in customers becoming increasingly sensitive to price, and when combined with the preference for customized products discussed earlier, this requires businesses to have a very strong grasp of their competition and their supply chain partners. Internet companies like Priceline.com have also changed the nature of pricing—consumers can now name their price and allow a company to accept or reject their offer. Auctioning sites have had a bigger impact on pricing, since auctioning has made its way into B2B through trading exchanges.

Customer Focus and Time to Market

The ability to create and deliver new products has become critically important in many industries. Not only is it necessary to be able to innovate and develop high-quality products, it is crucial to be able to do it quickly and continuously. Competitors Intel and AMD are examples of high-tech chip manufacturers that focus on time to market to maintain their coveted market share of the computer industry. A combination of research and development, partnerships, and supply chain management allows these companies to continually create high-quality products at "internet speed."

Just-in-Time Inventory and Inventory Reduction

Inventory reduction has been attempted for many years; however, the increasing use of the internet and internet protocols (such as TCP/IP) has reduced the difficulty for firms to share information with other supply chain members. Data sharing and communication have traditionally been major obstacles to reducing inventories. Having common information is most effective because all members of the supply chain can then work in concert to reduce inventories while meeting customer demands and maintaining order fill rates.

Enterprise Resource Planning

Enterprise resource-planning (ERP) applications have become the norm in large organizations and, to a great extent, help an organization to facilitate SCM. With legacy systems, firms could spend days or even weeks trying to integrate data from sales, inventory, and purchasing systems to effectively plan for future production. This lack of data integration has been largely overcome with ERP systems, which use centralized databases, allowing companies to ensure that everyone is using the same data and to make decisions in real time. Through the use of centralized data, and the linking of the applications that utilize that data, ERP is an effective tool for integrating the supply chain and thus expediting SCM.

Outsourcing

Outsourcing is increasing and requires supply chain managers to make important supplier selection decisions. For example, Nortel Networks signed a seven-year outsourcing contract in the summer of 2000 for its IT function.[1] Although it may seem ironic that an IT company would outsource its internal IT operations, this strategic decision allows Nortel to concentrate on its own customers and products. The decision to outsource is often made to focus on core competencies, but the supplier effectively becomes a partner who can dramatically affect the ability of the business to meet its objectives. Coupled with customization and time-to-market forces, outsourcing requires that the supply relationships be strong and well managed. The outsourcing partner must be willing and able to react quickly to required product changes and demand fluctuations. Many of the concepts discussed earlier in this book such as the use of extranets can be helpful in establishing effective outsourcing strategies by allowing the supplier to access crucial information on a timely basis.

Nortel Networks
www.nortel.com

When an entity outsources significant parts of its operations it can obtain significant benefits; however, it can also encounter risks such as loss of control over the outsourced operations, inability to monitor performance by the outsourcing service provider, conflicts of interest between the outsourcing service provider and itself over how outsourced services are provided and managed, and loss of in-house expertise in the outsourced functional areas. Thus, outsourcing contracts should be entered into only after a thorough analysis of the benefits and risks and provision should be made to enable the entity to oversee the outsourced operations to the extent necessary.

The Internet-Enabled Supply Chain

The internet economy has resulted in drastic changes to the entire supply chain. The current business environment often results in what has become known as a **pull system** of production. In a pull system the production of suppliers is determined by the needs of customers who request or order goods, necessitating production. In the internet-enabled supply chain (see figure 7.3), the customer drives the entire process by initiating an order (often for a specific or customized product) that results in information flows being passed upstream to suppliers from the firm, which may be a manufacturer, distributor, or wholesaler. In some organizations, no product is made until the customer order is known (e.g., Dell), while in others the customer order results in updates to supplier orders so that appropriate inventory levels can be maintained. The major change from the traditional supply chain is that the predominant information flow is upstream as opposed to downstream.

PULL SYSTEM
A supply chain in which the production of suppliers is determined by the needs of customers who request or order goods, necessitating production.

The internet supply chain has also resulted in substantial changes to more than just information flows. Early in the electronic age, some analysts felt that major changes to supply chains would result in disintermediation and that many businesses would fail if they did not counteract this phenomenon. **Disintermediation** is a change in the supply chain where the provider and con-

DISINTERMEDIATION
A change in the supply chain where the manufacturer or service provider and consumer interact directly with each other, thereby eliminating the need for an intermediary.

Figure 7.3   Internet-Enabled Supply Chain Information Flows

In the internet-enabled supply chain the customer drives the process, and information flows primarily upstream.

sumer interact directly with each other, thereby eliminating the need for an intermediary. The two major categories of disintermediation are (1) when the supplier
of a good or service circumvents another member of the supply chain, such as a
distributor, and provides the good or service directly to the end consumer, and
(2) when a new intermediary enters the market using a new business model (often
lower cost) to drive out existing intermediaries.[2]

The travel industry is an example of an industry that has seen some level of disintermediation take place in the area of bookings (see figure 7.4). In the past, nearly
all airline and other travel was booked through travel agents who had exclusive access
to information and provided it to the customer. The airlines provided information to
the travel companies which, in turn, rolled out that information to their agents. The
agents would then provide information to interested customers, which at times
would be inaccurate or out of date by the time the end consumer was reached.
Reliance on manual processes reduced timeliness and accuracy of information.

With the advent of internet communication, booking a trip has been completely transformed. Customers now have access to a great deal of information
from a variety of sources, including information directly from the airlines. Thus
the travel industry has undergone disintermediation in both major formats.
Customers can book flights now in a variety of ways: online directly with the airline, online with new services like Travelocity.com, or through a travel agent.
Essentially, the booking area of the travel industry has shifted from a push system
to a pull system, whereby the customer can extract information from a variety of
sources and make an informed decision.

Many travel agents feel that their services will remain in demand because
they are better able to offer travel packages and provide customized solutions and
recommendations to travellers than websites. While this may be true at present,
this balance of power is rapidly changing. Travel arrangements are one of the most
widely used services on the internet. Customers can comparison shop quickly and
easily in the comfort of their home at their own pace, forcing the industries
involved to ensure they offer a quality, valuable service.

Other industries are experiencing disintermediation. For example, recent
attempts have been made to disintermediate the grocery industry (see the E-
Strategy box). Not all attempts at disintermediation have been successful. Levi's
attempted to offer custom jeans directly to consumers through their website, but
was faced with difficulties when retailers and distributors became angry and when
demand didn't meet estimates (since customers preferred to try jeans on before
purchase). In contrast, Nike iD shoes sold through Nike's website appear to be a
hit and do not seem to have created the same conflicts with distributors. As business continues to change, we can expect many other industries to be affected by
changes in the internet-enabled supply chain.

Figure 7.4   Travel Industry Information Flows

The travel industry supply chain has been drastically changed by e-commerce and the internet.

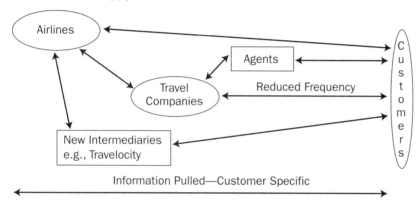

While disintermediation has significantly changed the travel industry, these changes simply force the industry to compete in different ways. This leads to a process known as reintermediation. **Reintermediation** is the process by which companies use the internet to reassemble buyers, sellers, and other partners in a traditional supply chain in new ways. Some examples include New York-based Newview Technologies and Houston-based ChemConnect Inc., bringing together producers, traders, distributors and buyers of steel and chemicals, respectively, in web-based marketplaces. The "e-tailers" in the book industry (Amazon.com, Chapters.Indigo.ca) are the pioneers of reintermediation.

REINTERMEDIATION
Using the internet to reassemble buyers, sellers, and other partners in a traditional supply chain in new ways.

Integration of Technology

As discussed above, changes in many aspects of the business environment have greatly impacted how an entity manages its supply chain, including technological changes. While SCM has been strongly affected by the growth of the internet, other technologies such as extranets, enterprise resource planning applications, business intelligence software, application service providers and other technologies also contribute to the evolution of SCM.

Use of Extranets

Sharing information between supply chain members has been made significantly more manageable through the use of extranet technologies. For supply chain members to reduce costs and increase efficiency, information needs to be shared in a reliable, cost-effective manner. Extranet technologies have reduced the usage of EDI as an information-sharing technology due to the simplified and more economical process of using TCP/IP. Even so, the cost of providing information on an extranet is much more manageable if an organization is fully integrated in its back office (likely through ERP), which allows provision of current inventory, demand, and other data.

Extranets allow for companies to share information in a much more timely manner than was previously available through EDI. The use of EDI required complex standards to be developed, and the request for an order would be sent to a supplier and require a reply. Extranet/internet technology allows for the demand forecast to be adjusted constantly, giving the supplier advance notice and allowing for production planning changes to take place sooner. This increase in timeliness of

E-Strategy

Online Grocery Shopping at Grocery Gateway

Grocery Gateway is a Canadian dot-com business started in 1996 by two university graduates. The online supermarket delivers orders to customers in the greater Toronto area. From failed competitors it has learned the importance of effective supply chain management, since effective handling and delivery of orders is the key to customer satisfaction. In addition to being quick, the process must reduce handling to prevent damage to produce and other items.

Grocery Gateway's 26 040 square metre customer fulfillment centre in Mississauga uses a combination of wireless scanners, high-speed conveyors, bar code readers, and well-trained pickers equipped with Bluetooth Palm handhelds—all controlled by a fully

integrated ERP system. The centre offers a good selection of popular food items and brands, grocery products, and delivery management. The facility has five temperature areas designed to keep all products as fresh as possible.

After the ordered items are picked, the products are packed inside a plastic delivery box that fits into racks built into the delivery trucks. Grocery Gateway's trucks are temperature-controlled, with three distinct sections, to maintain product freshness throughout the delivery process.

Using logistics software from Descartes Systems Group, Grocery Gateway plans each run based on delivery locations, order sizes, and time of day, allowing the firm to optimize costs while giving cus-

tomers a choice of 18 different 90-minute delivery windows. By acquiring Direct Home Delivery, and thereby its Staples Business Depot delivery business, Grocery Gateway can fully utilize its assets throughout the day when its grocery trucks are the least busy.

From failed competitors, Grocery Gateway also learned not to grow too fast or enter markets it could not serve profitably. Thus, it started by targeting affluent suburbs like North York and Richmond Hill, and has now moved into Mississauga. The company's $45 minimum order size and $8 delivery fee caters to customers who are more concerned about convenience than price and enables the company to make a small profit on each order.

Grocery Gateway
www.grocerygateway.com

Questions

1. Grocery Gateway's strategy is to be a leading logistics provider. Why don't they just contract that part of the operation out to UPS Logistics or another major logistics provider?

2. Do you think online grocery companies will be more successful than those that are already established in the industry?

SOURCES: Grocery Gateway website **www.grocerygateway.com**, accessed April 19, 2004; Jordan Kendall, "Grocery Gateway Masters Canadian Home Delivery," *The Forrester Brief* (August 8, 2001).

information should reduce the production-to-delivery timeframe and also reduce supply chain costs over the long run. Effective information sharing is allowing companies like Dell and Wal-Mart to become highly effective supply chain managers.

Wal-Mart is famous for sharing its information with suppliers. Its Retail Link system processes tens of thousands of supplier queries per week, providing updates about invoice status, product sales per store, effects of markdowns, and returns on inventory and other detailed information. Retail Link helped Wal-Mart shift responsibility for inventory management from in-store managers to suppliers. By sharing information gathered from store cash registers with suppliers such as Procter & Gamble, Wal-Mart encouraged quicker replenishments and leaner inventories, giving both suppliers and the retailer higher margins.

Thomson Consumer Electronics Inc. makes extensive use of an extranet to facilitate communication and information sharing in its supply chain. Analysis of Thomson's customers was carried out through a survey, which revealed that its supply chain effectiveness was considered weak in on-time delivery and stockouts. As a result, Thompson implemented an integration project by using an extranet and i2's supply chain management system (see figure 7.5). Customers such as Best Buy, Circuit City, and Kmart agreed to provide detailed information on sales and forecasts to Thomson. Thomson uses i2 to analyze the information internally and updates its plans and forecasts that are shared with suppliers. In effect, the extranet facilitates communications and allows supply chain members to improve planning. Thomson's supply chain strategy has improved its supplier relationships, increased sales, and reduced rush shipments due to last-minute decision-making.

ERP in SCM

Enterprise resource-planning systems have truly become the backbone of any e-business. To improve decision-making in the digital economy, it is absolutely essential to have access to up-to-date information. ERP systems allow for effective

Figure 7.5   SCM at Thomson Consumer Electronics

Thomson Consumer Electronics uses an extranet along with sophisticated applications to control its supply chain.

monitoring of the entire organization and provide essential information to the functions of SCM. Imagine trying to place orders to suppliers for a toy manufacturer without an ERP system. The major difficulty in legacy systems was coordinating and synchronizing data sets to ensure that inventory levels, purchasing requirements, and production plans were all based on accurate information to meet upcoming orders. In today's business world, a manager is constantly aware of customer demand information and can instantly revise purchasing, staffing, financial, and production information based on an integrated ERP system.

Business Intelligence Software

In an era of information overload, it is essential for companies to have strong data analysis tools to identify critical operating information. At Wal-Mart, data warehousing and data mining assist in better understanding which items sell and which do not; which tend to sell with other specific items; and what types of people shop at particular Wal-Mart stores. That means better decisions in merchandising, inventory and pricing.

A number of software tools and techniques have emerged to turn raw data into business information, such as data mining techniques, decision support systems (DSS), and most recently business intelligence software. As discussed in the previous section, ERP systems allow organizations to capture data, and many of these systems include analysis tools such as SAP's Business Warehouse (BW) and Executive Information System (EIS) modules. The SAP EIS functions enable high-level reporting of data and are intended to simplify the analysis of data for information appropriate to decision makers. Most organizations, however, have traditionally determined that custom reports are necessary for their specific organization, which is where the Business Warehouse module is targeted. This data warehouse allows for customized queries and reporting to be carried out, based on the SAP data.

Cognos Inc.
www.cognos.com

Business intelligence and specialized software makers such as SAS and Cognos Inc. have emerged to improve the usability, impact, and understanding of critical data. For example, Cognos products allow organizations to integrate any data source (such as ERP, legacy system, and website data) into one business intelligence system. Cognos products can then be customized with preset, company-specific information such as quality level warnings, whereby returns under warranty related to a specific supplier would be automatically flagged. This information can be more carefully examined through a drill-down interface to determine source locations, manufacturing dates, and other critical information that can then be passed back to the supplier. The system also allows the company to establish a web browser-based interface for suppliers to log into and analyze the data in their own way, thus providing a high level of information sharing.

Business intelligence software is primarily used to address critical issues in supply chain management, such as information analysis and information sharing. As the pace of change accelerates, the usefulness of business intelligence increases exponentially. Chapter 9 delves more deeply into the features, capabilities, and uses of business intelligence software.

Application Service Providers

The growth of application service providers (ASPs) is affecting SCM in a number of ways. ASPs are allowing companies to access software through the internet without hosting and maintaining the systems in-house. This method of providing technology is expected to grow rapidly for several years, since it enables businesses to select core components of ERP applications or other software at lower cost. To date, logistics and supply chain software have experienced difficulty in providing technology through the ASP model because customization is often required for each business. However, as standards develop and ERP providers increasingly move toward ASP models, the provision of SCM technology through the internet will become much more commonplace.

Strategic SCM

To operate effectively, an organization must employ its technology strategically. The adoption of leading-edge technology will yield little benefit unless it is used to facilitate corporate goals, and the same is true of SCM software and applications. The technology to be chosen for SCM must be carefully planned and coordinated so that benefits may be achieved through integration and information.

Boeing recognized that its supply chain was in crucial need of revision in 1997 when delays forced the closure of its production facilities. Since that time, Boeing has planned extensively to build its new technological infrastructure, which consists of its ERP backbone (provided by SSA Global Technologies Inc.), forecasting software (provided by i2 Technologies), factory floor software, and internet communication tools.[3] Each of the applications was implemented with a common goal in mind—to turn Boeing's assembly line and supply chain into a highly efficient operation. Starting with a backbone ERP system, Boeing added applications that would allow it to more specifically target areas crucial to its success. Given that the lead-time to order a plane was approximately three years in the late 1990s, it was essential to be able to forecast several years in advance to achieve supply chain effectiveness. As such, Boeing adopted i2 Technologies' forecasting software to allow for advanced planning, and also changed many manual processes to EDI and internet transactions. For example, customers can order parts through the Boeing PART webpage. In addition to adopting technological solutions, Boeing carried out product changes to streamline internal processes. The core components of the aircraft were redesigned to allow for a more "Henry Ford"-like production line, with customization taking place at the end of the process wherever possible.

Boeing provides a good example of a company that made strategic use of technology: it established a strategic vision for its supply chain, adopted technological applications in support of that vision, and made process changes internally and externally in support of its strategy. Strategy, not technology, must drive the business!

Boeing
www.boeing.com

SSA Global Technologies Inc.
www.baan.com

Business Process Reengineering

Business process reengineering (BPR) was popularized with Hammer and Champy's *Reengineering the Corporation*, and reflects the requirements of corporations to initiate change to fundamental business processes as a result of the changing business world. They define a business process as "a collection of activities that takes one or more kinds of input and creates an output that is of value to the customer."[4] In terms of SCM, business processes include procurement processes, internal operations, sales processes, and numerous other fundamental processes in the business. As discussed in the previous section, the evolution of e-business is requiring that companies change business processes as technological advances are made to achieve success. The adoption of ERP, forecasting tools, and e-procurement are all changes that will require an organization to re-evaluate and often revise its business processes.

An often-cited business process re-engineering initiative was taken by Ford Motor Company in the early 1990s. At that time, Ford's North American accounting department employed 500 people in its accounts payable area and management thought that by rationalization and automation this could be reduced to 400. However, it then noticed that Mazda (part-owned by Ford in Japan) had an accounting workforce of only five people doing essentially the same task! By reengineering the process, much of the paperwork and crosschecking associated with the department's tasks was either eliminated or automated. As a result, Ford achieved a 75 percent reduction in headcount, not 20 percent.

Ford used to have its purchasing department prepare a three-part purchase order, one part each for purchasing, the vendor, and accounts payable. When goods were received, the receiving department prepared a multi-copy receiving report and sent one copy to accounts payable and kept the other. The vendor prepared a multi-copy invoice and sent a copy to accounts payable. More than 500 people worked in accounts payable matching 14 different data items on the three documents and trying to reconcile all the mismatches. Payments were delayed, vendors were unhappy, and the process was time consuming and frustrating for all the parties.

In Ford's reengineered system, purchasing agents enter their purchase orders into a database application and forward an electronic copy to the vendor. Vendors ship the goods but send no invoice. When goods arrive, the receiving clerk enters three items of data into the system: part number, unit of measure, and supplier code. The computer matches the receiving information with the outstanding purchase order data. If they do not match, the goods are returned. If they match, the goods are accepted and the computer sends an electronic funds transfer payment to the vendor. The reengineered system has saved Ford a significant amount of money and time, and has been a widely quoted example of BPR.[5]

Business process change can occur at three major levels—streamlining, reengineering, or organizational change.[6] Streamlining involves relatively minor changes or "tweaking" of existing business processes to facilitate changes occurring in the business. Business process reengineering is defined as "fundamental rethinking and radical redesign"[7] of existing processes and is therefore a large undertaking. Organizational change has been described as the creation of a process organization by modification of organizational structure.

In a process organization, new management-level positions are created that focus on maximization of process efficiency. As discussed in chapter 4, ERP systems such as SAP require that specific processes be adopted to facilitate the technology's "best practices" model. The adopting corporation's current processes often determine the extent of change required, because streamlining may be adequate in cases where processes are similar.

Many organizations have achieved tremendous results through reengineering. IBM's senior vice-president of technology and manufacturing stated, "As we set out to reengineer our company, we knew that having world-class information technology simply wasn't enough. Since speed and efficiency were fundamental elements of our strategy, we needed entirely new approaches to our operations management."[8] Through technological innovation and reengineering of operations, IBM saved hundreds of millions of dollars (see the Global Perspective box for more information).

ERP systems are not the only cause of business process change. When organizations begin to more closely integrate with supply chain members, it is often necessary to align processes more closely with other organizations. For example, assume a key supplier of e-Co wishes to be able to quickly monitor demand to adjust its production plans. To facilitate this information sharing, e-Co

CASH-TO-CASH CYCLE
The length of time from purchasing materials until a product is manufactured.

E-Business in Global Perspective

Refining the Global Supply Chain and Service Call Management at IBM

International Business Machines (IBM) Corporation is one of the world's largest technology companies, operating in over 160 countries worldwide. The range of services and products provided by IBM includes manufacturing, software design/sales, personal computers, servers, and after-sales service. Revenues were over US$90 billion in 2004. Operating on such a large scale requires IBM to have an effective supply chain strategy in place, ensuring that research and development, purchasing, manufacturing, delivery, and sales channels are all properly integrated to deliver products on time, within budget, and of superior quality.

Global Supply Chain Reengineering

In the mid-1990s, IBM decided that inventory levels were too high and that customer service levels could be improved. Operations analysts began reviewing the supply chain and determined that the length of time from purchasing materials until the product was manufactured (called the **cash-to-cash cycle**) was excessive. The results of a long cash-to-cash cycle include increased inventory levels, customer service delays, excessive write-offs of obsolete inventory, and high dealer discounts.

To improve the global supply chain, IBM needed to develop a strategic approach to improvement. Management determined that in-house expertise within the IBM Research division would be able to assist in the development of a simulation tool that was named the Asset Management Tool (AMT). The AMT is a sophisticated optimization tool that examines inventory levels, forecasts, supplier information, and products to develop optimal supply chain plans. In addition, AMT must be able to integrate foreign currency transactions, duties, tariffs, and tax concerns to make accurate decisions. Given that IBM deals with such large volumes of product, the AMT needs to carry out many analytical functions. For example, AMT analyzes products manufactured in all countries to identify common parts requirements and carries out detailed analysis of shipping and purchasing costs, combined with activity-based costing methods, to determine whether all parts should be sourced from common locations or sourced from the nearest company. This analysis can now be carried out across the 3000 hardware and 20 000 software products and analyzed in further detail by supplier. Essentially, AMT demonstrates the need for advanced systems in large organizations that can accommodate uncertainty.

The global reengineering initiative has netted IBM in excess of US$750 million and reduced the cash-to-cash cycle by four weeks to six weeks. The goal of reduced cost and improved customer service was met, and IBM continues to improve its world-class SCM practices.

Service Call Management

IBM also recognized that the increasing complexity of its Global Services division was an area where effective planning could improve results. Dealing with approximately 22 000 service calls per day, more than 7000 service representatives need to be sched-uled throughout the world. At first glance, one could assume that this task could be simple—just give each representative three or four service calls per day. However, factoring in the diverse products, parts availability, language, location, call/problem complexity, and service representative expertise, the task becomes overwhelming.

Once again the IBM Research group was called in to help develop a customized solution, after a manager recognized the similarity of the situation's complexity to chess. The IBM Research group had been able to develop algorithms for the chess match between then-world-champion Gary Kasparov and IBM's Deep Blue computer. The programming was designed to handle the multiple iterations of moving chess pieces and was also able to develop an advanced call centre management system for Global Services.

The solution is able to analyze huge volumes of data to reduce customer response time and minimize idle time, travel costs, and delays by focusing on the integration of data. Available service reps are first assigned to service calls as they come in (by qualifications), and then the system begins to optimize the assignments through global and local locations by analyzing costs and other factors. The schedule needs to be recomputed every 10 minutes to ensure that new service calls are allocated in an optimal manner—often juggling the calls already within the system. IBM estimates that the time spent at service calls has been reduced by 10 to 35 percent through better assignment, and that idle time has decreased as much as five-fold in some locations.

IBM
www.ibm.com

Questions

1. In a large company like IBM, how can management be sure that the supply chain initiatives are improving operations?
2. Can other organizations effectively manage service calls like IBM without the use of high-technology systems?
3. What complications does the global operation of IBM add to the supply chain management process?

SOURCES: IBM United States website, **www.ibm.com**/, accessed April 19, 2004; Brenda Dietrich, et al., "Big Benefits for Big Blue," *OR/MS Today* (June 2000).

may decide to use an extranet to share inventory levels, customer orders, and sales forecasts with this supplier. However, e-Co has always been very cautious in releasing information related to sales and also guards its forecasts closely. In addition, e-Co's production manager meets with the purchasing department manager once every two weeks to establish appropriate purchase order amounts. For the extranet to provide useful information, e-Co will have to modify business processes such as budgeting and ordering. As such, the duties of the production and purchasing managers will also change. This simple example illustrates how information sharing and technology adoption can result in tremendous change within an organization—e-business must be willing to embrace change to achieve success.

Trust, and Partnerships of the Supply Chain

Throughout this chapter we have discussed the need to form supply chain partnerships to achieve success. Forming partnerships, however, is only partially facilitated through the use of technological tools discussed earlier. Sharing information is a difficult task in a business world where traditionally information has been safeguarded. In this next section, partnership formation is discussed in further detail from the perspective of managing relationships.

Forming partnerships and strategic alliances in the supply chain are as crucial to supply chain success as the technology and information systems. Appropriate sharing of critical information will not take place unless both exist. Establishing strong lines of communication is the first step in ensuring that supply partnerships will succeed. Since the technology is only an enabler of the information sharing, decisions need to be made about what information should be shared, when, and who is responsible for it. Clarifying these basic terms early will help to develop trust.

Supply chain success can often be attributed to the development of a relationship based on trust. Trust involves one party having confidence in or relying on another party to fulfill its obligations. The existence of trust in a relationship reduces the perception of risk associated with opportunistic behaviour and allows each party to believe that its needs will be fulfilled in the future by actions taken by the other party.[9] As in personal relationships, trust is formed over time and begins with honest and open communication among parties. Having appropriate managers involved in the partnership development is key to success.

A mere win–win agreement is not enough to ensure high performance. Measurements are need to test the performance of each link to establish an overall control whereby the actions truly support the global chain. The downstream links need to ensure fast response to any market opportunity, while the upstream links need to validate that sales are generated from what is already in the system.

One criterion that could be used to measure the performance of a vendor is late orders, and how late they were, along with the financial value of the order. A common problem at the seller's site is that orders that cannot be fulfilled are not registered, even though the specific sale has been lost! Hence, the full damage caused by the unavailability of products cannot be directly measured. This measurement is specific and motivates all the parties to do what is good for the chain as a whole.

The relationship of trust can be created more quickly if discussions centre on:

- realignment
- service level agreement
- performance measurement
- dispute resolution
- security

Realignment

The creation of a supply chain partnership does not simply entail setting up an extranet and sharing information. In many cases, realigning work responsibilities, selectively outsourcing, and realigning decision-making will help achieve success. For example, many organizations have realigned the decision-making related to purchasing by moving toward vendor-managed inventory. **Vendor-managed inventory (VMI)** is the process by which suppliers take over monitoring inventory levels through the use of technology and are responsible for replenishment of stock. Wal-Mart has adopted the use of VMI for many of its products, thus reducing the reliance on internal decision-making and allowing suppliers such as Procter & Gamble to be responsible for their own products. Research has shown that VMI often leads to reduced inventory levels and substantially lower stockout rates,[10] as suppliers are keen to ensure that consumers are always able to purchase their products.

Selective outsourcing may be necessary or economically feasible in some supply chains for functions that are traditionally problematic. For example, if both partners evaluate the outcomes as positive, transportation of rush orders may be outsourced to courier companies to reduce costs and improve delivery times. Outsourcing may also mean the movement of work from one organization to another in the supply chain to improve overall supply chain effectiveness. Outsourcing decisions will vary by industry but should always be made on the basis of improving customer value, reducing complexity, and/or controlling costs.

VENDOR-MANAGED INVENTORY (VMI)
The process by which suppliers take over monitoring inventory levels through the use of technology and are responsible for replenishment of stock.

Service Level Agreement

A service level agreement (SLA) is fundamental to service provision from the perspective of both the supplier and the recipient.[11] It essentially documents and defines the parameters of a supplier–customer relationship. The quality of the service level agreement is therefore a critical matter that merits careful attention.

An SLA is wide in scope, covering all key aspects of the service to be delivered and such issues as problem management, compensation (often essential in terms of motivation), warranties and remedies, resolution of disputes and legal compliance. It essentially frames the relationship, and determines the major responsibilities, both in times of normal operation and during an emergency situation.

Performance Measurement

Performance measurement is a complex task in any setting, and e-business changes the dynamics of performance measurement by changing the dynamics of information and rate of change. To allow supply chain partners to contribute positively to the partnership and later evaluate the relationship, partners should create joint metrics for performance measurement. Establishing the terms by which success will be measured at the onset allows partners to develop plans to meet those goals.

Performance measurement goals should be established for delivery timelines, decision effectiveness, quality procedures, and any other outcomes that are considered important to the relationship. The partnership can also make use of benchmarking studies to establish realistic goals, which can later be re-evaluated. For example, Wal-Mart uses BridgePoint software to assess supplier performance and identifies opportunities to improve cycle times and other performance measures. Suppliers can review these results in scorecards posted online.

Dispute Resolution

Given that we are in an age of lawsuits and expensive legal battles, it is wise, as with other business functions, to take dispute resolution into account in supply chain planning. Supply chain partners need to document and plan ahead for areas of concern such as security, copyright, and asset title when changes to the supply chain process take place. Trademark and copyright concerns need to be dealt with up front so that partners are willing to share critical information without the risk of losing a "trade secret." In addition, simple changes to the process can result in confusing terms of title that should be clarified with contracts and partnership agreements. As in health, prevention (of disputes) is the best medicine.

Security

Sharing information digitally poses additional concerns to security in the supply chain partnership. Security issues such as remote access and data warehouse sharing over extranets or virtual private networks should be clearly documented and monitored to ensure that security breaches do not occur. Partners need to establish policies that each is comfortable with and may monitor the compliance continually (and may be included in internal and external audits as well).

Essentially, trust will be the result of a well-planned and communicated supply chain partnership. Managing the changes in sharing of confidential information and job duty modification will often be a major task. As all of the issues are considered, we see that e-business and SCM are major business issues.

Order Fulfillment/Delivery

Order fulfillment has emerged as a critical component of the supply chain in the e-business era. In the early 2000s and the Christmas of 1999, fulfillment failures and difficulties tarnished the reputations of many e-tailers, including toy sellers and electronics retailers. The inability of many dot-coms to deliver goods on time for Christmas tarnished the growth of e-commerce and disappointed a number of children waiting for Barbie and Hot Wheels models, or computer systems. Since that time, a number of new fulfillment possibilities have emerged, and organizations—both bricks-and-mortar and dot-com—have dedicated substantial management and financial resources to modifying the fulfillment process.

The 1999 e-commerce problems were to a great extent the result of unexpected demand, combined with underdeveloped supply chains and inventory control, and unrealistic delivery promises. In addition, the relatively new supply chains often lacked full integration on the B2B end, which resulted in increased pressure on the e-tailers to take late shipments and turn them into on-time deliveries, often at excessive costs. Admittedly, at the early stages of e-commerce, demand was unknown; however, many of the early e-tailers had committed relatively little to planning and were focused on other important areas such as security and advertising. General business studies have taught us that a business is an integrated enterprise, and emphasis on select functional areas at the expense of others often leads to failure.

Order fulfillment is a set of processes involved in delivering a product to a customer. It consists of many procedures grouped into the main areas of order processing, warehousing, and shipping and transportation planning (see figure 7.6). Order fulfillment is the front-end and back-end processes necessary to convert an order into a sale by completing the company's responsibility of providing a product or service. **Order processing** includes activities that take place during the fulfillment of an order, such as credit checks, inventory availability determination, accounting, billing, and replenishment requests. A great deal of the work in order processing is now automated through ERP and web-based systems.

Warehousing refers to all tasks involved with handling inventory. This includes processes such as receiving orders of inventory from suppliers (if not previously in stock), picking, organizing, and packaging goods for delivery. Initial attempts by online sellers to have suppliers package orders for shipment direct to the consumer had to be revised as customers began ordering multiple products and were dissatisfied with receiving multiple deliveries. Consider, for example, Wine.com (originally Virtual Vineyards), an e-tailer of wines and other gift products. When a customer ordered wines from the California region, Wine.com would relay the orders to individual vineyards for shipment to the consumer. Ordering wine from more than one vineyard would result in an inconvenience to the customer who might receive delivery at various times. As a result, Wine.com needed to centralize its fulfillment centre into a warehouse to provide quality service to customers.

Shipping and transportation planning (STP) is the process of transporting finished goods to the consumer quickly and efficiently. STP requires

ORDER FULFILLMENT
A set of processes involved in delivering a product to the customer. It consists of procedures grouped into the main areas of order processing, warehousing, and shipping and transportation planning.

ORDER PROCESSING
Activities that take place during the fulfillment of an order. These include credit checks, inventory availability determination, accounting, billing, and replenishment requests.

WAREHOUSING
All tasks involved with handling inventory. These processes include receiving orders of inventory from suppliers, picking, organizing, and packaging goods for delivery.

SHIPPING AND TRANSPORTATION PLANNING (STP)
The process of transporting the finished goods to the consumer quickly and efficiently.

Figure 7.6 The Order Fulfillment Process

Order fulfillment includes many business processes in areas such as order processing, warehousing, and shipping and transportation planning.

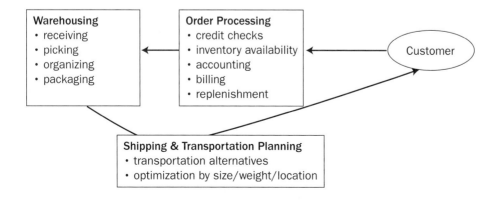

RFID TAG
Radio-frequency identification
tags placed on shipping crates
and pallets that contain embedded electronic product codes that
can be used for tracking and
identifying items at the individual
crate and pallet level.

Toys "Я" Us (online)
www.toysrus.com

businesses to coordinate all their orders cost-effectively by analyzing sizes, weights, packaging, and transportation alternatives. Like many other e-business functions discussed in this book, STP and order fulfillment require the use of sophisticated technologies to implement.

Wal-Mart announced in June 2003 that it plans to require its top 100 suppliers to put radio-frequency identification (RFID) tags on shipping crates and pallets by January 2005. This would result in the deployment of nearly 1 billion **RFID tags** with embedded electronic product codes (EPC) for tracking and identifying items at the individual crate and pallet level. RFID tags can gather and track a variety of data related to products, materials, and more, though Wal-Mart will initially concentrate on using the technology to further improve inventory management in the supply chain. The tags can store more detailed information than conventional bar codes, enabling tracking of items at the unit level. Wal-Mart's announcement provided a thrust to the wider adoption of RFID, as several companies announced their intention to start using the technology, which has so far had low adoption due to the high cost and a lack of standards.

Fulfillment is similar to the "moment of truth" in service organizations, whereby delivery of a quality service or product is the only thing that a customer truly sees. The moment of truth is the critical moment in a service transaction when the customer's expectations are met, exceeded, or disappointed. The customer is not aware of or concerned with how complex the supply chain is or the number of processes involved—the customer wants to receive what was ordered, when it was promised, and at the cost quoted. To meet these needs, many companies have chosen to outsource the fulfillment function to remain focused on core competencies. For example, Toys "Я" Us decided to outsource its fulfillment function for online orders to Amazon to focus on inventory management and procurement, which are complicated processes in the toy industry.[12] Amazon had strong fulfillment capabilities in place and could capitalize on existing infrastructure, allowing Toys "Я" Us to control internal functions, manage its upstream supply chain, and concentrate on its new e-strategy.

A growing number of outsourcing companies are emerging, including some of the well-known courier companies like FedEx and UPS. UPS signed an agreement with Samsung Electro-Mechanics Co. in the fall of 2000 to provide outsourced global supply chain management services. The UPS Logistics Group offers services such as supply chain analysis, transportation, brokerage, and financing to companies wishing to move SCM outside of the organization.[13] Samsung determined that its focus should remain on quality, production, and management, and UPS offered a competitive price, leading technology, and proven expertise.[14] Partnerships and outsourcing with firms such as UPS and FedEx have allowed many organizations to reduce the demands of SCM. While outsourcing is common, it can be an expensive alternative to in-house management and should be carefully evaluated. The size of an organization, product features, industry, and complexity of the supply chain will all affect the costs of carrying out SCM.

Large organizations with established management structures and supply chain expertise can develop top-performing fulfillment systems by capitalizing on technological structures already in place. ERP systems hold a great deal of the information required to develop efficient fulfillment, such as inventory information (quantities on hand and on order, delivery information, backorders), customer information (credit limits, shipping addresses), and financial information (sales prices, shipping cost information, etc.). To leverage the information in the ERP system it is necessary to ensure that fulfillment is based on ERP data and

Canadian Snapshots

Descartes Systems Group

Descartes Systems Group is a Waterloo, Ontario-based provider of inter-enterprise execution software for supply chain management. The company's products are geared towards delivery-sensitive organizations with short time-to-plan horizons. For these companies, successful execution is essential to success: delivery is a component of product value and failure to perform may be catastrophic to their business. Descartes' product family offers a complete portfolio of software solutions that streamline the entire order-to-delivery process.

Market Differentiation

Descartes differentiates itself through the broad functionality of its solutions, application of leading edge technologies, and its inter-enterprise focus on the supply chain. Descartes designs solutions from an inter-enterprise perspective for global companies with mul-

tiple trading partners. By approaching the supply chain from this perspective, Descartes has created a complete order-to-delivery solution that companies can rely on to manage their current and emerging supply chain requirements.

Descartes offers integrated solution for the highly fragmented software application market for logistics industries. Descartes offers three value-added networks (VANs) to serve as a central communications infrastructure for companies. Millions of logistics-related messages are exchanged via the Descartes VANs each month to provide companies with real-time visibility into their supply chains. These messages are also recorded in the VANs' data repositories. Descartes integrated Cognos' PowerPlay and Impromptu solutions to provide a means of querying the information about actual logistics activities that take place throughout a company's supply chain over

the VAN and analyzing the performance of their supply chain to identify inefficiencies and bottlenecks.

Customers and Markets Served

Descartes provides solutions for delivery-sensitive organizations that view delivery as a component of product value, recognize that failure to deliver may be catastrophic to their business, and have high velocity, complex or changing delivery chains. Initially, such companies were found in the food and beverage industries. However, Descartes has found that such "delivery-centric" companies represent an ever-broadening range of industry groups, such as courier services, newspapers, hotels, electronics, etc. To date, Descartes has implemented solutions for companies in over 35 industries and has built a client base of more than 2500 customers in 60 countries worldwide.

Descartes Systems Group
www.descartes.com

Questions

1. Why would companies use Descartes systems and services rather than implementing their own version of Descartes' systems?
2. What are the critical success factors for a company like Descartes?

SOURCES: Descartes Systems Group website, **www.descartes.com**, accessed April 19, 2004; Descartes Systems Group, Public Relations, Annette Van Gerwen, "Cognos Solutions Offered over the Descartes Network" *DSStar* 5, no. 32 (August 7, 2001).

integrated with the SCM system to deliver real-time updates. Order status information needs to be provided back to the ERP system from custom applications (such as shopping cart applications or shipping partner data, so that data need not be entered twice) and allows customer service to provide meaningful feedback to customer service calls. The Canadian Snapshots box explores one company's solution to the technological side of supply chain management.

Warehousing concerns have resulted in major changes within e-business as companies strive to reduce delivery times while controlling costs. The classic example is that of Amazon.com. Amazon's original business model was to operate as an online sales organization with no inventory on hand. Amazon chose to move from a "pure play" e-business model to a "bricks and clicks" business that holds some inventory in strategically located warehouses throughout the United States. Amazon now stocks high-volume books in high-tech warehouses and has the ability to better meet its objectives of shipping overnight for most customer orders. Wine.com has taken a similar approach by using warehouses as storage points for high-volume items and as a receiving point for integrating and packaging orders. Many online retailers have found that it is often necessary to hold some inventories to provide rapid customer service and delivery.

As shipping and transportation companies embrace technological advances in business it becomes easier to provide high levels of customer service. UPS and FedEx allow customers to track packages on the internet by entering an identification number. The ability of these transportation service providers to deliver information at all stages of the delivery channel is made possible through information systems and internet technology. In addition, wireless devices are enabling businesses to better provide services to customers. For example, AirIQ Inc., a Pickering, Ontario-based company, has developed a tool through which transporters set up tracking components in each truck. A central server customized to each transportation service provider captures fleet information with the aid of a global positioning system (GPS) and 24 satellites. The management of the transportation service provider then views fleet activities using a standard internet browser.

In an age where delivery speed is often measured in hours or days, this type of information becomes crucial to success. The combination of wireless and internet technologies is creating excellent opportunities for transportation and other companies to gain substantial benefits throughout the fulfillment process—improving customer service, increasing revenue, and controlling costs all at the same time.

AirIQ Inc.
www.airiq.com

Reverse Logistics

Internet research has demonstrated that returning products is both a concern for buyers and an important issue for sellers. **Reverse logistics** is the internal process through which customers can return items purchased, either for a refund or for repair or replacement under warranty. Having an effective mechanism for dealing with returns is helpful in making sales but also must be designed to guard against fraud.

Bricks-and-mortar businesses that have been in the catalogue sales business have dealt with the problem of returns for many years. However, pure online stores need to establish policies, drop-off locations, and credit procedures to effectively handle returns. For instance, clothing e-tailers quickly found that customers would purchase a medium and a large of the same style and then return the item that did not fit properly. Without proper procedures in place, the return of items can be very costly—incurring shipping costs, banking and transaction costs, and the expense of storing and dealing with excess inventory. Policies that assist with returns include many items that are common to retailing such as time limits on returns, responsibility for shipping costs, and reasonable use limitations for warranty-related concerns. Establishing clear policies and communicating them to customers assists greatly in controlling reverse logistics.

Outsourcing has once again become an important strategy in dealing with reverse logistics. For example, Buy.com Inc. determined that having an effective delivery system encouraged customers to purchase products and have confidence in the company. Initially, Buy.com allowed customers to make returns by calling

REVERSE LOGISTICS
The internal processes for handling customer returns, either for a refund or for repair or replacement under warranty.

and obtaining an authorization code, and then later a mailing label would be sent to the customer for the product's return. The process was cumbersome and slow, so Buy.com outsourced the function to UPS. Customers now obtain authorization for returns online and can enter their authorization code into the returns section of the website, which enables them to print out their own packaging label from UPS. The package can then be dropped off at a UPS location or picked up by the courier service. Once again, customer service has dominated.

C-Commerce: The Future

The Gartner Group coined the term **collaborative commerce** (c-commerce) in late 1999 in a strategic planning note examining the future of e-business.[15] C-commerce is the application of technologies to allow trading partners to synchronize and optimize their partnerships and is performed in collaboration. As SCM and other applications develop, we will watch c-commerce emerge as an extremely important component of the supply chain, facilitating strong relationships, fuelling efficiency, and driving customer-oriented decisions. For example, Wal-Mart's supply chain management program, also known as Collaborative Planning, Forecasting, and Replenishment (CPFR), aims "to sell as much product as possible without either the supplier or Wal-Mart having too much inventory." Some analysts believe that Wal-Mart saves 5 to 10 percent in cost of goods through the use of technology in its streamlined supply chain. The reason Wal-Mart has had so much success is that its supply chain management practices have benefited not only the retailer but its suppliers as well.

Essentially, c-commerce is the advanced stage of many of the topics discussed in this chapter. It involves employing technology to improve partnerships, gain efficiency in processes, make effective decisions, and satisfy the customer. Trading exchanges and customer relationship management are part of the development of c-commerce and are discussed later in this book.

COLLABORATIVE COMMERCE
The application of technologies to allow trading partners to synchronize and optimize their partnerships; performed in collaboration.

Chapter Summary

Supply chain management is the process of coordinating and managing the product, information, and financial flows among members of the supply chain. As e-business has emerged, SCM has become an important aspect of success by allowing businesses to gain efficiencies and improve customer service in a fast-paced environment. The internet-enabled supply chain has a customer focus from the beginning, whereby the entire chain is driven by the pull of the customer.

Technology is an important component of SCM. ERP systems provide the backbone for information exchange. The internet provides the medium through which much communication and "collaboration" take place. Extranets and other technologies allow partners to securely share information in a convenient, cost-effective, and user-friendly manner.

Strategy plays a key role in SCM by setting the direction for partners to work toward. Like many other aspects of business, technology is a critical tool for SCM, but success is achieved by making strategic decisions and effectively managing the people who employ the technologies. Companies like Dell have employed SCM to achieve their goal of providing the customer with customized products, at a competitive price, within a short period of time.

Key Terms

cash-to-cash cycle   [p. 134]
collaborative commerce   [p. 143]
disintermediation   [p. 127]
logistics   [p. 124]
order fulfillment   [p. 139]
order processing   [p. 139]
pull system   [p. 127]
push system   [p. 124]

reintermediation   [p. 129]
reverse logistics   [p. 142]
RFID tag   [p. 140]
shipping and transportation planning   [p. 139]
supply chain management (SCM)   [p. 124]
vendor-managed inventory   [p. 137]
warehousing   [p. 139]

Tools for Online Learning

To help you master the material in this chapter and stay up to date with new developments in e-business, visit www.pearsoned.ca/trites. Resources include:

- **Review Questions and Exercises**

- **Problems for Discussion**

- **Recommended Readings**

- **Updates to Case Studies and Textual Material**

- **Streaming CBC Videos with Cases**

Endnotes

1. Advertising Supplement, *Canadian Business* (September, 2000).

2. Philip Evans and Thomas S. Wurster, *Blown to Bits: How the New Economics of Information Transforms Strategy* (Boston, MA: Harvard Business School Press, 2000), 237.

3. Tom Stein and Jeff Sweat, "Killer Supply Chains," *Informationweek* (November 9, 1998).

4. Michael Hammer and James Champy, *Reengineering the Corporation* (New York: HarperCollins Publishers, 1994), 35.

5. J. Peppard and P. Rowland, *The Essence of Business Process Reengineering* (London: Prentice Hall, 1995).

6. Gerald Trites, *Enterprise Resource Planning—The Engine for E-Business* (Toronto: CICA, 2000).

7. Michael Hammer and Steven Stanton, *The Reengineering Revolution* (New York: HarperCollins, 1995).

8. Brenda Dietrich et al., "Big Benefits for Big Blue," *OR/MS Today* (June 2000).

9. Kevin R. Moore, "Trust and Relationship Commitment in Logistics Alliances: A Buyer Perspective," *International Journal of Purchasing and Materials Management* 34 (1988): 24–37.

10. Hau Lee, "Creating Value through Supply Chain Integration," *Supply Chain Management Review* (September/October 2000).

11. "The Service Level Agreement," *IT Infrastructure Library*, Office of Government Commerce, www.itil-itsm-world.com/itil-sla.htm, accessed April 19, 2004.

12. Bob Tedeschi, "Internet Merchants, Seeing Landscape Shift, Adapt to Survive," *The New York Times*, 18 December 2000.

13. UPS Global website, www.ups-scs.com, accessed April 19, 2004.

14. Samsung Digital World website, www.pressroom.ups.com/pressreleases/archives/archive/0,1363,3827,00.html, accessed April 19, 2004.

15. B. Bond et al, "C-Commerce: The New Arena for Business Applications," Gartner Group research document (August, 1999).

— CHAPTER **8**

E-Procurement, Trading Exchanges, and Auctions

LEARNING OBJECTIVES

When you complete this chapter you should be able to:

1. Explain the e-procurement process and why e-procurement is important in today's business world.

2. Outline the major benefits of e-procurement and what types of goods are often procured.

3. Describe trading exchanges and what functions they have.

4. Explain the issues exchange providers are facing.

5. Categorize auctions and explain how the different types could be used.

6. Identify the critical stages of the auctioning process and describe how an auction would be carried out online.

Introduction

Businesses have become increasingly interested in the area of e-procurement as a means of cutting costs and improving efficiency in the early 2000s. While the dot-com craze of the late 1990s corrected itself and disappointed many, the benefits of B2B transactions, e-procurement, and trading exchanges are starting to be realized. A variety of strategies have been adopted in the B2B arena in an attempt to capitalize on the benefits. For example, the Marriott and Hyatt hotel chains moved their procurement staffs outside the organization into a joint venture called Avendra LLC. Raytheon, a large U.S. defence contractor, has used its own in-house e-procurement efforts to "rationalize" its number of suppliers and cut costs, while also using outsourced procurement services from Ariba Inc.[1] While a variety of strategies are used, one thing is clear—e-procurement is a critical area of e-business that will continue to evolve for the next several years as companies strive to achieve completely digital, integrated B2B e-commerce. In this chapter we will examine the e-procurement process, trading exchanges, implementation challenges, and directions for future development.

Marriott
www.marriott.com

Hyatt
www.hyatt.com

Raytheon
www.raytheon.com

E-procurement can be defined broadly as the complete business process of acquiring goods through electronic means, from requisition through to fulfillment and payment. The process of e-procurement involves more than just the purchasing of goods, as it deals more broadly with the complete cycle, including selection and payment.

The E-Procurement Process

The e-procurement process can be illustrated by referring to figure 8.1. The process itself will vary somewhat by organization, but a simplified analysis of the components will allow us to better understand the concept. Once a firm identifies a need for a good or service, an employee would begin the selection process to find a good or service to fill the need. This process could be carried out through catalogues, either online or through the corporate intranet, through a trading exchange, or by examining websites of potential vendors. Other possibilities such as negotiated prices and auctions will be discussed later. Once the employee has identified the specific good or service to be procured and an appropriate supplier, he or she would create a requisition electronically and forward it to the appropriate signing officer if approval is required. Purchases of specific types of goods or within certain dollar limits may be automatically approved by the system.

The approval of the requisition will result in the creation of a purchase order that will be transmitted to the supplier firm. The transmission could take place in any number of formats including EDI, XML, or through a secure internet transaction in another format. The transmission of the purchase order may occur directly through a trading exchange, through the internet, or through a proprietary VAN, depending on the technologies of the firms involved.

The supplier firm may then carry out all of its fulfillment processes and arrange for transportation to the buyer firm, if required. In the case of a purchase of goods, once the buyer receives the goods, the payment process will begin. The receiving information should be entered in the buyer's ERP/accounting system to update inventory, and when the invoice is received it is matched to the receiving information and purchase order to confirm receipt of the entire order as well as pricing information. The accounts payable will be paid in the normal sequence by the buyer, and again the format of this would depend on the partic-

Figure 8.1   The E-Procurement Process

E-procurement encompasses numerous tasks that are increasingly being carried out in integrated, electronic formats.

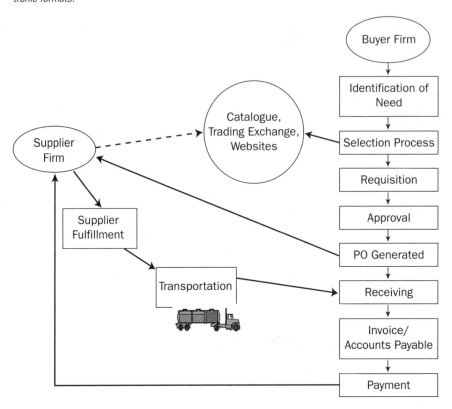

ular circumstances. Increasingly, the steps described in this process are carried out electronically and integrated into the back office systems.

Surprisingly, the level of integration achieved in these processes by many large companies is rather limited. Texas Instruments claimed that it wished to emphasize efforts on improving its own capabilities and those of its suppliers to integrate systems to expand the products acquired through e-procurement. A great deal of information was passed through e-mail and spreadsheets and then later re-keyed into their ERP system, leading to inefficiencies and errors.[2] Many organizations have identified improved integration as a key issue for stimulating B2B transactions through trading exchanges and e-procurement, thus creating a lucrative opportunity for technology firms in this area.

Goods and Services Procured

When e-procurement began, the most common use was for the purchase of office supplies and maintenance, repair, and operating (MRO) items. As businesses began to realize the potential for cost savings, the purchases expanded into computer equipment and corporate travel services, and later into production-related goods such as raw materials.

It is critical that processes for e-procurement be established when considering the types of goods and services being acquired so that e-procurement can be both efficient and effective. Like paper-based transactions, the dollar value and urgency of the purchase impact how processes function and how quickly they occur. Despite this, it is important to keep the electronic processes in check. Consider the following example from Microsoft, where Bill Gates discovered inefficiency within digital processes:

> I thought every company had this kind of explicit review for expense approval. I learned I was wrong when I demonstrated our intranet to a group of CEOs. Paul O'Neill of Alcoa, which is the world's leading producer of aluminum, came up to me after my talk and asked, "It's great that everything is digital and efficient, but why should you have to review expense reports? You've got better things to do with your time."[3]

This example illustrates exactly what businesses must be careful not to do— simply automate paper processes. In this case there was no need for Bill Gates to authorize the travel expenditures of senior-level VPs, even though it may have only taken a relatively short amount of time. As for many other aspects of e-business, processes often need to be reengineered for procurement when moving to electronic processes.

Businesses will not want to allow automatic approval on many types of goods being acquired but should consider carefully thinking through the approvals process. For example, it may be reasonable to establish budgeted amounts for basic office supplies that are purchased through specified vendors rather than dealing with individual purchase order review and approval. The expenses may be audited later for control purposes, but the time saved should exceed the cost of any potential employee wrongdoing.

Maintenance, Repair, and Operating Expenses Maintenance, repair, and operating (MRO) expenses are other areas where automatic approvals may be delegated to specific individuals. For instance, the production manager may have approval to create a purchase order up to a specific dollar limit so that machine breakdowns can efficiently be dealt with. If downtime within a manufacturing business is expensive, then allowing the production manager to quickly deal with a problem would benefit the business, whereas a detailed process of approvals could delay the repair and impact the bottom line. This example is not intended to imply that MRO should always be automatically approved, but simply that each business must carefully evaluate its processes when establishing e-procurement policies.

Travel Services Travel services and meals and entertainment costs represent a major expense for many of today's service-based businesses. Therefore, the ability to deal with travel services in an integrated fashion has the potential for major cost savings. Microsoft saw this potential in the late 1990s and established a partnership with American Express so employees could access negotiated rates and discounts through the e-procurement portion of the corporate intranet, dubbed "MS Market" (see the E-Strategy box). Allowing employees to book their own travel at approved rates resulted in more than just improved rates—it also satisfied employees who wished to manage their own schedules and have the flexibility to make changes if necessary.[4]

Computer Equipment The acquisition of computer equipment represents another major category where businesses have begun to employ e-procurement. Not only can computers be acquired through exchanges and vendors' websites, but increasingly, corporate intranets can be linked to specialized pages of the vendors. For example, Dell has created "Premier Pages" (see figure 8.2) for many of its customers, which allows a number of benefits, including negotiated pricing, pre-configured systems, and knowledge of corporate infrastructure. Arrangements such as this allow for computer systems within budget limits to be purchased with little involvement of supervisors and technical support staff.

E-Strategy

MS Market at Microsoft

Microsoft began its efforts in the e-procurement arena in the mid-1990s with MS Market. MS Market was an intranet project that Microsoft tied in with several of its other intranet-based initiatives, such as Microsoft Archives, MS Reports, and MS Sales. Recognizing early the importance of employee self-service to create increased efficiency, cost reduction, and employee satisfaction, Microsoft built an application for procurement that would address a number of important cost areas for the company, including office supplies and travel.

In *Business @ The Speed of Thought*, Bill Gates describes some of the "growing pains" that MS Market went through as well as how some problems were addressed. For example, then-President Steve Ballmer (who later became CEO) was hesitant to make use of the application and the MS Market product manager confronted him over his concerns. Ballmer was disappointed that he was unable to determine if other managers had already reviewed

and/or approved orders that he was responsible for, as no routing application was in place. In addition, he was unable to review supporting documentation for purchase orders. Within weeks the routing requirement was resolved, and documentation support was available within a few months.

The key reason that the MS Market issues were addressed was that the product manager was fully in control of the project and sought advice from the user group in a manner users understood. Issues were resolved quickly and users began requesting other functionality that both saved them time and saved Microsoft money.

Microsoft's digital capabilities allow it to manage employee time and information even before an employee is hired, from the point of application (through the online résumé tool) through to dealing with human resources information for the hiring process. After an employee has been hired he or she is able to use self-service for a number of functions including ordering office supplies, business

cards, and dealing with human resource issues like benefits selection and charitable donations, all through the corporate intranet.

The Microsoft and American Express travel partnership, AXI, is a 24/7 service that allows employees to book corporate-discounted fares on airlines and negotiated rates at preferred hotels. Travel policies are built into AXI so that routine travel is automatically approved, while non-routine requests are routed to the appropriate manager for review. Gates estimated that employee time to book routine domestic flights would be reduced "from seventeen minutes and six phone calls or e-mails to approximately five minutes."

MS Market was used to conduct over US$1 billion of transactions in its first year and was estimated to reduce administrative procurement costs by US$35 million—an e-procurement success. E-procurement implementation strategies, like all other implementations, need to be carried out with swiftness and flexibility in order to succeed.

Microsoft
www.microsoft.com

Questions

1. Does the fact that Microsoft was working on e-procurement before many other large businesses indicate that they should have made a lot of money by selling their expertise in this area?

2. Gates made several presentations to share information regarding MS Market with fellow CEOs. What would be the motivation behind this? What can Microsoft gain from these "show and tell" sessions?

SOURCES: Bill Gates with Collins Hemingway, *Business @ The Speed of Thought: Using a Digital Nervous System*, New York: Warner Books, 1999; David B. Harding et. al, "Site Server: Market Technical Deployment" White Paper, Microsoft Corporation (August 1999), www.microsoft.com/technet/prodtechnol/sscomm/reskit/deploy/msmarket.mspx, accessed November 20, 2004.

Figure 8.2   The Medium and Large Business Homepage of Dell.ca

Dell's Premier Pages allow corporate and other large customers to access tailored web pages and pre-configured systems, which provides excellent service and ease of use.

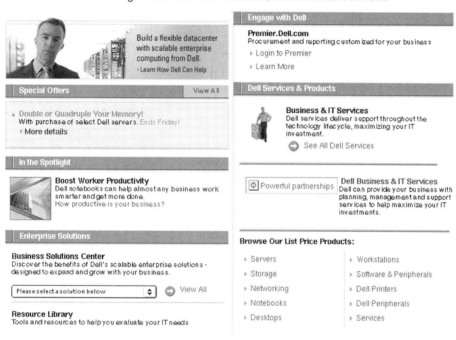

Production Items The cost savings and benefits obtained through e-procurement for non-production items have led many businesses to look to e-procurement for production items (also referred to as direct spending), such as raw materials and components. There are, however, some significant differences between production and non-production goods, making this transition more difficult. For example, non-production goods can be acquired more easily through poorly integrated systems since the co-ordination of the arrival date of the goods and the update of related information in the system are less critical. Production items need to be acquired within specific time frames to keep manufacturing schedules and maintain inventory levels, both for internal planning purposes and for customer notification. Also, production items may need to be customized. Therefore, production items need to be obtained and tracked through an integrated e-procurement system or information will need to be re-keyed.

In addition to currency of information, production items tend to have other important concerns that need to be addressed, such as product quality, payment terms, delivery arrangements, and supplier capabilities for collaborative product design. Essentially, the concern for using e-procurement, trading exchanges, or auction models to procure production goods is that price is only one part of the buying decision. Item quality, availability, and predictability and timeliness of delivery are also important considerations.

Supplier Selection and Approval

Supplier selection is critical in managing costs in the procurement process. There may be several vendors for any given product to be purchased, and considering the number of products purchased routinely by a company's purchasing department, unless careful attention is paid to costs, those costs could spiral out of control. For repetitive purchases, contracts should be negotiated with selected suppliers, and terms should be established for delivery, pricing, and quality. In the case of non-repetitive purchases, employee requests to purchase a product may involve a request for quotation (RFQ) being sent to suppliers inviting them to submit a bid for that purchase contract.

When the size of the purchase dictates that a detailed evaluation is required for a new purchase, supplier evaluation may be required. The potential evaluation of suppliers begins after determining that a purchase need exists (or is likely to exist) and the development of material specifications occurs. For routine or standard product requirements with established or selected suppliers, further supplier evaluation and selection is not necessary, and the approval process may be generated. However, potential sources for new items, especially those of a complex nature, require thorough investigation to be sure that purchasing evaluates only qualified suppliers.

Final supplier selection occurs once purchasing completes the activities required during the supplier evaluation process. Errors made in supplier selection can be damaging and long-lasting. After bids have been received, and/or the negotiation has taken place, the sourcing team will select a supplier, and then move on to authorize the purchase through the purchase approval process.

After the supplier is selected or a requisition for a standard item is received, Purchasing grants an approval to purchase the product or service. This is accomplished through an electronic drafting of a purchase order (PO), sometimes called a purchase agreement,. The purchase order details critical information about the purchase: quantity, material specification, quality requirements, price, delivery date, method of delivery, ship-to address, purchase order number, and order due date. Note that firms are increasingly using computerized databases to perform these processes, and are moving toward a "paperless" office.[5]

Several technology solution providers are targeting this area of strategic sourcing of purchases, also known as e-sourcing. These strategic sourcing solutions are designed to replace the traditional paper-based, labour-intensive processes of identifying and evaluating suppliers, automatically performing those processes to help enterprises identify the optimal supply network.[6]

The cost savings of consolidating purchases with a few suppliers can be substantial. For example, Bristol-Myers Squibb claims to have saved US$20 million per year by consolidating its purchases from both Dell and IBM with e-procurement.[7]

Benefits of E-Procurement

The benefits of e-procurement to businesses are still being discovered, but early indications are that the practice has a tremendous payoff. Some of the benefits involve cost and efficiency, strategic procurement, and authorized suppliers.

Cost and Efficiency The benefits of e-procurement are many, including price reductions and process efficiencies. Recent studies have found that companies reported benefits such as faster order times, convenience, time savings, easier price comparisons, and cost savings.[8] While the initial jump to adopt e-procurement was to create more competitive markets and reduce prices, a number of businesses claim that the "primary benefit lies in streamlining internal processes."[9]

It is interesting to consider how costs have been reduced from approximately US$120 to process a purchase order to the US$5 to $25 range. Paper-based procurement is laced with inefficiencies such as approvals of all purchase orders, despite the dollar amount or importance. In addition, the length of time to process a purchase order has been reduced by many businesses by nearly 75 percent due to the removal of "the paper chase." Microsoft claimed to have significantly reduced its paper forms related to procurement from 114 to 1.[10] The reduction in cost and increase in efficiency also results in a reduced administrative workload for procurement staff.

Strategic Procurement With the implementation of e-procurement in a business, the staff from the procurement area will be able to focus efforts on more important areas, such as strategic sourcing and supplier relations. As discussed in chapter 7, efficient supply chains depend on reliable suppliers, and the ability of staff to spend more time developing relationships is very beneficial. In addition, procurement staff may become involved in managing procurement processes that now occur through electronic means.

Authorized Suppliers Another area where benefits of e-procurement have been obtained is in consolidating buying from a small number of approved vendors. By controlling which suppliers employees may order from, the business should be able to demand improved pricing by increasing volume. For example, the impact of consolidation could be tremendous for a large business with tens of thousands of employees, each of whom purchases their own office supplies at the local supplier. Limiting employees to the suppliers in the e-procurement system can reduce maverick buying. **Maverick buying** is the unauthorized purchase of goods by employees through non-routine and poorly controlled means, such as acquiring office supplies with petty cash. In addition to potentially reducing the costs of goods purchased, controls required by e-procurement can reduce the volume of small transactions and payments required, thereby increasing the efficiency of related transaction processing operations.

MAVERICK BUYING
The unauthorized purchase of goods by employees through non-routine and poorly controlled means, such as acquiring office supplies with petty cash.

The benefits of e-procurement are broad in scope and will vary by organization. However, one thing is clear—e-procurement is a strategy that all e-businesses are working on now, or will be working on in the near future. See the Canadian Snapshots box to see how the Canadian government is moving into e-procurement.

Trading Exchanges

Business-to-business trading exchanges are internet-based sites in which businesses can sell or purchase products and services or share information to advertise products and services. Trading exchanges reduce reliance on other forms of communication in the procurement/selling process, as illustrated in figure 8.3. During the year 2000, the popularity of trading exchanges resulted in the formation of more than a thousand online exchanges; however, the limited growth in trading through these exchanges was unable to support this number, and by mid-2001 many of the startups had shut down. For example, Chemdex, which had

Canadian Snapshots

E-Procurement at Merx.com

The Canadian federal government is moving in the direction of e-procurement with the Government Electronic Tendering System (GETS), known as MERX. MERX is not a government service; rather MERX is the trademark under which MERX, a subsidiary of Mediagrif Interactive Technologies, is operating GETS. MERX combines GETS with e-procurement opportunities from the provincial, and MASH (municipal, academic, school, and hospital) sectors. MERX began as an initiative with Cebra Inc., a Bank of Montreal company, and now provides contractors and businesses (both large and small) with the opportunity to bid on tenders.

Essentially, MERX is an electronic tendering service, meaning that an Ottawa-based contractor can easily search for any contracts in the Ottawa area with the federal government, the City of Ottawa,

local municipalities in the region, or government agencies (a complete list of purchasers can be found on the MERX website). If tenders of interest are posted on the site, the contractor simply requests the tender documents and pays the shipping fees. In 2001 electronic bid submission was introduced, with reasonable charges levied for usage of these facilities. MERX has various subscriber service plans that start at $21.95 per month, and non-subscribers can pay a one-time-order fee.

In early 2001, MERX and the Canadian Chamber of Commerce signed a deal that would allow nearly 170 000 Canadian businesses to take advantage of MERX as part of their membership in the Canadian Chamber of Commerce. This agreement was expected to triple the number of suppliers able to access the site, taking into account that many of the Chamber

members were already paying users of the site. In late 2004, the agreement with the federal government changed, and MERX no longer charged a basic membership fee to suppliers of the Government of Canada but received an annual service fee from the Government of Canada instead.

An auction service was introduced by MERX in late 2001. The service creates a secure buyer and seller auction site and allows business-to-business transactions to be conducted through the internet. Renah Persofsky, CEO and President of MERX Inc., said, "Most of the auction sites available in Canada today are business-to-consumer or consumer-to-consumer focused. Through this auction solution we will be offering a service which is designed specifically for the B2B market."

MERX
www.merx.com

Mediagrif Interactive Technologies Inc.
www.mediagrif.com

Questions

1. What extensions to the existing e-tendering strategy should MERX be working on to improve the overall procurement process?
2. Should the government be getting involved in any fashion with the auction site? Why or why not?

SOURCES: MERX website, www.merx.com, accessed April 20, 2004; "Small and Mid-Sized Companies Big Winners Thanks to E-Tendering System," *CANOE—BIZchat*, Jan 25, 2001, www.canoe.com/BizChatTranscripts/010125_neumann-can.html, accessed November 20, 2004; "Mediagrif Announces Change to MERX Contract with the Government of Canada," press release, www.mediagrif.com/html/news/release_dtl_en.asp?id=87, accessed November 20, 2004.

been touted as one of the trading exchanges with great potential, discontinued operations in April 2001. Forrester Research predicts an exchange shakeout will leave fewer than 200 significant B2B companies in operation.[11] Despite this fact, a number of trading exchanges, both public and private, are operating successfully today and offer extended benefits to e-procurement activities on the buy-side and selling opportunities on the sell-side.

Figure 8.3   Trading Exchange Facilitating Role

Trading exchanges can consolidate numerous forms of communication into one medium.

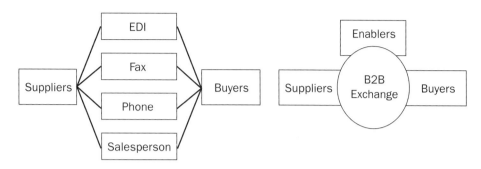

Trading exchanges may also be referred to by a number of different names in practice. Terms such as *hubs, e-hubs, marketplaces, consortiums,* and combinations of these (sometimes with B2B added) are used in trade literature and magazine publications. In this book, we will refer primarily to trading exchanges, that being the most comprehensive term.

Trading exchanges can be grouped into two major categories in terms of products and services exchanged: vertical and horizontal. **Vertical trading exchanges** are those that have an industry or specific market focus, such as healthcare or energy products and services. **Horizontal trading exchanges** are those that have a product or service focus, such as computers or office equipment, and do not target any specific industry. Figure 8.4 illustrates the concept of vertical and horizontal exchanges.

Trading exchanges are also categorized as either public or private, depending on the controls in place and any access limitations. A **private exchange** is a trading exchange that limits participation to specific buyers and sellers—normally related to the exchange provider's supply chain. For example, when General Electric first began its Global eXchange Services (GXS), it was limited to a few specific buyers who were soliciting goods and services from sellers who had been given access to enter the exchange. GXS has evolved over time and continues to provide exchange services such as network infrastructure, software, hardware, and consulting services

VERTICAL TRADING EXCHANGES
Trading exchanges that have an industry or specific market focus, such as healthcare or energy products and services.

HORIZONTAL TRADING EXCHANGES
Trading exchanges that have a product or service focus, such as computers or office equipment, and do not target any specific industry.

PRIVATE EXCHANGE
A trading exchange that limits participation to specific buyers and sellers—normally related to the exchange provider's supply chain.

Figure 8.4   Vertical and Horizontal Trading Exchanges

Trading exchanges are often categorized as either vertical or horizontal based upon the way they operate.

to major clients like JC Penney and Procter & Gamble.[12] (See the New Business Models box for more information on GXS). Private exchanges continue to evolve and vary in the methods by which they allow sellers and buyers to join.

Public exchanges are those in which buyers and sellers register to join, and there are few limitations to joining. Public exchanges have not had tremendous success in the B2B market, however, as enterprises have had difficulty integrating their ERP/EDI systems with the exchanges, especially since the enterprise would have to implement the integration itself. The E-Business in Global Perspective box shows another example of a public exchange.

PUBLIC EXCHANGES
Trading exchanges in which buyers and sellers register to join, and there are few limitations to joining.

Trading Exchange Functions

Trading exchanges operate with a variety of service levels and allow for varying degrees of integration. The functions of a trading exchange can range from simplistic, in which members share company information and then conduct transactions offline (similar to the brochureware phase of the internet), to catalogue sites, to fully integrated collaborative environments (see figure 8.5). In the collaborative environments, contract terms and payment can be carried out completely online and integrated with the buyer and seller back-end systems, and products and services may even be designed online.

In this section we will look at trading exchanges from the perspectives of buyers, sellers, and exchange enablers. To illustrate the points being discussed, the automotive trading exchange, Covisint, will be highlighted. Covisint was formed in the spring of 2000 by General Motors Corp., DaimlerChrysler AG, and Ford Motor

Covisint
www.covisint.com

Figure 8.5   Progression Stages for Trading Exchanges and Marketplaces

B2B trading exchanges range from basic brochureware sites to complex collaborative environments.

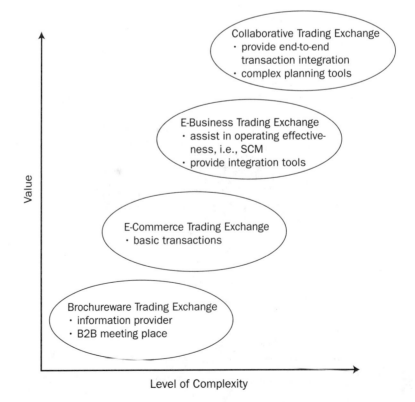

Collaborative Trading Exchange
· provide end-to-end transaction integration
· complex planning tools

E-Business Trading Exchange
· assist in operating effectiveness, i.e., SCM
· provide integration tools

E-Commerce Trading Exchange
· basic transactions

Brochureware Trading Exchange
· information provider
· B2B meeting place

Value

Level of Complexity

New Business Models

The GXS Trading Exchange at GE

General Electric (GE), at first glance, may not strike individuals as a particularly exciting company; however, their strengths in the world of e-business may just be unknown. GE's history is full of innovation, adaptation, and change, which are characteristics that should serve it well in the world of e-business. GE has a history of over 120 years and in that time has been involved with product innovation in the areas of lighting, aircraft engines, mainframe computers, and now B2B trading exchanges. GE is a very diversified company with business units dedicated to supplies, medical products, plastics, trucking, appliances, insurance, and other products.

In the late 1990s, GE began working on its own e-procurement processes by automating purchases through the internet. As the pure-play dot-com businesses expanded into trading exchanges, GE realized that its work on its own Global eXchange Service (GXS) could be a very valuable asset. The company's CEO, Jack Welch, recommended major innovation and devotion to the project and in early 2000 spent several hundred million dollars on the GXS project.

What makes GXS different from many of the other dot-com trading exchange enablers is its core strength in working with EDI. While many other enablers struggle with integration, GXS uses the experience of GE with EDI to allow integration to take place over the internet. By early 2001, approximately 5 percent of trading exchanges had the processes integrated with ERP systems of users. To expand the possibilities of GXS, partnerships were formed with leading companies in the area, including Commerce One Operations, Inc. and TIBCO Software Inc.

The GXS private exchange successfully built exchanges for large bricks-and-mortar businesses such as JC Penney and DaimlerChrysler, and realized that it had the ability to provide excellent service in the area.

Despite its involvement in trading exchanges, both use and design, GE has opted not to become involved in public exchanges with its own products. GXS sees that a great opportunity in the exchange area will be to create means of integration between separate exchanges that will create better experiences and processes for

users. The old bricks-and-mortar organization known as GE has shown clearly that the world of e-business is not just for startups.

New Developments

GXS was acquired by Francisco Partners in June 2002 and now operates as an independent firm. GE retains 10 percent ownership in the new company, and GXS continues to operate the GE Global Supplier Network, one of the world's largest private marketplaces, serving a majority of GE's business units and their trading partners.

In March 2004, the Hong Kong subsidiary of Global eXchange Services, Inc. (GXS) entered into an agreement with ChinaECNet to establish a B2B electronic transaction exchange, named "e-Hub," to enhance information exchange between original equipment manufacturers (OEMs) in China's electronics industry. Among China's most ambitious logistics and procurement exchange platforms, e-Hub will connect Chinese electronics OEMs with other China-based manufacturers as well as international customers and suppliers.

Commerce One Operations, Inc.
www.commerceone.com

TIBCO Software Inc.
www.tibco.com

GXS
www.gxs.com

Questions

1. Why would GE choose not to engage in selling its own products through public exchanges?
2. Should GE abandon its "traditional" product lines of appliances and lighting products to focus on its technological capabilities? Why?
3. At a time when outsourcing has become extremely common, does it make sense for GE to focus its attention on the development of trading exchanges?

SOURCES: Jon Burke, "Is GE the Last Internet Company?," *Red Herring*, no. 88 (December 15, 2000): 55; General Electric website, **www.ge.com**, accessed April 20, 2004; Global eXchange Services website, **www.gxs.com**, April 20, 2004; Global eXchange Services press releases, **www.gxs.com/gxs/press/release/press20040318**, accessed April 19, 2004.

Company. The exchange had previously been known as the Automotive Network Exchange (ANX). Covisint is currently owned by Compuware Corporation. This industry consortium aims to create a business community of buyers, sellers, designers, engineers, and third parties within the global automotive industry.[13]

Covisint developed plans for expansion during the year 2000 and early 2001 to begin facilitating its role by mid-2001. Renault SA and Nissan Motor Company later joined the Covisint exchange as automotive partners and both Oracle and Commerce One joined as technology partners. By May 2001, Covisint said it had more than 250 customers on the exchange carrying out some functions of auctions, quote management, and collaborative design. Products and services, however, at this point in time were focused primarily on procurement and the supply chain.[14]

Covisint has a development plan that aims to move far beyond the use of the exchange for procurement. The Covisint trading exchange aims to move toward the collaborative environment by providing services for supply chain management, collaborative product development, and e-procurement capabilities. Covisint's goals relate back to figure 8.5 as well, where the progression is from an e-commerce trading exchange to a collaborative exchange.

For Buyers Trading exchanges offer buyers the ability to search, select, and acquire goods and services in an efficient manner from numerous suppliers. Suppliers can register with an exchange to list their products in catalogue form on the exchange so that buyers may seek their products.

In addition to hosting catalogues, exchanges can facilitate trade by providing additional services that the buyer may consider valuable. For example, the exchange may provide services related to the review of potential suppliers in terms of quality and past customer satisfaction. Trading exchanges may also work closely with buyers to deal with issues of integration, technology requirements, and training, as well as numerous other offerings. See Table 8.1 for a listing of a number of services that can be offered by trading exchanges.

Covisint offers a number of services to its buyers (such as Ford and GM), who are also the founding members of the exchange. Members of the exchange can carry out procurement activities through catalogue methods or use auction or

Table 8.1 Potential Trading Exchange Functions

Trading exchanges have the potential to provide numerous value-added services to members on both the buy-side and sell-side of transactions as they increase in complexity.

• Supplier certification, reputation	• Contract administration
• Transportation management	• Tariffs and duties assessment
• Product life cycle management	• Planning, scheduling, forecasting
• Warehousing and inspection	• Promotions/campaign management
• Risk mitigation services	• Profiling and personalization
• Catalogue display/maintenance	• Authentication/security
• Financing	• Complex pricing
• Product configuration	• Private markets, negotiated terms
• Derivative instruments	• Post-sale support, warranty programs
• Community news, employment, etc.	• Receivables management
• Returns processing, repair claims	• Scrap management/reverse logistics
• Payment processing/order management	• Inventory availability
• Order explosion/routing	• Partner/team selling and promotions
• Workflow and business rules	• Backorder management

reverse auction methods (these will be discussed later in the chapter). Other services at Covisint include supply chain optimization, integration of supply chain technologies, and hosting of applications to allow for collaborative design and development of new products in a virtual workspace. This industry-led consortium essentially allows buyers to deal more efficiently with suppliers, to reduce costs, and to make gains in effectiveness by using collaborative tools designed specifically for the industry.

For Suppliers Suppliers to trading exchanges are attempting to attract additional business through a medium that allows for efficient sales to take place. By listing products and services on a public trading exchange, a supplier may be aiming to reach new customers across a range of industries. On the other hand, a supplier may join a private trading exchange to more efficiently and effectively deal with customers it has sold to previously. See the E-Business in Global Perspective box to further examine the potential benefits of exchanges to buyers and sellers.

Covisint offers suppliers access to a huge market as well as an exchange backed by leading players in the automotive industry. Suppliers can look forward to accessing customers on a more cost-effective basis as well as begin using collaborative functions over the next few years to become more closely involved in the design process. Covisint also allows suppliers who deal with several of the major automakers the ability to use one major interface to conduct business, thus simplifying the process for employees. These functions should develop strong bonds between trading partners who successfully participate and demonstrate their ability to provide input and meet commitments (which may be tracked and disclosed by the exchange).

Issues for Exchange Providers

Business-to-business exchange providers have a huge challenge ahead of them to deliver on the demands of both buyers and suppliers over the coming years. In addition, those exchanges that have gone through the initial public offering or IPO process, whereby they raised capital to fund their operations by selling shares to the public, have high expectations from shareholders. The challenges ahead for B2B exchange providers include integration, profitability, governance, and legal issues.

Covisint, for instance, has not been as successful as was expected when it was created. After having financial problems it was purchased by Compuware in March 2004. Compuware CEO Peter Karmanos Jr. believes Covisint could be made more robust in its role through the removal of the auction function, which was used by automakers to reduce prices. As a result of the sale, some legal issues have been dealt with and Covisint now plays more of a third-party role.[15]

Integration: Making It Work Early participants in B2B exchanges provided only basic services, such as corporate information on products and contact details. Exchanges, however, have moved quickly beyond that point and participants now demand the ability to conduct transactions in real time and integrate the data into their own back-end systems. By early 2001 only about 5 percent of companies involved in trading exchanges had achieved full integration of processes with back-end ERP systems.[16] The difficulty is that exchanges may facilitate transactions between companies that use dozens of different back-end systems.

One initiative aiming to make the process of integration a little easier is the **Universal Description, Discovery, and Integration (UDDI) initiative**. UDDI is a collaborative effort among several technology companies that aims to improve

UNIVERSAL DESCRIPTION, DISCOVERY, AND INTEGRATION (UDDI) INITIATIVE
A collaborative effort that aims to improve the ability of businesses to carry out electronic transactions with each other.

E-Business in Global Perspective

Industry Exchange at TransLease Pro

Fleet management for leasing companies and other fleet operators in Britain has become much more efficient since the introduction of TransLease Pro. TransLease Pro was a product/service of Cap Gemini Ernst & Young that was launched in Britain and is growing steadily.

The general manager of fleet operations for TransLease Pro's largest customer, Motability Fleet Limited, stated, "The reduction in paperwork and administrative time resulting from TransLease Pro will deliver substantial annual cost savings in excess of £9 million by 2002 compared with what we would have spent using a traditional fleet management process." Benefits to the e-procurement/exchange service are numerous and the product has become well accepted by fleet managers as well as repair and maintenance providers.

Assume for a moment that you lease a vehicle in London and are travelling to a nearby city when your vehicle breaks down. Since repairs on many of the leases are included in the cost, you must call the leasing company and get an approval for repair work at the nearest garage. Then the repair garage can either charge you for the work (and you can be reimbursed by the leasing company later) or the leasing company can pay the garage directly if the repair garage is comfortable with the account receivable.

TransLease Pro was developed to streamline the process described above as well as provide additional valuable services to the leasing companies. A customer with a problem now can call a central location and be directed to an approved repair garage nearby. The garage can use its internal system to authorize the transaction and then receives payment very rapidly. Vehicle owners, garage operators, and fleet managers are all happy with the improvements in the process created by streamlining the procurement of repairs. By mid-2000, TransLease Pro had nearly 600 000 vehicles in the database (growing by 10 000 per month) and 2400 registered maintenance and repair garages.

TransLease Pro provides an extensive array of services |such as:

- approving garages to carry out work based on experience and basic business requirements
- analyzing trends and costs for vehicles across multiple companies to allow improved analysis of model/repair information
- handling the payment process to dealers, thus reducing the work involved for its customers (the leasing companies)

It seems that TransLease Pro has created a new intermediary in the fleet management and leasing industry, which provides services that satisfy a number of members of the supply chain.

New Developments

Epyx, a company providing e-solutions for the automotive industry, acquired TransLease in May 2003 for an undisclosed sum. After the takeover, Greg Connell, managing director of Epyx, said, "We are seeing tremendous growth in electronic invoice processing, with our combined platforms set to process invoice transactions in excess of £200 million this year alone!" This statement highlights the extent to which electronic authorization and invoice processing was mature in the automotive industry in the UK. Epyx has since renamed and expanded TransLease Pro to the 1link series of products.

Epyx
www.epyx.co.uk

Cap Gemini Ernst & Young
www.capgemini.com

Questions

1. Why couldn't the leasing companies use a standard B2B trading exchange to facilitate the processes described here?
2. Are there any concerns for the leasing companies with respect to privacy of data held by 1link?

SOURCE: Cap Gemini Ernst & Young website, **www.capgemini.com**, accessed April 20, 2004; "Motoring-UK: Epyx Acquisition of TransLease Will See 200 million of Transactions Processed this Year," **www.motoring-uk.co.uk/mot_news.taf?_function=detail&_record=149994&_ UserReference=B1513AF4303ABE9AC29ACF71&_start=1**, accessed April 20, 2004.

UDDI
www.uddi.org

the ability of businesses to carry out electronic transactions with each other. The UDDI Business Registry (UBR) is a free, public UDDI registry currently jointly operated by IBM, Microsoft, NTT Communications, and SAP. Essentially, it is a listing of businesses involved in B2B e-commerce that describes in a standardized manner how each business handles electronic transactions. As active participants in the B2B arena, trading exchange providers must get involved in this initiative to provide value-added services to users. OASIS is a global not-for-profit consortium for the development of e-business standards in this area.

UDDI is part of a new paradigm for e-business that is expected to change the way business applications are developed and interoperate, termed web services. The primary goal of web services is to provide a mechanism for applications to communicate with each other from different systems across the internet, based on emerging standards such as XML, SOAP (simple object access protocol), WSDL (web services definition language) and UDDI. In essence, a **web service** consists of four key components: a message that is exchanged, an application software that acts as a service requester or a service provider, shared transport mechanisms that enable the flow of the message, and a service description of these components such as a description of the service, a description of the messages that are exchanged by the service, and a description of the service's interface. These descriptions may be machine accessible and processable for use in service discovery systems and in service management systems. Since the service is wrapped up in an interface with a service description, one service is independent of the interaction of other services.

Advances in technology and improvements to existing standards will assist in the process of integration; however, like most areas of technology, complexity also continues to rise. The promise of extensible markup language (XML) to assist in integration was initially hailed as very strong, but unfortunately many of the ERP systems were unable to adequately deal with the language. Other attempts to standardize formats such as EDI have been largely unsuccessful. Exchange enablers like Ariba and Commerce One have established partnerships with leading ERP vendors such as SAP and Oracle to address these very issues. Collaboration in the technology area must continue to be developed in order to facilitate B2B integration.

Profitability B2B exchange enablers are struggling with issues similar to many of the failed dot-coms—notably, how to charge for services. It is essential that exchange enablers adopt pricing schemes that will allow them to become profitable enough that they can continue to grow and invest in new technologies. An oft-quoted example of an exchange enabler that failed to find an appropriate revenue model is the New York Stock Exchange, which facilitates over US$7 trillion in trades but has revenues of just US$100 million.[17] Similarly, online exchange providers struggle with similar issues—whether fees should be based on per-transaction amounts, dollar amounts traded, or a membership signup fee.

Covisint, for example, began by charging no fees to encourage participation, but later changed to a fee per transaction to cover the costs of operating the exchange. Other exchanges tie fees more closely to services offered and utilized by the particular customer. Establishing a pricing model for an exchange is not dissimilar to pricing in any other business—determine what drives costs, estimate costs, evaluate the market, and establish a profitable pricing system.

Governance Trading exchanges run into additional complexity when they attempt to establish policies and procedures to govern their operation. Some of the concerns that may arise include: Who can join the exchange on both buyer and supplier sides? Is data owned by the exchange or individual members? Do members have the ability to demand access to data? Are members restricted in their rights to participate/own other exchanges?

Addressing issues such as those outlined above will vary depending on the format of the exchange. Private exchanges and public exchanges will address these

OASIS
www.oasis-open.org

WEB SERVICES
A mechanism for applications to communicate with each other from different systems across the Internet.

concerns in different manners but each has the same objective—to provide the most value possible to all members of the trading community.

Restricting membership in an exchange may be necessary. As mentioned previously, the exchange may provide a service of supplier accreditation, which effectively limits membership to those suppliers who pass the codes of accreditation established. In other circumstances, however, exchanges will experience pressures from members not to allow competitors to join, in an effort to keep a competitive advantage. Exchanges must clearly document methods by which membership is restricted and enforce policies to achieve consistency and provide a valuable service to members.

Data confidentiality will be a key concern to all members. Consider the repercussions if DaimlerChrysler were to find out through Covisint that Supplier X had been giving General Motors a better price and higher service levels. In this age of litigation, this situation would likely lead to several costly lawsuits. Confidentiality of data and details of its ownership must be clearly laid out in the exchange's policies to prevent situations such as those described here.

The rights of members are another area of concern for exchange governance. The Covisint exchange members, for example, are not restricted from using other exchanges but the question of their commitment arises when you consider that several of the founding members also operate their own private exchanges. Private exchanges will need to address the issue of member rights if they want to stimulate a community of collaboration where members are not competing directly with the exchange and/or borrowing valuable resources from the exchange itself.

Legal Issues The growth in the size of trading exchanges and the establishment of Covisint has brought attention to legal issues surrounding B2B trading. The sheer magnitude of Covisint sparked the U.S. Department of Justice and the U.S. Federal Trade Commission to examine the impact of such exchanges on competition and antitrust laws. Covisint was given approval to go ahead based on its policies, which did not strictly limit competition, despite some concerns by suppliers that they would be heavily pressured to reduce prices. Legal issues that could arise are far-reaching and should be carefully considered in advance by exchanges, both public and private.

Auctions

Internet-based auctions have been popularized by the success of eBay in developing a model for trading goods between disparate individuals. The development of internet-based auctions, however, has not been limited to consumer-to-consumer transactions, as businesses have begun to embrace the concept for purchasing and procuring all types of goods. Auctions have been built into trading exchanges as one major method of carrying out transactions and have also been employed by government organizations to conduct commerce online, as discussed in the MERX example earlier in this chapter.

History of Auctions

The internet has brought attention to auctions recently, but they do not have a short history by any means. Some historical researchers claim that auctions actually date back to 500 BC, when marriage and slave auctions were carried out. Other auctions are also tied to Ancient Rome around AD 100, where auctions took place in the atrium auctionarium. Documentation of auctions was limited, and approximately a thousand years passed before information regarding auctions was again written. By the mid-1500s auctions again were documented in France, the Netherlands, and China for slaves, estate auctions, and fine art.[18]

Modern auction giants such as Sotheby's and Christie's were formed in the late 1700s in Britain to sell books, art, and other valuable collectibles. Globalization began to take place in the auction industry in the post-World War II era, as Sotheby's and Christie's expanded internationally with their high-quality and prestigious auctions.

Auctions made their way to the internet in 1995 when Aucnet, a Japanese company, began selling automobiles at auction. eBay followed closely in September 1995, with its storybook beginnings as a technology to assist the fiancée of Pierre Omidyar (eBay's founder) to sell Pez dispensers over the internet. During 1999, eBay purchased Butterfield & Butterfield to transform itself into a bricks-and-clicks organization, and Sotheby's formed a joint venture with Amazon.com.[19] By 2001 hundreds of auction sites had begun to replicate and expand upon the model of eBay, including internet giants like Yahoo! and Amazon.com.

Sotheby's
www.sothebys.com

Christie's
www.christies.com

Types of Auctions

Auctions, both physical and virtual, can take a variety of formats in terms of how the process is conducted and how the winner is determined. The auction format is generally tied to the type of product being sold and the audience where the auction is taking place in an effort to achieve the maximum revenue for the seller of an asset or the lowest price for the purchaser of an asset.

A number of different names have been assigned to auction formats, but six types are readily apparent:[20]

1. **English auction.** In the **English auction** the bidding occurs through an ascending price process when buyers gather in a common location (physical or digital) during specified periods of time. This is the form of auction most would be familiar with, as both estate auctions and online auctions are usually run on this model.

2. **Yankee auction.** The **Yankee auction** is similar to an English auction except that multiple items are sold by price, quantity, and earliest bid time. This form of auction can be used by businesses that are buying products where price is not the only factor to consider and quantity available is a key consideration, such as purchasing supplies where a small quantity would be insufficient and would necessitate buying from multiple suppliers.

3. **Dutch auction. Dutch auctions** use a descending price format whereby the auctioneer begins with a high price and buyers can bid on specific quantities of inventory as the price falls. This type of auction can be used for perishable goods or any other type of commodity in which the process is predicted to have good results. The buyers must purchase the goods they wish to obtain before the price falls to a level such that demand rises enough to deplete the inventory.

4. **Reverse auction. Reverse auctions** again use a descending price format but in this case the buyer creates the auction to receive bids from potential suppliers. Suppliers must bid lower than the most recent bid in order to gain the sale in this auction-type format, which has been

ENGLISH AUCTION
An auction in which the bidding occurs through an ascending price process when buyers gather in a common location (physical or digital) during specified periods of time.

YANKEE AUCTION
An auction format similar to an English auction except that multiple items are sold by price, quantity, and earliest bid time. This form of auction can be used by businesses that are buying products where price is not the only factor to consider and quantity available is a key consideration.

DUTCH AUCTION
An auction that uses a descending price format, whereby the auctioneer begins with a high price and buyers can bid on specific quantities of inventory as the price falls.

REVERSE AUCTION
An auction that uses a descending price format, but the buyer creates the auction to receive bids from potential suppliers.

SEALED-BID AUCTION
An auction form often used for products/services where price is only one consideration to the decision. For example, construction contracts often go through a sealed-bid process, as the buyer will consider capabilities, product quality, timelines, and past experience of the contractor before awarding the contract.

VICKREY AUCTION
An auction using an ascending price format in which the highest bidder wins the auction but must pay the price submitted by the second place bidder.

used quite frequently on the internet through trading exchanges and other formats.

5. **Sealed-bid auction.** The **sealed-bid auction** is often used for products/services where price is only one consideration to the decision. For example, construction contracts often go through a sealed-bid process, as the buyer will consider capabilities, product quality, timelines, and past experience of the contractor before awarding the contract. Many of the auctions conducted on MERX, which was discussed earlier, use the sealed-bid format.

6. **Vickrey auction.** The **Vickrey auction** format is an ascending price format in which the highest bidder wins the auction but must pay the price submitted by the second place bidder. The objective of this auction type is to encourage the price upwards by allowing the buyer to pay the next highest price.

A number of variations on these auction types exist where conditions of anonymity, "opting out," and restrictions are used to control the process. A number of studies have been conducted that indicate that the outcomes of many of the auction formats are very similar in nature, with a few minor exceptions.[21]

The most common formats of auctions used on the internet to date have been English auctions for consumer-to-consumer (C2C) transactions (such as those on eBay) and reverse auctions for B2B transactions (such as those often used at Ariba's FreeMarkets). The English auction format appears to work well in the C2C arena and could also be used in the B2B arena for selected products and services. In addition, governments are being strongly advised to adopt auction models to become more efficient and effective in carrying out their mandates.[22]

The reverse auction model, as noted above, suits itself particularly well to addressing the needs of buyers looking to procure products and services in a cost-effective manner. Ariba's FreeMarkets, for instance, assists numerous customers through the reverse auction process and claims to reduce costs—often by as much as 50 percent.[23]

REQUEST FOR PROPOSAL (RFP)
The first stage in a procurement process whereby the buyer communicates its needs to potential suppliers, who will then submit tenders based on the requirements.

eBreviate
www.ebreviate.com

EDS Canada
www.eds.com/canada/

EDS Canada used a reverse auction to acquire contract technical staffing services after first issuing a **request for proposal (RFP)**. An RFP is the first stage in a procurement process whereby the buyer communicates its needs to potential suppliers, who will then submit tenders based on the requirements. The RFP process was used to short-list qualified suppliers in terms of qualitative aspects such as service capabilities, experience, and guarantees. Initial requests for pricing information were included in the RFP, but it was made clear to suppliers that pricing details would be dealt with later. In association with eBreviate, the procurement solutions arm of A.T. Kearney, Inc., EDS provided the six short-listed candidates with information on the auctioning process. In discussing the time involved to carry out the reverse auction, Patricia Moser, Director of Global Purchasing, commented that turnaround time was quite impressive since, "We knew that the bids we were receiving reflected the going market rate for our size and type of organization. Instead of having to go through a research house for this information, we were able to get this information during the auction."[24] EDS Canada was able to successfully carry out the auction and within two months had hired a labour contractor for a two-year period, using a new purchasing strategy. Previously, this process would have taken up to six months, and would have involved a lot more administrative work.

E-Auction Requirements

To successfully carry out online auctions either to sell or acquire products or services, it is necessary to properly plan and administer a process that uses the appropriate technologies. For auctions to be fair to participants, the process requires full disclosure and security procedures, which prevent the "rules of the game" from being broken. In addition, e-auctions must provide the capability to integrate data, notify users of recent information, and process/facilitate payments.

Full Disclosure To function efficiently, auctions must provide participants with all relevant information related to the prospective purchase or sale. In addition to basic descriptions of product or service types and quantity information, it is necessary to provide details of quality levels, warranty programs, transportation agreements, payment terms, and after-sale support mechanisms. In essence, an auction will only work properly when participants are aware of what they are getting involved in. Similar to the "viewing period" in traditional auctions, where buyers are given time to view the items for sale and determine their own preferences, the disclosure of information in an electronic auction will yield better results and create more active participation. Where possible, emerging technologies such as streaming video and collaborative discussions should be used to provide visual support to the disclosure of information.

Integration The use of auctions creates some unique considerations for integration of the auctioning system with the back-end ERP system. For sellers, it is important that the ERP system can be integrated with the auction's front end or auction provider's system to capture details of pricing and shipping information so that the transportation-planning process can be carried out effectively. Buyers also can benefit from integration as details of incoming shipments can be captured, as well as cost information for acquired assets or upcoming expenses.

Notification Mechanisms Auction providers, whether external (such as FreeMarkets) or internal, must develop notification mechanisms that are effective at ensuring that all participants in an auction are up to date at all times. Early auction sites used e-mail extensively for communication, but developments in the area have led to the use of push technologies, which allow the auction server to frequently update clients directly through the internet browser. Information relating to the current status of the auction can be critical in gaining new business for sellers or cutting costs for buyers, so it is essential that mechanisms are in place to provide details. EDS Canada's first e-auction made use of timed bidding, whereby if any bid was placed during the last 10 minutes of the auction time block, a 15-minute extension would be added to ensure that other suppliers had an adequate opportunity to resubmit.

Auction Security Auction security is crucial to ensure that the process is executed appropriately and that hackers are unable to sabotage an auction. In addition, it is necessary to ensure that information that is meant to be confidential is in no way breached or the use of auctions in the future could be compromised. For example, if a product's design and manufacturing details are released to a potential buyer but the auction mechanism inappropriately released the information to a competitor in the auction, the reputation of the auction provider and buyer could be damaged. To prevent mishaps such as this, the auction process will need to use cryptographic techniques similar to other electronic transactions. In addition, the system will need to adequately create audit trails so participants can develop confidence that the technology will conduct the auction according to the rules and award business to the appropriate supplier.

Figure 8.6   The Auctioning Process

The auctioning process must be carefully executed to be efficient and effective.

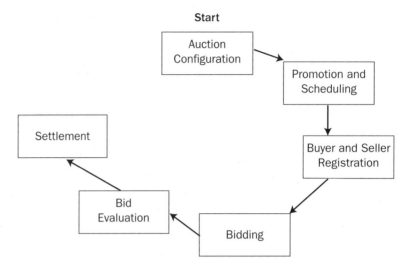

Payment Capabilities The requirement for payment capabilities differs depending on the nature of the auction, the products or services, and the participants (whether B2B or C2C). However, the ability for auction providers to facilitate payments will become increasingly important. Early in the life of eBay, the potential for the business was limited due to the lack of convenient payment mechanisms. The growth of numerous payment schemes for online commerce (such as PayPal), however, has allowed eBay to successfully grow and for consumers to sell to one another by paying for goods through online mechanisms. Similarly, B2B transactions with unknown suppliers have been limited by payment mechanisms. Technology advances are helping in this area as well (see chapter 6), while other services like escrow payments and funds transfer are also helping to make these transactions possible.

The Auctioning Process

Auctions are used extensively in B2B trading exchanges, as discussed earlier, to procure all types of goods and services. The process of conducting an auction online varies depending on the type of auction and the rules adopted, but a basic process is as demonstrated in figure 8.6.

Auction Configuration The auction initiator (who may be either the buyer or seller) and auction enabler must establish the preliminary requirements for the auction at the beginning of the process. The auction type (English, reverse, etc.) must be decided upon, as well as the details of the products or services involved (quantity, quality, etc.). In addition, the configuration will control the timing details of the auction, minimum bid amounts, minimum bid increments, auction closing rules, and other details.

Promotion and Scheduling In coordination with the auction enabler, the initiator will carry out promotion and advertising consistent with the strategy for the auction. This may involve simply notifying a number of potential participants that the initiator is familiar with or an advertising campaign to a broad or targeted audience. This stage of the process may also involve soliciting participants from other exchange or auction providers to expand the number of participants to improve the outcome of the auction.

Buyer and Seller Registration In this step of the process, both the buyer(s) and seller(s) must register with the auction provider and deal with such concerns as sharing of cryptographic keys, contact information, and other basic details. At this stage, the process can be either "open" or "by invitation only" depending on the preferences of the initiator of the auction. Participants may be investigated or evaluated at this phase as well to ensure that they meet standards they have claimed (e.g., ISO certification) and to verify credit if necessary.

Bidding The bidding phase of the auction may last for minutes, days, or weeks depending on the parameters outlined at the configuration stage. While this stage is primarily concerned with carrying out the auction and executing the process, it may also include a training element. For example, new participants may be able to use a demonstration to evaluate the bidding process and train members of their firm. There may also be a number of standby mechanisms such as the ability to use fax or voice in the event of bidding process problems. Once the bidding has begun, this stage essentially carries out the details of the configuration by controlling minimum bid increments and notifying participants of changes in auction or bid status.

Bid Evaluation The evaluation of bids may be automatic or may involve human intervention depending on the format of the auction chosen. For example, a reverse auction may automatically notify the "winner" at the end of the bidding time period, whereas a sealed-bid auction would simply notify participants that their information had been received and they would be contacted later. If factors other than price are involved at this stage, the process is complicated; however, alternative methods can be utilized such as pre-screening participants for qualitative factors (as EDS Canada did).

Settlement The final stage of the process involves settlement of contractual terms, payment, and transfer of goods. The ordering and method of carrying out this stage may differ based on a number of factors, but the key is to execute payment and enter a valid contract. This stage may be entirely electronic (besides delivery of tangible goods) or may involve an in-person meeting, again depending on the preferences of the parties involved.

The auction process as described here could take only a few hours in total or could occur over a period of months. The importance of the process is that each of the stages needs to be thoroughly planned and executed, taking into account the auction requirements discussed earlier for the auction to be successful.

The Future of Auctions

The use of auctions in the procurement and sale of goods is projected to increase dramatically over the next few years. Some pundits go so far as to predict the demise of fixed prices in business, with a move to **dynamic pricing**.[25] Dynamic pricing is the use of market-based, negotiated prices for transactions, which some analysts argue can be easily accomplished through internet-based auction technologies. While the demise of fixed pricing may be unlikely, the increasing use of auction models for conducting business will continue to occur.

To facilitate the improved use of auction models to carry out commerce, the idea of metamarkets and meta-auctions has been discussed. Essentially, a metamarket would result in the linking of all related auctions and markets together to form

DYNAMIC PRICING
The use of market-based, negotiated prices for transactions.

Figure 8.7   An Automotive Metamarket

The consolidation of auctions and B2B exchanges may lead to the creation of metamarkets such as this automotive market.

Automobile Metamarket

Fully integrated, informational and transactional marketplace

- Auto manufacturers
- New car dealers
- Used car dealers
- Newspaper classifieds
- Auto magazine
- Peer and expert opinions
- Financing companies
- Insurance companies
- Mechanics
- Service shops
- Spare parts dealers

a large base of participants with common interests. Figure 8.7 provides an example of a metamarket for the automotive industry. The difference between this concept and the concept of industry exchanges is that the metamarket would allow for various exchanges and auctions to integrate all of their participants to achieve a critical mass, which would lead to a more efficient market of "frictionless commerce."[26]

E-procurement, trading exchanges, and auctions will continue to converge and be more easily integrated with back-office technologies over the coming months and years. The creation of metamarkets is an ideal that may be in the distant future, but it gives competitors in this area something to strive for.

Chapter Summary

E-procurement has become an important e-business initiative in the last few years. Recognizing the potential for reduced administration costs, increased turnaround time, and improved pricing, businesses have begun to embark upon e-procurement initiatives to automate paper processes. The major success factors for e-procurement are the ability of organizations to integrate digital procurement data into the ERP system and the flexibility of the organization to modify existing business processes.

Trading exchanges form an important part of an overall e-procurement strategy. Exchanges provide a medium through which buyers and suppliers can transact business in an efficient manner. Horizontal exchanges are those that target business across numerous industries, such as an office supplies exchange. Vertical exchanges are those that target business within a specific industry throughout the supply chain, such as a healthcare industry exchange. As trading exchanges evolve, they progress towards a medium through which e-procurement, supply chain management, and customer relationship management are conducted.

The growth of the online auction industry sparked by consumer-to-consumer giant eBay has resulted in increased awareness of auctioning applications. The business-to-business community has commenced the use of auctioning techniques in the e-procurement process as an efficient means of executing transactions for many types of goods and services. B2B transactions have commonly been carried out through the use of reverse auctions, and as the industry and technologies develop many of the trading exchanges are facilitating auctioning processes.

The auctioning process employs numerous technologies to operate efficiently and effectively. For all auction participants to be treated fairly, it is essential that auction policies are provided and that bidders are kept up to date throughout the auction period. Auctions in the future are predicted to increase the use of dynamic pricing in business, possibly in both B2B and B2C transactions.

Key Terms

Dutch auction   *(p. 163)*

dynamic pricing   *(p. 167)*

English auction   *(p. 163)*

horizontal trading exchanges   *(p. 155)*

maverick buying   *(p. 153)*

private exchange   *(p. 155)*

public exchanges   *(p. 156)*

request for proposal (RFP)   *(p. 164)*

reverse auction   *(p. 163)*

sealed-bid auction   *(p. 164)*

Universal Description, Discovery and Integration (UDDI) initiative   *(p. 159)*

vertical trading exchanges   *(p. 155)*

Vickrey auction   *(p. 164)*

web services   *(p. 161)*

Yankee auction   *(p. 163)*

Tools for Online Learning

To help you master the material in this chapter and stay up to date with new developments in e-business, visit www.pearsoned.ca/trites. Resources include:

- **Review Questions and Exercises**

- **Problems for Discussion**

- **Recommended Readings**

- **Updates to Case Studies and Textual Material**

- **Streaming CBC Videos with Cases**

Endnotes

1. Tim Wilson, "e-Procurement Revisited—More than Cheap Supplies," *Internetweek* (April 23, 2001).

2. William Atkinson, "Web Ordering, Auctions Will Play Limited Role," *Purchasing* (April 5, 2001).

3. Bill Gates with Collins Hemingway, *Business @ The Speed of Thought: Using a Digital Nervous System* (New York: Warner Books, 1999).

4. Bill Gates with Collins Hemingway, *Business @ The Speed of Thought: Using a Digital Nervous System* (New York: Warner Books, 1999).

5. Rob Handfield, "E-Procurement and the Purchasing Process," *Hot Topics,* Supply Chain Resource Consortium, NC State University, October 22, 2003, scrc.ncsu.edu/public/DIRECTOR/dir102203.html, accessed November 20, 2004.

6. Heather Harreld, "Optimizing Supplier Selection," *InfoWorld* (November 16, 2001).

7. John Geriant, "Drug Company Triples Cost Savings via E-Procurement," *Supply Management* (March 15, 2001).

8. "E-Procurement Savings," *The Controller's Report*, New York, New York (April 2001).

9. "E-Procurement Saves," *Internetweek* (April 2, 2001).

10. Bill Gates with Collins Hemingway, *Business @ The Speed of Thought: Using a Digital Nervous System* (New York: Warner Books, 1999), 49.

11. "eMarketplaces Boost B2B Trade," Forrester Research (February 2000).

12. Jon Burke, "Is GE the Last Internet Company?," *Red Herring*, no. 88 (December 15, 2000): 55.

13. Compuware Corporation website, www.covisint.com, accessed April 20, 2004.

14. Jeff Bennett, "Covisint Becomes Corporation: Online Parts Exchange Defies Doubters in Europe," *Detroit Free Press*, 12 December 2000.

15. Jeff Bennett, "Compuware Has Ideas for Covisint: Streamlined Exchange Expected to Earn Big," *Detroit Free Press*, 6 February, 2004.

16. Jon Burke, "Is GE the Last Internet Company?," *Red Herring*, no. 88 (December 15, 2000): 55.

17. Jon Burke, "Is GE the Last Internet Company?," *Red Herring*, no. 88 (December 15, 2000): 55.

18. Vendio Services Inc., website, www.vendio.com, accessed April 20, 2004.

19. Vendio Services Inc., website, www.vendio.com, accessed April 20, 2004.

20. David Wyld, *The Auction Model: How the Public Sector Can Leverage the Power of E-Commerce Through Dynamic Pricing*, monograph (Southeastern Louisiana University: November 2000).

21. M. Kumar and S. Feldman, *Internet Auctions,* Iac report (IBM T.J. Watson Research Centre: November 1998).

22. David Wyld, *The Auction Model: How the Public Sector Can Leverage the Power of E-Commerce Through Dynamic Pricing*, monograph (Southeastern Louisiana University: November 2000).

23. David Wyld, *The Auction Model: How the Public Sector Can Leverage the Power of E-Commerce Through Dynamic Pricing*, monograph (Southeastern Louisiana University: November 2000).

24. William Atkinson, "IT Firm Uses Reverse Auction for Big Contract Labor Buy," *Purchasing* (December 22, 2000).

25. David Wyld, *The Auction Model: How the Public Sector Can Leverage the Power of E-Commerce Through Dynamic Pricing*, monograph (Southeastern Louisiana University: November 2000).

26. Mohanbir Sawhney, "Making New Markets: Sellers Need to Better Understand Buyers to Achieve the Promise of the Net Economy," *Business 2.0* (May 1999).

CHAPTER 9

Customer Relationship Management

LEARNING OBJECTIVES

When you complete this chapter you should be able to:

1. Describe the process of customer relationship management (CRM) and explain its relevance to e-business.

2. Identify the sources of data for CRM and how that data can be turned into information.

3. Outline the goals of CRM and how technology helps to achieve those goals.

4. Name and describe the core internet-enabled CRM technologies.

5. Describe how CRM fits into systems integration.

6. Identify the potential issues that may arise during CRM implementation and how they may be addressed.

Introduction

Today's business world has adopted a customer-centric approach to strategy, following several years of cost-reductions and downsizing. The advent of e-business, with its need for speed in meeting—even anticipating—the wishes of customers, has increased the need for a customer-centric approach. The key to finding out what the customers want, developing relationships with them, and managing those relationships lies in the careful application of appropriate technologies.

Customer relationship management (CRM), in an e-business context, is the use of technologies to establish, develop, maintain, and optimize relationships with customers by focusing on the understanding of needs and desires.[1] Besides technology, CRM also necessarily involves business processes, human resources, and strategies to enable businesses to focus on customers to deliver better profitability. CRM technologies allow customer information to be gathered through a single point and then used throughout an organization to improve the relationship with customers (either businesses or end consumers).

Blue Martini Software
www.bluemartini.com

Customer relationship management has been adopted recently by organizations large and small, online and offline. For example, Canadian Tire Corporation adopted some of Blue Martini Software's CRM applications to better serve and interact with customers both online and through its call centre. Online customers are able to benefit from Canadian Tire's loyalty program and Canadian Tire Money, and the company can track and understand its customers' online shopping habits using the CRM software. In addition, the online store can customize prices based on the shopper's postal code, since prices at each store vary because each store's independent franchise owner can set its own prices. This enables customers to see prices that correspond with the prices at their local stores. Offline customers who phone the Canadian Tire call centre are better served because customer service representatives (CSRs) are automatically provided with account histories and information on the customer. The application of CRM technologies is helping Canadian Tire retain its competitive position in the retail market for automotive, sports, and home products.

Although CRM is a relatively simple concept, successfully carrying out a CRM implementation and developing the appropriate attitudes with employees can be very challenging. Similar to other major technology implementations such as ERP systems and e-procurement systems, changes required in business processes are always a challenge. While the basic idea of focusing on the customer has existed since business began, CRM offers a revolutionary means of fully understanding, predicting, and responding to customers and potential customers. See the E-Strategy box for an example of CRM by an online retailer.

The CRM Process

CRM must include the major functional areas (such as marketing, sales, and service) across the organization to create a framework that will allow employees of the organization to better fulfill customer needs. Marketing can use CRM to establish new relationships as well as develop and optimize existing relationships through a better understanding of questions such as:

- Who are our customers?
- What do these customers really want from us?
- What advertising methods are most effective?
- Which channels are likely to be most successful in gaining repeat business?

E-Strategy

eBags Focuses on the Customer

eBags is an online retailer of bags, luggage, and travel accessories based in Denver, Colorado. The company's management feels that the key to maximizing profitability is understanding the customer and designing advertising campaigns and websites based on their customers' needs.

eBags decided that a customer loyalty program was required to retain existing customers and chose Kana e-Marketing for its program. As well as focusing on the loyalty program, eBags is integrating its front-end website and its back-end applications (J.D. Edwards ERP and Oracle database) with the Kana CRM applications. Other information sources such as e-mail, chat interactions, and telephone conversations are also being captured to add to the information eBags possesses about customer behaviour.

The president and CEO of eBags, Jon Nordmark, describes the importance of the CRM initiative as follows:

Conversion rates are the best measure of customer satisfaction. Improving those rates means making continuous improvements on click-throughs on e-mails, getting more browsers to put items in their shopping carts, and getting more shopping carts all the way to the order desk.

The CRM application allows eBags to more quickly analyze the customer information it gathers, up to five times as fast as previous analytical tools, which can save the company numerous lost opportunities.

Once the website redesign and customer analysis techniques were in place, eBags began to employ e-mail marketing and campaign management using its CRM application. By capturing all data related to the campaigns, including response rates, buy rates, and customer analysis, eBags aims to gain 10 to 30 percent on its conversion rates while improving customer service levels—potentially improving the incidence of return visits.

eBags has learned a number of important facts about its customers through the use of technology, such as how its e-mail campaigns work. The analysis of data has led eBags to the conclusion that customers are much more likely to buy items placed at the beginning or end of an e-mail ad. This information allows eBags to design more profitable campaigns by placing high-margin items at the beginning and end of e-mail campaign messages.

eBags didn't stand still after successfully employing its CRM application; in fact Nordmark stated that he wanted the company to link its databases and share information extensively with those of its suppliers and partners. Since the eBags system is already automated, Nordmark argues that collaboration is simply the next logical step.

Looking to expand its online presence and brand image, eBags has partnered with notable companies such as Amazon.com and United Airlines. The United Airlines partnership, which includes a special co-branded site at **united.ebags.com**, provides customers with the opportunity to earn United Mileage Plus bonus miles for their eBags purchases. Through a partnership with Amazon, eBags is able to offer its products to even more potential customers. The partnership with Amazon, however, is somewhat different. Instead of sending customers directly to the eBags site, eBags merely acts as a distribution partner for Amazon.

eBags
www.ebags.com

Questions

1. What possible advantage could eBags see in sharing its CRM data with suppliers and partners?

2. Do partnerships such as the United Airlines one complicate the CRM process and data capture? How?

3. From a CRM perspective, which of the two partnerships has more potential? Why?

SOURCES: www.ebags.com; www.kana.com/casestudies/default.aspx?cid=EBags.

In addition, marketing can better develop and manage campaigns by using centralized customer data, rather than the piecemeal information that is often used in the absence of an organized CRM process. The concept of e-marketing is explored more fully in chapter 11.

The sales area will benefit from CRM by providing sales representatives with better information that they can use to **up-sell** or **cross-sell** products and services. Up-selling is the process of encouraging customers to purchase higher-priced products or services. Cross-selling is the process of encouraging customers to purchase complementary or additional products or services from the firm. If a business customer phones a salesperson and the CRM application can automatically provide the customer's purchase history, credit details, and other information, the salesperson may be able to generate more sales dollars than would be possible without the information. If the salesperson can up-sell a customer from a mid-level product to a higher-quality product, sales will increase and the customer will have a better product offering. The salesperson may also be able to cross-sell by providing customers with information regarding optional equipment that is available or details of how products can be combined to enhance their capabilities. In advanced systems, these selling opportunities may even be scripted and provide additional details the customer may wish to know, such as how the product compares to the competition.

The customer service area of many businesses also offers the opportunity to become involved in selling while providing valuable customer service. For example, when a bank customer phones looking for information on current interest rates, a CSR can see that the customer has outstanding credit card debts for the past few months but has a strong credit rating. A scripted discussion may appear on the CSR's screen that guides them through the process of "selling" the customer debt services by consolidating high-interest credit cards into a personal loan. This situation essentially can turn a service-based interaction into a selling opportunity. Increasingly, organizations will be using techniques similar to this to improve their customer relationships and their bottom line.

An illustration of the CRM process will provide a clearer understanding of the processes and technologies involved in CRM. Figure 9.1 illustrates the core components of CRM and illustrates the integration of internal departments. Data are gathered utilizing advanced technologies for data capture. Integration of internal processes across the organization must include all potential areas that may directly or indirectly impact the customer. For example, sales would be an obvious area to include in CRM, but research and development (R&D) is another important integration point. Information on customer feedback needs to be linked to the design process, while information about R&D relating to new products and product improvements needs to be communicated to sales and marketing internally, and selectively to customers—establishing two-way communication through a central medium.

The process of CRM can be described as data capture, data analysis, strategic decision making, and implementation (see figure 9.2).

Data Capture

The first stage, data capture, occurs from each of the touch points in figure 9.1 including online sources (web forms and e-mail), offline sources (warranty registration cards), and back-office data integration. Data are stored in a **data warehouse** and will generally be formatted and modified to suit the particular requirements of the organization by removing unnecessary data elements and adding any necessary data descriptions. A data warehouse is a central data repository utilized to organ-

UP-SELL
The process of encouraging customers to purchase higher-priced products or services.

CROSS-SELL
The process of encouraging customers to purchase complementary or additional products or services from the firm.

DATA WAREHOUSE
A central data repository utilized to organize, store, analyze, and report upon data for decision-making purposes.

Figure 9.1   CRM Integration

CRM requires integration of data and access to the application to occur seamlessly across multiple systems.

ize, store, analyze, and report upon data for decision-making purposes. In some organizations, data from each touch point may be stored in a **data mart** prior to being transferred to the data warehouse. A data mart is a data repository that is dedicated to specific user groups and is often integrated into the data warehouse.

DATA MART
A data repository that is dedicated to specific user groups and is often integrated into the data warehouse.

Data Analysis

CRM applications offer a number of tools to analyze and understand customer data. The second step of the CRM process, data analysis, involves the use of CRM applications to explore the data to identify relevant customer information. Some organizations refer to this component of CRM as **customer intelligence**. While some predefined settings will assist in identifying trends or alerting management to areas needing attention, the data analysis stage requires customization and the involvement of individuals who have a strong understanding of the business strategy and the industry. Essentially, data will not be turned into relevant information without the application of logic to identify key areas of concern. This analysis may be carried out by any of sales, marketing, service, or other personnel. Collaboration across departments will often lead to discovery of important factors that may not be learned without a team approach.

CUSTOMER INTELLIGENCE
The use of CRM applications to explore the data to identify relevant customer information.

Strategic Decision Making

The information identified in the data analysis stage of the CRM process may lead to the identification of numerous areas where management can or should make

Figure 9.2 The CRM Process

The CRM process is a cycle that begins and ends with the customer touch points.

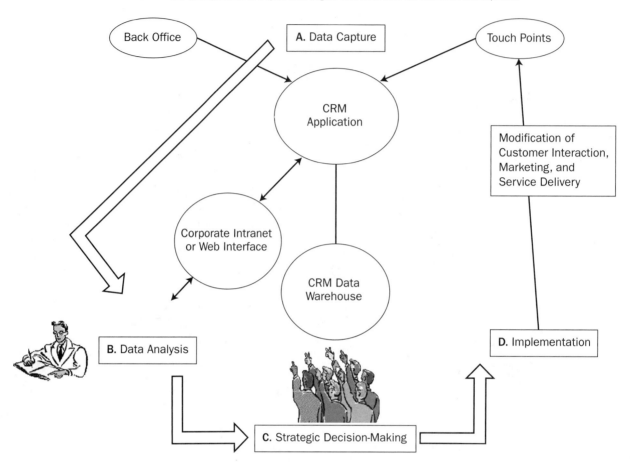

changes. It is critical, however, that the management team review the analysis and compare the planned initiatives to corporate and departmental strategy. Marketing analysis may highlight an opportunity to sell a new upscale product, but management's strategic objective may be to focus on cost-effectiveness. Therefore, the opportunity may be dismissed in favour of another that, for example, offers the delivery of product and service information through electronic media as a cost-reduction measure. In essence, the appropriate process is to narrow the initiatives identified by data analysis to those that most directly relate to current strategic objectives.

Implementation

Once strategic objectives have been clarified, the implementation of change can begin. This may involve change in the methods by which information is delivered to customers, modification of marketing campaigns, revisions to the online store, or numerous other possibilities. Implementation, however, is a critical stage in the process, where objectives must be clearly understood and outcomes should be predicted. Predicted outcomes should be measurable, so that ongoing evaluation of any process changes can be measured. Sometimes, cross-departmental teams are necessary to effectively implement change, while in other cases implementation may only require a single group or individual.

CRM vs. Business Intelligence

While CRM makes use of data warehousing technology and data analysis techniques it is not the same as business intelligence (BI). CRM data may be used within a BI application but would only form one component of the system. As illustrated in figure 9.3, business intelligence is broader in scope and carries a different focus than CRM. As technologies continue to converge, CRM applications are becoming offerings within BI applications. Business intelligence is examined fully in chapter 10.

Goals of CRM

The goals of CRM are many and can be organized into a number of key areas, such as marketing, sales, and service. The overall goal of any CRM implementation should be to improve upon customer relationships by providing better service, improved sales efforts, and reduced marketing costs.

Marketing Goals

The goals for CRM in the marketing area are extensive and in many cases overlap with other areas. Some of the marketing goals include improved marketing planning, sales forecasting, competitor intelligence, trend analysis, and performance analysis. While many of these goals are related specifically to marketing, others are cross-functional because of the integrative nature of CRM.

Sales Goals

In the sales area, CRM strategies aim to improve the sales process by increasing efficiency, improving customer interaction and service, and simplifying the process for salespeople. In addition, the sales goals include the redirection of sales to the most efficient and effective selling channels (e.g., telesales, internet sales, trading exchanges, etc.).

Figure 9.3   CRM and Business Intelligence

CRM overlaps with BI but has a different focus and narrower scope.

SALES FORCE AUTOMATION (SFA)
The process of simplifying sales in the field and the integration of sales activity into the corporate information structure.

CRM efforts have developed naturally from some firms' efforts in the area of sales force automation. **Sales force automation (SFA)** is the process of simplifying sales in the field and the integration of sales activity into the corporate information structure.[2] CRM is a much more encompassing strategy than SFA, but the two share some common goals. SFA efforts began with simplistic tools such as contact managers, and later emerged into sophisticated technologies to track leads, integrate databases, and share information with back-end systems. Some of the leading CRM application providers have evolved from being SFA providers in the past.

Service Goals

Service departments and customer service representatives have the capability, through the use of technology, of becoming effective sales contacts by developing an enhanced understanding of customer needs. As with other areas in the organization, customer service needs to examine its role as a customer touch point and learn which service methods are most effective for particular customer groups. (See the Canadian Snapshot box for a look at customer service goals at Hydro-Québec.)

CRM Metrics

CRM involves gathering large volumes of data for analysis to better understand the customer. The large volumes of data, however, will lead to storage capacity problems and result in slow response times if unnecessary data are not purged from the system.

The CRM metrics commonly used are centred on the areas of marketing, sales, and service. Each of these areas can be used to structure the types of outcomes and information that the CRM system should be able to provide. The basic metrics for CRM may be programmed as standard reports within the application. While these metrics provide useful information, the most valuable information will often be obtained through custom queries and analysis that are linked to the company's specific industry and strategic goals.

Internet-Enabled CRM

CRM has become much more powerful with the increasing use of the internet. Internet technology allows e-businesses to efficiently gather and distribute customer data as well as provide a new medium for communicating with customers. Websites were originally used as simplistic marketing tools, but the increasing use of multimedia and other components allows businesses to transmit large volumes of data, provide customer support online, and reach potential customers through a flexible interface.

The data capture process described earlier is simplified by technology that can easily gather data from customers and prospects. Information typed into online forms or through e-mail can be automatically moved to the data warehouse through automated tools. While a bricks-and-mortar retail business may never realize that potential customers were in the store but couldn't find the product they were looking for, online stores can find this out through click-stream analysis, log-file analysis, and efficient feedback systems (discussed below).

Online Contact Management

Internet-based contacts can be a valuable resource for developing customer relationships. A number of methods exist to establish contacts, but gathering infor-

Canadian Snapshots

Hydro-Québec Improves Customer Service

Hydro-Québec is one of Canada's largest providers of energy, with more than 3.5 million customers throughout North America. With the deregulation of the energy markets, Hydro-Québec has decided to adopt a proactive strategy to deal with customer service and relationship management.

Hydro-Québec's vision statement includes the following statement: "Customers are the reason we are in business and we must show them that, at Hydro-Québec, the customer comes first. Whether in Quebec or on international markets, we want to satisfy our customers by supplying energy products and services of a quality that meets their needs at competitive prices." While numerous companies may have statements similar to this, Hydro-Québec has taken action by adopting Siebel applications to assist in CRM.

Hydro-Québec adopted Siebel Sales to improve relationships with corporate customers and improve information sharing among sales and service staff. Realizing that

deregulation might bring substantial competition, the company began implementing its CRM strategy with corporate customers, who make up a large portion of sales and offer a stronger opportunity for relationship development than residential customers.

Siebel Sales allows company representatives to consolidate and share customer information in a manner that was never before possible. Previous attempts to automate the system based on periodic updates resulted in little success due to missing information and lack of timeliness. The adoption of CRM has allowed employees to work more successfully as a team, and management claims that customer service has been improved with more accurate and up-to-date information available.

Sales contact in the past had been primarily in person, and Hydro-Québec realized that customers were beginning to demand more personalized and timely service. The company is improving on its CRM strategy by adopting addi-

tional products from Siebel, including Siebel eChannel and Siebel Handheld. Siebel eChannel allows customers to communicate with the company by internet, e-mail, and cellular channels while continuing to capture data and provide seamless customer service. Siebel Handheld is an application that lends support to sales staff so they may interact with the CRM application anytime, anywhere.

Hydro-Québec's implementation of Siebel applications is being integrated with both the back-end ERP system (Oracle, in this case) and the front-end applications, allowing efficient transfer of information. One of the key selling points of the Siebel applications to Hydro-Québec was the integration of French-language support that was well designed and reduced requirements for translation.

The benefits of CRM at Hydro-Québec include improved customer service, enhanced information sharing and team selling, faster sales cycles, and an increase in customer retention rates.

Hydro-Québec
www.hydro.qc.ca

Siebel Systems, Inc.
www.siebel.com

Questions

1. Should deregulation have been the motivator for Hydro-Québec to get involved in CRM?
2. What types of communication are likely to take place through Siebel eChannel with corporate customers? How is this more efficient?
3. Will CRM assist Hydro-Québec in any way to develop relationships with residential customers? How?

SOURCES: www.hydro.qc.ca; www.siebel.com.

mation from and about them is important in an e-business context. It is common, for example, to be contacted by salespeople after registering online for free demos and product white papers. The CRM systems at these businesses were designed to capture the information needed on prospective buyers so that a salesperson could later follow up with the individual. Some studies have indicated that personal follow-up to such contacts has resulted in a 20 to 37 percent increase in sales. The internet can be a tremendous means of gathering information on prospects, but it is necessary to use that information in an effective way—either through e-mail, mail, or telephone follow-up.

Online Marketing Campaigns

CRM analyses should lead to the ability to create targeted online marketing campaigns by better understanding who the online customers are, how their needs may differ, and what predictors of buying are relevant. As businesses move to an online sales channel, historic information regarding customer segments and buying patterns may need to be completely re-evaluated. Customers making use of internet technologies for purchasing may have different demographics and new prospects may be found who would not have been identified through traditional campaigns.

E-Mail Campaigns The use of e-mail for sales is a controversial but important area for e-businesses to consider. Sending a large volume of general-interest e-mails will likely result in negative attitudes by customers; however, targeted e-mail can be very beneficial. Past customers are known to be those who are most likely to buy again, so e-mail offers to existing customers, if done appropriately, can result in additional sales. The use of e-mail in online marketing is discussed more fully in chapter 11.

CRM applications such as those offered by Siebel Systems include advanced tools for creating, managing, and analyzing e-mail campaigns. To benefit from experience, it is essential that e-mail campaigns be carefully monitored. Details of sales arising from e-mail campaigns should be integrated with both online and offline sales to evaluate campaign success, and any past analysis techniques should be re-evaluated based on the outcomes.

Real-Time Chat The internet brings a number of technologies to the table to create relationships with customers or potential customers, an important one being the use of chat technologies. A number of service providers are available that can integrate live chat into a website so that a user can ask to chat immediately with a human being. For example, HumanClick Ltd. provides chat applications that can be used to provide improved customer service on a website.

Chat technologies have a reputation as a way to waste time online with groups of people with common interests; however, the potential business applications of this technology are impressive. A prospective customer can get information immediately from a sales representative, for instance, rather than having to dial a 1-800 number (potentially having to go offline to do so). Many "browsers" would not go the extra step to phone with a question, but the live chat session makes the inquiry convenient and hassle-free, potentially leading to new business. Existing customers can also utilize real-time chat for assistance with finding specific product information or to learn about special offers to existing customers.

Advanced technologies also allow chat sessions to be interactive, with the support person actually guiding the user through the web. A support person can see on the screen what the user is looking at and is able to give detailed advice on where to find something. In some applications the support person can actually move the user interactively through the site—effectively taking them to the site they are looking for. These capabilities are allowing businesses to establish stronger relationships by providing customers and prospects with service when they need it.

VOICE OVER INTERNET PROTOCOL (VOIP)
The use of an internet telephony protocol that relays voice signals across the internet, whether in a computer-to-phone call or a computer-to-computer call.

Voice over Internet Protocol Similar to the usefulness of real-time chat sessions, **Voice over Internet Protocol (VoIP)** is an application that can enhance service to customers and prospects. VoIP is an internet telephony protocol that relays voice signals across the internet, whether in a computer-to-phone call or a computer-to-computer call. VoIP allows users to phone a customer service representative through the internet by clicking on a "Phone us now" button on a website. As broadband technologies improve, the application of VoIP is likely to increase, allowing users a convenient, low-cost method of connecting with businesses to receive service.

Intelligent Agents Also known as "web bots" or "bots" (from robots), **intelligent agents** allow companies to implement tools that can assist users to find products or information throughout their site and may result in automated up-selling and cross-selling of products. For example, if a truck owner is searching a supplier's site for a needed part and has difficulty identifying the specific part required, an intelligent agent could pull information about the customer's existing truck, past buying patterns, and other details to select web content that may be useful to provide. The intelligent agent may come back with a few options that would work for the customer, including higher-quality products or supplemental items that can be purchased. While intelligent agents are still in their infancy, integration with CRM systems is a promising prospect.

INTELLIGENT AGENT
A program designed to assist users on the web to carry out tasks such as searching for information or to automate tasks such as up-selling or cross-selling products.

E-Mail Management The volume of e-mail requests sent to many organizations with a successful web presence quickly outpaces the capability of the organization to respond. An effective CRM strategy would require that e-mail requests be handled in a very reasonable period of time. User and customer expectations are leading to faster and faster response times. E-mail management technologies are available which can assist in dealing with the mass of e-mails that are sure to come with growth.

E-mail represents one of the many customer/prospect touch points discussed earlier and as such is a form of data that must be captured. Leading CRM providers' applications integrate e-mail data into the CRM applications so that call centre staff who later receive contact from a customer can review former correspondence, thus remaining up to date with all business/customer information.

Incoming e-mail can be sorted and redirected to appropriate individuals by applications that seek out keywords in the e-mail and identify those within the organization who can address the concern or question. In addition, many applications can put together draft responses to questions based on pre-defined templates (or FAQs), which employees need only review quickly prior to responding to the customer or prospect. Other features such as auto-acknowledgement of requests, statistical analysis, and standard e-mail system integration are also available.

Customer Self-Service

Another important aspect of internet-enabled CRM is the ability of customers to "serve themselves," thus reducing costs and simplifying service. Customer self-service may take many forms but is essentially the application of technologies that allow customers to easily identify problems, seek out service information, and in some cases solve their own problems (e.g., software downloads). Technology-based products are particularly well-suited to customer self-service since customers often have expertise related to the product and may be happy to identify and solve difficulties on their own. Allowing those customers who are content to service themselves to do so also allows the business to focus its time on those customers who wish to have personal (person-to-person) service.

Internet-enabled CRM is an important area of CRM that includes numerous tools and applications to better serve the customer. (See the New Business Models box to see how Eddie Bauer is coping with the vast changes in the CRM area). Ranging from simple tools like e-mail applications to complex integrated systems, internet-enabled CRM is growing in importance and will continue to develop over the next several years.

New Business Models

CRM at eddiebauer.com®

Eddie Bauer Inc. is a retailer of casual lifestyle clothing, accessories, and home furnishings, and has a history as an excellent service provider for more than 80 years. The company had stores around the world and extensive sales through catalogues as the e-business era approached. To maintain its foothold in the retail industry, the company launched eddiebauer.com in 1995 to begin selling many of its products over the internet.

The traffic on the website increased rapidly and Eddie Bauer became concerned about the level of customer service being provided. Customer service representatives began to be overwhelmed by the volume of e-mail questions, and telephone queries related to the website were on the rise—dramatically increasing costs while customer service was getting slower. To combat this problem Eddie Bauer began seeking new technology in the hope of capturing some of the upcoming, lucrative 1999 holiday season.

Eddie Bauer chose Kana to provide it with CRM applications that could assist in improving online customer service. The initial concern by Eddie Bauer staff was regarding the e-mail volume that was being handled on a first-come-first-served basis by the CSRs—so an e-mail application was added that sorted the queries based on CSR expertise and forwarded them to the appropriate in-box.

Intelligent agent technology, known as "Ask Eddie Instant Help," was added to the site as well. Ask Eddie is an intelligent agent that can respond immediately to customers seeking self-service by compiling standard responses from FAQs and employee e-mail responses. By 2001, up to 80 percent of the users of Ask Eddie had no further questions, indicating "Eddie" had adequately answered their requests. This resulted in reduced demand on CSRs to respond to routine requests and allowed the e-mail requests to be

answered within two hours rather than one or more days.

Eddiebauer.com also employs live chat technologies to improve customer service. Chat is available both in the service and sales areas of the site. In service, chat allows the customer to immediately query a knowledgeable CSR without the use of the telephone and while still on the site—potentially increasing the likelihood of purchasing on the site or strengthening the relationship with the customer. In the sales sections of the site, chat is available throughout the purchase process so that nervous buyers can discuss the checkout process with a CSR.

Utilizing internet-based technologies and CRM applications, Eddie Bauer has now transformed itself from a bricks-and-mortar retailer to a leading bricks-and-clicks retailer. Eddie Bauer has embraced the changes brought forth in the era of e-business and has utilized technology to become a leading player in the field.

Eddie Bauer
www.eddiebauer.com

Kana
www.kana.com

Questions

1. Do you feel the application of technology such as intelligent agents can actually improve the business–customer relationship?

2. Would the company require as many CSRs as in the past? What other roles could those employees take on?

3. Eddie Bauer is an upscale retailer. Does online selling impact that image?

SOURCES: www.kana.com; www.eddiebauer.com.

Technologies and Integration

Many of the technologies discussed in this book are used to allow CRM applications to operate in an integrated fashion. Businesses are investing heavily in the development of integrated systems and CRM efforts require a number of integration points to be considered. To develop customer relationships, it is necessary to capture, process, and share information across the enterprise. The information may originate in the ERP system, the SCM application, within legacy systems, or be drawn from external data sources.

The ERP system is the cornerstone source for data on the internal side of the business. For example, all current information related to the customer (such as orders placed, in production, or being shipped) should be up-to-date within the ERP system. These data need to be available to the CRM system so salespeople or customer service representatives can discuss issues in a current fashion at the various touch points they deal with. The integration of the CRM application and ERP system is critical and its implementation will vary depending on the particular systems employed.

The integration of data from the supply chain will also be important in successful CRM applications. For customers to gain access to information regarding expected delivery dates or other factors, the CRM application must be interfaced with the SCM system. Much of the data within the CRM system will also be useful for SCM processes such as forecasting and demand analysis. In order for the entire value chain to operate effectively, it is essential that internal and external data be integrated.

The use of external data sources is one that complicates the process of data integration. As more companies integrate their systems with each other, the intricacies of each ERP system and other applications can create major roadblocks to data sharing. Some of the tools used to overcome these difficulties are discussed in the next section.

The integration of data must be carried out as a critical component of developing a CRM strategy. Identification of relevant data sources must be followed by developing an understanding of the technologies to be employed and creating data structures that will allow the data to be easily analyzed. The complexity of the data must not be allowed to encroach on the usefulness of the information that can be obtained through analysis.

Implementing CRM

Implementation of CRM is a project that requires planning similar to other major technology projects, but also requires managers to deal with a number of implementation concerns. The implementation process may take from several months to several years to complete and will progress through a number of stages as the "learning curve" takes place.

Implementation Concerns

Many of the implementation concerns related to CRM projects are similar to those that arise in ERP projects and can result in very expensive, failed projects. It is important when undertaking such an implementation to consider the political, cultural, and technological concerns that are likely to arise as the project progresses. Like ERP implementations, technology is important, but it is critical that business strategies, processes, and people considerations drive the implementation.

Political and Cultural Concerns Political and cultural concerns can get any technology project into trouble as employees struggle with changes in responsibilities and processes. Team-based approaches with strong buy-in from management tend to reduce the concerns in this area, but they will still invariably arise. For example, CRM implementation will require various departments such as sales, service, and marketing to review their data requirements, processes, and customer touchpoints to plan for the implementation. As these and other topics are considered, the "ownership" of customer touch points is likely to become an issue, necessitating management to deal with the changes that are inherent in developing a true customer-centric approach.

CRM implementation will also require a number of employees to adjust their responsibilities when dealing with customers. For example, customer service representatives may now become responsible for selling products or services, as described earlier in the chapter. This change alone may require the development of new compensation arrangements within the firm, whereby the traditional "salesperson" is no longer the only employee receiving commissions or performance bonuses based on sales. These types of cultural changes are likely to cause difficulties as the CRM strategy is adopted, but can also be valuable learning tools for adept managers who identify means by which customer relationships can be improved throughout the enterprise.

Technological Concerns Technological concerns for a CRM implementation project focus on integration with existing technologies and planning for new technologies. As discussed earlier in this chapter, the CRM system needs to be integrated with ERP, SCM, and other applications to be an effective tool, and this can create difficulties for information systems departments dealing with numerous other applications. CRM applications vary a great deal in structure as well, ranging from typical client-server approaches to web-based designs.

Many of the linkages required to integrate CRM will be based on enterprise application integration (EAI) tools such as middleware. Middleware is software that allows communication between different systems by reformatting data into a form that can be interpreted by the other system. In addition to middleware, XML has been touted as a language that will simplify the integration of technologies by permitting applications to read and understand the self-described format. Despite the capabilities of middleware, EAI, and XML to allow organizations to integrate systems, some analysts claim that possibly only 10 percent of organizations have achieved integration at a sophisticated level.[3]

Other technology concerns will focus on the integration of the numerous touch points and processes involved in CRM. Customer contacts that occur, for example, at a wholesale outlet or via a website should generate similar data from the customer and store it within the data warehouse. In addition, call centres need access to integrated customer data that may require the business to adopt computer telephony integration.

COMPUTER TELEPHONY INTEGRATION (CTI)
A technology that allows telephone systems to integrate with computer systems to aid in customer service and data capture.

Computer telephony integration (CTI) is a technology that allows telephone systems to integrate with computer systems to aid in customer service and data capture. An example of CTI in action would be a customer service request coming in by phone. As the phone system recognizes the caller (through caller identification), the call is redirected to an appropriate CSR within seconds, and information is pulled from the CRM system related to the customer and output to the CSR's computer screen. Without any demands being placed on the CSR, the customer is now ready to be serviced by a knowledgeable employee who has a great deal of information related to the customer. This information can be used to provide service and potentially to sell products or services that the customer is likely to buy, based on the system's analysis.

Technological concerns will vary in complexity and cost but must be considered in relation to the implementation project's objectives. The critical stages of implementation for technologies include the CRM application selection stage and integration stage. CRM application selection will dictate how the project proceeds and the capabilities of the system for integration. Once again, the use of cross-functional teams at the planning stage is critical to allow the best application to be chosen for the organization.

Implementation Stages

The implementation of CRM will evolve through a number of stages over the term of the project. Some implementations will end up with only basic functionality, while others will evolve into advanced systems that are used extensively throughout the organization. Various methodologies exist but most CRM implementations will progress through the following stages: planning, process redesign, integration, education, analysis, and change implementation. See the E-Business in Global Perspective box for a discussion of the implementation process at National Australia Bank.

Planning The planning phase of CRM adoption and implementation is an important foundation to the entire project. Setting the stage for the remainder of the implementation, planning will address such areas as needs analysis, software selection, project responsibilities, and project timelines. The planning phase may consider some preliminary requirements for process change and will evaluate and have input into the CRM strategy.

The planning process should be carried out by a cross-functional team of employees (and consultants) to establish input from the entire enterprise. As discussed earlier, the team approach will allow concerns of various departments to be raised early in the process and establish a communication process for the implementation. It is important to have consultants involved at the planning process as well so that the project goals and timeline are reviewed for reasonableness. Consultants will also be able to offer important advice as to how departments can plan for the implementation and what process revisions are likely to be required.

Process Redesign Business processes are likely to change as the CRM implementation project moves forward, accommodating technological requirements and revised employee/departmental responsibilities. Process redesign and business process reengineering (BPR) will occur throughout the implementation of CRM and often afterwards as well, but should be planned for early in the implementation process.

Early planning for BPR will allow employees and their departments time to consider the changes and provide feedback on the proposed changes. Some process changes may be dictated by the CRM application that is chosen, but others will be necessitated to achieve the strategic goals of the CRM implementation. Feedback and discussion of the process redesign will allow employees to have input into the process and will often result in suggested improvements that better the overall implementation.

Integration The implementation project's technological aspects will focus on integration of data once the CRM application has been installed. Relating back to the goals established at the planning process, the implementation team will work towards integrating any systems required for project success. This integration

E-Business in Global Perspective

Implementing CRM at National Australia Bank

National Australia Bank Limited (NAB), formed in 1858, is a leader in the employment of CRM. NAB has holdings in Australia, New Zealand, Ireland, United Kingdom, and the United States and has developed a CRM strategy over the past several years that allows it to manage customers globally by segments.

As a large financial institution, NAB may not have been a likely candidate to lead the CRM charge, but it began working on its CRM initiatives in 1988. At that early date, NAB began developing its strategy for CRM and a management and profitability system that would integrate customer-related information. Over the next seven years, NAB continued to develop its CRM systems, expanding to additional product lines and customer categories. By 1999 NAB implemented a complete CRM data warehouse, which linked customer data from Australia, New Zealand, and the United States, and had begun to identify important information to capitalize on opportunities across a number of countries in its holdings.

During 2000 NAB began a global implementation of a CRM solution to allow it to focus on its "franchise strategy." NAB, unlike many other banks, had organized its holdings to operate primarily as franchises rather than completely independent companies. Each franchise, such as the National Irish Bank, would look after its own regional and country-specific initiatives, but the management of customer segments was done on a global basis using all CRM data.

The franchise strategy approach allowed NAB to enable participation in strategic initiatives by all of the banks it controlled but recognized that customer segments tended to perform in a similar manner globally.

In progressing to the stage where NAB is a progressive manager of CRM data, the company has gone through a series of developments and revisions. The early initiatives focused on learning who customers were and what types of services the customer segments tended to use. Later the company explored the profitability of customer segments and how customer contact and follow-up

impacted the likelihood to buy. A number of technologies have been used during the years that CRM strategies were implemented, including NCR's Teradata data warehouse, NCR's Relationship Optimizer, and Siebel's eBusiness Applications.

NAB attempts to approach CRM as both a proactive and a reactive process. The company proactively uses information from its data warehouse to conduct custom campaigns and implement targeted selling strategies. Reactively, NAB looks for customer trends to reduce risk, increase customer loyalty, and attempt to respond to customer concerns in a reasonable manner. For example, a reactive approach may take place after the CRM system notifies an investment advisor that a major customer has accumulated a large deposit balance in the past week, resulting in a sales call that can benefit both NAB and the customer.

While NAB doesn't claim to know all there is to know about CRM, the company has developed an advanced system and a strategic operational approach to focusing on the customer.

National Australia Bank Ltd.
www.national.com.au

Questions

1. What customer segments might NAB analyze that are similar in all of its markets?
2. What role should the subsidiary banks (e.g., National Irish Bank) have in the CRM strategy?
3. What other complications do you see in operating a CRM strategy on a global basis?

SOURCES: www.national.com.au; K. Khirallah, "CRM Case Study: Optimizing Relationships at National Australia Bank, Ltd.," research note (Tower Group, January 2001).

stage will often continue to evolve as further stages of the implementation take place. Future investments in integration will occur once management and employees buy into the CRM approach and continue to demand further capabilities from the system.

Education The implementation of any new technology will involve a learning curve and an educational process. For CRM implementations, the educational process will involve both technology training and CRM-focused learning. The training required of most employees can be minimized by adopting systems that are web-enabled, allowing basic point-and-click interaction. However, despite ease of use, training for advanced queries and capabilities will be required for those users who will be responsible for aspects of the CRM application beyond basic reporting.

CRM-focused learning sessions should be provided to all employees who will interact with customers to implement a common strategy of customer contact. The CRM strategy's goals can only be achieved if employees are aware of the requirements and understand the customer-centric approach being adopted. The learning sessions also serve to inform and educate staff on the process revisions adopted so that customer touch points have common service levels.

Analysis The analysis stage of CRM implementation comes once the implementation has reached a stage where data are collected and the CRM application can begin to provide useful information. An interesting analysis of the stages of growth for CRM was written by Ronald Swift, who outlines the stages as reporting, analyzing, and predicting.[4]

Reporting The reporting stage of analysis is characterized by the use of pre-configured reports and queries on the data. In this initial phase of implementation, users become familiar with the system by developing an understanding of the customer, what products and services sell in particular areas, and other basic analysis. The reporting phase is primarily historical in focus with the limited use of ad-hoc querying.

Analyzing The analyzing stage is a step up from reporting, whereby managers and users begin to ask questions such as why events are occurring. This stage of implementation begins to truly develop a CRM mentality, whereby users ask what the causes of specific events and trends have been. Analyzing data may look more specifically at understanding why specific product lines did not meet targets, why a marketing campaign was so successful, or other similar kinds of questions.

Predicting The final stage of the analysis phase of a CRM implementation is the predicting phase, in which the business begins to truly capitalize on the CRM initiative by utilizing the data for strategic purposes. In the predicting phase, businesses begin to set marketing strategy, service goals, and modify touch points based on analysis from the CRM system. For example, the marketing and sales departments may perform analysis to identify which customers are most at risk of going to alternative suppliers and carry out proactive relationship measures to retain them. In this phase of CRM implementation, users are very familiar with the system and have developed an appreciation for the value of CRM.

The analysis stage of implementation is one that will proceed concurrently with other activities such as education and process redesign. The time that individual businesses will spend at each stage will vary and, despite large investments, those who don't spend adequately on education and change management efforts will never progress to the predicting stage of analysis.

Change Implementation The change implementation stage of CRM implementations is the point at which businesses begin to capitalize on their investments. This will normally occur after the business has been able to reach either the analyzing or predicting phases, described above, and truly understands customers.

At this stage, businesses will focus on efforts such as redesigning processes after successful or unsuccessful efforts have been evaluated. For example, a firm may run an internet-based advertising campaign based on CRM analysis, which has identified a target group likely to buy through this channel. If this campaign is successful, the firm may continue with this strategy by modifying processes that strengthen and support the use of this channel by specific groups, such as creating specialized websites for their use. This implementation of change should further develop customer relationships by making it easier for them to deal with the company through the channel of their choice.

Chapter Summary

Customer relationship management (CRM) is the process of establishing, developing, maintaining, and optimizing relationships with customers by focusing on the understanding of customers' needs and desires through the use of technology.

The key functional areas for CRM include marketing, sales, and service. The customer service area of many businesses also offers the opportunity to become involved in selling, while providing valuable customer service. The process of CRM can be described as the capture of data, data analysis, strategic decision-making, and implementation.

CRM applications offer numerous tools to analyze and understand customer data. Data analysis is the use of CRM applications to explore the data to identify relevant customer information. Some organizations refer to this component of CRM as customer intelligence.

While CRM makes use of data warehousing technology and data analysis techniques, it is not the same as business intelligence (BI). As technologies continue to converge, CRM applications are becoming offerings within BI applications. The overall goal of any CRM implementation should be to improve customer relationships by providing better service, improved sales efforts, and reduced marketing costs.

In the sales area, CRM strategies aim to improve the sales process by increasing efficiency, improving the customer interaction and service, and simplifying the process for salespeople. The service areas of businesses pursuing CRM strategies strengthen and develop the customer relationship from the date of original sale.

Internet technology allows e-businesses to efficiently gather and distribute customer data, as well as provide a new medium for communication with customers. The data capture process described earlier is simplified by technology that can easily gather data from customers and prospects.

Leading CRM providers' applications integrate e-mail data into the CRM applications so that call centre staff who later receive a contact from a customer can review former correspondence and thus remain up to date with all business/customer information. This ability to integrate data to aid in customer service is a major development for companies in the e-business arenas.

The critical stages of implementation for technologies include the CRM application selection stage and integration stage. The implementation project's technological aspects will focus on integration of data once the CRM application has been installed. For CRM implementations, the educational process will involve both technology training and CRM-focused learning. To implement a common strategy of customer contact, CRM-focused learning sessions should be provided to all employees who will interact with customers.

Key Terms

computer telephony integration (CTI)   *(p. 184)*

cross-sell   *(p. 174)*

customer intelligence   *(p. 175)*

data mart   *(p. 175)*

data warehouse   *(p. 174)*

intelligent agent   *(p. 181)*

sales force automation (SFA)   *(p. 178)*

up-sell   *(p. 174)*

Voice over Internet Protocol (VoIP)   *(p. 180)*

Tools for Online Learning

To help you master the material in this chapter and stay up to date with new developments in e-business, visit **www.pearsoned.ca/trites**. Resources include:

- **Review Questions and Exercises**

- **Problems for Discussion**

- **Recommended Readings**

- **Updates to Case Studies and Textual Material**

- **Streaming CBC Videos with Cases**

Endnotes

1. Tricia Fox and Steve Stead, *Customer Relationship Management: Delivering the Benefits*, White Paper (CRM (UK) Ltd., and SECOR Consulting Ltd., 2001).

2. R. Kalakota and A. Whinston, *Electronic Commerce: A Manager's Guide* (Toronto: Addison Wesley, 1996).

3. R. Kalakota and M. Robinson, *e-Business 2.0: Roadmap for Success* (Toronto: Addison Wesley, 2001).

4. Ronald Swift, "The Stages of Growth for CRM and Data Warehousing," *DM Review* (September 2000).

CHAPTER 10

Business Intelligence

LEARNING OBJECTIVES

When you complete this chapter you should be able to:

1. Explain the importance of business intelligence to business strategy.

2. Compare and contrast how business intelligence and ERP systems handle data.

3. Name and describe the major functions of business intelligence systems.

4. Explain the types of technologies used in business intelligence systems.

5. Discuss the implementation of business intelligence systems and what stages need to be followed.

6. Describe how businesses may use data warehouses and data marts within the business intelligence infrastructure.

Introduction

Globally, corporations are struggling to keep pace in the "information economy," and the rapid growth of the internet and related technologies is strengthening the demand for data management strategies. Business intelligence (BI) has emerged as a powerful tool that allows businesses to capture, analyze, interpret, and report on data—thus creating valuable information for the enterprise. Massive investments in ERP systems over the past decade have resulted in huge data storage mechanisms. In addition, the deployment of electronic commerce strategies on the internet results in large volumes of data, such as click-stream information. Business intelligence is the environment that supports analysis of data from any source (internal or external) to provide valuable information for making operating, tactical, or strategic decisions.

The concepts of business intelligence are not entirely new and have emerged from data-mining techniques, decision support systems, data warehousing, knowledge management, and other business tools that have been used for many years. Business intelligence differs from these other tools in that it is a completely integrated approach to data management and has been made possible by advances in technology such as the internet, ERP, and database systems.

Telus Mobility has adopted BI technology as a means to improve its decision-making capabilities in the highly competitive wireless communications industry in Canada. After a careful evaluation of the various business intelligence technologies available on the market, Telus Mobility chose a solution by Cognos Inc. Based in Ottawa, Cognos is one of the leading developers of business intelligence applications. Telus Mobility's strategy was to develop a data warehouse that would allow for user-friendly data analysis and reporting while also being powerful enough to allow ad-hoc queries and analysis to be carried out. Telus Mobility adopted the Cognos Impromptu and PowerPlay products, which met the company's needs and were very flexible in their deployment. Using Cognos business intelligence tools, Telus Mobility can more quickly analyze its business and leverage data.[1]

Telus Mobility
www.telusmobility.com

Business intelligence applications can be closely related to CRM strategies, as discussed in the previous chapter (see figure 9.3 on page 177), and in many instances the two go hand in hand. For example, Telus Mobility may use Cognos tools to identify customer segments that are highly profitable and develop strategies to ensure that it retains those customers (a CRM activity). In a similar light, however, a business analyst may use business intelligence applications to identify wireless infrastructure that is most likely to become problematic based on historical data in the system and deploy additional service and upkeep in that area (an operating activity). Essentially, business intelligence can be used any time that an organization wishes to better understand its data to improve decision-making. See the Canadian Snapshots box for a discussion of decision-making capabilities and relationship building with business intelligence technology at the Bank of Montreal.

Business Intelligence Functions

Business intelligence has evolved from previous data management systems such as data warehousing. As businesses struggle to gain a competitive advantage, BI offers the potential to improve decision-making and improve profitability. However, many organizations have recently undergone massive investments in ERP systems, which promised an integrated data environment—leaving many wondering why BI is even necessary.

Canadian Snapshots

BI at the Bank of Montreal

The Bank of Montreal (BMO) is one of the largest banks in North America, with over $200 billion in assets and 30 000 employees. During the late 1990s, BMO recognized that its huge IBM DB2 database had excellent potential to provide management with the information they needed to compete in the increasingly competitive financial services industry.

BMO was worried about common bank concerns such as customer attrition, profitability, and risk and wished to utilize business intelligence technology to provide a user-friendly method to better manage key areas. BMO formed an implementation team and selected the MicroStrategy platform to provide the BI functionality from its IBM data warehouse.

BMO's successful implementation resulted in numerous improvements in business analysis, customer service, and risk management. Each day the BI platform performs over 500 queries against the database and provides detailed reports to the appropriate employees. The capabilities in reporting are much greater than previous reporting systems and easily allow users the ability to drill down for further details.

Customer service has been improved in a number of ways. BMO has a separate CRM strategy but utilizes BI information to understand which customers are at risk of leaving the firm, which are most profitable, and similar important analysis. The information gleaned from the BI system allows BMO to proactively work with customers to identify their needs and attempt to reduce attrition. BMO has developed point-of-sale interfaces for its employees that provide them with key customer metrics from the BI application when they are meeting with clients. This custom interface provides the employee with details that previously would have taken hours to research, and allows for easier negotiation of interest rates and terms of service.

Risk analysis is a key factor in the financial services industry but is also a very complex and data-rich area. BMO's BI application has been custom designed to allow executives and high-level users to quickly spot business segments that are approaching or exceeding predefined risk levels by the use of colour-coded symbols. A yellow or red indicator would let the executive know, for example, that a decision made to extend a loan in a Calgary branch has increased the overall credit risk in the Alberta segment to an unacceptable limit. While the executive would not likely override the approval of a specific loan arrangement, the analytical information would allow BMO to actively reduce credit risk in other areas of Alberta to compensate for the overall increase in risk.

The BI application at BMO has provided the opportunity to make improved decisions in multiple areas of the business. In competitive industries such as banking, this information may be the only thing that can help sustain profitability and growth.

Bank of Montreal
www.bmo.com

Questions

1. Does the BI initiative at BMO give it a competitive advantage?
2. How does Bank of Montreal's BI strategy differ from CRM?
3. What other major types of analysis would BMO likely carry out within the BI application?

SOURCES: "Success Story: Bank of Montreal," MicroStrategy website, **www.microstrategy.com/Customers/Successes/bankofmontreal.asp**, accessed November 23, 2004; Bank of Montreal website, **www.bmo.com**.

ERP vs. BI

Enterprise resource planning (ERP) systems promised businesses a single data environment to capture transaction data and integrate all parts of the business. ERP implementations have ranged widely in their successes but in the reporting and analysis area have lacked the ability to satisfy users. A number of important reasons exist as to why ERP systems are not suitable for data analysis, reporting, and decision support—the most important being that ERP was designed as a transaction-based processing system.

ERP transaction systems capture data from the operation of a business into a complex structure of thousands of tables and fields. The structure of ERP is in part dictated by the need to service multiple industries from a single system. The disparate structure of the data results in difficulty attempting to create reports specific to the company, since the data fields need to be selected from numerous tables. In addition, the ERP data structure cannot be "cleaned" to a structure more compatible with reporting, since the transaction system would be impacted.[2] While ERP systems have succeeded in integrating the transactional systems of business, they have been unable to satisfy all of the information needs—leaving a place for business intelligence strategies.

In addition to the complexity of the ERP data structures, the demands on the transaction system also severely limit the reporting capabilities. If you consider a large organization that operates globally, there could be virtually no time during the day when transactions are not being processed. By adding numerous complex queries into the database, analysts could easily hinder the performance of the transaction system. Slow processing time within the transaction system could result in lost sales, data errors, employee frustration, or other difficulties.

Other ERP insufficiencies in the intelligence area include the difficulty in incorporating additional data. Reporting and analysis requirements today reach far beyond the basic debits and credits in the accounting system, demanding information on competitors, e-commerce statistics, and the supply chain data, which is often not found within the ERP system. It is conceivable that ERP systems could be modified to include other data needs, but due to the reasons already cited, an external data warehouse is a superior solution. Although business changes at a rapid pace, it can be important to carry out analysis over numerous years to identify important trends. Maintaining several years of data within any environment can be difficult, and within ERP huge storage capabilities would be required that can be reduced by adopting BI. With BI systems the data can be "cleaned" and stored in more efficient formats than possible with ERP.

ERP vendors have recognized the weaknesses of their systems in this regard, and many have begun to address the needs of their customers with new products. For example, SAP has addressed the limitations of its R/3 application in the reporting area with its own data warehousing/business intelligence application, known as SAP Business Warehouse (BW). SAP BW is designed to integrate with R/3 so customers who have not modified the standard ERP system can implement an advanced BI solution relatively easily. SAP has also incorporated SAP BW into its product offering known as Strategic Enterprise Management (SEM), which allows users to integrate ERP data with BW data in a process-oriented and strategic manner for analysis.[3] SEM is intended to replace former Executive Information System reporting, which was limited in capability by the ERP system. In addition to offerings from ERP vendors, numerous business intelligence application providers have created customized interfaces to simplify the data extraction process from ERP systems. For example, Cognos has an extraction application designed to simplify the process of gathering data from an SAP R/3 system (see the New Business Models box for an example). Other leading business intelligence providers, such as MicroStrategy, Business Objects, and Hyperion, have similar applications for various ERP systems.

New Business Models

BI and ERP at NB Power

New Brunswick (NB) Power is the primary supplier of electricity to over 350 000 customers in the province of New Brunswick. The company is a Crown corporation that generates its power at 15 generating stations using nuclear, thermal, and hydroelectric generation. As the energy industry prepared for deregulation and increased competition in the 1990s, NB Power adopted a proactive technology strategy that would assist the company in remaining competitive.

Similar to other businesses that had long histories, NB Power faced increasing complexity within its IT infrastructure as it continued to grow. The numerous legacy mainframe and mid-range computer systems were difficult to administer and use—resulting in a severe backlog in reports. The information systems department was running reports that end-users were unable to do on their own if they couldn't program, and the delay meant waiting from a few days to up to a

month to get the information requested.

Realizing that this scenario was unacceptable, NB Power set out to modernize its business and develop a technology platform that could carry it into the new millennium. The company set out to modernize its financial systems and its analysis/reporting capabilities by adopting both an ERP system (SAP R/3) and a data warehousing/BI technology (Cognos Impromptu and PowerPlay).

The data warehousing initiative began prior to the ERP implementation, as the company recognized that much of the legacy data would be required in the system. The software selections did, however, provide the opportunity to simplify future integration since the Cognos applications (Cognos SAP HeadStarts) had the ability to quickly migrate much of the SAP data into the data warehouse.

In addition to internal integration, NB Power's BI initiative pulls

external information deemed important into the system. For example, the data warehouse loads data from the local telephone company in the region to simplify employee work and improve customer service at the company's call centre. Integration of the external data with internal records has improved the efficiency at the call centre dramatically.

The ERP and BI initiatives have placed NB Power among the leading companies in the world. The implementation has improved decision-making, customer service, and even operational planning. The analysis of data has allowed the company to identify areas where power outage risk is higher, based on numerous factors, thus allowing for targeted preventive maintenance to be carried out. This type of information reduces repair costs and improves customer service at the same time.

New Brunswick Power
www.nbpower.com

Questions

1. What benefits would the business intelligence implementation provide to NB Power that would not have been available in the ERP system itself?

2. Why would a Crown corporation with a monopoly over energy in a province be so progressive? Is there a real threat of competition in this industry?

3. How could NB Power expand its e-business strategy to utilize the power of the internet?

SOURCES: www.cognos.com; NBPower.ca.

Functions

A number of functions have emerged as business intelligence solutions continue to evolve and business needs for reporting and analysis change. Business intelligence tools should be considered an extension of the power of the ERP system and focus on data integration and organization, data analysis, performance analysis, information dissemination, and collaboration (see figure 10.1).[4]

Figure 10.1   Business Intelligence Functions

The tools of business intelligence can be categorized into data integration and organization, data analysis, performance analysis, information dissemination, and collaboration.

Data Integration and Organization The business intelligence application performs a key function of integrating and organizing all data considered relevant for managing the enterprise. The sources of data for business intelligence can be numerous, including both internal and external data sources. Internal data sources can include ERP systems, CRM systems, e-procurement systems, legacy systems, and call centres. External data sources may include supply chain partners, industry information regarding competitors, or other external information such as economic indicators (see figure 10.2). The business intelligence application serves to integrate all of these data sources in a manner optimized for reporting and analysis.

A data warehouse is a central data repository used to organize, store, analyze, and report upon data for decision-making purposes. Essentially, a data warehouse is a system that exists outside the online transaction processing (OLTP) system or ERP and is dedicated to the analytical aspects of the organization. An **online transaction processing (OLTP) system** is a program that facilitates and manages transaction-oriented applications, typically for data entry and retrieval transactions across a network. In some organizations, data warehouses are also divided into smaller, dedicated databases known as data marts. BI solution providers structure their warehousing solutions in a variety of ways, with some focusing on data marts while others focus more specifically on the larger data warehouse.

Whether the business intelligence system is based upon a data mart or data warehouse is of little significance when considering the importance of BI. In either case, the data in the system will be structured around metadata. **Metadata** is a structured definition of data—it is data about data. For example, a number of data tables within an ERP system may be consolidated with e-commerce data into a single table when the data is extracted. The extraction process would involve the movement of the data and may also remove unnecessary fields and combine other fields. The changes and combinations of the data may then be described by metadata so that an end-user or data warehouse administrator can better understand where the data has originated and how it has been formed.[5]

ONLINE TRANSACTION PROCESSING (OLTP) SYSTEM
A program that facilitates and manages transaction-oriented applications, typically for data entry and retrieval transactions across a network.

METADATA
A structured definition of data; it is data about data.

Figure 10.2   Data Sources for Business Intelligence

Numerous data sources contribute to the BI data warehouse, including internal and external sources.

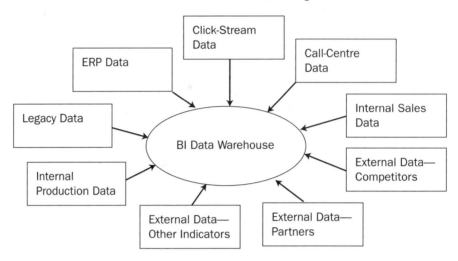

EXTRACTION, TRANSFORMATION, AND LOADING (ETL)
The process of gathering data from a system, such as an ERP system, which can be simplified and stored within the data warehouse.

The integration of data occurs through a number of methods, as the data warehouse consolidates data from numerous sources. **Extraction, transformation, and loading (ETL)** is the process of gathering data from a system, such as an ERP system, which can be simplified and stored within the data warehouse. Many sources of data will require ETL so that data from systems such as ERP and legacy can be combined into a common database. The frequency with which ETL will occur within a given organization will depend upon the industry and the type of reporting environment desired. If management wishes to have very up-to-date information ETL could occur daily, while if the reporting is for several past periods, weekly or monthly, less frequent extraction may be acceptable. Most e-businesses would require frequent updates of data to stay on top of crucial trends and performance indicators necessary to manage the business.

Data Analysis The many users of BI applications in organizations have a great variety of needs in terms of data analysis capabilities. The levels of data analysis may range from basic reporting upon pre-configured **data cubes** (multidimensional database structures that allow quick drill-down and reformatting of data) to ad-hoc queries or data mining. Since the demands for data analysis range drastically, it is important that BI applications are flexible and user-friendly. See the E-Strategy box for an example of data analysis.

DATA CUBES
Multidimensional database structures that allow quick drill-down and reformatting of data.

Many BI applications make use of data cubes. Essentially, a data cube packages data into a cube-like format that has data elements as blocks and data fields within each block (see figure 10.3). If a user performs an analysis on sales in the Atlantic Canada region, the user would be quickly able to drill down and receive information regarding each province within the region or by sales channel as well. While data cubes are a common format for data warehouses, some critics feel that they lack flexibility and reduce the ability of users to create custom reports. Other more advanced design formats for data warehouses include star and snowflake schemas.

BI allows users to have access to reports and information that previously resided only in the information systems group. By moving the data access directly to users, businesses allow for reduced demands on information systems for routine reporting needs and allow users to more quickly analyze data in the fashion they wish. Information systems staffs can focus their attention on the appropriate

E-Strategy

Business Intelligence at Monsanto

Monsanto Company is an international company with over 30 000 employees in more than 100 countries. Monsanto operates in the agricultural, pharmaceutical, and food ingredients businesses as a leading biotechnology firm. The diversity of operations and abundance of data led Monsanto to look at business intelligence technologies.

The procurement area at Monsanto operated with disparate systems, and procurement personnel had difficulty consolidating data from each of the operating areas and countries the company operated in. The difficulty of determining, for instance, the volume of purchases from a specific vendor made it difficult to negotiate prices and improve procurement efficiencies. Monsanto decided to begin its BI initiative by adopting MicroStrategy technology and focusing on improvements in its procurement area.

The Monsanto BI initiative began by building a procurement data warehouse to consolidate and organize the multiple sources of data. The data warehouse was built using Oracle, and MicroStrategy applications were added as the user interface and BI technology to query the Oracle data warehouse.

In addition to reporting functionality, Monsanto was looking for improved decision-making and control with its BI project. The technology succeeded in these areas by allowing procurement professionals to monitor information for both decision-making and control purposes. For example, Monsanto can now identify consolidated purchase volumes from vendors worldwide to improve price negotiations and partnership agreements.

The data also allows procurement professionals to control the processes used by procurement employees to acquire goods in more detail than before. Acquisitions can be summarized and queried by type to identify instances where inappropriate processes have been used, such as purchase order usage for small purchases when a credit card transaction would be more cost-effective.

The BI initiative carried out at Monsanto has been successful to date, with the company claiming savings in the millions of dollars. These savings were derived with a focus purely on the procurement area, which indicates that significant additional savings from BI should be possible as the tool is rolled out to other areas within the business.

Monsanto Company
www.monsanto.com

Questions

1. Was the application of BI to just one area of Monsanto a wise decision? Why?
2. What difficulties might Monsanto encounter as it rolls the BI initiative out to other areas of the business?
3. What specific concerns might arise due to Monsanto's global presence?

SOURCES: MicroStrategy.com; Monsanto.com.

hardware, software, and integration issues for which their expertise is required. The types of data analysis and reporting required range from standardized reports through to data mining (see figure 10.4).[6]

Standard Reports Users will commonly wish to access standard reports such as income statements and inventory lists that may be available within the ERP system as well as the BI system. The data warehouse should provide numerous standard reports for users to reduce the need for ad-hoc queries and ERP-based reporting. Many standard reports are provided with purchased business intelligence applications. Custom-designed systems will require programmers to create

Figure 10.3   Illustration of a Data Cube

This illustrates how a data cube may structure data for an Atlantic Canadian company selling via differ-ent channels to allow drill-down and data analysis in a structured format.

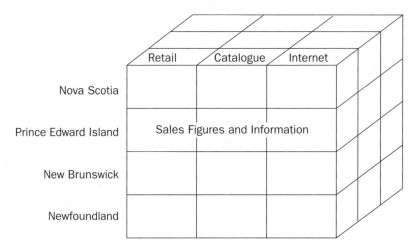

the standard report lists. Standard reports can be considered low value to deci-sion-making, since they tend to lack detail and often necessitate further analysis.

AD-HOC QUERY
The ability for users to generate any type of query or report they wish within the system.

Ad-Hoc Query **Ad-hoc query** is the ability for users to generate any type of query or report they wish within the system. To carry out ad-hoc queries, users will require sufficient understanding of the data structure and may require additional training with the BI system. The purpose of ad-hoc query is to allow users who have limited understanding of programming languages to create custom reports using the querying capabilities of the BI system.

ONLINE ANALYTICAL PROCESSING (OLAP)
A process that provides the abil-ity for users to perform detailed, summary, or trend analysis on data and allows for drill-down into that data.

OLAP Analysis **Online analytical processing (OLAP)** provides the ability for users to perform detailed, summary, or trend analysis on data and allows for drill-down into that data. Most users will be familiar with drill-down, as it works in a similar manner to the hypertext format of the internet (in fact, some of the BI providers use HTML as the interface).

Figure 10.4   Data Analysis and Reporting Methods

The value of BI increases as the complexity of the level of analysis increases beyond standardized reporting.

Data Mining Data analysis techniques such as data mining are those that can have drastic impacts on transactional system performance and are, therefore, best suited to BI. **Data mining** is the analysis of data for relationships that may not have previously been known. For example, data mining of sales data at a sports retailer may reveal that customers who buy particular golfing equipment are likely to buy a specific type of hockey equipment in the fall or winter. Discovery of information from data mining can be useful within many areas of the business, from customer analysis to production planning and cost control.

DATA MINING
The analysis of data for relationships that may not have previously been known.

E-Business in Global Perspective

Fighting Terrorism with Business Intelligence Software

Since the World Trade Center attacks of 2001, the war against terror and the prevention of future attacks have become increasingly important. Security has been tightened substantially around the world and immense efforts are undertaken to identify potential terrorists long before they can do any harm. Information technology, and data-mining systems in particular, is playing an increasing role in this effort. The approach is similar to how companies link internal and external databases to identify new opportunities or to anticipate potential problems. By linking government databases from various sources, for example immigration and law enforcement, data mining techniques can be employed to identify "persons of interest." The federal government in the United States has introduced a system that could be used to make air travel more secure. The program requires all airlines to electronically submit passenger information to the U.S. government before a flight

begins. The information demanded by the government is quite comprehensive and has been subject to a heated privacy debate: in addition to name, nationality, and age of the passenger, additional information such as credit card number, telephone number, and even the type of meal are among the data requested. This information is cross-referenced with government databases as well as external sources such as credit card databases. Instead of only matching passenger data with "wanted lists," the data is analyzed to find potential terrorists, even if they do not appear suspicious on the surface.

According to the U.S. government, every passenger would be assigned a colour, depending on what "score" they are assessed by the system. Green means that no further checks are required. Yellow means that additional screening is necessary. If a passenger is flagged as "red," he or she will not be permitted to board a flight. The announcement of the program has

sparked substantial controversy, both by privacy groups and by foreign governments. Groups such as the American Civil Liberties Union in the United States claim that the program is too intrusive and violates individual rights. The European Union has strong reservations about the system, since privacy laws in Europe do not permit such extensive sharing of data, especially with a foreign government. The scope of the system is still subject to a fierce debate. Supporters of the system argue that the threat of terrorism is more important than privacy concerns and that every available technology should be used to identify suspects. Others are more cautious and only want the system to match passenger data with lists of known suspects. No matter what the ultimate capabilities of the system are, it does give an interesting outlook into the future. Will business intelligence software be used to identify potential criminals before they ever committed a crime?

U.S. Transportation Security Administration
www.tsa.gov/public

Questions

1. What other government uses can you see for data mining systems?
2. What are the implications of using data mining technologies to prevent terrorism? What are the benefits? What are the dangers?
3. Do you think Canada should introduce laws that govern the use of data mining by the private sector and the government?

SOURCES: *Wired*; American Civil Liberties Union; U.S. Transportation Security Administration.

The level of analysis utilized by users will vary with their skill levels both technologically and analytically. While the technology will allow nearly unlimited analysis of data, users need to understand the relevance of reports and output if it is to have any impact on decision-making. For this reason, business analysts within various departments are becoming valuable individuals who can identify important information for management decision-making.

Performance Analysis Performance analysis and monitoring have become important in measuring success as well as evaluating prior decisions to improve future decision-making. **Key performance indicators (KPIs)** are important measures that a company measures its performance against in relation to goals, competitors, and the industry. KPIs will vary substantially by industry and firm, depending upon the products or services offered and the corporate strategy. Some common examples of KPIs include market share percentages, revenue growth, and quality deviations. In many cases, the KPIs are linked to a **balanced scorecard**, which is a multidimensional measurement tool aimed to capture performance measures related to accounting and finance, human resources, internal processes, and customers. Robert Kaplan and David Norton developed the balanced scorecard as a means to reduce the limitations of the traditional financial-based performance measures used in business.[7]

The use of KPIs and/or balanced scorecards for performance measurement and analysis require the capture of large volumes of data. BI and data warehousing technologies aim to capture data for decision-making and performance analysis and, therefore, are well suited to be combined into KPI monitoring or balanced scorecard creation. BI applications can be configured to automatically notify individuals of specific changes in KPIs or other indicators deemed important by management.

Several of the BI and data warehousing vendors have configured their applications to easily support the use of both KPIs and balanced scorecard analysis. SAP's Strategic Enterprise Management suite and Cognos's Visualizer products both use colour-coded information (green, yellow, red) to allow users to quickly identify indicators that are operating within or outside predefined or historical limits. As technology improves, users continue to have additional information at their fingertips for decision-making, and BI provides the perfect environment for performance analysis.

One company that has achieved success in employing BI technology for performance analysis is Grand & Toy. Grand & Toy is one of the largest office supplies companies in Canada and is based in Toronto. Recognizing the need for improved information management at the company, management set out to establish a data warehousing system as they moved away from the use of mainframe technology and standardized reports. Speaking of historical decision-making, the director of marketing commented, "Profitability analysis was based on a combination of dated information, educated guesses, and opinion." The weak reporting system and data was unable to even distinguish retail from commercial sales or easily identify increases in sales attributable to promotions or discount prices.

Grand & Toy selected Cognos PowerPlay and Cognos Impromptu to build its business intelligence applications. The system was built upon a new data warehouse, and numerous reporting capabilities from standard reports to OLAP analysis are available. The implementation team created customized reports for product profitability analysis and customer analysis that can be monitored easily by the merchandising and sales departments. Analysts can report on products by dimensions such as location, promotion type, stock-keeping unit (SKU), and weekly sales. Customer analysis is similarly powerful. Grand & Toy has recognized gains in both its gross margin on products and overall profitability, which it attributes to improved decision-making based on business intelligence technology.

Information Dissemination Communicating information to users and partners on a timely basis is critical to facilitate decision-making at key points in the process. Information dissemination tools are developing which integrate closely with BI applications to carry out this function. For example, MicroStrategy's Narrowcast Server is an application dedicated to delivering the right information to the right user in a personalized format and on a timely basis.[8] The growth in technological tools means that this dissemination of information is now necessary in numerous formats, from e-mail to cellular phones, PDAs, and pagers.

MicroStrategy
www.microstrategy.com

The dissemination of information can be configured to a number of different criteria. For example, a production manager may wish to receive notification of changes in demand above a specified limit. Furthermore, he may want to receive the information using wireless technology so that set-up or other necessary modifications on the shop floor can be planned or commence immediately. Partners of the supply chain may wish to be notified immediately of any changes in production or delivery schedules so that customers can be updated or orders can be revised to reflect the change in circumstances. The application of intelligence technologies to ongoing operations has limitless potential, as managers increasingly require up-to-date information to make important decisions.

Collaboration The management of organizations has progressed to the point where focusing on only one enterprise limits the ability to reduce costs and increase sales. Supply chain management, e-procurement, and customer relationship management all require that data and information be shared among members of the entire supply chain. While some of the information to be shared can be facilitated by ERP systems, business intelligence and data warehousing applications provide businesses with the opportunity to share and collaborate on information useful for decision-making.

During 2001, Home Depot began sharing detailed data with some of its suppliers in an attempt to increase sales and efficiency within the supply chain. Home Depot is marrying information regarding employees, inventory, and sales to allow its major suppliers, such as Georgia-Pacific Corp., to better understand the operations at the shop floor level.[9] This form of collaboration in the analysis and interpretation of data has continued to grow as new technologies simplify the process, and will continue to blossom as the successful outcomes increase profitability.

Collaboration can occur in any aspect of inter-enterprise management and should result in value to all enterprises involved. Retailers and dealers can share detailed information with manufacturers and wholesalers (and vice versa) so that analysis of correlation among variables, such as production costs and rush orders or retail sales trends and manufacturing overtime costs, can be carried out. As businesses learn to embrace collaboration, numerous benefits should be achieved, leading to improved customer satisfaction and supply chain efficiency.

Technologies of BI

To fully appreciate the value of business intelligence applications, it is necessary to consider the technologies that underlie the user interface. While many vendors have accomplished the goal of simplifying the ease of use of their technologies, it is important to understand the core and enabling technologies employed for the full potential of BI to be obtained. The major technological elements in BI can be

Figure 10.5 Business Intelligence Architecture

The business intelligence architecture includes core technologies, enabling technologies, and solutions that allow the transformation of data into valuable information for management.

described as core technologies, enabling technologies, and solutions.[10] Figure 10.5 illustrates the technological components of a BI architecture.

Core Technologies

CORE TECHNOLOGIES
Those technologies that provide the basic infrastructure for business intelligence.

Core technologies are those that provide the basic infrastructure for business intelligence. Included in this category are basic networking technologies that facilitate the entire system as well as database management systems (DBMS) and the data warehousing technology. Core technologies create the operating environment within which BI operates and their design and structure will have a significant impact on the success or failure of BI initiatives. In most companies the existing networking infrastructure will be utilized for BI since local area networks (LANs), intranets, or other networking technologies will already be in place.

The use of internet technologies and protocols such as TCP/IP has significantly reduced the complexity of linking numerous systems. BI implementations where the application chosen uses an HTML interface (such as the MicroStrategy example provided earlier) can capitalize on internet technology when dealing with integration issues.

The networking design of a company has substantial impacts on performance in the BI environment as well as the transactional or ERP applications. The number of network servers, their ability to distribute workloads, and overall size of a network are all factors that will impact network performance. Numerous networking technologies such as routers, firewalls, and even operating systems will also need to be evaluated as the deployment of BI and any other corporate applications can cause substantial increases in network traffic. The concept of network design and management is a large area and is examined in numerous other texts. The key here is to understand that as a core technology for BI, networking can have dramatic impacts on performance, flexibility, and integration.

RELATIONAL DATABASE
A database that uses numerous tables and can relate fields or tables within the database to one another and can easily be reorganized or extended.

The type of core technology chosen for DBMS can vary as well and will be based on numerous factors. The most common form of database is the relational database. A **relational database** is one that uses numerous tables and can relate fields or tables within the database to one another and can easily be reorganized or extended. An example of how a relational database can reduce data duplication can be explained by thinking of a typical sales transaction. A customer order transaction for specific quantity of inventory items could be typed out by an order entry clerk with all fields necessary including date, customer, customer information (address, contact, etc.), purchase order number, inventory items ordered (item number, description, location, etc.), quantities, and numerous other details necessary for an organization to record and track sales. If this same customer were to call again the following day, however, several of the data fields above, such as customer address and inventory descriptions, would be duplicated several times, thus resulting in additional data to store, back up, and manage.

The relational database would reduce this duplication of data by storing different types of data within separate tables and then relating each table to the other to identify additional data elements (see figure 10.6). The order would be entered with a unique order number and date, but the only customer information required is the customer number. The orders table would then relate the customer number to the customer table if additional information is necessary for invoicing, analysis, or reporting. Similarly, an inventory number is entered into the orders table that relates to the inventory table for details of description, size, weight, and so on. The efficient design and management of a database strategy for BI is crucial to achieving success.

Microsoft Access represents an example of a common relational database you may have seen before. The use of database technologies such as a relational database management system (RDBMS) provides a data warehouse with the flexibility to add additional data sources in the future and redefine the structure of the data if necessary. The data warehouse structure will also be designed so as to reduce the amount of replication of data within the database.

Other forms of databases include distributed databases and objected-oriented programming database systems.

Enabling Technologies

Enabling technologies are those that provide the ability of the BI applications to interact and perform tasks within the core technologies, such as the data warehouse. Some of the key enabling technologies for data warehousing and BI are OLAP, structured query language (SQL), XML, security, messaging/workflow systems, and data mining technologies. The enablers for BI essentially allow either

ENABLING TECHNOLOGIES
Technologies that provide the ability of the BI applications to interact and perform tasks within the core technologies, such as the data warehouse.

Figure 10.6   Relational Databases

The use of relational databases reduces data redundancy and errors by minimizing duplication and the amount of information that needs to be entered into a system. The database can link to other fields in the customer and inventory tables to get other information necessary, such as price or shipping addresses.

Customer #	Name	Address	Phone	Contact Name
1000	Acme Co	Toronto, ON	416-555-5555	John Summers

Inventory Code	Description	Manufacturer	Weight	Price
986756	Disk Drive	Seagate	1kg	99.99

Transaction Record			
Customer #	Item	Quantity	Date
1000	986756	5	01/01/05

a BI user or a specific BI solution to carry out tasks of reporting, analysis, or modelling within the system.

OLAP (online analytical processing) enables a user to easily and selectively extract and view data from numerous angles and provides the ability for drill-down or drill-up through data. An example of the drill-down capability within OLAP was reviewed earlier in this chapter. The OLAP enabling technology is designed to create ease of use, flexibility, and improved performance in the system by simplifying data structures and organizing standard data elements into data cubes. OLAP applications can require the use of multidimensional as opposed to relational database technology to organize data for analysis. OLAP is carried out in numerous ways by different BI solutions including client-side OLAP, relational OLAP (ROLAP), multidimensional OLAP (MOLAP), and other hybrid forms of the technology.[11]

CLIENT-SIDE OLAP
Processing where the data warehouse passes the data from the server to the client machine, where the majority of the processing occurs.

Client-side OLAP, also known as "desktop OLAP," is where the data warehouse passes the data from the server to the client machine, where the majority of the processing occurs. Client-side OLAP is useful for laptop users who can effectively move selected information offline for analysis or use and also can reduce server demands for repeated analysis of the same data, such as through drill-down and report reorganization. Both Hyperion and Business Objects are examples of BI vendors who make use of client-side OLAP.

RELATIONAL OLAP (ROLAP)
Applications that allow multidimensional analysis within a relational database. The data processing may take place either at the server, intermediary, or client level.

Relational OLAP (ROLAP) applications allow multidimensional analysis within a relational database. The data processing may take place either at the server, intermediary, or client level. Depending on the networking infrastructure in place, ROLAP can be configured differently, thus allowing for strong flexibility. ROLAP can require larger storage capacity and additional query times due to its use of relational data, but it does have a large capacity. ROLAP is often used in situations where the data changes rapidly or within larger data warehousing environments for analysis purposes, as the ROLAP application can more quickly perform iterative queries than numerous clients could.[12] MicroStrategy's products make use of ROLAP technologies to provide scalable capabilities in the BI marketplace.

MULTIDIMENSIONAL OLAP (MOLAP)
Applications that make use of data cubes to perform analysis on multidimensional databases.

Multidimensional OLAP (MOLAP) applications make use of data cubes to perform analysis on multidimensional databases. MOLAP queries can be faster than ROLAP, due to the pre-configured data cubes, if the data is well defined; however, MOLAP runs into scalability difficulties in larger implementations due to its structure. Definition of data cubes and the multidimensional database format are critical stages of creating an efficient MOLAP application. Hyperion Essbase and SAS business intelligence applications make use of MOLAP technology.

HYBRID OLAP
Forms of OLAP that combine various other formats, such as ROLAP and MOLAP.

Hybrid OLAP forms are those that combine various other formats, such as ROLAP and MOLAP. Since ROLAP has strong scalability features and MOLAP has improved performance, it is natural that some vendors have attempted to consolidate the use of the two technologies to get increased benefits. Hybrid applications are more complex in format and development but offer excellent flexibility, scalability, and performance. Microsoft SQL 2000 Analysis Services and IBM DB2 OLAP server are both hybrid applications that provide the benefits described here.

BI Solutions

BI solutions are those technologies that provide the reporting and analysis of data at the client or user end of the process. The focus in this chapter has been on business intelligence applications but, as discussed earlier, the reporting and analysis may take place within other specialized applications as well. Customer relationship and supply chain management technologies may be integrated into or operated separately from the BI application and as such may also share data warehouses or data marts.

The BI solution chosen certainly does not have to be vendor specific. Several companies have adopted products from more than one vendor to suit their particular needs most effectively. Once again, internet and networking technologies, application programming interfaces, and other technologies can allow numerous systems to be tied together to best accomplish corporate goals.

Implementation

Implementation of a BI initiative requires many common IT project management tools to be employed, as well as numerous BI-specific concepts. The focus of the implementation of BI, similar to ERP, is on business issues and understanding which technological applications can best support the business needs. The basic structure of an implementation will follow a planning phase, architecture design, and execution.

Planning Phase

The planning phase of BI implementation must first focus on establishing reasonable goals for the project and aligning BI goals with corporate goals and strategy. It is essential that this phase clearly identify what areas of concern the BI implementation is attempting to address so that the system is designed appropriately and so that the success of the project can later be determined.

The goals established will assist the project team in defining the scope of the project. As described earlier in this chapter, BI initiatives rely upon data warehouses and data marts. The choice of departmentalized data marts versus deployment of a corporate-wide data warehouse will impact the scope of the project and all implementation phases dramatically. The selection of a major data warehouse does not prohibit the utilization of data marts by departments at a later date, but calls for specific database design and integration tools to be employed. Similarly, the development of a BI initiative that attempts to allow departments to implement data marts that will later be integrated does not prevent the company from developing a corporate-wide BI strategy. This method, however, does require that the individual data mart projects be carried out in unison with strong communication ties so that roadblocks don't develop later (e.g., by using different metadata definitions within each data mart for similar data elements).

The planning phase of BI implementation must also consider specific success factors required for BI. The analysis of industry practices and technological requirements for success will help to prevent the investment of time and money into a project that later needs to be abandoned.

Critical Success Factors for BI To be successful, business intelligence applications, similar to other technological tools, must meet a number of requirements. As technologies such as ERP systems, databases, and the internet continue to evolve, BI will need to keep pace to continue providing value to the firm. The critical success factors for BI include ease of use, scalability, flexibility, performance, and security.

Ease of Use The growth in use of the internet came with the rise of the World Wide Web's graphical interface; similarly, BI technologies will grow in value as they become easier to use. Much of the same data being used in BI applications today has been available for decades, but it was locked within legacy systems. In the mainframe environment, querying data for ad-hoc reports involved a detailed understanding of the data structure within the system, as well as an ability to program in a query language. For these reasons reporting was an expensive task and often took extended periods of time.

Several advances have been made already in improving ease of use of BI tools. The adoption of HTML or web interfaces by many vendors has improved the ability of most users to navigate and find reports. In addition, the use of BI applications drastically reduces the need for programming employees to develop queries into the data. Ad-hoc queries can be carried out by most users with little input from information systems staff, thus reducing costs and time to carry out reporting.

Fannie Mae
www.fanniemae.com

Fannie Mae, the largest financial institution in the world, has adopted data warehousing and BI technologies to allow its employees to more easily create reports. Historical data in the financial industry is critical for long-term analysis, and Fannie Mae maintains large volumes of data back to 1979. In addition to its own data, Fannie Mae stores data from over 70 external sources. In the past, a report requiring access to historical data could take weeks and require several programmers. The mainframe backup system was used to restore data from tapes where programmers would then need to consolidate and query the data to produce the requested reports. Today, Fannie Mae employees can access historical reports directly through their SAS Institute system (a BI provider) within minutes, thus reducing the time for analysis and increasing customer satisfaction.[13]

SAS Institute Inc.
www.sas.com

Ease of use will continue to develop as users request additional functionality and the volume of data increases. The conversion of data from complex ERP systems into data warehouse information supplemented by metadata descriptions will assist users to better understand the reports and data they analyze as systems begin to provide additional help functions. High-level analysis and data mining, however, have limited abilities to become easier. While performing data mining can be simplified by technology, the interpretation and understanding of the results is left to the user.

BI applications have simplified reporting and data analysis through web interfaces and must continue to improve value through ease of use. For example, standard reports must be easy to create and share with other users, tools such as wizards can assist users to build custom reports, and advanced users should be able to share interpretations of data with the user community in a simplistic manner.

Scalability Companies must ensure that the system they implement is extremely scalable. This capability is partially determined by the approaches followed in the implementation phase as well as the configuration of the system, but needs to remain a priority. The volume of data that an organization captures can grow rapidly as the value of BI is realized throughout the enterprise. Scalability and performance are similar and interrelated but not the same. **Scalability** is the ability of the system to maintain a set rate of performance as the number of users or volume of usage increases.

SCALABILITY
The ability of the system to maintain a set rate of performance as the number of users or volume of usage increases.

Many data warehousing/BI projects integrate data from ERP and legacy systems from the outset. This scenario can result in a relatively predictable volume of data that can be used for reporting and analysis. Once the value of BI is discovered, however, many users will begin to request that additional data from e-commerce transactions, click-stream data, and external sources be captured as well to increase the usefulness of BI for decision-making throughout the firm.

Hardware and software implications must be considered when evaluating the scalability of the BI solution. An obvious hardware issue is hard disk capacity, which can easily reach into the terabytes as data capture grows. In addition, the scalability of hardware performance should be considered as the potential increase in the number of users could bring the speed of the server to a standstill. The hardware selection will likely not be driven by distant future demands on the system, but it is important to be thinking at least a couple of years ahead to avoid wasted capital investments.

Software issues range from operating system selection to BI application selection. As the BI application is chosen, it is important that the entire environment be considered so as to simplify integration and improve compatibility. Other software concerns will include database selection and the use of customized ETL tools. Throughout software evaluation, it is crucial that planned and future demands be considered carefully.

Flexibility The flexibility of the BI system may be put to the test as the adoption of the technology throughout the firm grows. Varying data sources will often place demands on BI applications, and software and hardware selection must consider the needs for flexibility. The number of known data sources at the beginning of implementation will often necessitate specific technology choices, but businesses must plan ahead for potential external sources of data such as web-based data or partner data.

The BI system should also be flexible in allowing multiple data models within large enterprises. Advanced users and data warehousing specialists often disagree on the "best" models to be used for the database design, and flexibility in this regard can be very important. Some data warehouses are constructed so that data is standardized within the warehouse and then data marts are utilized to test alternative models.[14]

Performance Fast and accurate access to information will increase the value and use of BI applications. As with scalability and system selection, performance must be evaluated on an ongoing basis to ensure user satisfaction. Performance can be seriously hindered within a data warehouse by numerous data mining or large-scale analyses. If data mining is to be a common occurrence, policies should be established to control the impact on performance, and alternative system designs should be evaluated.

Performance may also be impacted by the chosen update frequency for the data warehouse. Frequent updates can hinder system performance; however, they result in more up-to-date information. A balance needs to be established in this circumstance.

Data warehouses can be broken down into data marts, as was discussed earlier in the chapter, to provide specific data to divisions or areas within the company. To improve performance of the system as the number of users increases, information systems departments may look to moving highly queried, specialized data into data marts. The performance of the BI system needs to be monitored carefully and is more easily improved if the system is scalable and flexible, as discussed earlier.

Security A data warehouse is designed to allow users to gain information and knowledge from data. However, the presence of confidential data in the system necessitates some level of security to be in place. The security level can range from all users having full access to read, write, and change data records (not reasonable) to only one "superuser" having complete access to the system (not practical). Within this range, each business will need to evaluate the objectives of its data warehousing/BI strategy and consider the implications of security on the rest of the implementation.

In examining BI objectives, the business must keep in mind that users with higher decision-making potential should have higher availability to information. Despite the ease of giving all users access to the data, it is not reasonable to allow a payables clerk to examine the payroll records for the entire company or to "borrow" corporate knowledge for personal gain. As such, the data warehouse needs to be designed with some reasonable security controls over data access to prevent misuse of data.

Consultants in the field of data warehousing have seen significant impacts on performance caused by inappropriately designed security measures. One consultant has observed a 20 to 500 percent increase in query run times as a result of a security implementation.[15] This indicates that although general database design is important, security system design is also important for both authorization and performance purposes.

One of the key decisions in establishing the security framework is deciding whether the security should be built into the business intelligence application or directly into the database (see figure 10.7). The security design will be impacted by several factors, including the number of users, the number of applications with data access, and the operating environment. If ODBC (online database connectivity) is available from the data warehouse, it will be necessary for the security to be built at the database level to ensure protection of data access from other connected databases.

Designing security for a data warehouse can be difficult since user access in this environment is much different from the objectives of security in the transactional (ERP) environment. Within the financial environment, the user's role is clearly defined and the requirement for access outside of the functional area is rarely necessary. In the data warehouse environment some users will be limited to the functional area, while others will need the ability to analyze and report upon company-wide data. Numerous security types can be established, but the increase in types leads to increased complexity and upkeep.

In addition to the design of security for employees, it will be necessary to determine what type of access is required for outside users. Some business intelligence proponents argue that sharing specific information with customers, suppliers, and partners has tremendous value from a complete supply chain and relationship perspective. Opponents argue that other methods of overcoming the lack of digital communication can be more successful and less costly. Each organization must decide which approach to information sharing it prefers to take. If outside users will access information, additional security concerns need to be addressed. In most circumstances, outside users will be able to access only infor-

Figure 10.7 Two Major Approaches to Security in Data Warehousing

Data warehouse security can be established at the application or database level, with the appropriate design depending on many other factors within the organization.

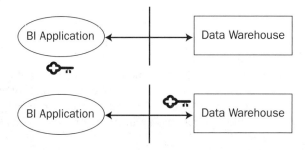

mation regarding their own relationship with the business. Basic or summarized information regarding supply and demand may also be shared in some organizations. The feeling of many in this regard is that more information leads to better knowledge, which then leads to improved decision-making.

The complexity of security and its potential impact on data warehouse performance suggest that it is not an issue to take lightly. To facilitate implementation in an efficient manner, the security should be designed along with the data warehouse. Building both the security framework and the data warehouse format concurrently may allow for both to occur more efficiently, since database design impacts on security and security impacts database design. Despite the importance of concurrent design of the security and data warehouse, consultants point out that rarely are security issues addressed until later stages of implementation, thus leading to increased complexity, time, and costs.[16]

Architecture Design

The design of the system for intelligence applications will be considered at the initial planning phase of the implementation but will need to be revised into achievable project requirements at this stage. Two critical issues to be determined include database design and system architecture.[17]

Database design will be tied in part to the outcomes and analysis methods to be employed. However, the database design will also be closely tied to the vendor applications chosen, meaning that the architecture design stage will be carried out in concert with software selection and consultant recommendations. As discussed previously, the database type and structure can be impacted by the vendor's OLAP type and may also vary if the implementation uses a data warehouse or data mart approach. The design of the database at this phase of implementation also needs to take into account the concerns over security design described earlier.

System architecture is a second critical issue to consider, since the system will impact several of the functions and abilities (flexibility, performance, scalability, etc.). The architecture decisions will also be linked to such factors as software application choice, number of users, hardware selection, and existing corporate infrastructure. One of the considerations to be made at this stage will be whether to use a two-tier or three-tier access design for the data warehouse/data mart (see figure 10.8). Two-tiered structures are simpler and often less costly, but if the number of users is high, performance can easily degrade. A three-tier structure allows the servers within the system to balance the load of user requests and is also required for some specific vendor products.

Execution

The execution phase of the intelligence implementation is where numerous common management techniques come into play. Top management commitment needs to exist throughout the project to ensure adequate resources are dedicated and to gain employee buy-in. In addition, a team approach to the entire project is necessary to allow departmental input and evaluation of the project planning and implementation.

Project management techniques should be embraced throughout the implementation so that costs, human resources, and consultants are controlled in a reasonable fashion. Use of project management techniques will assist the project to maintain reasonable timelines and also allow for evaluation of success at critical stages of the implementation.

Figure 10.8   Two-Tier and Three-Tier Data Warehouse Structure

Two-tier and three-tier structures for data warehouse design can impact system performance dramatically. The three-tier structure is more easily scaled as the number of users grows.

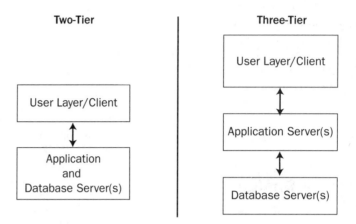

The implementation of any new technology will also require management to plan its approach to the implementation, that is, they must engage in "change management." The implementation of BI can create tensions among departments over data ownership issues and user frustration with new applications. Management must ensure that issues of data ownership are addressed to allow the project to be implemented successfully. In addition, the later stages of the implementation should involve strong commitments to training since users will be employing new technologies in their work.

Training will allow users to develop an appreciation for the BI applications and also may provide training in analytical approaches to top-level users. The importance of training is to allow users to truly take the onus of reporting and analysis from the information systems department. Appropriate training will also allow high-level users to understand the impact of data mining and other complex queries on system performance.

During the execution phase of implementation, the business should ensure that it has given consideration to the goals and outcomes defined at the planning stage. Return on investment (ROI) is a common tool used to evaluate business investments, and many companies have employed ROI as a basis to measure BI implementation success. A study by International Data Corporation found that the overall ROI on data warehousing/BI initiatives among 62 large organizations was 41 percent, with payback periods ranging from two to three years.[18] While ROI is a difficult measure to quantify, it can be used as an overall assessment of the project. Other metrics should also be employed to help assess the project's outcomes, such as query response time, number of users actively using the system, and analyses of important information discovered. Each organization will need to assess the metrics according to their objectives to determine the appropriate mix of financial and operating measures to evaluate.

One organization that has successfully implemented a BI solution and measured its success with primarily non-financial measures is the Vancouver Hospital and Health Services Centre. The Vancouver Hospital is the second largest in Canada and manages over 37 000 acute-care and 81 000 emergency visits per year, in addition to a growing number of surgeries and other medical services. Like other hospitals in Canada, Vancouver Hospital has increasingly found difficulty in keeping up with demand for many of its services, leading to long patient wait times and difficult employee scheduling. Having collected numerous data sources for several years, the Vancouver Hospital began searching for a solution that would allow it to improve its decision-making and patient service. After evaluating their options, the hospital chose Cognos BI as their solution provider to utilize browser-based decision-making and analysis tools.

The implementation utilized a team approach of executives, key users, and consultants to ensure all needs were clearly identified and communicated. The decision was made to utilize data marts rather than a fully integrated data warehouse, since the specific objectives identified did not require full integration within the short term. The solution was built around the parameters outlined at the planning stage, and Vancouver Hospital wished to use metrics such as improved utilization of patient-beds and reductions in wait times for surgery to determine success. In monitoring the overall hospital services, the BI solution employs the balanced scorecard approach to performance measurement. The Vancouver Hospital implementation team has been successful at the initial stages of BI implementation by following logical, business-oriented strategies and working in a team environment.

Chapter Summary

The growth in the knowledge economy has led to the need for a much more sophisticated understanding of business processes, statistics, financial information, and other "information based on data." Business intelligence is the environment that supports analysis of data from any source (internal or external) to provide valuable information for making operating, tactical, or strategic decisions.

The primary enabling technologies of business intelligence systems include both data warehouses and data marts. Data warehouses are repositories of data that have been designed and optimized for analysis and enquiry rather than transaction processing. Data marts are similar to data warehouses but are designed to satisfy the needs of a specific user group within the organization. Implementations of BI applications may make use of both data warehouses and data marts and can take several different forms.

The analysis of data can be carried out in numerous ways with BI systems. Data mining is a common technique used in BI, where the analyst attempts to discover important trends or information within the data. In addition to advanced analysis forms such as data mining, BI can be used to monitor key metrics for the organization—often called key performance indicators. Many organizations also employ BI to gather information to create balanced scorecards, tools that monitor numerous financial and non-financial KPIs important to the industry.

The implementation of a BI system is a complex task requiring sophisticated project management. The design of the system will be driven by the desired outcomes, software applications chosen, data warehouse/mart design, and several other factors. Similar to other technology projects, it is crucial to have management buy-in, team support, and a strong focus on the business processes involved.

The critical success factors for BI include ease of use, scalability, flexibility, performance, and security. For the application to be useful and meet the objectives established, it is critical that the implementation and software selection carefully consider these factors. The cost and time required for successful BI implementations can be substantial, so it is necessary to put substantial time into the planning process.

Key Terms

ad-hoc query   *(p. 198)*

balanced scorecard   *(p. 200)*

client-side OLAP   *(p. 204)*

core technologies   *(p. 202)*

data cubes   *(p. 196)*

data mining   *(p. 199)*

enabling technologies   *(p. 203)*

extraction, transformation, and loading (ETL)   *(p. 196)*

hybrid OLAP   *(p. 204)*

key performance indicators (KPIs)   *(p. 200)*

metadata   *(p. 195)*

multidimensional OLAP (MOLAP)   *(p. 204)*

online analytical processing (OLAP)   *(p. 198)*

online transaction processing (OLTP) system   *(p. 195)*

relational database   *(p. 202)*

relational OLAP (ROLAP)   *(p. 204)*

scalability   *(p. 206)*

Tools for Online Learning

To help you master the material in this chapter and stay up to date with new developments in e-business, visit www.pearsoned.ca/trites. Resources include:

- **Review Questions and Exercises**

- **Problems for Discussion**

- **Recommended Readings**

- **Updates to Case Studies and Textual Material**

- **Streaming CBC Videos with Cases**

Endnotes

1. www.telusmobility.com; www.cognos.com.

2. K. Wyderka, "Unlocking Your ERP Data: Business Intelligence for ERP Systems, Part 1," *DM Review* (July 14, 2000).

3. SAP website, www.sap.com.

4. R. Kalakota and M. Robinson, *e-Business 2.0: Roadmap for Success* (Toronto: Addison Wesley, 2001).

5. J. Wu, "What Is This Data? End User Presentation of Meta Data," *DM Review* (October 2000).

6. J. Wu, "User Requirements for Enterprise Query and Reporting," *DM Review* (April 2000).

7. J. Oliveira, "The Balanced Scorecard: An Integrative Approach to Performance Evaluation," *Healthcare Financial Management* (May 2001).

8. MicroStrategy website, www.microstrategy.com/Software/Products/Narrowcast_Server, accessed November 25, 2004.

9. P. MacDougall, "Companies that Dare to Share Information Are Cashing in on New Opportunities," *Information Week* (May 2001).

10. R. Kalakota and M. Robinson, *e-Business 2.0: Roadmap for Success* (Toronto: Addison Wesley, 2001).

11. R. Kalakota and M. Robinson, *e-Business 2.0: Roadmap for Success* (Toronto: Addison Wesley, 2001).

12. Whatis.com website, www.whatis.com, http://searchdatabase.techtarget.com/sDefinition/0,,sid13_gci214582,00.html, accessed November 25, 2004.

13. J. Ryan, "Cost-Effective Performance, Smarter Decision Support—Alpha Brings It Home to Fannie Mae," Techguide.com.

14. C. Kelley, "Stars and Snowflakes: Do You See a Snow Storm or Constellation Coming Your Way?" *Data Warehousing* (February 2001).

15. C. Silbernagel, "Data Security: Protecting the Warehouse from Within," *DM Review* (June 1999).

16. J. Cunningham, "Data Warehousing: A Security Perspective," *DM Review* (November 2000).

17. Bruce Love and Michael Burwen, *Business Intelligence and Data Warehousing: Crossing the Millennium* (Palo Alto, California: Palo Alto Management Group, February 1999).

18. J. Ryan, "A Practical Guide to Getting Started with Data Warehousing," Techguide.com.

Supply Chain Management

Although eBay is widely known for the auctioning of goods between individuals, it has become much more than that. Since its beginning, eBay has extended into the supply chains of established businesses of all sizes, facilitating both the purchase and sale of goods. In fact, this e-business startup may have started a new approach to the automation and integration of business supply chains. As of the end of 2003, more than 430 000 businesses were selling on eBay, either full-time or as an additional sales channel for their businesses. Business purchases on eBay grew to roughly US$2 billion in 2003, approximately double that of the preceding year.

One example of a business using eBay as a sales channel is Reliable Tools Inc., a machine-tool shop that listed some items on eBay in 1998 because of an industry downturn. The products included heavy machinery, such as a 2300-pound milling machine. The items, even the huge machinery, sold quickly and since then Reliable has become a regular eBay customer. By 2003, they were up to $1 million in monthly eBay sales, which constituted 75 percent of its total business. Prompted by this success and others, eBay established an industrial products marketplace that it feels may exceed US$500 million in gross sales in 2004.

eBay also has established a market for selling automobiles online, called eBay Motors. To start this line of business, eBay bought an existing auction company that specialized in cars for collectors, Kruse International, for US$150 million in stock. Then they arranged a deal under which they would include listings from the online classifieds site AutoTrader.com. They also arranged insurance and warranty plans, and shipping and inspection services.

In a related move, Toyota Motor Sales U.S.A. Inc. has signed a contract to become the exclusive automotive manufacturer sponsor on eBay. As part of the agreement, Toyota launched a site at http://ebay.toyota.com, from which it showcases its entire new vehicle line-up, links to items listings on eBay, and special promotional offers.

As a result of these initiatives, sales of cars and car parts through eBay topped the US$5 billion mark, putting eBay ahead of the No. 1 U.S. auto dealer AutoNation in number of used cars sold. About half of the sellers are bricks-and-mortar dealers.

Other big companies are into the act as well. Motorola started selling excess and returned cell phones in large lots on eBay. While this area accounts for less than 5 percent of eBay's gross sales, it has brought in many new customers for

eBay Toyota Showroom
http://ebay.toyota.com

eBay. With this kind of help, eBay's wholesale business jumped ninefold to US$23 million in the first quarter of 2003.

eBay also started another line of business when it began offering third-party equipment financing through a new service on its site provided by Direct Capital Corporation. This new service provides business buyers with financing options for industrial equipment and information technology. The equipment financing applies to a broad range of categories, including computers, networking, telecom, construction, agriculture, metalworking, restaurant, commercial printing, and medical equipment.

"Buyers can preserve working capital, leverage significant tax advantages, and bundle in shipping costs," said Jim Broom, CEO of Direct Capital Corp. "Sellers benefit from the reimbursement of eBay final value fees, attracting more buyers, and have the added assurance of selling to pre-approved bidders."

Use of the equipment financing program is streamlined for both sellers and buyers. Sellers simply enrol in the program and include a link to the financing service within their eBay item listings. Buyers complete an online application and, once approved, are able to purchase items on eBay up to a specified financing amount. Once a transaction is completed on eBay, Direct Capital will remit to the seller, via PayPal, the purchase price of the item, the eBay final value fee, and any associated PayPal fees. The Equipment Financing for eBay program can be accessed directly at eBay Business (www.ebaybusiness.com). More recently, eBay has also been in negotiations with a major partner to provide small-business lines of credit.

eBay Business
www.ebaybusiness.com

A very significant aspect of all the new big business entrants into eBay is that they are not all using the auctioning method, which of course was eBay's signature from the beginning. Giant companies such as Sears Roebuck & Co. and Walt Disney Co. are selling brand-new items there as well. More than a quarter of the offerings are listed at fixed prices familiar to mass-market consumers. In this way, eBay is entering the mainstream of mass retailing, probably the largest market segment in the economy.

As a result of all this new activity, eBay is morphing into something quite different than what it was when it started. It has changed from an auctioning site used largely by individuals selling off used and odd-lot items, to one that has become a large scale collaborative e-business. In 2004, at least 30 million people will have bought and sold over US$20 billion in merchandise—more than the gross domestic product of all but 70 of the world's countries. eBay's President and CEO, Meg Whitman, who joined eBay in March 1998, has referred to this new role of eBay as "the eBay economy."

A collaborative business requires a collaborative approach to management. It's important to make all the participants feel like they are in charge of their own business activities, and not to annoy them to the point that they want to leave. The big-business participants are really customers of eBay as well.

The whole eBay environment is very transparent. Through the web, eBay's participants have access, 24/7, to every trend, every sale, and every new regulation in the eBay world. The spread of information means that everyone has more power, but this can make life miserable for managers who fail to adapt. The key for management is to embrace the transparency and use it to turn customers and vendors into collaborators and colleagues.

One of eBay's more unique institutions is called the "Voice of the Customer." Every couple of months, eBay brings in a dozen or more sellers and buyers to ask them questions about how they work and what else eBay needs to do. Also, at least twice a week, it holds hour-long teleconferences to poll users on almost every new feature or policy, no matter how small.

This means Meg Whitman must take a laissez-faire approach to management, based on cooperation and finesse rather than coercion and force. eBay's executives must follow this approach as well, polling the populace through online town hall meetings and providing them with the services they identify or appear to need. It's a very dynamic approach, a different approach to management, and one that Whitman says often takes six months or more for new managers to adjust to.

The collaboration also extends to collaboration among the customers themselves. By rating each other on transactions, for example, both buyers and sellers build up reputations they must then strive to maintain. This sets standards of behaviour that reinforce eBay's business model—and its appeal. Other companies can learn from this approach. Some have, such as Microsoft. Its world of software keeps growing as a result of the thousands of companies and programmers who add their own applications. As Harvard Business School professor David B. Yoffie has observed, "You get the incredible leverage of other people doing all your work for you."

While eBay has grown tremendously in the world of big business, it still has a strong interest in maintaining its customer base among the individual users who like to use it to buy and sell items online on an auctioning basis. This is arguably what made eBay what it is in the first place. Therefore the activities that eBay gets into to accommodate the big customers must not alienate its huge traditional customer base. It's a high wire balancing act.

In addition, eBay wants to continue to expand its traditional business, which means it needs to continue to try to attract new customers, many of whom find the process of registering, listing items on the site, packing them up, and mailing them to be cumbersome and confusing. Moreover, there is the problem of fraud, which has been well-publicized and acts as a deterrent for some. This issue is detailed in part 4 of the eBay case.

The more eBay moves into the big business arena, the more difficult it will be to balance the needs of its two major groups of constituents. Can its laissez-faire, collaborative approach survive? Also, they have the problem of how to make eBay as easy to use as possible, to enable it to attract more of the small and individual customers. It may well require simplifying payments, reducing the hassles of shipping goods, and cracking down on the rising number of crooks who are prowling the site. But this would require management to push through the necessary reforms, which may require a more forceful management approach.

Meg Whitman sums it all up this way: "We don't actually control this. We are not building this company by ourselves. We have a unique partner—millions of people."

The future of eBay depends on maintaining that partnership into the future.

Questions for Discussion

1. What lessons does the eBay experience have for the management of other e-businesses?
2. What are the implications of moving to fixed price retailing for eBay? Is this line compatible with the traditional auctioning approach?
3. How can Meg Whitman and her team structure the strategic initiatives of eBay so as to balance the interests of the small and individual participants with those of the big business participants?

— CHAPTER **11**

E-Marketing and Advertising

LEARNING OBJECTIVES

When you complete this chapter you should be able to:

1. Describe how e-marketing and online advertising tools fit into the strategy of a business.

2. Describe the e-marketing process and its components.

3. Describe the types of online research tools that an e-business may use and how they can be used to understand user behaviour.

4. Discuss the implementation process for an e-marketing strategy and identify common marketing tactics.

5. List and describe the major online advertising tools available to e-businesses.

Introduction

The concept of e-marketing has gone through a rapid cycle of development, from introduction to craze, decline, and stabilization over the past few years. Initially, the promise of global markets, unlimited customers, and an improved communication medium led many to the conclusion that internet marketing and online tools would guarantee rapid growth and business success. The potential of e-marketing was perhaps misunderstood in these initial stages, and more recently the development of the internet's use for marketing purposes has settled into a more reasonable approach: the internet represents one important component of an overall marketing strategy.

E-MARKETING
The utilization of internet and electronic technologies to assist in the creation, implementation, and evaluation of marketing strategy.

E-marketing is the utilization of internet and electronic technologies to assist in the creation, implementation, and evaluation of marketing strategy. This chapter will review e-marketing concepts such as online research, internet advertising technologies, and online consumer behaviour, with reference to the e-marketing strategy process outlined in figure 11.1. The e-marketing process progresses through a cycle similar to other business initiatives, but may cycle through the process rapidly and numerous times prior to settling on any major strategy. The flexibility of the internet medium allows for the strategy to be fluid in nature, but numerous changes can still be costly and result in poorer than expected performance of future tactics.

The concept of e-marketing is closely related to customer relationship management (CRM) but is a broader concept that businesses need to consider (see figure 11.2). CRM and business intelligence (BI) are tools that may be used throughout the e-marketing process. The CRM/BI data may assist in the strategy-creation stage to define a target market, CRM tools may be applied in the implementation stage to provide specific service to customers, and the CRM application may be the tool used to evaluate the success of specific marketing campaigns. CRM and BI applications were discussed in detail in chapters 9 and 10, and throughout this chapter, areas where the applications hold particular value will be discussed.

Online Branding

Ask any individual what five companies they think of when they think of the internet and you are likely to hear Amazon.com as one of the responses. Why is that? Amazon has developed a successful marketing strategy that incorporates online,

Figure 11.1 The E-Marketing Strategy Process

The e-marketing strategy process includes strategy creation, implementation, and evaluation—all within the larger context of overall business strategy.

Figure 11.2   The Relationship Between CRM and E-Marketing

The relationship between e-marketing and CRM can be closely related in firms pursuing both strategies, but each is a unique aspect of e-business.

print, and other advertising methods that have successfully built its brand name as the leading online provider of books, CDs, and many other products. Internet startups like Amazon focused initially on the e-marketing components of their marketing strategy, while bricks-and-mortar competitors like Barnes and Noble stuck to more traditional marketing tactics. As the brand recognition of Amazon rose, Barnes and Noble moved towards an online presence with an e-marketing strategy, and Amazon branched out into more traditional media to continue to capitalize on its brand recognition. This example of the development of the online book industry illustrates an important point—whether a company originates as a bricks-and-mortar firm or an internet startup, e-marketing must form one important component of the business strategy.

An important focus of e-marketing is brand creation and brand reinforcement. A **brand** is a name, term, sign, symbol, design or a combination of these attributes that is used to differentiate a product or service from its competitors. E-marketing can help create brand awareness and brand associations that can help attract visitors to an e-business website and can help convert visitors to buyers. There is controversy about the degree of importance that should be attributed to online brands given the opportunities to send traffic to various sites through rating services, banner ads, and comparison shopping sites. Yet many analysts believe that branding of online businesses is critical due to their lack of physical presence, their remoteness from customers, and customers' need to trust the parties they do business with. A strong brand can build customer confidence, loyalty, and satisfaction and, in the long run, it can help an e-business reduce its marketing costs, improve its margins, and extend the developed brand to new products and services. Developing a strong brand requires an understanding of the target customer and key leverage points in the customer's e-business experience, monitoring competitors, a compelling communication program with regular feedback systems, and consistently reliable performance of e-business activities.

BRAND

A name, term, sign, symbol, design, or a combination of these attributes that is used to differentiate a product or service from its competitors.

Strategy Creation

The creation of an e-marketing strategy will require the use of both traditional and online tools. Similar to any other strategic plan, the development of an e-marketing plan will require the analysis of competition and other environmental factors. One of the major areas of concern at the strategy creation stage will be to evaluate the environment in terms of the legal, ethical, and taxation issues related to the strategy to be devised. These topics are explored in more detail in chapter 13. In addition, the firm may carry out market opportunity analyses such as a PEST analysis, which considers the political, environmental, social, and technological aspects of the environment in which an e-business operates; a Porter Five Forces analysis, which considers the competitive landscape in the industry in which the e-business operates (discussed in chapter 2); and a SWOT analysis which considers the entity's strengths, weaknesses, opportunities, and threats to identify potential areas of focus. The formulation of the e-marketing strategy must also examine the relationship between the e-marketing strategy and the overall organizational strategy in an attempt to achieve synergies that benefit the business. See the Canadian Snapshots box for an example of an internet strategy that includes marketing concepts as part of the business model.

The research process should provide management with the information necessary to segment the market. A **market segment** is a group of customers who share common needs and/or characteristics the selling firm may be able to satisfy. The primary means of segmentation for marketing purposes include demographics, geography, psychographics, and behaviour.[1] Developing an understanding of the market segments that exist will assist the business to identify its target markets and move forward into marketing strategy implementation.

Many services have been developed to assist businesses in many industries to analyze market segments. The automotive industry is one that relies heavily on demographics, and numerous companies aim to lead the demographics analysis segment. DemographicsNow has created a large automotive section within its website that provides detailed demographic information as well as geographic breakdowns across vehicle categories.[2] The creation of services such as this provides a wealth of information with which marketers can analyze and predict future sales across numerous markets.

Other categories that are used to create market segments are psychographics and behaviour. Increasingly, research methods aim to gather details about the psychographics of users—such as personality, values, and activities. The understanding of psychographics and online user behaviour, combined with demographic information and geographic analysis, provides the ability to create numerous market segments, which in the past would have taken much more extensive research to gather.

The internet opens up a strong channel for the development of strategy and is a crucial component of successful e-marketing plans. Since the internet is a developing medium, it is important that firms carefully evaluate their strategies in the context of both traditional customers and online customers. The processes that may be carried out at the strategy creation stage include online research, user behaviour analysis, and advertising planning.

MARKET SEGMENT
A group of customers who share common needs and/or characteristics the selling firm may be able to satisfy.

DemographicsNow Automotive
auto.demographicsnow.com

Online Research

The internet offers a tremendous opportunity to carry out research to develop marketing strategies. An abundance of information is available dealing with demographic trends, social and cultural climates, competition, industry statistics, technological innovation, economics, legal data, and political environments.[3] The sources for these types of data are many, and much information can be obtained for free, while other information will be fee-based. These data sources are forms of secondary data that are useful in carrying out the environmental and market opportunity analyses in the strategy creation stage.

Canadian Snapshots

Discount Brokerage at eNorthern.com

In early 2000 the CEO of Digital Gem Corp. became so frustrated with his online brokerage provider that he decided to start his own. It was this frustration that led to the creation of eNorthern.com, a website owned and operated by Northern Securities Inc. Northern Securities Inc. is a Canadian full service investment dealer, and the website provides online discount brokerage services. This new entrant into the highly competitive market needed to do what many other internet startups had failed at—attract and retain new customers.

eNorthern describes itself as an online brokerage and financial solutions website that aims to provide a quality service to investors at reasonable rates. The company offers Canadian investors a platform for trading Canadian and U.S. securities, including stocks, options, and mutual funds, to satisfy a range of investors from beginner to experienced. While these traits make eNorthern a competitor in the market, they by no means separate them from competitors like eTrade, Datek, TD Waterhouse, and many other online discount brokerages.

The uniqueness of eNorthern's business model was in its approach to reducing the costs of trading—to sell advertising space similar to Amazon and many other online start-

ups. To reduce its trading fees eNorthern sells advertising space to other e-businesses in a targeted manner, based on an understanding of their client's individual preferences, lifestyle, and other information. This strategy allows the company to provide targeted marketing to users and reduce the fee that users pay to execute trades.

eNorthern has also used some other interesting marketing approaches in an effort to gain customers and build customer loyalty. For example, the company aimed to negotiate a deal with a large ISP to provide free internet access services to eNorthern users. eNorthern also aimed to create partnerships with financial-planning software makers. These efforts all led eNorthern to broaden the scope of its offerings while keeping costs under control.

Competitors in the industry, however, are doing many of the same things as eNorthern, and some claim that the number of free giveaways and products won't really help. For example, BayStreetDirect.com's director claims that Canadians seem content to put up with poor service and unfair prices and are, therefore, very difficult to lure away from their traditional service providers. Despite this negativity, eNorthern has gained a small share of the market, and in a Canadian Business review of

Canada's discount brokers, it scored ahead of many of its competitors in categories such as cost and response time but scored poorly in the telephone service category.

As the financial services industry evolves, eNorthern is also attempting to shed its parent company's history. Digital Gem began as a mining company and attempted to move into the financial services and e-commerce industry through efforts of the then-CEO, Nadir Desai. In 1999, Digital Gem attempted to sell sapphires over the internet and then in 2000 it moved into financial services with the creation of eNorthern.

The CEO of Digital Gem, Nadir Desai, resigned in August 2000 but continues to be chairman of the board. The company is now led by Vic Alboini, a prominent Toronto specialist in mergers and acquisitions. In September 2000, Digital Gem changed its name to Northern Financial Corporation in an effort to distance itself from Digital Gem's past and to better reflect the primary business of the company.

The company needs to continue to innovate as it charges base fees of $24 a trade, resulting in minimal financial tools available on its website. The future of this non-traditional financial services company will continue to evolve.

eNorthern.com
www.eNorthern.com

Questions

1. What unique marketing challenges does eNorthern face?
2. How should eNorthern focus its e-marketing efforts in this new business environment?
3. Should the marketing efforts attempt to stay distinct from the Digital Gem past?

SOURCES: J. Gray, "Some Strings Are Attached," *Canadian Business* (March 6, 2000); "Trades and Grades: The Best and Worst Discount Brokers Rated by Criteria," *Canadian Business* (October 16, 2000); Rob Carrick, "BMO InvestorLine Top Pick Among Online RRSP Brokers," *The Globe and Mail*, 9 February 2003; eNorthern.com website, **www.enorthern.com**, accessed April 28, 2004.

SECONDARY DATA
Data that has not been developed specifically for the task at hand but may be useful for decision-making.

Strategis
www.strategis.gc.ca

Secondary data is data that has not been developed specifically for the task at hand but may be useful for decision-making. The abundance of secondary data on the internet provides marketers with information that can be used in crafting a strategy but needs to be used cautiously. For example, the Canadian government's major data centre, Strategis, provides a great deal of information that is from reliable sources such as Statistics Canada. Many of the research firms, such as Forrester Research and Gartner Group, also provide access to some of their research online. However, many other databases and surveys exist online that have been created using unknown and often questionable practices that should not be relied upon without careful review. The key to the use of secondary data is to examine the reliability of the source and ensure that the use of the data within a specific context doesn't reduce its reliability.

The strategy creation stage in most organizations will also lead marketers to gather primary data. **Primary data** is information that is gathered in an effort to better make a specific decision. Typically, primary data will be of a more specific nature than secondary data, and since it is proprietary it will often be more expensive to gather. Many businesses gather primary data on an ongoing basis to assist in evaluation and future planning for their e-marketing strategies. For example, some online retailers ask customers to complete a satisfaction survey after each experience they have with the company. Some of the common methods of gathering primary data online include surveys, experiments, focus groups, and observation.[4]

PRIMARY DATA
Information that is gathered in an effort to better make a specific decision.

Surveys Surveys can be conducted online either through the use of e-mail or web-based methods. Early users of online surveys used e-mail extensively; however, the use of e-mail technologies requires the surveyors to develop means of capturing the data in a database for analysis, which can be more difficult than with internet technologies such as forms. Researchers still use e-mail to reach users for their research, but often the e-mail now directs users to a website to complete the survey.

The process of collecting data through the internet is relatively simple with the use of modern technologies. Users simply enter the responses into a survey form, and upon clicking "Submit" the responses can be loaded into a database in the format pre-configured by the data collector. Surveys can be designed and hosted on the internet using readily available software applications, which significantly reduces the cost of research when compared to postal-based research. In addition, many researchers are finding that the response rates to e-mail and internet research are very similar to paper surveys.

The use of online surveys allows for significant reductions in time for data collection and analysis. If the data input is automated, the need for data entry and error checking are reduced. Users tend to respond to e-mail and web-based surveys either very quickly or not at all. The flexibility of design for online surveys also simplifies the completion process for users. Question formats can be customized to responses given in previous questions, and the use of drop-down boxes, radio buttons, and other online tools can make surveys very user-friendly.

Experiments Online experiments are those research methods that attempt to determine a cause-and-effect relationship by exposing participants to different stimuli.[5] The researcher may, for example, ask participants to conduct a search on a particular website and subsequently ask for information regarding the advertising that was on the site. This could lead the researcher to better understand the success of various advertising formats in building brand awareness online. Numerous other types of experiments could be carried out to test website designs, advertising media success, and other characteristics of importance.

Focus Groups The use of online focus groups has emerged as a successful application of internet technology. The ability to reach disparate areas at a low cost is one of the major advantages of the internet for conducting focus groups. Advances in web technologies such as chat, collaboration tools, and browsers allow a focus-group leader to carry out effective research at a reasonable cost. Participants in online focus groups can provide feedback based on their analysis of an online presence and are less likely to be influenced by the comments of others.

Critics of online focus groups claim that technology gets in the way of important face-to-face discussion. For many who have conducted focus groups in person, much of the value obtained is the interpretation of actions and facial expressions that often accompany participant feedback. Some critics are also concerned with the ability to confirm the identity of participants; however, advances in technology can overcome this problem relatively easily.

Observation The use of observation in understanding user behaviour online is very valuable. The internet provides an excellent medium for monitoring user behaviour through such technologies as click-stream analysis. Click-stream analysis forms an important component of CRM strategy, as well as website design and e-marketing strategy. The primary importance of observation online is to understand how users navigate websites and then utilize that information to improve the likelihood that users will change their behaviour in a favourable manner, such as staying on the site longer or increasing the likelihood of a purchase. Click-stream analysis is also an important input into e-business performance measurement, as will be discussed in the next chapter.

User Behaviour Analysis

The data-collection methods we have just discussed provide data for use in user behaviour analysis as well for other primary data collection. Online user behaviour includes search methods, types of internet usage, shopping patterns, e-mail usage, and other characteristics. The understanding of online user behaviour is extremely important to organizations whether they sell products and services online or not. The value of understanding user behaviour in addition to demographic and geographic information is the enhanced ability to create effective marketing and advertising strategies. If a particular user is very unlikely to buy a product online but commonly seeks information through the internet, a strategy may be to offer specific discounts for the first online purchase. The key to understanding if this is a valid strategy is to better understand users' behaviour.

To better understand user behaviour, companies also may be able to rely on secondary data. For example, much research is being carried out regarding the success rates of banner ads in capturing the attention of web users. This type of data may not specifically be designed for a particular company's products but can often be generalized to many different industries. The findings from secondary data analysis may also assist companies in developing the appropriate primary data research tools. The next chapter discusses user behaviour analysis in more detail for assessing the performance of an e-marketing strategy or evaluating the overall performance of an e-business.

Advertising Planning

One of the major planning components that will take place once the target markets have been identified is advertising and communication planning. Numerous advertising possibilities exist through the internet, traditional media, and wireless applications, and the business will have to tie the planning to each of the specific target markets identified at this stage. The target markets chosen will impact whether the advertising strategy is mass marketing, niche, or multi-segment, which in turn determine the types of advertising methods to choose from. Advertising options and technologies are discussed in more detail later in the chapter.

The strategy creation stage should conclude with a comprehensive e-marketing plan. The analysis should have identified proposed budgets and outcome measurements so that the campaign can be analyzed. If the business is involved in CRM, the planning phase will incorporate the marketing strategy and CRM application into the overall plan of action as well. Often the strategy creation stage will necessitate outsourcing to be organized and may also require changes to internal processes as e-marketing and CRM applications are integrated within the enterprise. The e-marketing strategy must be coordinated with all other marketing efforts and evaluated with regard to overall corporate strategy prior to implementation.

Implementation

Implementation of the e-marketing strategy is a stage of both execution and preparation for evaluation. The strategy must be put into place, but at the same time e-marketing allows the collection of data to occur during implementation and after the strategy is implemented. Since the e-marketing process can occur rapidly and is flexible in nature, it may be possible for changes to be made during a campaign as well, based upon preliminary analysis. See the E-Business in Global Perspective box for an example of the flexibility of the internet in marketing.

The internet's flexibility allows businesses to move from implementation back to strategy creation relatively quickly. For example, Chapters.ca may decide to reorganize its website, focusing first on the e-business books category, to improve the ease of use and improve its branding effects. After preliminary evaluation, however, the company may find that the changes reduced the time spent on the site while not improving the purchases-to-visitors ratio. In this case, Indigo Books & Music may decide to re-evaluate the site revisions and branding strategy prior to moving the new design into other areas of its site. Similarly, organizations conducting promotions through banner ads may decide to abandon banner changes if the click-through rates fall during the campaign.

The implementation of the marketing strategy will focus on a number of interrelated components within each target market. The strategy developed will include plans of action for website design, online advertising, affiliate programs, promotions, partnerships, public relations, and pricing. To examine the complex task of e-marketing implementation, we will examine each of these components below. Keep in mind, however, that the implementation of each of these interrelated components will impact the overall success.

Website Design

The concept of website design has developed very rapidly during the tremendous growth of the internet from the mid-1990s through to the early 2000s. The basic phases of site design that have occurred include the brochureware, interactive, and personalization phases.[6] Early site design was essentially the digitization of existing marketing materials—a phase known as the **brochureware phase** of the internet. The brochureware phase was the most logical step at the time since it was cost-effective and the use of the internet for commercial purposes was in early development. This phase of site design lasted only briefly for the online

BROCHUREWARE PHASE
An early stage of the internet's development where commercial enterprises primarily put existing marketing brochures in digital format.

E-Business in Global Perspective

Change in the Air at Reebok.com

The world's second largest footwear and apparel company, Reebok, has made several changes to its internet and marketing strategy over the past several years. After witnessing the boom in internet stocks and feeling the pressure to "be online," Reebok established a web presence in the mid-1990s, and by the late '90s had developed an e-tailing component to the site where selected merchandise could be purchased. The e-tailing segment contributed less than 1 percent of sales, and by the early 2000s it was irking some traditional retailers.

Recognizing that the potential to the company for online sales was limited and that Reebok's core business was not retail but wholesale, the company set out to revitalize its website along with its new marketing campaign. The new marketing campaign, known as "Defy Convention," was launched in late 2000/early 2001 and traditional media ads included the website URL reebok.com to encourage viewers to visit the site. Reebok also used popular websites like Yahoo! to increase hype for its Super Bowl 2003 Terry Tate advertisement. In the three days following the game, Reebok CEO Paul Fireman said over 800 000 people visited the site. Of those coming to the website, he said 750 000 downloaded the film, which required registration. Perhaps more importantly, Fireman said most viewers were men aged 18 to 34, the most important demographic for the shoe and clothing manufacturer. He added that Reebok's research showed 69 percent said they were likely to buy a Reebok product.

In a subsequent campaign, to support the launch of a new collection of shoes, Reebok created a game called WhoDunIt. It ran two or three TV commercials that played like a fictitious crime show. One of the clues was a tread pattern. Viewers had to register on Reebok's website to guess which of four players was responsible. They would print out a tread pattern from the website, then go to stores to compare it against the shoes in the store. According to Mickey Pant, Reebok's vice president of global marketing, "The interest level was tremendous and the website was very active . . . We use TV not to communicate a message but to direct traffic to the website and create promotions online. That creates a multiplier effect beyond reckoning."

Reebok, however, didn't just use traditional media to drive traffic to the site; it also built the new web presence with the intention to increase loyalty and improve customer service. For example, the website was revised to include not only the ability to search for Reebok retailers within an area but also to find retailers that sell a particular product type. This allows a potential customer to go directly to a store that sells the sneaker line that they are looking for—potentially reducing lost sales.

Reebok
www.reebok.com

Questions

1. Why would e-tailing be difficult for Reebok?
2. What other applications could be used by Reebok on its website besides providing end consumers with product information and marketing materials?
3. Visit the Reebok site and determine if they have modified their strategy from the one outlined in this scenario.

SOURCES: D. Lewis, "Reebok Defies Convention, and It Pays Off," *InternetWeek* (February 19, 2001); "Super Bowl Ads Use Web to Maintain Buzz," *Internet Magazine* (2003); Reebok website, **www.reebok.com**, accessed April 28, 2004; Dawn Anfuso, "Reebok's Micky Pant," iMedia Connection, **www.imediaconnection.com/content/2782.asp**, accessed September 30, 2004.

innovators who quickly learned that the interactive medium of the internet offered much more opportunity than simply broadcasting information.

Website innovators began to create sites that were more interactive than early sites and offered two-way communication. Many of the sites in this **interactive phase** began collecting information through e-mail and online forms and established the ability to conduct e-commerce transactions. The interactive phase of the

INTERACTIVE PHASE
A stage of the internet's development when websites began to allow two-way communication through e-mail and web forms.

internet site design has progressed from simple form-based e-commerce transactions over insecure connections to sophisticated shopping cart transactions over secure networks. Many businesses continue to work within the interactive phase.

The improvement in web programming and site design software, along with a desire to move to "one-to-one" marketing strategies, has led many businesses to the **personalization phase** of the internet. The personalization phase develops one-to-one marketing techniques through the use of cookies and other tracking tools. The personalization of websites allows marketers to tailor the site to the specific wants of the user in an attempt to both improve the chances of making a sale and to improve the relationship with the customer. For example, Yahoo! offers its users the ability to create a My Yahoo! customized page where the user can specify preferred sources for information about the news, entertainment, weather, stock portfolios, and so on.

The personalization of websites allows users to see advertising and information closer to their preferences, which increases the likelihood they will stay on a site—known as **site stickiness**. In addition, the personalization allows the business to create more appropriate, targeted ads for the user based on historic transactions combined with preferences.

Personalization has resulted in mixed feedback from users over its adoption by businesses. The key concern over personalization is whether the user can truly control what they see. In many instances the user would prefer to block most advertising and simply focus on information relevant to their internet usage. However, sites such as My American Express are designed to allow for improved marketing efforts and to increase site stickiness.

Online retailers such as Chapters.Indigo.ca and Amazon have carried out other personalization efforts. The booksellers have attempted to personalize websites by the use of cookies and user registrations to allow for customized web pages based on users' transaction histories. The difficulty in employing automated tools for personalization is in understanding what preferences truly are. A user who enjoyed reading about golfing and hiking would be happy to see suggestions for reading in this area upon returning to a bookseller's site. However, users complained that booksellers' websites would often tailor the pages with advertising for extended periods of time for items purchased as a one-time event. If, for example, a father purchased a child's friend a Pokémon book for a birthday gift and was inundated with ads for related products for months afterwards, neither the retailer nor consumer would benefit.[7] Personalization offers the potential to improve marketing efforts but must be used carefully.

Many aspects of website design are based on demographic, cultural, and technological considerations. The nuances of multimedia design, fonts, colour schemes, templates, and other website design issues all need to be considered to portray an image of professionalism and encourage users to fully utilize the features of the site. To more fully address these concerns, the complementary website to this book provides additional information on website design.

Making a Website Visible on the Web

Since the web is so large and widespread, simply launching a new website does not provide any assurance that people will find it. There are numerous considerations that must be kept in mind to ensure that a website is visible. These include:

- obtaining a good domain name
- metatags

PERSONALIZATION PHASE
A stage in the internet's development when websites began to develop one-to-one marketing techniques through the use of cookies and other tracking tools.

SITE STICKINESS
A term describing the amount of time and likelihood that users will stay on a particular website.

- registration with search engines
- launching an e-business marketing program

Obtaining a Good Domain Name The internet offers the opportunity for businesses to adopt and use domain names in numerous formats. The growth in e-commerce and internet startups, however, has led to the registration of many domain names. The primary domain name extensions of *.com*, *.net*, and *.org* had limited availability and additional extensions (e.g.,*.shop*) have been proposed to increase the ability of organizations to select names related to their business.

Domain names are controlled internationally by InterNIC. InterNIC is organized under the U.S. Department of Commerce, but it allocates domain name registration for the *.com*, *.org*, and *.edu* domain names. It also licenses various other organizations around the world to provide these domain names. For example, in Canada, domain names can be purchased from A Technology Inc., Tucows Inc., and ZiD.com, among others. These organizations also provide the .ca domain name for Canadian companies. Domain names take the user to a particular IP address, and are, in fact, just a simple way of naming web server locations, one that is easier to remember than an IP address. For example, the domain name for the *Globe and Mail* newspaper is globeandmail.com, and the IP address for that web server is 199.246.67.250. The website can be accessed by entering http://www.globeandmail.com or by entering http://199.246.67.250. The domain name is much easier to remember.

The selection of a domain name may not seem to be the most critical area of e-marketing but, as with product naming decisions, can be very important to branding. A domain name is portable from one server to another, so the possession of a domain name adds stability to the name of a site. The IP address, however, changes from time to time. It is generally desirable to have a domain name that is similar to the business name, but this is not always possible because many names have been taken by others.

The first domain names to be taken tended to be those with a short descriptor and the *.com* extension (e.g., Buy.com) to aid in ease of recall. Numerous domain names have been acquired by businesses, sometimes for substantial sums, after the value of their "brand" was recognized. For example, the Business.com domain was purchased for US$7 million to capitalize on the easy-to-remember name. Many factors must be considered when looking into domain name usage, such as competing names, spelling errors, and anti-company sites.

The use of a domain name that is also held by other businesses or internet users with different extensions can be a risky endeavour. For example, a politician in Nova Scotia registered a domain of his own name with the *.net* extension prior to an election. He was soon embarrassed to discover that the *.com* extension with the same domain name (where many constituents ended up in error) was a self-promoting porn star—not exactly the kind of publicity he was looking for. Several businesses have run into difficulties with similar scenarios, and for this reason it is often important to register more than one name and attempt to control other similar names.

The ease of registering domain names results in the ability of individuals to capture potentially valuable sites—a practice known as **cybersquatting**. Cybersquatting involves registering a domain name with the intention to use the name for financial gain, without legal right to its use. This concept has become problematic and its legality is addressed in chapter 13.

Despite popular misconception, however, there is some control over this practice. If a company owns a copyright to a name, such as Loblaws, it is very difficult for another company to obtain that domain name. Various national and

InterNIC
www.internic.net

Tucows Inc.
www.tucowsinc.com

ZID.com
www.domain-name-canada.com

CYBERSQUATTING
Registering domain names with the intention to use the name for financial gain without legal rights to their use.

international committees have been set up to control the distribution of domain names. Initially, there was a brisk trade in domain names of various companies. A famous case took place in 1994, when a young technology writer noticed that the domain name *mcdonalds.com* hadn't been registered. When McDonald's Restaurants wanted to register it, it was, of course, taken, and so a legal battle ensued. After much expense, the dispute was settled by McDonald's giving a donation to a charity. After this high-profile case, much better control was exerted over domain name distribution, and now, companies who have a trademarked name, such as McDonald's, have priority rights to domain names using that name.

Despite the potential legal means of getting domain names back, many businesses have planned ahead for misspellings and anti-business sites. An example of a company not planning for its web presence is Nissan Motors. North Carolina-based Nissan Computer Corporation registered the domain www.nissan.com in 1994; www.nissanauto.com, and www.nissaneurope.com have been acquired by a used car online quote website. Nissan Motors has not been successful in several appeals to acquire the nissan.com domain name and has had to settle for www.nissanmotors.com and www.nissanusa.com. The registration of multiple domain names should always be considered when misspellings are likely. In addition to misspellings, some businesses have taken proactive measures to register various "___sucks.com" domains and other anti-business sites that may damage the brand image on the web.

Metatags Search engines look for many different words to find sites of interest, so it is important that the most critical words, those that most likely would be the search terms that users would enter into a search engine when searching for the types of goods or services that the site offers, be strategically located at or near the top of the main pages, or within metatags. For example, one of the metatag lines on the site for the *Globe and Mail* is:

> META NAME="Keywords" CONTENT="canadian news, national newspaper, daily news, breaking news, political news, world news, canadian business news, canadian newspapers online, international news, report on business, national news, canadian sports, travel information, globe and mail, globe & mail"

This metatag line enables search engines to find the site if any of these search terms are used.

Registration with Search Engines One of the major means of driving traffic to a website is through search engine registration. Using search engines to identify sites of interest is one of the primary means that users find sites that they are not already familiar with; therefore, being registered with the engines is critical if a website is to be found. In addition to being listed, it is important that sites also show up high on the list of search results—a fact that requires different tactics with many of the different search engines. For example, registration with the Yahoo.com search engine will make the site show up on searches in the United States and other countries that use that site. If the sole intent is to do business in Canada, then registration with Yahoo.ca is needed. Similar reasoning applies to doing business in Europe and Asia.

Online Advertising

The evolution of website design and online technologies has led to tremendous improvements in the capabilities for online advertising. The understanding that online media are unique and require innovative approaches has led to the development of creative new means to capture attention, create brand strength, and modify payment methods in the advertising area. In this section the common forms of online advertising including banners, interstitials, Superstitials, interactive tools, e-mail, and multimedia are discussed.

Banners Banner advertising has existed on the internet for several years and has grown and changed over time. The first banner ad on the web appeared on the HotWired site in 1994. Banner ads are graphical images, which may include interactive applications that appear on websites to attract users to click-through to other websites or sections of the present website. Buttons are similar to banners and could be used to submit data on webpages or as a means of clicking through to another webpage. Businesses can charge other sites through various arrangements to host banners and buttons on their pages that can link users to other organizations.

The rising use of banner ads has led to the development of standard sizes and formats for banners. The Coalition for Advertising Supported Information and Entertainment (CASIE) organization, a joint effort of the Association of National Advertisers and the American Association of Advertising Agencies, in conjunction with the Interactive Advertising Bureau, developed the Universal Ad Package, which contains standard dimensions that more easily allow website designers to integrate banners and allow users to readily identify them.[8] As the technologies used in banner advertising have advanced, new standard formats have been developed that are better suited to interactivity, animation, and multimedia tools within the banners as well.

Banners are easily created using software applications. Many banners are designed and stored as animated GIFs. **Animated graphic interchange format (GIF)** is a file that consists of a series of frames that are shown in a particular sequence. The animation attempts to both capture the user's eye and deliver a more complete message than can be delivered within a single banner's image size. For example, Ameriquest Mortgage Company, a debt consolidation, mortgage, and home loan financing company, includes its animated banners on several sites such as Excite.

Other banners include the ability to select specific sections of a target site by drop-down boxes and other interactive applications. Higher-quality banners can be created in HTML formats or using Flash technology to create so-called "rich media" that include dynamic motion. Some industry observers have recorded major improvements in click-through rates based on the usage of these forms of rich media in banners.[9]

Banner advertising is the most dominant form of online advertising despite criticism that it is a relatively ineffective selling tool. Critics of banner advertising cite low click-through rates of less than 1 or 2 percent as proof of the ineffectiveness of banners. However, some researchers have claimed that exposure to banner ads online has significantly improved brand image and brand perception.[10] The low click-through rates, therefore, may be justified by brand building and explain why companies continue to engage in banner advertising. Banner success measurement (besides click-through rates) is not unlike much media advertising whereby the effectiveness is difficult to measure. DoubleClick Inc., however, has built its business model around measurement of banner ads and other advertising tools (see the New Business Models box).

The cost of banner advertising varies dramatically depending on the location of the advertisement, the host company, and any barter deals that are in place. Costs of advertising are often measured in **cost per thousand (CPM)** impres-

Interactive Advertising Bureau
www.iab.net

ANIMATED GRAPHIC INTERCHANGE FORMAT (GIF)
A file that consists of a series of frames that are shown in a particular sequence.

COST PER THOUSAND (CPM)
A standard measure of impressions. Charges are set for each thousand users who visit the site or see an advertisement.

New Business Models

Hot Water at DoubleClick Inc.

DoubleClick Inc. was founded in 1995 and aims to assist companies to improve their marketing online. DoubleClick founded the DoubleClick Network, the first and leading advertising network that allowed marketers to conduct advertising through a growing network of companies. In 1999 DoubleClick merged with Abacus Direct, an offline direct mail service.

DoubleClick describes its major capabilities in the e-marketing area as the ability to:

- deliver a more complete understanding of the customer
- effectively reach and influence customers
- measure the results of marketing efforts with a new level of accuracy

The company offers a broad range of technology, media, direct marketing, e-mail, and research solutions. Most likely, if you have clicked on a banner ad on the internet, you have become a DoubleClick statistic. The company uses banner ads, cookies, and proprietary technology to understand user behaviour online.

One of the company's major products is DoubleClick AdServer software, which allows sites to maximize their revenue while controlling the ad-serving process internally. The process of managing banner ads and other online advertising is a major task for those organizations that wish to capture relevant data as well as effectively control the income received through hosting advertising.

DoubleClick provides not only access to advertising on leading internet sites but also uses advanced technology to target markets effectively. DoubleClick's DART (Dynamic, Advertising, Reporting and Targeting) technology provides the capability for a company to specify target audiences and effectively focus advertising campaigns and, therefore, control costs. The advanced tracking of advertising through the Network also allows DoubleClick to gather massive amounts of data regarding online user behaviour and has led it to develop its own research division. The research garnered by DoubleClick allows it to improve its customers' advertising effectiveness and therefore improve its own brand image.

Having first focused on banners and other online advertising, DoubleClick recognized the importance of offering a full suite of services and in 2001 acquired Flonetwork Inc., and MessageMedia, both e-mail marketing providers. The acquisitions gave DoubleClick an advanced move into the e-mail marketing area, where it had not traditionally focused. DoubleClick now had the capacity to send 700 million e-mails per month on behalf of over 500 clients. DoubleClick utilized its DART technology in combination with e-mail to improve targeting and research capabilities across the e-mail frontier as well. DARTmail features dynamic content and offer management functionality so targeted offers could be sent to customers.

With these moves, DoubleClick became the leading digital marketing solutions company, taking the lead in building standards in the loosely-controlled internet advertising industry, and offering an entire suite of solutions to their clients. One of DoubleClick's technologies enabled it to track web users anonymously to create a database of some 100 million profiles and then serve targeted ads based on those profiles. DoubleClick's idea was to charge premium rates of US$10–$12 CPM for such targeted ads due to their potential to more effectively and more efficiently convey desired advertising messages to target audiences, compared to standard rates for randomly displayed ads of US$3 CPM.

As speculation grew that the databases DoubleClick was using could be merged between online, anonymous data and offline data with names, the company came under fire by privacy advocates. But in early 2001, the U.S. Federal Trade Commission (FTC) closed its investigation into these privacy concerns, leaving the way clear for the company to merge online and offline data—providing that health and financial information was not be used, and users must be informed of the uses of the data and have the opportunity to opt out. However, by December 31, 2001, DoubleClick abandoned its intelligent targeting service to pursue marketing research, data management, and technology opportunities instead.

DoubleClick.com
www.doubleclick.com

Questions

1. **What advantages does the DoubleClick Network provide to marketers? Why?**

2. **Do you agree with the privacy concerns raised? Do you agree with the FTC's conclusion?**

3. **Why do you think DoubleClick abandoned its profiling service? Was it the right decision? Why?**

SOURCES: N. Sperling, "DoubleClick Tries to Regain Credibility," *RedHerring.com* (December 28, 2000); J. Welte, "DoubleClick Grabs Email Firm," *Business 2.0* (February 23, 2001); DoubleClick website, **www.DoubleClick.com**, accessed April 28, 2004; Stefanie Olsen, "DoubleClick Turns Away from Ad Profiles," CNET news.com, (January 8, 2002), **http://news.com.com/ 2100-1023-803593.html?legacy=cnet**, accessed September 30, 2004.

sions. Charges are set for each thousand users who visit the site or see an advertisement. The range in costs can be from less than US$10 to US$100 CPM, and on premium, targeted sites may even exceed these amounts.[11] The CPM for online advertising is often compared to traditional media costs, but marketers must be careful to ensure that the rates are compared based on media-specific terms. For example, the ability to use targeted marketing online is much higher than through broadcast media such as television. Running an advertisement during a prime-time television show is expensive and only results in limited targeting due to the wide demographic bases on television. On the other hand, the use of banner ads would allow the ad to appear on websites specifically targeted to audiences and often related to products that users are searching for.

Banner ads are often run on websites through bartering arrangements. The trading between sites of banners often allows for sites to cooperatively increase traffic and reduces the cash cost of e-marketing. The barter of banners and other advertising has resulted in difficulties in measuring the size of the online advertising market and also has caused complexities in accounting for the costs and revenues associated with online advertising.

One of the major strengths of banner advertising is the ability to measure the effectiveness of advertising in various locations. Banner ads can be created with unique identifiers so that the click-through rates can easily demonstrate which ads have been most effective, what hosting sites have provided the referrals, and other comparisons among numerous criteria. These capabilities offer marketers a substantial improvement over the methods of measuring direct marketing initiatives in the past.

Interstitials The use of interstitials is another common form of online advertising that has been used by many businesses. **Interstitials** are web-based windows that pop up as a user enters an internet site aiming to catch the user's attention. These pop-up boxes, also known as **daughter windows**, commonly promote a specific product of a site or aim to gather survey data (see figure 11.3). The requirement for users to pay attention to an interstitial either to use it or to close it is one factor that proponents of interstitials claim as part of their effectiveness. This same factor is what annoys many internet users—the requirement to click and close boxes to which they do not wish to pay attention. Interstitials are now facing a period of turmoil, as advertisers find them powerful, but often visitors to websites do not want them, and various companies are offering tools that embed in a web browser and block any pop-ups from being displayed. While the fact

INTERSTITIALS
Web-based windows that pop up as a user enters an internet site, aiming to catch the user's attention.

DAUGHTER WINDOWS
Another name for interstitials or pop-up windows.

Figure 11.3   Illustration of an Interstitial Ad

Acer uses interstitials to promote various initiatives that it is presently undertaking. The daughter window appears above the main page that had been selected by the user.

SOURCE: Acer Inc. website, **http://global.acer.com**, accessed May 5, 2004. Reprinted with permission.

remains that pop-ups remain one of the best means of increasing traffic to a website, retaining that traffic is dependent upon other factors such as website design, content, and interest to users. Planned use of interstitials allows advertisers to gather attention—the key is to find a balance between use and overuse.

Superstitials   The rise of internet advertising led one innovative company, Unicast, to create an advertising format tailored to the web—Superstitials. **Superstitials**® are internet advertisement spots that load into a user's browser while the internet connection is idle and then launch as a daughter window showing a short, TV-like advertisement. A study by Harris Interactive in the summer of 2001 concluded that Superstitials demonstrated performance equivalent to television ads in terms of recall, communication, and persuasion.[12]

Unicast created the Superstitial format to provide advertisers with an improved medium over banner ads and interstitials. The benefit from a user perspective is that the ads do not use up bandwidth while you are attempting to use your internet connection (see figure 11.4). Advertisers will be pleased with the findings in the Harris Interactive report demonstrating the capabilities of online advertising—thus leading to increased use of Unicast's product and the development of similar technologies in the near future. Major companies including Coke, NBC, and Kia, along with hundreds of others, have already adopted the use of Superstitials in their online advertising initiatives. The format not only offers a broadcasting capability but also allows interactivity and direct links to purchasing products—an ability promised but not widely delivered by webTV for the past several years.

Samples of Superstitials can be viewed at unicast.com or linked through the website accompanying this text.

SUPERSTITIALS®
Internet advertisement spots that load into a user's browser while the internet connection is idle and then launch as a daughter window showing a short, TV-like advertisement.

Unicast
www.unicast.com

Figure 11.4   The Superstitial Process

Unicast's Superstitial format is an efficient process designed to minimize user disruption and maximize advertiser effectiveness.

SOURCE: Yahoo!, **www.yahoo.com**, accessed December 16, 2004. Reprinted with permission of Yahoo! Inc. © 2004 by Yahoo! Inc. YAHOO! and the YAHOO! logo are trademarks of Yahoo! Inc.

Interactive Tools   The creation of interactive tools is leading internet innovators to develop multiple new formats for advertising online. One notable creator of interactive ads is Ad4ever, the creator of Toplayer® technology. This technology provides advertisers with numerous capabilities such as branding, interactive selling, and other advertising techniques by using technology that seemingly floats ads over the existing web browser. Interactive advertisements allow marketers to carry out targeted marketing and branding techniques in numerous formats. An example of the use of Ad4ever's technology is tying brand awareness into search engines. In 2001, a user who searched for information at a search engine site or entered the toys section of Walmart.com saw the Energizer bunny venture across the screen and rest in a location where the user could follow up. These types of targeted strategies and innovative uses of technology will be major components of online advertising as companies continue to allocate budgets to e-marketing strategies.

Yahoo's website displays an interactive advertisement of a new movie that, when clicked, plays the trailer of the movie.

E-Mail   The use of e-mail for corporate advertising and marketing campaigns is an important area but also needs to be used very carefully. The overuse of the ability to send unsolicited e-mail has led to consumer revolt in several instances and can also result in legal problems in some locations. This phenomenon is known as spamming. **Spam** is the name given to unsolicited e-mail sent in an attempt to gain commercial advantage. The rising problem with spam was created by the relative ease of gathering large numbers of e-mail addresses over the internet

SPAM
The name given to unsolicited e-mail sent in an attempt to gain commercial advantage.

Figure 11.5 Example of a Spam "Business Opportunity"

Spam offers continue to spread through e-mail, disrupting users and weakening the effectiveness of e-mail marketing.

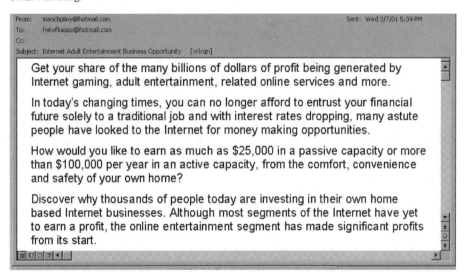

through newsgroups, chat sites, and other websites. Many ISPs and online e-mail services (e.g., Hotmail, Yahoo!) now provide some protection against spam by blocking largely distributed e-mails and attempting to shield users from the disruptions caused by spam. Despite these efforts, users are still often in receipt of spam offering numerous products and services (see figure 11.5).

To utilize e-mail advertising, marketers need to be careful not to be mistaken for spam. The use of e-mail advertising is commonly carried out through permission marketing. Permission marketing occurs when users are able to opt-in to receive e-mail offers and advertising, for example when registering on a website for the first time and agreeing to receive offers related to computer products. The use of permission marketing can be witnessed on many sites and allows users to select the types of advertising that they are willing to receive. This assists marketers in targeting potential customers, but because users must opt-in first it results in much less reach. Google's innovative email service GMail is a cross between a free e-mail account and search engine advertising. It is a form of permission marketing whereby Google provides users with an email service with a large amount of storage space in return for the right to provide advertising similar to the advertising on its search engine. The advertising is targeted on the basis of key words identified by scanning the emails, just as Google scans the results of a search engine request.

The use of e-mail marketing has been heralded by some advertisers as a powerful tool. To take advantage of e-mail without getting confused with spam, Nick Wreden identified several points that should be kept in mind.[13]

1. *The customers should have opted in* to receiving the e-mail and have the ability to opt-out at any time. The spam example in figure 11.5 contained an unsubscribe option; however, repeated attempts to be removed from the list failed and attempts to contact the "spammer" were unsuccessful.

2. *E-mail is not the same medium as direct-mail advertising and should not be treated the same.* The design of e-mail campaigns needs to be carried

out differently from mail ads, which are often long with various type-faces and "free" offers. The growth of promotions on the web has led many of these "free" campaigns and is reducing their success rate as users become frustrated with the volume. Another difficulty with the design of e-mail campaigns is the incompatibility of various e-mail applications. The formatting of an e-mail due to word-wrap and other functions can be altered by each recipient's software, resulting in an unprofessional appearance if design is not carefully planned.

3. *Giving information away can be a powerful form of e-mail marketing.* Many businesses offer electronic newsletters or information services that provide a great opportunity to build brand image and also sell products and services. For example, Air Canada offers e-mail notification of discount fares on selected destinations to users who have opted to receive the information. The provision of this service allows Air Canada to tout its brand and sell off discount flights to customers.

4. *E-mail marketing is a learning process.* It is important that organizations use the information they have gleaned from other sources such as previous campaigns, CRM, and/or BI initiatives to improve their marketing campaigns. For example, the identification of target markets and preferences of opt-in customers may allow marketers to develop specific campaigns and use trial-and-error methods. It is important that the trial-and-error attempts do not tarnish the brand or lead to categorization as a spammer but are used to determine what campaigns have been most effective for click-through or sales increases.

5. *Ensure adequate resources for e-campaigns.* To carry out e-campaigns, human resources, technology, and financial resources will be required. Organizations must balance the commitment of resources toward e-mail campaigns and may wish to look at outsourcing as an option to reduce the human and technology resources required in-house.

6. *E-mail isn't free.* Despite the ease with which we are able to click "send," e-mail campaigns can truly become costly. The use of e-mail for advertising will require extensive upkeep of lists and integration with other applications and may also demand investments in design.

   As discussed earlier, the use of various e-mail applications by users will require that design is carefully carried out—a job often completed by outsourcing. Whether in-house or outsourced, the successful use of e-mail for marketing and advertising will have a cost.

7. *Always look ahead.* The rapid changes in technology and the internet will continue to demand a forward-looking firm. The use of wireless technologies, PDA, and voice e-mail access will require that advertisers carefully design campaigns to be effective across numerous media now and in the future. Shifts in demand and demographics will continue to impact advertisers for the foreseeable future—necessitating forward-looking plans.

Multimedia The internet provides a dynamic medium through which advertising can take on a multimedia approach relatively easily. Several technologies such as Shockwave, Java, and Flash provide the capability to integrate animation, sound, and interactivity into web page design. For example, Disney's internet presence makes use of Flash to build sound and pop-up boxes into its site in numerous places.

Disney Online
www.disney.com

The use of multimedia and advanced software on websites has led to some criticism in the past. Multimedia results in increased transfer of data between the web server and the user's computer and also requires the user to have specific plug-ins installed on their system. The increased transfer of data requires advertisers to consider their strategy carefully, as dial-up internet users may easily become frustrated with slow-loading graphics. The use of multimedia, therefore, requires the consideration of segmenting dial-up versus broadband internet users and may require alternate website design. This is commonly seen on corporate sites where users may select, for example, Flash-enabled or non-Flash sites.

RSA Security Inc.
www.rsasecurity.com

Multimedia tools are also useful in providing service and information related to the company. For example, RSA Security offers numerous Flash demonstrations that explain security applications and concurrently promote the RSA brand. The use of demonstrations and other information online takes advantage of the unique aspects of the internet by allowing users to interactively move from a demonstration to additional product details or to purchase the product.

Affiliate Programs

AFFILIATE PROGRAMS
Agreements between website operators whereby delivery of customers or prospective customers to another company's site results in compensation becoming due.

The use of affiliate programs as part of a strategy to increase website traffic and sales has become a common component of e-marketing strategy. Popularized first by CDnow, **affiliate programs** are agreements between website operators whereby delivery of customers or prospective customers to another company's site results in compensation becoming due. CDnow owners became interested in the concept of affiliate programs when it was at an expensive stage of its life cycle and the cost of banner ads seemed risky. CDnow's affiliate program has grown to over 250 000 members and provides a major source of customer acquisition (see the E-Strategy box).[14]

Many companies have created affiliate programs in an attempt to increase traffic to and sales on their websites. The concept is similar for many of these programs but payment amounts can differ. For example, chapters.indigo.ca offers an affiliate program that nearly any site can join and earn commissions of 5 to 20 percent for click-throughs that lead to sales. The ease of joining and potential for commissions makes affiliate programs attractive. Chapters.indigo.ca provides numerous helpful tools such as pre-designed banner ads and custom HTML codes that allow even novice web designers to integrate the affiliate program.

The affiliate program becomes operational as an internet user clicks on a banner ad or button at an affiliate site and is redirected to another site (such as chapters.indigo.ca). As the user arrives, the affiliate's referring address is tracked so that if the user purchases a product, the affiliate will be eligible to receive the commission they are due. For the affiliate program providers, one of the major benefits of these programs is that the cost of acquiring customers is only paid if the user actually purchases something. In addition, the affiliate program gains a new customer who may come back to the site directly on the second visit (either through brand recall or e-mail advertising), which results in only paying the affiliate commission once.

Partnerships

The internet offers unique capabilities for companies to enter into partnerships that can fit into the e-marketing strategy. Online partnerships can be used to create increased traffic or to target specific products and services to a market segment. For example, eBay and Sympatico have formed a partnership in Canada that

E-Strategy

Affiliate Marketing at CDnow

CDnow is an online music retailer that started out of the basement of a home in Pennsylvania in 1994. Aiming to assist other music lovers to find specialty and hard-to-find music, 19-year-old twins Jason and Matthew Olim started CDnow. CDnow had sales of US$387 in its first month of business, when the only major form of promotion available was to be listed as a website on NCSA Mosaic's "What's New" page. CDnow has grown to be one of the three largest e-commerce sites on the internet. It is owned by Bertelsmann AG, the third largest media company in the world.

Early in the company's development, the Olims recognized that the substantial customer acquisition costs of up to US$500 being paid by some firms were unsustainable, so CDnow began to focus on developing new acquisition tactics. In an era when repeat purchases were not guaranteed and selling products of low-dollar value was

common, CDnow aimed to reduce customer acquisition and marketing costs to a very low amount per customer. Banner ads were still a relatively expensive form of advertising and CDnow was uncomfortable paying for advertising costs that didn't guarantee paying customers. The Olims attempted to get sites to guarantee click-throughs on the banner ads but achieved only limited success.

In late 1994, CDnow and Geffen Records formed a partnership in which Geffen put links to CDnow's site to enable customers to purchase the music of Geffen's artists. The entire concept made sense and CDnow created the Buyweb program, an early affiliate marketing program. The early edition of the program paid referring sites a commission of 3 percent of sales (which later increased to 7 and then to 15 percent), which provided CDnow with its desired outcomes—pay an "advertising" cost only when the customer actually buys. Later known as the Cosmic

Credit and C2 programs, CDnow had an extensive affiliate program with over 250 000 members.

CDnow's overall strategy was as follows:

Offer the most comprehensive selection of music in the world at great prices and with the best service and delivery; build communities of music fans; and strive to always stay at the cutting edge of music distribution technologies. (CDnow.com)

In 2002 CDnow.com formed a partnership with Amazon.com and it has now become an Amazon company. Under the terms of the agreement, Amazon.com provides inventory, fulfillment, site content and customer service. CDnow.com customers have access to Amazon.com features, including free Super Saver Shipping on orders over $25, editorial and customer reviews, personalized features and recommendations, and 1-Click ordering.

CDnow
www.cdnow.com

Questions

1. Why do you think two young men in their parents' basement were the first to develop an affiliate program?
2. What factors would lead Bertelsmann to acquire CDnow? Bertelsmann is the operator of the BMG music club as well, so why didn't BMG have its own online presence?
3. Is Amazon's takeover of CDnow a positive decision for e-business? Do customers benefit by this decision?

SOURCES: D. Hoffman and T. Novak, "How to Acquire Customers on the Web," *Harvard Business Review* (May/June, 2000); Ina Steiner, "Amazon and CDnow Relaunch CDnow.com," *AuctionBytes* (December 5, 2002); and CDnow website, **www.cdnow.com**, accessed April 28, 2004.

allows eBay to improve its user-base by increasing its use on the popular Sympatico service. Other prominent partnerships have been formed that allow businesses to work together and capitalize on each other's strengths. For example, Amazon and Toys "Я" Us formed a partnership that saw Amazon use its existing technologies and e-commerce capabilities to facilitate online transactions with Toys "Я" Us.[15] Partnerships can allow businesses to benefit in a number of ways in the online world.

Promotions

The use of promotions is an important aspect of e-marketing and advertising. Promotional tools such as coupons, discounts, contests, points programs, and demos/free trials are all easily employed over the internet. Several online companies provide tools to create these types of promotions or provide the services for a fee. In addition to using web pages to provide these promotional tools, it is possible to integrate promotions into e-mail campaigns. For example, a targeted and timely advertisement by an optical care provider reminds the customer that it is time to replace their disposable contact lenses, and offering a discount at the same time. The e-mail ad also attempts to establish new business by providing compensation for referring a friend to the company.

A large number of companies offer points programs and customer loyalty programs online. These programs range from the more traditional airline miles/points to online cash such as the online currency created by Beenz.com. Beenz currency was earned by web users for shopping at selected sites, registering for services, and completing surveys. The Beenz could then be spent at specified sites for products and services available. (Beenz.com ran into financial difficulties and is no longer in operation.) Bricks-and-mortar companies that have loyalty programs have also begun to move their programs online to both increase usage and develop online strategies.

The internet is loaded with locations where users can access free trials and demos. Perhaps most common are software demos that can be downloaded at sites like CNET Download.com. The provision of software demos provides many software businesses with a powerful avenue to display their products and allow users to ensure that they are satisfied with the products prior to purchase.

Companies also use chat communities to promote their products. For example, Johnson & Johnson uses teen chat communities as an avenue to provide trials of its Clean & Clear skin-care products. The company provides teenage girls with the opportunity to send their friends electronic postcards that offer samples of Clean & Clear.[16] While tangible products require either physical shipment or customer pick-up, the internet provides the opportunity to target customers and profile these products at a reasonable cost.

Public Relations

Public relations is the activity of creating goodwill or positive company image. Typically, public relations aims to please a wider audience than advertising alone—targeting shareholders, employees, communities, the media, and the public. As an efficient and effective communication tool, the internet offers numerous methods for satisfying a company's public relations strategy. A review of most corporate websites will reveal a news or press release section whereby current information can be disseminated easily and cost-effectively. In addition, online delivery of information such as annual reports and shareholder information allows for the integration of multimedia and internet enhancements, along with additional details that cannot be as easily delivered in print.

The proliferation of internet sites, online magazines, news services, and industry organizations offers tremendous potential for public relations online. Many companies encourage employees to become involved in writing articles for publication on the internet (and in print) in order to portray an image of excellence and industry leadership. In addition, publication on the internet is often accompanied by a link to the writer's or employer's website. The combination of published material and interactivity may lead to improved brand image, increased website traffic, and potentially increases in sales.

A key objective of public relations is to instill trust in an e-commerce site. Trust can allay market participants' fears about the riskiness of conducting business on the internet. Such fears stem from the lack of physical presence for many entities involved in e-commerce; the anonymity of many internet users; widespread users of outsourcing of various e-commerce functions, which creates a complex web of relationships; demonstrated vulnerabilities of some e-commerce sites to security, availability, integrity and privacy abuses. Those fears can relate to the internet as a whole, as well as to specific concerns about particular e-commerce sites or participants in an online marketplace. A number of mechanisms can help reduce such concerns and help signal that an e-commerce entity or individual participant is trustworthy. Interestingly, website design and look has been found to be one of the most important factors associated with a website's credibility, despite the fact that fraudsters can create professional looking sites to deceive their victims.[17] Payment escrow services and credit card guarantees discussed in chapter 6 contribute to trust in e-commerce. Two mechanisms that are particularly noteworthy because they provide external evidence about a site's trustworthiness are trustmarks or "seals of approval" and online feedback mechanisms, also called "digitized word of mouth."

Trustmarks Many sites use trustmarks or seals to convey a positive company image and help overcome customers' fears that a seller may not fulfill its commitments to them, that the security of their credit card numbers may be compromised, or that their personal information will be misused. **Trustmarks** or seals are graphic representations similar to logos that are placed on websites to indicate that the entity complies with certain recommended e-commerce practices and is therefore a trustworthy business partner. Due to the graphic nature of the web, there are many such seals or logos on the internet with a variety of meanings that are often not clear to customers. For example, the WebTrust seal is a certification mark which is intended to be more authoritative than a registered mark or logo; however, this distinction would not be visible to customers viewing the graphic image. We will consider four programs designed to label e-commerce sites as being trustworthy—TRUSTe, BBB*OnLine* (both Reliability and Privacy) and WebTrust. Figure 11.6 illustrates the trustmarks or seals associated with each of these programs.

TRUSTe The TRUSTe seal was developed by TRUSTe.org to indicate that an entity follows privacy principles that comply with the fair information practice principles approved by the U.S. Federal Trade Commission. In particular, the entity must clearly disclose on its website its collection and use practices regarding personally identifiable information (PII). Users must be given choice and consent over how their personal information is used and shared. Finally, access and data security measures should be in place to safeguard and update PII. Websites that display the TRUSTe privacy seal must agree to comply with ongoing TRUSTe oversight and its dispute resolution process. TRUSTe monitors licensees to ensure compliance with their stated privacy practices and TRUSTe program requirements. The oversight process includes periodic website review, "seeding," and online community monitoring. Seeding involves signing up on an ecommerce site under a dummy user ID that is solely used for that purpose, and explicitly opt-

TRUSTMARK
A graphic representation similar to a logo that is placed on websites to indicate that the entity complies with certain recommended e-commerce practices and is therefore a trustworthy business partner.

WebTrust
www.webtrust.org

TRUSTe
www.truste.org

Figure 11.6 Trustmarks

Trustmarks are graphic symbols used to represent authoritative sources that testify to the trustworthiness of an e-commerce site.

SOURCES: TRUSTe and the seal are trademarks of TRUSTe; BBB*OnLine* logos reprinted with the permission of Better Business Bureaus, Inc., copyright 2003. Council of Better Business Bureaus, Inc., 4200 Wilson Blvd., Arlington, VA 22203. World Wide Web: **www.bbb.org**; WebTrust logo reprinted courtesy of The Canadian Institute of Chartered Accountants.

ing out of any sharing of personal information by the company. By monitoring whether the dummy user ID receives unwarranted e-mail, it is possible to determine whether the entity honoured the user's request.

BBBOnLine
www.bbbonline.org

BBBOnLine BBB*OnLine*, an arm of the Better Business Bureau (BBB) that is devoted to websites, offers two main types of seals—reliability and privacy. The BBB*OnLine* Reliability Seal indicates that a company is a member of their local Better Business Bureau, has been reviewed to be truthful in advertising and follows good customer service practices, that the site complies with the BBB Code of Online Business Practices, has at least one year of operating history, a satisfactory complaint handling record, prompt response to consumer complaints, and agrees to participate in the BBB's advertising self-regulation and dispute resolution programs. The BBB*OnLine* Privacy Seal indicates that a company's online privacy policy is presented accurately, and that the BBB*OnLine* program requirements with respect to the handling of personal information are met.

WebTrust The WebTrust seal was developed by the American Institute of Certified Public Accountants and the Canadian Institute of Chartered Accountants to provide assurance on e-commerce system security, availability, processing integrity, and privacy. Security means that the system is protected against unauthorized access (both physical and logical). Availability means that the system is available for operation and use as committed or agreed. Processing integrity means that system processing is complete, accurate, timely, and authorized. Privacy means that personal information obtained as a result of e-commerce is collected, used, disclosed, and retained as committed or agreed.

As table 11.1 illustrates, the WebTrust criteria are structured into four categories of criteria and each category has four layers: policies, communications, procedures, and monitoring. Each layer has specific criteria related to the respective categories. The criteria in the policies layer are similar from category to category, as are the criteria in the monitoring layer. Security is a base for all the other categories, and so the security criteria in the procedures layer are repeated in each category so that they could be audited individually if desired. Thus, there is some overlap in the categories which would be eliminated during an actual audit. Online privacy has the most criteria, due to the extensive disclosure requirements in the communications layer.

The *policies layer* considers whether the entity has defined and documented its policies in each category. In the context of WebTrust, the term "policies" is used to refer to written statements that communicate management's intent, objectives, requirements, responsibilities, and/or standards for a particular subject. Such com-

Table 11.1   Structure of WebTrust Criteria

The WebTrust criteria include 113 specific requirements structured into four categories of issues (security, availability, processing integrity, and online privacy) and four layers of criteria within each category (policies, communications, procedures, and monitoring).

CRITERIA	Layers	Security	Availability	Processing Integrity	Online Privacy	Total
	Policies	3	3	3	3	12
	Communications	5	5	5	10	25
	Procedures	12	15	19	18	64
	Monitoring	3	3	3	3	12
	Totals	23	26	30	34	113

munications may be explicitly designated as policies, whereas others (such as communications with users not otherwise documented as policies, or written procedures) may be implicit. Policies may take many forms but should be in writing.

The *communications layer* considers whether the entity has communicated its defined policies to authorized users both external and internal to the entity.

The *procedures layer* considers the procedures the entity uses to achieve its objectives in accordance with its defined policies. Procedures are the activities that are actually performed by system components, not merely desirable procedures documented in manuals or other guidelines. Procedures may be manual, automated, or a combination of manual and automated activities.

The *monitoring layer* considers whether the entity monitors the system and takes action to maintain compliance with its defined policies.

A WebTrust seal on a website means that the site has been certified by authorized CA/CPA WebTrust licensees, adequate disclosure of the company's business practices is provided, and that these practices have been audited against the stringent criteria established by the WebTrust task force.

Digitized Word of Mouth It is generally believed that word of mouth is one of the most powerful promotion methods. The internet offers important new possibilities for **digitized word of mouth** advertising and promotion and for building trust in e-commerce sites through formal online feedback mechanisms. Perhaps the best known example of such feedback mechanisms is eBay's buyer and seller ratings following a transaction. Such ratings help establish buyer and seller reputations on eBay for repeat business activity. Other examples include Epinions Inc., which provides an online forum for users to write reviews about products and services and others to rate the usefulness of those reviews. At Elance, Inc., a professional services marketplace that helps buyers/contractors requiring services match up with freelancers offering services, contractors rate their satisfaction with sub-contractors. Slashdot is an online discussion board owned by the Open Source Technology Group, where postings are prioritized according to ratings they receive from readers.

Online feedback systems can help promote e-commerce activity on a particular site, as well as the broader e-commerce community. Creating opportunities for digital word of mouth can be an important trust building tactic for many e-commerce sites, especially online marketplaces and exchanges that might otherwise be viewed as too risky for transacting business. However, to be effective, the site needs to attract a sufficient number of participants to neutralize attempts by

DIGITIZED WORD OF MOUTH
Mechanisms for recording feedback about e-commerce sites, products, and market participants and sharing such feedback with others.

Epinions, Inc.
www.epinions.com

Elance, Inc.
www.elance.com

Slashdot
www.slashdot.org

some users at manipulating the feedback mechanism.[18] In this regard, an important recent development has been the creation of artificial word of mouth by marketers seeking to leverage the power of this promotional device. For example, marketers have started to pay bloggers (authors of **blogs**, which are websites containing personal posts available to be read by web surfers) to promote certain products in their blogs, thereby creating word of mouth for those products. Another recent development is the recruiting of volunteer "buzz agents" to create word of mouth through a variety of online and offline activities. BzzAgent Inc. has more than 60 000 volunteers, while Tremor, a division of Procter & Gamble, has an astounding 240 000 volunteers spreading word of mouth about products ranging from TV shows to consumer products. One concern that has been expressed by critics of these developments is that the volunteers and the marketers that recruit them to "manufacture" word of mouth using a variety of covert techniques are abusing the trust that their acquaintances place in them.[19]

BLOG
A website containing personal posts available to be read by web surfers.

BzzAgent, Inc.
www.bzzagent.com

Tremor
www.tremor.com

Pricing

Establishing prices that maximize profitability is a difficult task for businesses. The internet offers a new medium within which businesses must establish pricing policies that capture potential sales and maximize profits. The traditional practices of establishing prices that remained in effect for extended periods, however, are no longer necessary. The internet offers the capability of changing prices relatively rapidly and offering varying prices to customer segments. As discussed in chapter 8, the use of auctions has led many transactions to occur with flexible pricing arrangements.

One concern of many companies to date has been how to deal with pricing between online versus offline sales channels. The online channels originally were thought to become extremely competitive based on price, but the low prices charged by many pure-play competitors forced them out of business. The establishment of multichannel pricing requires a focus on customer segments and also can create additional complexity within an organization. Prices online have not fallen as drastically as some pundits had predicted and, in fact, some online companies claim to use higher prices in their online channel due to convenience, additional services, and appropriate segmentation. In contrast to claims regarding the importance of low prices on the internet, a McKinsey study found that most online buyers actually do very little shopping around and many tend to return to sites used in the past—suggesting that brand may be as important as pricing.[20]

Low prices may not be the most important factor online, but a solid pricing strategy can lead to substantially improved profitability and market share. For example, some B2B sellers have indicated that they segment customers by the extent with which the customer conducts business with them. Those customers who carry out the majority of their purchases with the seller receive improved pricing, while those who use the seller only as an alternate means of supply may pay a premium price. This form of segmentation led an electronic components company to charge a premium of up to 20 percent to some customers, with little impact on volumes sold.[21]

The internet provides an opportunity for e-businesses to conduct test pricing and price-related research in an effort to optimize prices. The difficult aspect of altering prices, however, is to do it in a fair manner. As part of a price test, Amazon offered potential customers discounts that ranged from 30 to 40 percent, but was criticized when consumers became aware of the actions. The bad publicity associated with such research requires that companies carefully consider any test pricing strategies they plan to carry out. E-businesses may also optimize prices by making adjustments related to supply and demand on an ongoing basis. The adjustment of prices online can be much simpler than in the traditional sales channels, where price lists, signage, and multiple sales channel firms may all need to be updated with regard to changes.

Evaluation

The ability to modify or refine marketing campaigns is simplified online and can occur several times per week or even per day. Staples measures its online marketing campaigns by the hour according to a number of key metrics. If those metrics indicate that a particular strategy is not working, the marketing campaign is quickly revised. In addition, Staples adjusts the allocations of its marketing budget on a weekly basis to focus on the most crucial elements within a set dollar budget.[22] The development and understanding of key metrics can help businesses adjust e-marketing strategies in internet time.

The metrics to be used will vary drastically by industry and the particular strategy being pursued. Some metrics that may be considered are banner click-through rates, website view-to-buy ratios, pricing effectiveness measures, market share, revenue growth, and numerous other factors. In developing the e-marketing strategy, the business should determine which metrics are relevant and ensure that an appropriate measurement process exists to evaluate the success of strategy implementation. Chapter 12 contains an in-depth discussion of various metrics that can be used to assess the performance of e-commerce sites.

Chapter Summary

E-marketing is an important component of the overall marketing and business strategy of e-businesses. While many dot-com businesses have failed and the spending on online advertising has dropped from its peak, the importance of having an e-marketing and advertising strategy is still widely acknowledged. The e-marketing process includes strategy creation, implementation, and evaluation.

The e-marketing strategy is developed at the strategy creation phase whereby research is carried out, target markets are identified, and a strategy is devised. Secondary research information may be gathered through the internet as well as other methods, while e-businesses may also engage in primary research. Primary research may be carried out through surveys, experiments, focus groups, and observation.

As in any business, e-businesses must aim to use the data they have gathered to segment the market and identify target markets. The unique aspect of e-marketing is that targeted marketing is often more easily conducted than through offline businesses.

The e-marketing and advertising strategy should be implemented in a fluid manner to capitalize on the capabilities of the internet. If implemented and carefully monitored, the strategy can be revised mid-stream to better meet the needs of customers. Implementation will include website design, advertising, affiliate programs, promotional techniques, partnerships, public relations, and pricing.

Advertising online has changed dramatically as software and hardware improvements have been made. While simple banner ads are still commonly used, the internet now allows advertisements to take on television-like appearances with multimedia and interactivity added in. Many advertising tools such as e-mail require careful monitoring, design, and execution to be effective—often requiring trial-and-error or outsourcing.

The e-marketing and advertising strategy must be evaluated on an ongoing basis to ensure that the desired outcomes are being met. In addition, the fit of the e-marketing strategy within the general marketing strategy and overall business strategy must be kept in mind as online and offline operations continue to converge.

Key Terms

affiliate programs   *(p. 236)*

animated graphic interchange format (GIF)
   (p. 229)

blog   *(p. 242)*

brand   *(p. 219)*

brochureware phase   *(p. 224)*

cost per thousand (CPM)   *(p. 229)*

cybersquatting   *(p. 227)*

daughter windows   *(p. 231)*

digitized word of mouth   *(p. 241)*

e-marketing   *(p. 218)*

interactive phase   *(p. 225)*

interstitials   *(p. 231)*

market segment   *(p. 220)*

personalization phase   *(p. 226)*

primary data   *(p. 222)*

secondary data   *(p. 222)*

site stickiness   *(p. 226)*

spam   *(p. 233)*

Superstitials®   *(p. 232)*

trustmark   *(p. 239)*

Tools for Online Learning

To help you master the material in this chapter and stay up to date with new developments in e-business, visit **www.pearsoned.ca/trites**. Resources include:

- **Review Questions and Exercises**

- **Problems for Discussion**

- **Recommended Readings**

- **Updates to Case Studies and Textual Material**

- **Streaming CBC Videos with Cases**

Endnotes

1. Judy Strauss and Raymond Frost, *Marketing on the Internet: Principles of Online Marketing* (Upper Saddle River, NJ: Prentice Hall, 1999).

2. "Auto.DemographicsNow.com Provides Marketing Data for Auto Industry," *Direct Marketing* (April 2001).

3. Judy Strauss and Raymond Frost, *Prentice Hall's e-Marketing Guide* (Upper Saddle River, NJ: Prentice Hall, 2001).

4. Judy Strauss and Raymond Frost, *Marketing on the Internet: Principles of Online Marketing* (Upper Saddle River, NJ: Prentice Hall, 1999).

5. Judy Strauss and Raymond Frost, *Marketing on the Internet: Principles of Online Marketing* (Upper Saddle River, NJ: Prentice Hall, 1999).

6. Adapted from Ward Hanson, *Principles of Internet Marketing* (Cincinnati, OH: South-Western College Publishing, 2000).

7. M. Hicks, "Getting Personal: E-biz Firms Search for Better Ways to Customize Content," *eWEEK* (October 2, 2000).

8. Interactive Advertising Bureau website, www.iab.net/comm/adsizes.asp, accessed April 28, 2004.

9. L. Hughes, "Rich Media Spicing Up Online Buying Choices," *Advertising Age* (February 2001).

10. R. Briggs and N. Hollis, "Advertising on the Web: Is There Response Before Clickthrough?" *Journal of Advertising Research* (March/April 1997).

11. JDA Software Group, Inc. website, www.jda.com, accessed April 28, 2004.

12. Harris Interactive, marketing study (June 2001), Unicast website www.unicast.com/research/pdfs/effectiveness_of_superstitial_relative_to_tv.pdf, accessed April 28, 2004.

13. Nick Wreden, *Mapping the Frontiers of E-mail Marketing*, Harvard Management Communication Letter (September 1999).

14. D. Hoffman and T. Novak, "How to Acquire Customers on the Web," *Harvard Business Review* (May/June 2000).

15. Amazon.com website www.amazon.com, accessed April 28, 2004.

16. D. Kenny and J. Marshall, "Contextual Marketing: The Real Business of the Internet," *Harvard Business Review* (November/December 2000).

17. B.J. Fogg et al., "How Do People Evaluate a Web Site's Credibility? Results from a Large Study," research report (November 11, 2002) www.consumerwebwatch.org/news/report3_credibilityresearch/stanfordPTL.pdf, accessed November 29, 2004.

18. C. Dellarocas, "The Digitization of Word of Mouth: Promise and Challenges of Online Feedback Mechanisms," *Management Science* (October 2003).

19. Rob Walker, "The Corporate Manufacture of Word of Mouth," *The New York Times Magazine* (December 5, 2004): 69–75, 104, 130 131.

20. W. Baker et al., "Price Smarter on the Net," *Harvard Business Review* (February 2001).

21. W. Baker et al., "Price Smarter on the Net," *Harvard Business Review* (February 2001).

22. N. Aufreiter et al., "Marketing Rules: What Sets Winners Apart? More Than Anything Else, It's Lightning Fast Marketing," *Harvard Business Review* (February 2001).

— CHAPTER **12**

Metrics for Performance Measurement in E-Commerce

LEARNING OBJECTIVES

When you complete this chapter you should be able to:

1. Explain the benefits that metrics provide to an e-business.

2. Identify and describe the importance of the major types of metrics.

3. Explain how traffic metrics can help an e-business assess its internal processes.

4. Explain how marketing-oriented metrics can help an e-business plan its marketing efforts.

5. Identify the major types of financial metrics.

6. Identify other performance metrics.

7. Describe the major sources of information for creating performance metrics.

Introduction

The focus of this chapter is measurement of e-business performance. E-business performance can be measured in several ways, ranging from measures of traffic on an e-commerce site, to measures of customer behaviour, and ultimately, to measures of e-business effectiveness. One of the great benefits of the internet is that it enables tracking and measurement of business activity. In this chapter we will consider the benefits provided by well-designed metrics, what aspects of e-commerce can be measured, and what are the sources of information for such measurements.

Benefits of Metrics

Management and measurement go hand in hand. Commonly heard expressions in business are, "If you don't measure it, you cannot manage it" and "If you don't measure it, it doesn't get done."

Metrics can help an entity to better understand its business model—to understand the customer base and thereby better target the content of the e-commerce website, to better target promotions and discounts, product placements, up-selling and cross-selling, and to better manage price points.

Metrics can serve as a communication device to provide guidance to the personnel who are assigned the responsibility for achieving strategic objectives on what they are expected to do, since implicit within metrics are the variables that must be acted upon to positively affect those metrics.

Metrics also act as an incentive to motivate certain types of performance. We all pay attention to the things for which we know we are going to be held accountable. So if you are given marks for a task in a course, then you're more likely to do that task than an optional task for which there are no marks assigned. If a sales agent is paid a higher commission for certain types of sales than others, then the agent is more likely to focus on generating those sales.

Metrics provide a basis for analyzing performance. In the absence of metrics, performance assessment would be based primarily on qualitative observations of behaviour. Such observations could be haphazard and subjective, resulting in performance assessments that are biased or indefensible. Also, they could focus unduly on easily observed or surface aspects of behaviour rather than on desired outcomes. For example, metrics can be used to determine whether promotions are actually working. Every time an entity has a promotion, it is giving something of value away in order to attract business, hoping that the new business attracted will pay for the promotion. Simply observing that a great deal of effort went into planning and organizing a series of weekly promotions does not provide the entity with knowledge of the effectiveness of all that activity. If the entity doesn't keep track of the outcomes of promotions in terms of increased traffic or revenue, it will never know whether its promotions add value, or are simply a drain on value. The Canadian Snapshots box describes the use of metrics for assessing the maturity of e-government services.

Another important benefit of metrics is that they provide a basis for holding people accountable. They provide guidance as to what tasks ought to be performed, motivation to do those tasks, and subsequently, a standard against which performance can be evaluated and rewarded and non-performance can be addressed.

Aligning Metrics with Business Objectives

Measurement should align performance with objectives. If an entity has set objectives and knows how to measure them, then this is an indication that it knows how to link its activities to its business objectives. Accordingly, the metrics that are established in this way provide part of the roadmap to achieving strategic objectives; they define the actions required to meet objectives. For example, if an e-business wishes to grow its customer base then it can establish a metric of traffic volume for its e-commerce site such as the number of visits per week during the campaign to attract customers. Such a metric immediately focuses attention on bringing traffic to the website and entity personnel will be focused on tactics to achieve this objective. The effectiveness of chosen tactics will be assessed by the number of visits per week that resulted, aligning the activities with the objectives.

An e-business may have different objectives at different times in its life. For example, maximizing traffic might be an objective early on when an e-business is trying to get established and it just wants to get attention from potential shoppers. However, maximizing traffic may not necessarily lead to maximum profit; in

Canadian Snapshots

Using Metrics to Rate E-Government Maturity

According to a research study by global management consulting firm Accenture Ltd. (released Tuesday May 4, 2004), Canada has placed number one out of 22 countries globally in e-government maturity for the fourth consecutive year. The study found Canadian e-government practices ranked first in all categories including service breadth, service depth, and customer relationship management, earning 80 percent out of a possible score of 100—13 percent better than its closest challengers Singapore and the United States.

Accenture studied the e-government practices of 22 countries including Canada, Australia, the United States, the United Kingdom, Singapore, Brazil, France, and Germany.

Accenture researchers in the countries used the internet to obtain access to and use 201 services that national governments typically provide in the human services; justice and public safety; revenue; defense; education; transport and motor vehicles; regulation and democracy; procurement; and postal sectors. The researchers

focused on the functionality, quality, and maturity of services offered. Services were categorized into three levels—publish, interact, and transact—reflecting the level of service maturity. Services also were evaluated on the basis of the extent to which the government used customer relationship management (CRM) to manage their customer (citizen and business) interactions. Scores in these areas were combined with 70 percent weighting allocated to service maturity and 30 percent weighting to CRM to derive an overall rating for the maturity of e-government services.

Additionally, telephone interviews were conducted with senior executives in agencies with customer-facing responsibilities for welfare, immigration, revenue, licensing, and employment services in a subset of the target countries. This research was supplemented with information about the e-government environment in each of the countries, including the details about the country's e-government program, recent political and legal developments related to e-government, and other details about the

processes being used to implement e-government.

According to Graeme Gordon, an Ottawa-based partner with Accenture's government practice in Canada, the nation has earned its top spot based on the fact that its e-government vision is predicated on customer centricity and a "whole of government" approach, which incorporates the different levels of government to deliver the best possible service to the user community.

"Canada's action plan is built on a solid foundation of fact based on the known information from the customer base," Gordon said. "It regularly surveys citizens and businesses for indications of attitudes and needs, and the processes [Canada] has appear to be the most extensive compared to other countries in the survey, in terms of gathering and understanding the needs of the citizens."

Canada also actively markets its e-government services. It advertises on TV and radio, and places ads in airline magazines and newspapers to get citizens to use its portal, canada.gc.ca.

However, despite Canada's leading role in e-governance, the study found that advances in maturity on the whole are slowing down around the globe and even countries like Canada—with the most advanced e-government practices—have a long way to go to achieve dramatic results.

Government of Canada
www.canada.gc.ca

Questions

1. Should the Canadian government be spending tax dollars on external consultants to evaluate e-government services? Why?

2. What are the strengths and weaknesses of the scorecard used to evaluate e-government maturity?

3. How can metrics be used to address the finding that advances in e-government maturity are slowing down?

SOURCES: Carly Suppa, "Study: Canadian E-Gov Maturity Ranks First Globally," *The Industry Standard* (May 5, 2004), **www.thestandard.com/article.php?story=20040505163338275**, accessed May 25, 2004; "The Government Executive Series: eGovernment Leadership: High Performance, Maximum Value," research paper, **www.accenture.com/xdoc/en/industries/ government/gove_egov_value.pdf**, accessed May 25, 2004; "eGovernment Leadership: Engaging the Customer Study," press release, **www.accenture.com/xd/xd.asp?it=enweb&xd=newsroom\ epresskit\egovernment\egov_epress.xml**, accessed May, 25 2004; Eric Chabrow, "Canada Is Still No. 1 in E-Government Rankings" *InformationWeek* (May 6, 2004), **www.informationweek.com/ story/showArticle.jhtml?articleID=20000010**, accessed May 25, 2004.

fact, it may lead to losses because there might be significant customer acquisition and promotion costs associated with generating that traffic. But during the business startup phase, maximizing traffic may be a legitimate objective and the costs involved may be considered an investment for the future.

Although traffic is definitely a key metric for e-commerce, even more important is the conversion of traffic into customers. By customer we mean an entity that fulfills the main objective for the site, which could be content consumption, lead generation, sales or customer support. For example, for sites that provide content, traffic alone might be an insufficient measure of content consumption. Instead, the average length of visits, the average number of page views per visitor, and net subscriptions (new subscribers minus cancellations) could be useful metrics. For lead-generation sites, useful metrics might be white paper downloads, number of opt-ins for future e-mail contact, and average length of visit.

For a product sales site, maximizing revenue could be the main objective. Maximizing revenue is not the same as maximizing traffic, because maximizing traffic is focused on getting visitors to a site, whereas maximizing revenue is focused on selling products and services by converting visitors into buyers. For example, generating traffic but not having the products that customers want in stock would not help generate revenue. So having a revenue maximizing objective would focus attention on products and services as well as traffic. Revenue related metrics such as sales per visitor rate the website's success in converting visitors to buyers.

For a customer service site, two paradoxical goals are to have more traffic on a self service site than on more expensive call centre sites, but progressively less traffic and shorter visit times on both types of support sites, with constant or increased levels of customer satisfaction.

Increasing market share is a little different than maximizing sales because it involves competition. Metrics of market share by definition involve competing with others, trying to take some of their business. That is a very different objective than simply creating sales. For example, an entity can attempt to generate sales through joint advertising with a competitor. Such an approach could increase the size of the sales pie, but the entity's share of the pie may not get any bigger.

Minimizing transaction costs is an objective that is aimed at reducing the costs of doing business. At the startup phase of a business or launch of a particular product or service, it might be beneficial to provide a significant level of support to customers through dedicated call centre support and so on. But that support translates into significant transaction costs. Over time, the objective would be to minimize those costs by reducing the number of people in support functions or keeping the same number of people but putting through much more business activity. A metric such as cost per visitor would focus attention on transaction costs.

Maximizing return on investment (ROI) deals with earnings relative to the investment incurred to develop an e-commerce site. That could be an important objective as an e-business matures. During the dot-com bubble the conventional wisdom was that entities were supposed to spend a lot of money maximizing traffic and sales, without worrying about return on investment. Huge sums of money were spent on developing e-commerce sites and on advertising to attract customers to e-businesses that never generated a return on the huge investments made. Metrics that recognize that expenditures on e-commerce sites are investments will focus on return rather than income alone. A marginal income stream could satisfy revenue and expense metrics but might not satisfy requirements based on ROI.

In summary, objectives must be linked to strategy and must be specific. If they are vague it will be difficult to establish metrics for assessing their level of achievement. And if an entity doesn't know how to measure an objective, then it won't know how to deliver it.

Limitations of Metrics

Although metrics can help a business achieve its strategic objectives by guiding, motivating, and holding personnel accountable for their actions, metrics also have limitations that should be recognized. For example, when strategies change rapidly, as is the case for many startups, metrics can quickly become irrelevant or even misleading. Some measures may be ambiguous or susceptible to faulty analysis and interpretation. For example, website stickiness may be good in some circumstances and bad in others.

Also, it is important to recognize that measurement can be costly, consuming the time of key personnel or funds if external sources of information are used.

Online measures are vulnerable to tampering by insiders or external parties as well as eavesdropping and therefore the data sources should be safeguarded against unauthorized access. A case in point is Air Canada's contention that certain WestJet executives accessed and used performance measures posted on Air Canada's intranet to gain an unfair competitive advantage over Air Canada on certain routes.[1]

Soft metrics are sometimes not as well accepted as hard data, but may be as important. Hard data may reflect attributes that are easy to measure rather than the most important attributes. Also, some metrics may need to be subjective; for example, supervisors' ratings of their employees, visitors' ratings of their overall experience on a website, and so on.

What to Measure

Now that we have considered the value of measuring performance, let's consider what aspects should be measured. There is much that is still not well understood about various metrics and the metrics that are "in" on one day may be "out" on another. Nevertheless, there are several broad categories of measurements that should be considered for use in assessing performance of e-commerce units:

- traffic and site usage metrics
- marketing metrics
- financial metrics
- other performance metrics
- multi-dimensional scorecards

Traffic and Site Usage Metrics

Traffic Metrics The earliest form of online business measurement related to traffic measurement. While such measures can be very crude, they can provide a surprising amount of useful information about traffic volumes, site usage, sources of traffic, and visitor attributes.

Traffic is the most basic unit that financial backers, advertisers, and affiliates look for. In the early days of e-business, companies spent any amount necessary to generate interest in or traffic on their sites, because this translated into financial support, share price growth, and so on.

Site traffic analysis can help determine the volume of traffic on a website, as well as which sections of a website are visited, when they are visited, by whom they are visited, and where the visitors came from. Traffic volume can be measured in a variety of ways: hits, page views, ad views or banner impressions, visits, and unique visitors.

Hits The oldest traffic metric involves measuring hits. A **hit** is counted anytime that something is requested from the web server. It can be a page, a picture, or just a link to another location. Anytime that you click on a page, that would be called a hit. A hit is a very broad piece of information. When somebody creates a hit, you don't know what they looked at and what they saw. Also, a single web page can account for a dozen hits if it has many photos, while a text-only page could generate just a single hit. As a result, the relevance of hits for measuring traffic on a website has been questioned and alternative measures of traffic volume have been widely adopted.

HIT
Each download of any information from a website.

Page Views The next type of information that is used is a **page view**, which occurs when an entire page of information is downloaded. That would be considered more valuable because all of the information that is displayed on that page would be viewed, or at least presumed to be viewed, by the user.

PAGE VIEW
Each download of an entire page of information.

Ad Views, Ad Impressions, or Banner Impressions **Ad views**, ad impressions, or banner impressions are a more focused measure of the number of times a page with a banner ad or other advertisement is viewed during a period of time. This measure would be particularly useful to advertisers who pay for a specified number of such views as part of a marketing campaign.

AD VIEWS
A measure of the number of times a page with a banner ad or other advertisement is viewed during a period of time.

Visits A **visit** is not just a single page view, it's a whole collection of pages that are viewed by a single user during a period of time—usually 30 minutes. By gathering all of those pages into one unit, called a visit, that is identified with a particular user, an entity can get better information than by looking at thousands of potentially unrelated hits.

VISIT
A collection of webpages a visitor views in a time period while on a website.

Unique Visitors The number of non-repeating visitors in a specific timeframe measures the volume of activity in terms of purported individuals, although it is really

Figure 12.1   WebTrends Dashboard

Illustration of a WebTrends dashboard.

SOURCE: WebTrends website, **www.webtrends.com**, accessed May 2004. © 1995 WebTrends from NetIQ Corp.

computers (i.e., IP addresses) rather than individuals that are counted in this type of analysis (i.e., many individuals may share a single computer or a single IP address).

Traffic analysis tools normally rely on the IP address to group various hits and attribute them to the same user. However, proxies and "floating" IP addresses make this method inaccurate. Since it is possible to store the content of a cookie in the log file, some tools allow for more precise tracking by assigning a unique ID in the cookie, then dumping the cookie content to the log file at every hit, thereby being able to more accurately track the user session.

Traffic analysis tools are available as shareware as well as formally licensed software. For example, StatCounter offers shareware traffic analysis tools whereas NetIQ Corporation offers licensable software such as WebTrends (see figure 12.1).

StatCounter
statcounter.com

Site Usage Metrics Traffic is a general indicator of a site's potential; however, to obtain meaningful insights, the analysis must get deeper. Site usage metrics help an e-business assess the effectiveness of its e-commerce website. The "Marketer's Common Sense Guide to E-Metrics"[2] uses the analogy of the leaky bucket to describe the sales losses that result from a poorly designed website. Website traffic is like water that fills a bucket. Website design problems are like holes that permit visitors to escape without fulfilling the sales objectives of the website. Site usage analysis can help trace the losses at various points in the pathways through the website from entry point to exit and help eliminate the holes that permit "leaks" instead of converting visitors into buyers.

Site usage can be analyzed spatially or temporally. Spatial usage analysis can identify visitor behaviour according to:

- *top entry pages*—pages most commonly entered
- *top exit pages*—pages most commonly exited from (exit pages can represent leakage from a website, indicating premature exit by visitors)
- *most visited pages*—pages most frequently visited
- *least visited pages*—pages least visited
- *single visit pages*—pages only visited once (these may represent trouble spots in the website)
- *paths within site*—most common paths taken by visitors (these may represent design problems if the most common path does not lead to successful completion of an e-commerce transaction or other site objective)

Temporal site usage analysis can identify traffic by month, week, day of week, and hour of day. Such breakdowns can be useful to correlate with the timing of promotions or website changes to determine their efficacy. In fact, most traffic measurements should be reported for a specified and consistent time period to ensure comparability of metrics.

Marketing Metrics

The purpose of marketing measurement is to help market the entity's products and/or services better. With the advent of CRM systems, collaborative filtering, and personalization tools, sophisticated customer-focused methods have been developed for gathering important marketing information. We will discuss marketing measurements under four main headings:

- referrer analysis
- location analysis
- customer profile analysis
- shopping basket analysis

Referrer Analysis Web server log files contain information about a visitor's previous URL. Referrer information can also be purchased from infomediaries such as DoubleClick. From this information, it is possible to determine where traffic is coming from and thereby measure the effectiveness of advertising campaigns. If an entity is advertising on a website but not receiving traffic from it, then the advertising expenditure may not be effective. Conversely, if the traffic is coming from places where the entity is not advertising, then it should consider what factors may be responsible for attracting that traffic.

Location Analysis Location analysis involves a breakdown of customer behaviour by geographical origin. Location analysis has great importance for marketing, since some promotions/advertising have regional reach. Location metrics can also help assess the performance of managers of different geographical regions and the effectiveness of local marketing efforts in generating traffic and revenues. In the absence of explicit data, rough location can be inferred by IP address; however, proxies pose a severe limitation to this method. Increasingly, user surveys or visitor registration are used to obtain information such as location and, of course, purchasers provide their location as part of their shipping information.

Customer Profile Analysis Customer profile analysis involves a breakdown of visitor behaviour by profile attributes. We have previously discussed user behaviour analysis in chapter 11 in connection with marketing and advertising. This section continues that discussion by focusing on analyzing user behaviour relative to the actions taken by an e-business to attract visitors and to persuade them to purchase goods and services, provide information, or otherwise contribute to the objectives established for an e-commerce website. As we have already noted, the internet allows real-time or quasi-real-time sampling of a target audience. New visitors come in to an e-business website as "anonymous," but are immediately profiled by their actions. Every action is recorded in the web server log file. By interacting with the e-commerce site, visitors provide information that can be used to form "user profiles," which in turn can be used for marketing purposes such as selecting what products to display, etc.

The entity's marketing efforts can be significantly aided by creating a profile of the typical user or classes of users, by tracking attributes such as age, gender, household income, average purchase, total purchases, etc. Customer profile data can be derived from data provided by customers explicitly or inferred from the implicit information inherent in the customer's attributes or behaviour. *Explicit information* is surrendered by the user when subscribing to a service, making a purchase, completing a survey form, etc., for example name, address, and marital status. *Implicit information* can be inferred from the user's actions and/or purchase history, for example favourite colour, age group, or preferred topics. Such inferences may require the use of data mining tools to identify key patterns of interest to the entity. For example, if a customer buys three red shirts and only one blue shirt, the implicit information is that the customer prefers the colour red to blue. A system may not have explicit gender information about a customer. However, if the customer purchased male fashions then the system could conclude that the customer is male. These types of inferences are obviously fraught with all kinds of limitations, but nevertheless, data mining tools attempt to make such inferences.

User profile analysis can help an entity assess whether it is reaching its target audience and, thereby, the efficacy of its marketing campaigns.

Shopping Basket Analysis Shopping basket analysis involves a breakdown of the items purchased in a sample transaction. Shopping basket analysis can help develop an understanding of customers' purchasing behaviour and customers' value reasoning. *Itemsets* are sets of items that appear together in many transactions. Knowledge of itemsets and their frequency can be used to improve product placement or for cross-sell and up-sell. For example, by using shopping basket analysis, a company may offer a recommendation to a customer such as, "Customers who purchased X, also purchased Y" that you see on Amazon.com. Shopping basket analysis can help an entity assess and predict product demand and, thereby, the efficacy of its marketing campaigns.

Financial Metrics

Financial metrics track revenues, expenses, return on investment, and shareholder value creation.

Revenue Revenue streams in a typical e-business include the sales revenue from products and services, advertising revenue (e.g., $3 CPM), affiliate commission (e.g., 15 percent of order generated for an affiliated site via a clickthrough or other referral), and database marketing (e.g., customer name sales to others for $10 to $1000 per name).

Sales analysis involves a breakdown of revenue streams per period, product category, referrer, time of day, etc. Sales analysis can be extended to identify top selling products, least selling products, and product margins. It can also include a breakdown of sales by shopper profile, demographics, geographical location, etc. Advanced sales analytics can involve analysis of product clusters, purchase patterns, shopping basket analysis, and the prediction of future sales based on the patterns observed.

Expenses Expense metrics include fixed costs, operating costs, and marketing costs. Fixed costs include infrastructure costs and operating costs. Infrastructure costs include store development (e.g., $250 000–$1 million), catalogue development (e.g., $5–$10 per stock-keeping unit or SKU), store hosting services (e.g., $50 000–$200 000 per year). In addition, credit card companies typically require a merchant account deposit which can range from $10 000–$50 000. Although it is not really a cost, it nevertheless requires a cash outflow.

Operating costs include site maintenance, advertising/promotion, marketing, and operations. Variable costs include product/service costs, per unit licensing costs, commissions on clickthrough sales, etc., and distribution costs for non-electronic goods or services.

Return on Investment (ROI) Return on investment is calculated as **(Revenues – Expenses)/Assets**. A strength of this metric is that it combines three key financial measures into a single composite metric. A weakness is that it omits non-financial measures such as customer service, operational quality, and innovation. Calculating ROI is simple; however, deciding what numbers to quantify can be difficult. The difficulties arise when economic benefits of e-business endeavours are intangibles such as customer service, competitiveness, communications, and content management.[3] These softer benefits (intangibles) are much harder to measure, but firms such as GE Capital IT Solutions are working on ways to factor intangible benefits into its analyses of e-commerce initiatives to create a more effective and accurate measure of payback; for example, conducting customer satisfaction surveys either directly or over the internet to learn how customers are interacting with their systems.[4]

Other Performance Metrics

Other performance metrics can be used to assess the performance of internal e-business units as well as the performance of e-business partners ranging from IT service providers such as ISPs and website hosting services to other outsourcing service providers such as transaction processing services, logistics service providers, payment processors, and others. For example, performance metrics may relate to network availability, system response time, transaction processing accuracy, transaction processing timeliness, responsiveness to requests for system changes, help desk effectiveness, security incident handling, customer satisfaction, degree of innovation, and so on. Typically, such metrics are embedded in service level agreements that define performance criteria tailored to the services being provided, as well as penalties for non-performance.

Multi-Dimensional Scorecards

Multi-dimensional scorecards bring several metrics together to create a multi-dimensional measure of performance. Such scorecards can be created externally, as illustrated by the Watchfire and Gómez scorecards referred to in the E-Strategy box. Or, they can be created internally using approaches such as the balanced scorecard.

Internal Scorecard The best known prescription for internal scorecard creation is the balanced scorecard format developed by Robert Kaplan and David Norton

E-Strategy

Watchfire Acquires Gómez Scorecard and Website Assessment Business Unit

On March 8, 2004, Watchfire Corporation, a provider of software and services to manage online business, announced the acquisition of GómezPro, the benchmarking and website assessment services business unit of Gómez Inc., the Internet Performance Management Company. The acquisition extended Watchfire's growing portfolio of online business management solutions and financial services offerings and expertise. Gómez, in turn, was able to focus on internet performance management.

Gómez, named after its founder, offers products and services to Global 1000 companies to improve the effectiveness and profitability of their internet operations through improved performance monitoring, measurement, and analysis. Founded in 1997, Gómez has provided performance measurement, benchmarking, and competitive insight to help build successful e-businesses. Gómez publishes widely accepted indices that measure relative internet performance in many industries, including financial services, e-tailing and

hoteling, which adds context to individual site performance.

Significant growth in its Internet Performance Management services (bookings increased 82 percent in 2003) prompted Gómez to focus exclusively on this business. Gómez sought a partner intent on extending GómezPro services to meet clients' heightened demand for broader and deeper website functionality and usability assessments.

Watchfire provides Online Business Management software and services to manage the online brand and risk of online business. Four of the five most valuable brands in the world and over 200 enterprise customers, such as AXA Financial, SunTrust Banks Inc., ChevronTexaco, and Dell rely on Watchfire to optimize their online business investments and to help them gain competitive advantage. Watchfire's alliance partners include IBM Global Services, PricewaterhouseCoopers, Mercury Interactive, CA, Microsoft, Interwoven and Documentum. Watchfire's headquarters are in Waltham, Massachusetts.

Watchfire's solutions help protect an organization's online brand and help enable privacy, regulatory, and accessibility compliance by automating the manual process of identifying website issues. Watchfire's quantitative site analysis, combined with rigorous best practices from GómezPro and internet performance data from Gómez, creates a powerful offering. The synergies derived by this combination provide customers a more complete offering to improve the effectiveness, usability, and functionality of their online business.

"To better manage their online business, customers are demanding consolidated solutions that bring together multiple web measures," said Peter McKay, president and CEO of Watchfire. "Watchfire and Gómez are leaders in their respective markets, with particular expertise in financial services. GómezPro's experience and technology complements Watchfire's market leading online brand and risk management capabilities, and enables us to expand our offering and provide our customers the most full featured services available."

Watchfire Corporation
www.watchfire.com

Gómez Inc.
www.gomez.com

Questions

1. Why would firms hire Watchfire to rate their e-commerce websites?
2. What strategic advantages do you see in Watchfire's acquisition of Gomez scorecard and website assessment units?
3. Why would Gomez give up its scorecard and website assessment units?

SOURCES: Gomez Inc. website, **www.gomez.com/**; "Gomez Inc.: A Look at One of the Major Players in the Web Rating Business," **www.realtor.org/webintell.nsf/0/ e0988fd68e653c4386256aa9005a48a1?OpenDocument**, accessed December 3, 2004; Lauren Gibbons Paul, "Browser Beware," *Inc.com*, **www.inc.com/magazine/20010615/ 22794.html**, accessed May 25, 2004; "Watchfire GómezPro Industry Benchmark Services," **www.watchfire.com/resources/gomezpro-industry-benchmark.pdf**, accessed May 25, 2004; "Watchfire Acquires Gómez Pro Scorecard and Website Assessment Business Unit," **www.gomez.com/main.aspx?m=6&s=4&sub=1&aid=9641**, press release, accessed May 25, 2004.

Figure 12.2   Example of a Balanced Scorecard for an E-Business

Financial Metrics	Customer Metrics	Internal Process Metrics	Learning and Growth Metrics
· Online revenue per customer	· Level of service delivery	· Availability of systems	· Staff productivity & morale
· Cost per online customer	· Satisfaction of existing customers	· Volume of transactions processed	· # of staff trained in new services
· Cost-efficiency of e-business processes	· # of new customers reached	· # of errors	· Value delivery per employee

out of a concern that business managers were overly focused on financial metrics and were insufficiently motivated or guided by other performance metrics such as customer satisfaction that would determine the entity's long term success.[5] While financial metrics are important, they represent the financial results of marketing operations and other actions taken that should also be measured and assessed. A good set of metrics should incorporate measures of those actions rather than ignoring them. Kaplan and Norton created a "scorecard" with four major sections: customer, internal process, learning and growth, and financial performance. The idea is that a small number of metrics must be identified in each of these four areas to guide and motivate managers to focus on long term drivers of business success.

Customer-oriented metrics include market share, traffic analysis, shopping analysis, acquisition cost, awareness, and satisfaction/loyalty. Internal process metrics include innovation, efficiency, effectiveness and economy of e-business operations, and system reliability. Learning and growth metrics address employee capabilities and motivation. Financial metrics focus on revenues, expenses, and return on investment (ROI).

In summary, the balanced scorecard approach involves taking measurements in four different areas rather than focusing solely on financial performance measures, as illustrated in figure 12.2.

Since it is not solely financial, it gives personnel a balanced perspective on the actions required to achieve strategic objectives. The main difference between scorecards used by different entities would be which metrics are selected in each of the four categories and how well those metrics align with the entity's strategic objectives—in other words, how well they guide and motivate personnel to take specific actions that will lead to achievement of those objectives.

External Scorecards   There are numerous organizations providing scorecard services on the internet. For example, the Watchfire GómezPro scorecard referred to in the E-Strategy box considers 150 or more different variables to arrive at a rating of an e-commerce website's quality. To create the quality criteria, Watchfire GómezPro first reviews all of the features and services that are delivered online (and to some degree offline) across an industry. While practices can vary across industries, Watchfire GómezPro typically identifies criteria in at least four categories:

1. **Ease of use:** demonstrations of functionality; simplicity of account opening and transaction process; consistency of design and navigation; adherence to proper user interaction principles; integration of data providing efficient access to information commonly accessed by consumers.

2. **Customer confidence:** availability, depth, and breadth of customer service options, including phone, e-mail, and branch locations; privacy policies, service guarantees, fees, and explanations of fees.

3. **Online resources:** availability of applications for specific products; ability to look up account information for each product; ability to transact in each product online.

4. **Relationship services:** online help, tutorials, glossary, and FAQs; advice; personalization of data; ability to customize a site; re-use of customer data to facilitate future transactions; support of business and personal needs such as tax reporting or repeated-buying.

Unlike services such as BizRate that base their ratings on consumer feedback, Watchfire GómezPro relies on its analysts to assess the various features of each website and make the decisions on each of the criteria. The company believes its experts have the capabilities to "define the elements of quality in the internet delivery of services." This methodology of using analysts is the exact opposite from BizRate, which uses consumer surveys to compile ratings. The overall result of the rating process is a scorecard, with each website given a ranking between 1 and 10, with one being the lowest, and 10 the highest.

Watchfire GómezPro believes that it is able to maintain objectivity across firms and create objective and comparable rankings by making metrics very objective and unambiguous; for example, a site either offers Saturday telephone customer service or it does not. The rankings are posted on the Watchfire GómezPro website. High scoring companies also often post their Gómez rankings prominently on their website.

Sources of Information

Users browsing the website, users clicking on banner ads, users interacting with surveys and polls (see discussion of Greenfield Online in the New Business Models box on page 262), shoppers making product selections, shoppers making purchases, shoppers contacting customer service—all these customer activities can be tracked and analyzed to better understand customer behaviour and align the design of the e-business with customer behaviour. The data for all the analyses discussed in this chapter is available from four main sources. The most obvious place is user-stored data found in cookies and wallets. The next most used source is the data found in web server log files. A third key source is the transaction databases that record information about sales. A fourth source is user profile databases created by the entity or infomediaries.

Click-Stream Analysis

CLICK-STREAM ANALYSIS
A method by which a user's path through a website can be tracked and analyzed.

Click-stream analysis is a method by which a user's path through a website can be tracked and analyzed. The key here is to analyze the data to identify important trends such as difficulty in finding specific sites or information, searches that yielded no results, or constant "back" movement through the site. By analyzing click-stream data, an e-business can identify website design errors, which can be corrected before other customers run into them. In other circumstances, click-stream analysis may be correlated with other factors about the customer, such as demographics or business industry, that may lead to the discovery of trends related to specific target markets. For example, the correlation of user registration data, such as industry type, or other offline information, with click-stream analysis may lead an organization to the conclusion that its website is not organized in a manner well suited to particular industries. The site could then be reworked to better suit specific industries or a specialized design could be developed to address this problem.

E-Business in Global Perspective

Nielsen//NetRatings

Nielsen//NetRatings (NetRatings) was founded in July 1997 to track audience exposure and behaviour related to online advertising. All of the products and services are designed to assist companies in making critical business decisions regarding their internet strategies and initiatives. It is an infomediary that builds on the economic value of information about people's internet behaviours and is one of the leading providers of internet audience measurement and analysis in the United States and around the world.

Products and Services

The products and services provided by NetRatings include NetView, an internet audience measurement service; AdRelevance, an online ad measurement service; @Plan, a target-marketing platform for internet media planning, buying, and selling; webRF, a comprehensive media reach and frequency planning tool; and custom research and analysis on a variety of internet-related subjects. These services are designed to help customers make informed decisions regarding their internet strategies. For example, information provided by NetRatings about the size of specific target groups and their gender or age characteristics can help clients determine which sites are best to advertise on depending on their target audience. The products are sold primarily on an annual subscription basis.

NetView Service

This service provides comprehensive reports about online audiences to internet advertisers, agencies, marketers, and publishers using advanced tracking technology. These clients make use of such audience information to strategically plan and deploy their online advertising and marketing efforts towards specific target groups. NetView classifies websites according to content rather than technical structure so that a client can easily analyze information in a logical user-friendly manner. NetView measures all activity in what it calls the "Digital Media Universe" which includes web-based traffic, internet applications and browser data, and even measurement of AOL proprietary channels. Further, the Digital Media Universe also encompasses the measurement of instant messaging such as MSN Messenger, media players, media sharing applications, web phones, news and information toolbars, connected games, weather applications, auction assistants, and shopping assistants. NetView has a list of 33 predefined reports that it produces for clients but also has the capability to produce reports for user-specific queries. Reports can cover a myriad of areas including demographics targeting, audience profile, daily or hourly traffic metrics, average usage, access locations for websites, and even loyalty and retention of users. A client can specify exactly which reports it wishes to receive on a regular basis and have the most current information delivered to them each week or each month.

NetRatings offers products and services in 17 countries. As a result, it currently tracks over 70 percent of the internet usage around the world.

Nielsen//NetRatings
www.nielsen-netratings.com

Questions

1. What are the strengths of NetRatings offerings?
2. Do you see any weaknesses in NetRatings' global reach?
3. Are there any threats that could dislodge NetRatings from its apparent globally dominant position?

SOURCES: Nielsen//NetRatings, "Products and Services," **www.nielsen-netratings.com/mktg.jsp?section=ps**, accessed May 24, 2004.

Cookies

Click-stream data is enabled by a number of technologies. **Cookies** are small text files stored by a website on individual computers that allow the site to track the movements of a visitor.[6] Cookies are often added to an individual's computer the first time that a site is visited and can track a great deal of information, such as time

COOKIES
Small text files stored by a website on individual computers that allow the site to track the movements of a visitor.

spent on a site, passwords, shopping cart information, preferences, and the most recent site visited. The use of cookies can personalize a website, by remembering the user's profile and organizing the presentation of the websites. Privacy concerns have often been raised about cookies; however, many people are satisfied that they are not harmful and do not invade privacy. The primary concern over cookies is the fact that they are stored on the user's computer and can potentially provide information regarding other sites visited, preferences, and shopping habits. However, information in a cookie is not generally readable by anyone except the entity that placed it there; it is typically numbers and letters that would mean nothing to anyone except when it is combined with the information that is already stored on the web server side. The use of cookies as an online technology has become standard practice but will continue to evolve as privacy concerns are worked out.

The privacy concerns tend to relate to the use of cookies to analyze the user's shopping habits and create targeted marketing. For example, after searching for several books related to golfing on Chapters.ca, a user may notice that the banner ads on the site are for several golf-related products and that featured books the next time the user visits the site are golf-related. The personalization of websites by this means can be beneficial to the user but to some is too intrusive to be acceptable. Privacy concerns are considered more fully in chapter 13.

It is important to note that data stored in a cookie can be easily erased by the user, or the user can decide not to accept cookies at all. Therefore, cookies are often used to store non-critical data such as personalization for anonymous users, login information (login name only, not password), the date the user last logged on, and so forth.[7]

Electronic Wallets

ELECTRONIC WALLET
A file that securely stores a user's information such as name, address, credit card number and ship-to address, for frequent use in executing e-commerce transactions.

Electronic wallets are a more elaborate version of cookies, because a cookie may only have two or three items of information whereas a wallet could contain quite a bit more information. Electronic wallets initially provided a more secure method to transmit credit card information over the internet, but have evolved to more general uses as well. An electronic wallet could contain the user's credit card number, name, address, ship-to address and so forth. Having that information available in an electronic wallet would be particularly useful for a frequent shopper because it would eliminate the necessity of having to retype that information each and every time the user wanted to buy something. Also wallet information could be kept very secure at a specially designated storage location that is neither at the online store nor on the user's own computer (where it could be perhaps read by someone who has access to the computer). The use of an authority for storing digital wallets can provide both security and convenience when shopping.

There are two or three different versions of wallets that are competing to become the standard that governs everyone's use. In the end there may be two or three different types of wallets, and some may be stored locally on the user's computer, whereas others, particularly ones involving financial transactions, might be stored at the bank. For example, a user's wallet could be stored at the Royal Bank in a database. If the user was shopping at Chapters.ca, then, instead of Chapters requiring the user to type in a list of information it would ask the user for his or her key. Chapters would use that secret key to contact the bank, which would in turn use it to process the payment transaction, and then transmit payment directly from the Royal Bank to Chapters and deduct the amount from the user's account. Encryption techniques would make sure that when they provide the key, users can send the key but they can't read the key.

Web Server Log Files

Log files contain details of every action that has occurred on a website, and are one of the most widely used data sources for traffic analysis. Web server log files are text files stored in the web server. Every line represents a "hit" containing the following information: HTTP request, date, time, OS, browser type, and referrer URL. The referrer URL is the source that that request came from. This information is very useful. With just this little information an entity can determine where a visitor came from, whether it was a referral from a banner ad or another advertising vendor. Other information that can be retrieved from the log includes, for example, which browsers people are using (for example, Internet Explorer, Netscape, Opera, etc.), which operating systems are being used (for example, Macintosh, Windows, Unix, Solaris or Linux), which computing platforms, etc.

LOG FILE
A file stored on a web server containing details of every action that has occurred.

    Log file analysis is the process of analyzing information regarding the movements of users throughout a site based upon data captured in server log files, and can be carried out by a number of means including basic database techniques or advanced internet-based products such as those offered by WebTrends (see figure 12.1 for an illustration of a sample WebTrends display).

LOG FILE ANALYSIS
The process of analyzing information regarding the movements of users throughout a site based upon data captured in server log files.

    Log files are often used for other purposes, not just for performance analysis. Log files are often used to recover from a system failure. If a server crashes while processing a transaction, the log file can be used to reprocess the transaction or at least to get the system back to the state it was in before it crashed.

Web Bugs

Web bugs (also known as clear GIFs) are image files embedded into a web page that can track user movements without the user knowing. Essentially, web bugs are clear images or images that blend in with the background of a page you are viewing. The web bug sends information to a server (belonging to the company itself or an advertising firm) each time you request a new page and thus tracks your movements. This allows the analyzing firm to understand your movements throughout the site and is one method of capturing click-stream data.

WEB BUGS (CLEAR GIFS)
Image files embedded into a web page that can track user movements without the user knowing.

Transaction Database

A transaction database is the accounting data file that keeps track of the items that were sold, the quantity, the means of settlement, the terms, the date, and so on. This type of information can be useful for understanding shopper behaviour; however, the richness of the information contained in such a database is implementation-specific. As in the case of user profile data, there will be explicit data reflecting the transaction, and implicit data inferred by analysis of the user's behaviour. Such inferences may require the use of business intelligence or data mining tools to identify key patterns of interest to the entity.

User Profile Database

The user profile database contains information about visitors and shoppers. (There are many more visitors than there are shoppers.) The database can contain explicit data provided by users, for example, information about their address, their name, or their age, if they answered requests for this information on forms or provided information in their wallet. The database could also have implicit data, data that is inferred by analysis of user characteristics, as described previously. Such inferences may require the use of data mining tools to identify key patterns of interest to the entity.

New Business Models

Greenfield Online

Greenfield Online Inc. was founded in 1994 to serve the online data collection needs of more than 300 marketing research firms by gathering consumer opinions through online research surveys and focus groups. According to the company, "We realized that the internet is an ideal environment for consumers to speak out and be heard as they can participate at their leisure—rather than respond to ill-timed or intrusive telephone surveys. As one of the first in marketing research to recognize the value of online interviewing, we offer a state-of-the-art

system of hardware and software designed specifically to:

- create survey instruments that incorporate the types of questions and features required to execute complex research methodologies
- operate a real-time web-based reporting capability
- maintain secure and redundant systems
- launch fully functional recruiting/panel websites internationally
- profile, in detail, the Greenfield Online panel of 1.7+ million

member households and manage multiple sample sources

Last year, General Mills conducted 20 percent of its research online. That number is projected to grow to 60 percent next year because of the company's belief that the web produces up to a 50 percent cost-savings and speeds up research up to 75 percent." "Surveys that used to take four weeks can be completed in 8 to 10 days," says Gayle Fuguitt, Vice President of consumer insights at General Mills.

Greenfield Online
www.greenfield.com

Questions

1. What are the apparent strengths of Greenfield Online's offering?
2. Are there any threats that could dislodge Greenfield Online from its leadership position?

SOURCES: www.greenfield.com.

Infomediaries

Infomediaries are organizations that monitor, analyze and report on web activity for a fee. There are numerous organizations that track important metrics ranging from traffic on the web to e-business performance to industry performance to financial reports. The best known traffic analysis entity is NetIQWebTrends. Market research is provided by organizations such as BizRate, comScore Networks, ACNielsen (see the E-Business in Global Perspective box on page 259), Gomez, and Watchfire (see the E-Strategy box on page 256). Analyst reports are available from market research entities such as Forrester Research, Jupitermedia Corporation, Aberdeen Group, Frost & Sullivan, and IDC. Finally, financial information is available from EDGAR Online Inc., Standard and Poor's, and other providers.

Chapter Summary

The internet enables an unprecedented degree of activity measurement. E-business performance can be measured in several ways, ranging from measures of traffic on an e-commerce site, to measures of customer behaviour, and ultimately, to measures of e-business effectiveness.

Performance metrics linked to specific objectives can help management achieve its strategic objectives by providing guidance, motivating performance, analyzing outcomes, and holding personnel accountable for their actions. However, metrics must be synchronized with business realities, should be unambiguous, and should involve a reasonable cost.

Metrics used to assess performance of e-commerce websites fall into five main categories: traffic and site usage metrics, marketing metrics, financial metrics, other performance metrics and multi-dimensional scorecards. Traffic metrics can be based on hits, page views, ad views, and visits. Site usage metrics can be spatial and temporal measures of traffic in various sections of an e-commerce site. Marketing metrics provide information about sources of visits, visitor shopping behaviour, user profiles, and product purchase patterns. Financial metrics provide information about revenues, expenses, and return on investment. Other performance metrics measure website availability, processing integrity, service quality, and so on. Multi-dimensional scorecards attempt to bring a number of metrics together for use in performance assessment to prevent the excessive focus on one particular category of metrics.

There are many sources of information for metrics, including clickstream data, cookies, electronic wallets, web server log files, web bugs, transaction databases, user profile databases, and infomediaries.

Key Terms

ad views   *(p. 251)*

click-stream analysis   *(p. 258)*

cookies   *(p. 259)*

electronic wallet   *(p. 260)*

hit   *(p. 251)*

log file   *(p. 261)*

log file analysis   *(p. 261)*

page view   *(p. 251)*

visit   *(p. 251)*

web bugs (clear GIFs)   *(p. 261)*

Tools for Online Learning

To help you master the material in this chapter and stay up to date with new developments in e-business, visit www.pearsoned.ca/trites. Resources include:

- **Review Questions and Exercises**

- **Problems for Discussion**

- **Recommended Readings**

- **Updates to Case Studies and Textual Material**

- **Streaming CBC Videos with Cases**

Endnotes

1. David Paddon, "Air Canada Suit Adds WestJet CEO Clive Beddoe, Others as Defendants in Suit," www.cp.org/english/online/full/Business/041105/b1105122A.html, accessed December 5, 2004.

2. Bryan Eisenberg and Jim Novo, "The Marketer's Common Sense Guide to E-Metrics," white paper, http://download.netiq.com/CMS/WHITEPAPER/NetIQ_WP_WRC_MarketersGuidetoEMetrics.pdf, accessed May 9, 2004.

3. Toby Ward, "Measuring the ROI of Intranets: Mission Possible?" *Intranet Journal* (November 8, 2002), www.intranetjournal.com/articles/200211/pij_11_08_02a.html, accessed December 4, 2004.

4. B. Violino, "Payback Time for E-Business—Net Projects No Longer Too 'Strategic' for ROI," *InternetWeek* (May 1, 2000): 1.

5. Robert Kaplan and David Norton. "The Balanced Scorecard—Measures That Drive Performance," *Harvard Business Review* (January–February 1992): 71–79.

6. Interactive Advertising Bureau, www.allaboutcookies.org, accessed December, 4, 2004.

7. Interactive Advertising Bureau, www.allaboutcookies.org, accessed December, 4, 2004.

— CHAPTER **13**

Privacy, Legal, and Taxation Issues in E-Commerce

LEARNING OBJECTIVES

When you complete this chapter you should be able to:

1. Explain the importance of law in the context of e-commerce on the internet.

2. Identify and describe the major issues surrounding online privacy.

3. Discuss how organizations can comply with Canadian privacy legislation.

4. Describe how intellectual property issues impact e-commerce.

5. Identify the major legal issues that companies need to be concerned with on the internet.

6. Discuss the taxation issues that e-commerce has created.

Introduction

The rapid growth in e-commerce and increase in globalization over the past several years has given rise to several new issues in the areas of law and taxation. The legal and tax systems of Canada and most countries worldwide were not designed for the complications of commerce conducted through electronic means. While the existing legal system had previously addressed many similar issues to those raised by e-commerce, the legislation and legal infrastructure have numerous areas where the concerns over e-commerce are not well addressed. Substantial effort has been directed at legal and taxation issues related to e-commerce in the past few years, and progress has been made; however, there remains a great deal of change to be made in the future. This chapter will review the issues, progress, and remaining challenges of the law and e-commerce.

The concerns over e-commerce legal issues were perhaps brought to the forefront by the Napster situation, although it focused on only one major area of concern—intellectual property. The Napster service was essentially brought to a halt by the rulings of the court system, which stated that the music copying application violated the intellectual property rights of musical artists and other copyright owners by allowing the illegal copying of MP3 files. As an important and developing area, intellectual property issues such as copyright, trademarks, domain names, and patents are all being addressed by the legal systems within countries worldwide.

The improvements in technology and e-commerce applications have given rise to serious concerns over privacy on the internet. The tracking of users and potential identification of individuals through technology threatens the right to privacy of all internet users and thus is a growing area of importance. The Canadian federal government has also addressed the issue of privacy through comprehensive legislation, as discussed in more detail below. Other countries and international organizations are also monitoring issues with regards to privacy and many have adopted similar legislation and guidelines that both consumers and businesses need to be aware of.

The legal system is also addressing numerous other issues with regard to e-commerce. Some of the principal concerns are in relation to jurisdictional issues, which also impact taxation. In addition, electronic contracts, enforcement, liability, and unfair competition issues all arise as the use of the internet and globalization of commerce change the competitive landscape of business. These issues will be discussed throughout this chapter with an aim to highlight areas of importance for management of e-businesses—in specific cases, it is important to consult professional legal counsel.

Internet Privacy

The concerns over privacy have grown immensely as e-commerce has developed and consumers and businesses provide a growing amount of information to often-unknown sources. The major concerns in this regard are wide-ranging, since many types of private information could impact employment, personal finances, and other aspects of life. For example, medical information is a key privacy concern. Imagine if an individual's medical records became available to a potential employer when that individual had a serious illness—the individual could be turned down for a job based on what should be confidential information. In less serious cases of privacy infringement, advertisers may gather details about an individual and flood that person with ads and other information—a serious annoyance. Despite the severity of the issue, one thing is for sure—individuals have a right to privacy and the internet has changed the landscape in which privacy must be protected.

Information of a personal nature can be gathered through numerous means over the internet. For example, while surfing the web, users' movements can be tracked by the use of cookies, web bugs, and other tracking tools, as described earlier in this book. Other data/information can be collected or revealed about an individual through chat groups, news boards, or e-mail. The number of potential sources of information available makes it quite possible that a person's privacy can be inappropriately handled through the internet. The ability of online businesses to gather data has also been complicated by the issue of merging the online data with offline data, as was the case with DoubleClick (see the New Business Models box on page 230 in chapter 11). DoubleClick was essentially given the approval to merge data—with the exception of medical and financial information—as long as users are made aware of the use and have the ability to opt-out.

The increasing concerns over privacy have led to the development of legislation within Canada and abroad. The Canadian government developed the Personal Information Protection and Electronic Documents Act (originally Bill C-54 and later introduced and approved as Bill C-6) as a component of Canada's Electronic Commerce Strategy. The strategy recognized that one important component of assisting Canada to become a world leader in e-commerce was to instill confidence in the internet through legislation and other means.[1] The **Personal Information Protection and Electronic Documents Act (PIPEDA)** provides privacy protection for personal information, and came into full effect on January 1, 2004.

PIPEDA is federal legislation that applied initially to federally regulated organizations including airlines, banks, telephone companies, and broadcasting companies. In addition, all businesses in Nunavut, the Yukon, and the Northwest Territories were subject to the act as of January 1, 2001. The second phase of implementation for PIPEDA took effect on January 1, 2002, when all organizations that collect, use, or disclose personal health information come under the legislation. The final phase of implementation was January 1, 2004, when the act became applicable to all commercial activity,[2] unless a firm is operating in a province that has passed privacy legislation that is substantially similar to the federal legislation—an attempt by the federal government to encourage harmonization within Canada. The standards for assessing substantial similarity were established by the Privacy Commissioner of Canada. As of January 2004, British Columbia, Alberta, and Quebec had all passed provincial private sector privacy legislation, and by November 2004 all three had been reviewed and deemed to be substantially similar by the federal Privacy Commissioner.

PIPEDA is designed to protect any personal information that is collected, used, or disclosed within the private sector. The privacy rights of Canadians are protected by the Privacy Act (1983) with regard to the personal information collected, used, or disclosed by federal governmental organizations. Most of the provinces have similar legislation in effect with regard to provincial government organizations. **Personal information** is defined within the act as information that could identify an individual and could potentially be used to discriminate against or invade an individual's privacy, such as:

- name, age, weight, height
- medical records
- income, purchases, and spending habits
- race, ethnic origin, and colour

PIPEDA on the Web
www.privcom.gc.ca/ekit/index_e.asp

PERSONAL INFORMATION PROTECTION AND ELECTRONIC DOCUMENTS ACT (PIPEDA)
Canadian legislation that provides privacy protection for personal information and has come into full effect since January 1, 2004.

PERSONAL INFORMATION
Information that could identify an individual and could potentially be used to discriminate against or invade an individual's privacy.

- blood type, DNA code, fingerprints
- marital status and religion
- education
- home address and phone number[3]

The definition of personal information covers each of these specific items to ensure that individuals' privacy is respected and not used inappropriately. The misuse of this information can lead to inappropriate business practices, identity theft, and discrimination and is, therefore, of critical importance.

The privacy principles within PIPEDA are based upon the 1996 standards established by the Canadian Standards Association (CSA) in its "Model Code for the Protection of Personal Information." This code, similar to the new legislation, establishes the rights of individuals to access personal information about themselves held by organizations and to have that information corrected if it is incorrect.

The 10 principles included in the CSA Model Code are as follows:

1. *Accountability.* Organizations are responsible for all personal information under their control and shall establish procedures to ensure that the organization complies with all of the 10 principles.

2. *Identifying purposes.* Organizations will identify the purpose for which they are collecting personal information to individuals prior to or at the time that the information is collected.

3. *Consent.* The individual must give consent to the collection, use, or disclosure of their personal information.

4. *Limiting collection.* All information must be collected by fair and legal means and should be limited to information deemed necessary by the organization for the purposes outlined to the individual.

5. *Limiting use, disclosure, and retention.* The use of personal information should be limited to the purposes outlined to the individual at the time of collection unless further consent is obtained and information should only be retained for as long as deemed necessary by the terms outlined.

6. *Accuracy.* Organizations shall keep personal information accurate, complete, and up to date.

7. *Safeguards.* Appropriate security and internal controls should be in place to protect personal information.

8. *Openness.* Organizations should make their policies readily available to individuals with regard to the handling of personal information.

9. *Individual access.* Individuals have the right to request whether information about them exists and to request the ability to review that information and challenge its accuracy and completeness.

10. *Challenging compliance.* Individuals are able to address their concerns over compliance with the above principles to a designated individual or individuals. In the Canadian context this principle now leads ultimately to the Privacy Commissioner, who has the right to investigate concerns where individuals do not receive satisfaction from the company or organization itself.[4]

The principles set out in the CSA code are, of course, only a set of guidelines that can be interpreted differently by different organizations and individuals. The PIPEDA legislation aims to give the Privacy Commissioner the authority to handle complaints related to privacy whereby individuals are not satisfied with the outcomes of their discussions with an organization. One example of the type of issue that can arise within the legislation that is subject to interpretation is the Toysmart issue that arose in early 2001. Toysmart had filed for bankruptcy protection and the receivers were considering the sale of customer lists and marketing data as one means of recovering funds owed to creditors. The concern that arose was that Toysmart's collection of information had indicated that personal information would not be disclosed to other parties without the express consent of the individual—now that information was potentially going to be sold. The courts ruled that customer information could not be sold separately, but could be sold as a package with the rest of Toysmart assets, as Toysmart had stated in their privacy statement that they do not share customer information with any third party. The Toysmart case focused around principle five in that use should be limited to that which was identified at the time the information was collected. A court decision was not reached in the case as Walt Disney Co., a major shareholder, bought the list and destroyed it to deal with the issue quickly.[5] This case illustrates how privacy issues can be an ongoing concern and how illegitimate use could have an adverse effect on e-commerce.

Establishing a Privacy Policy

The enactment of PIPEDA has led to the need for all businesses and organizations to establish a privacy policy that can be disclosed and communicated to internet users and customers. To comply with the principles in the act and to provide customers with relevant information, the web pages of many businesses now include a "Privacy Policy" link that leads to a full disclosure of the company's policy. For example, Bell Canada would have had to comply with PIPEDA and established a privacy policy and other disclosures on their website as shown in figure 13.1, prior to January 1, 2001, as they are a federally regulated organization (now PIPEDA applies to all businesses engaged in commercial activity in Canada). Included in the privacy policy is a discussion of the types of information collected by Bell, the companies that may share the information (related parties), and an opt-out clause to prevent sharing with other subsidiary firms. The privacy policy also discusses the company's use of cookies, PIPEDA, and discloses how customers may direct their concerns both inside and outside the company (e.g., the Privacy Commissioner's office).

Other Privacy Legislation

The development of legislation in Canada and other countries has been somewhat pressured by the lead taken with regard to privacy in Europe. The European Union's Privacy Directive went into effect in 1998 and established relatively strong privacy regulations for members of the European Union (EU). In addition, the legislation restricts the flow of personal information outside the EU by permitting its transfer only to countries that provide an "adequate" level of privacy protection.

Prior to PIPEDA Canada had little protection for privacy. However, once passed, the EU approved the federal legislation as "adequate" for the purposes of transferring personal information held by EU-governed organizations to Canada-based organizations governed by PIPEDA. However, other countries like the United States were primarily using policies of self-regulation or sector specific legislation. The EU's approach led to extended negotiations with the United States and many other countries to establish what has become known as the "safe harbour" agreement.[6] Agreed upon in July 2000, the safe harbour provisions allow for

Figure 13.1   Example of an Organization's Online Privacy Policy

Bell's website includes detailed information about its privacy policy to users and discusses the means by which users may address their complaints or concerns.

SOURCE: Bell Canada, "Security and Privacy," **www.bell.ca/shop/application/commercewf?origin=noorigin. jsp&event=link(goto)&content=/jsp/content/cust_care/privacy_home.jsp,** accessed December 17, 2004. Courtesy BCE IP Group, Bell Canada Law Department. Tel.: 416-353-4265; e-mail: ilya.kalnish@bell.ca.

specific companies to be certified as complying with the EU requirements by becoming voluntarily compliant. This will permit U.S. businesses to obtain personal information from EU businesses and effectively conduct business in EU nations.

Another major issue of concern in the privacy area is the protection of privacy for children. The internet is an open network and the growth in its use has brought many children to become avid users. While children can often learn to use the internet quite quickly, they are less likely to understand the risks and concerns over privacy protection than adults are. The United States established the Children's On-line Privacy Protection Act, which establishes privacy requirements for websites that target children. The Children's On-line Privacy Protection Act applies not only to U.S. sites but to any website that is perceived to be targeting U.S. children and, therefore, can have wide-reaching effects on the operation of any website in Canada or elsewhere. For example, a toy company established in

Canada may decide to sell into the United States to expand its market. If that company's website could conceivably be used by children and aims to sell to that market the company must be aware of the Children's On-line Privacy Protection Act and its implications on information collection and use. The growth in concerns over privacy protection will continue to give rise to legislation and policies that businesses must consider as they operate outside their own country's boundaries through the internet.

Privacy and Wireless Devices

The increasing use of wireless technologies is bringing additional privacy concerns to the forefront. Users of cellular phones, personal digital assistants (PDAs), and other wireless devices may be subject to all of the concerns over internet privacy but may also be subject to additional concerns. The use of wireless technology can potentially allow a user's exact location and movements to be tracked, in addition to websites visited, telephone calls placed, and other information transferred. These issues are of critical importance as an individual's location and activities are very private information that needs to be protected from misuse.

The use of wireless technologies also brings with it concerns over security. The security of internet access through telephone, cable, and other access methods has been developing for several years, and just as users are beginning to feel comfortable with these systems, wireless adds a new dimension. Consider the use of a PDA to conduct financial transactions through a bank—requiring the user's password and other personal information to be transmitted. This information is now transmitted through the airwaves and therefore can be much more susceptible to theft or misuse if appropriate security mechanisms are not in place.

The risks of misuse of wireless technologies and infringement of privacy need to be balanced with what may be considered useful to the individual. For example, some advertisers hope to be able to deliver discounts to wireless devices in the appropriate location, such as in a specific mall. If a wireless user walks into the West Edmonton Mall and receives a list of discounts for various stores in the mall, the advertiser has potentially delivered a valuable service. On the other hand, that delivery indicates that the individual's movements are being tracked by at least one organization (wireless service provider) and the information could be passed to advertisers or other organizations, potentially compromising the individual's privacy and freedom of movement. These types of privacy concerns will continue to evolve but represent important issues for individual consumers to investigate fully and for organizations to develop policies around.

Privacy and Technologies

The concerns over privacy on the internet have stimulated some entrepreneurs to develop software and applications designed to assist users to avoid privacy issues. David Sobel, general counsel for the Washington, DC-based Electronic Privacy Information Center, stated, "Technologies that facilitate anonymous use of the internet are really critical to the survival of the internet as an open and democratic forum."[7] The technologies that can be used to protect an individual's privacy online are many but most attempt to accomplish a similar goal—to make the user an anonymous web surfer.

Programs that can reduce privacy issues include solutions provided by Zero-Knowledge Systems Inc. (ZKS), Anonymizer, SafeWeb (owned by Symantec), IDzap, Somebody, and several others. ZKS solutions, for example, are geared

Electronic Privacy Information Center
www.epic.org

towards internet service providers to allow their users to surf anonymously by removing information regarding the user's IP address and other identifying information. ZKS' Privacy Manager scans all outgoing communications for sensitive or identifiable information to prevent its release without user consent. Users can also release information to trusted parties by asking to unmask some information to complete a purchase or fill out a particular form online. See the New Business Models box for a discussion of the privacy protection issue and some of the concerns it raises.

The use of technologies to protect privacy can take numerous forms. Some applications allow users to control cookies and web bugs while surfing the internet. Other programs such as Webwasher® and AdSubtract can be used to block out banner ads to reduce the amount of advertising one is subjected to. The growing concern over advertising and privacy has led a relatively small percentage of people to sign up for services such as these.

The technological tools that are designed to protect privacy don't come without their costs and complications. Many of these tools can impede the speed of web usage, since information must pass through a specific server and be rerouted to the user. In addition, the tools can require service fees to be paid depending upon the services selected. Cookie management applications can result in the inability to use some websites and limit the capability to use personalization tools and other aspects of some websites. You can see the impact of cookie management by altering the settings within your web browser to "Do not accept cookies" or "Confirm cookies" and surfing through some websites. The disadvantages of privacy protection tools, as described here, are why privacy advocates are pushing for stronger legislative controls to automatically protect users' privacy.

Intellectual Property

INTELLECTUAL PROPERTY
A creation of the mind such as an invention, artistic work, symbol, name, image, or design used in commerce.

COPYRIGHT
A category of intellectual property that includes literary and artistic works such as books, poems, films, and musical works.

INDUSTRIAL PROPERTY
A category of intellectual property that includes patents, trademarks, and other industrial designs.

The environment of the internet, full of "free" resources and shared information, has led to a great deal of confusion and controversy surrounding intellectual property. **Intellectual property** is a creation of the mind such as an invention, artistic work, symbol, name, image, or design used in commerce. Intellectual property can be divided into two primary categories—copyright and industrial property. **Copyright** includes literary and artistic works such as books, poems, films, and musical works. **Industrial property** includes patents, trademarks, and other industrial designs.[8] Most countries have dealt with intellectual property law for many years and established laws that have become well interpreted. The internet has changed the circumstances by complicating the issues around intellectual property. See the E-Strategy box for a strategy by an internet startup to aid businesses in addressing intellectual property issues.

The issues surrounding intellectual property on the internet have a much wider range than just illegal copying of music files. In fact, there are issues with regard to patents, trademarks, books, and most other forms of intellectual property—both copyright and industrial property.

Metatags

The dispute between former rivals Chapters Online Inc. and Indigo Online Inc. provides a good example of the types of issues that can arise on the internet as competitors strive to gain a captive audience. Chapters had inserted the term "Indigo" within its metatags on its website so that users searching for that term would see the Chapters website listed. As discussed in previous chapters, metatags

New Business Models

Privacy Fighting at Anonymizer

The technologies of the internet bring both positive and negative changes to the world. One of the most serious concerns in recent history has been the protection of privacy and the rights of individuals to use the web without being tracked and monitored. One of the leading applications for protecting one's privacy online is Anonymizer, Inc.

The ability for employers to track employee use of the internet while at work is an issue that has led to much debate. With no clear legal ruling on the issue, companies like Anonymizer have developed a business model that aids web users in "masking" their identity from employers, governments, ISPs, and even the websites they visit. Anonymizer essentially masks a web surfer's IP address and allows surfers to visit sites that may be banned or controversial.

The use of anonymous surfing technologies has led to concerns by those who seek to protect specific groups from material on the internet. Few would disagree with schools aiming to block children from reaching pornographic material online, but tools like

Anonymizer can allow web-savvy students to circumvent the protective controls if those sites themselves are not blocked. Anonymizer has a variety of services, including private surfing, e-mail, chat, and telephony, with the fee for service depending upon the options chosen. Some of its competitors offer similar services—some for free.

Other uses of monitoring and blocking tools online are much more controversial. Many countries and governments severely restrict the use of the internet for citizens and monitor their usage. For example, Saudi Arabia restricts its citizens from accessing material that is pornographic or contrary to the state system by routing all internet traffic through a central server with filter mechanisms. Other countries such as China severely restrict internet use by requiring ISPs to block sites of Western media, Taiwan and Hong Kong newspapers, and human rights groups. From a Western perspective these practices seem questionable, but tools like Anonymizer can allow web users in these countries to circumvent the rules—at least until the government catches up.

The use of Anonymizer and SafeWeb has created much concern for governments in some countries. Essentially, these tools make it appear to the government filters that the user is visiting the IP address of Anonymizer, even if the user actually accesses pornography or other banned materials. Anonymizer simply encrypts the material and uses a framing mechanism to display the user's destination. Attempting to prevent use of these tools, governments have attempted to block access to Anonymizer's IP address. Anonymizer however, feels that the internet should be an open forum, and to allow users to continue to use its services, it cycles through various domain names and IP addresses so that users effectively stay one step ahead of their governments.

Some governments and employers are likely very upset with applications like Anonymizer, since their ability to control and monitor use of the internet is diminished. Privacy advocates, however, congratulate such services on protecting the rights of individuals and keeping the internet an open medium.

Anonymizer
www.anonymizer.com

Questions

1. **Does Anonymizer appear to be providing a valuable service?**
2. **Should this service be provided to individuals in countries where the government controls internet use?**
3. **Should Anonymizer restrict the sites that its users can access, such as forbidding access to pornography, since its tool allows web surfers to waste time at work?**

SOURCES: J. Lee, "Punching Holes in Internet Walls," *The New York Times*, 26 April 2001; R. Van Horn, "The Crazy Business of Internet Peeping, Privacy, and Anonymity," *Phi Delta Kappan* (November 2000); Anonymizer Inc., **www.anonymizer.com**.

E-Strategy

Online Monitoring at Cyveillance Inc.

The cost to build a strong brand image can be very high and, in the world of the internet and e-commerce, that cost can skyrocket. As well, today's technologies make it increasingly easy for that brand image to be compromised through the piracy of software, misuse of brand names, and copyright abuse to name a few of the issues. Two young entrepreneurs recognized this issue in 1996 and began developing software that could help businesses protect their brand.

The Cyveillance tools can search millions of webpages per day for trademarks, logos, keywords, graphics, software, music, and videos that may be displayed on sites that don't have approval. The misuses of these items can cost companies tremendous amounts in lost sales, and

Cyveillance has signed on major clients like Ford Motor Company, Bell, and Levi Strauss to assist them in their online efforts.

Cyveillance describes their services as enabling "businesses to capture revenue by taking control of their online brand identity, digital assets, and corporate reputation." The application can even search out protest sites and sites that are defamatory in nature, and then assist clients to address issues in the best manner possible. Much of the concern clients express involves loss of sales due to misuse of corporate assets. For example, Cyveillance located numerous sites that were using the Dell brand name and/or image to sell their own products, which Dell estimated was costing it millions in lost sales.

Another example of the use of Cyveillance was for The Washington Post Company, where it was discovered that numerous websites were copying stories directly from the company's newspaper to develop their own content. While Cyveillance doesn't specifically address the legal issues in court, the company's technologies enable businesses to gather the evidence they need to pursue legal action or out-of-court settlements.

Online brand protection can be a major concern for often-criticized large corporations like Nike and Microsoft. Cyveillance allows these businesses to monitor what is being said online and, where possible, to develop methods of counteracting negative publicity.

Cyveillance Inc.
www.cyveillance.com

Questions

1. Why would these large firms hire Cyveillance to conduct the web searching rather than perform the analysis in-house?
2. What rights should businesses have in protecting their brand name online?
3. Should upset consumers be legally entitled to establish complaint sites that criticize corporations?

SOURCES: Cyveillance Inc., **www.cyveillance.com**; "Marketing: Helpline Service," *Marketing*, June 21, 2001.

are sets of keywords in the source code of a HyperText Markup Language (HTML) page that help search engines to categorize websites. Once Indigo discovered that Chapters had used its trademarked name in the metatags, it threatened to sue, and Chapters quickly removed the term from its website.[9] Ironically, these two companies merged in 2001 and combined their affiliate programs and advertising efforts. The issue of metatags has not been completely dealt with in all courts of law, but indications can be drawn from cases completed to date. It appears that the use of any trademarked name in an attempt to draw traffic to a site for commercial purposes is inappropriate. The U.S. court system has ruled on several occasions that use of a trademark within metatags for commercial purposes is copyright infringement.

Some cases have begun to provide guidance as to what is acceptable use of trademarks in metatags within Canada and abroad. For example, in early 2001 a British Columbia court ruled that the use of the trademarked names "British Columbia Automobile Association" within the metatags of a criticism and protest site did not constitute copyright infringement. Also at issue in the case was the use of the letters BCAA within the domain name of BCAAonstrike.com (not in operation now). The union in the case had been on strike and had established websites to provide public information related to their concerns. The court found that the use of the trademarked terms did not infringe on copyright, primarily based upon three key factors:

1. The domain name was not identical to the trademark and should not create confusion.

2. The union was providing public information and not competing with the BCAA and, therefore, not attempting to take business directly from the trademark owner.

3. The union's site displayed a disclaimer that clearly indicated that the site was not a BCAA site, and the court liked that the disclaimer clearly removed any confusion over the identity of the site owner.[10]

This case appears to give website owners, social activists, and critics the right to use trademarks to attract visitors, as long as the public is not confused as to who the owner is and the content of the site is not defamatory in nature. The right of free speech has been upheld here and provides some guidance for the future.

The results of this case also provide some guidance to commercial enterprises. The use of a domain name that causes confusion, use of a trademark to lure business away from another, and lack of a disclaimer for discussion of a trademark are all risk factors for commercial enterprises. In general, domain names should not be closely related to another's trademark (as will be discussed shortly) and metatags should not include the trademark of another firm where the nature of the website in question is commercial.

Trademarks

The previous section considered some of the issues related to trademark use with regard to metatags; however, trademark issues can arise in many other ways online. A **trademark** is a distinguishable feature such as a word, symbol, picture, logo, or design that can be used to identify the products or services of a specific individual or organization. A trademark provides the owner with the exclusive right to use the mark within the jurisdiction of the appropriate governing body.[11] Another major area where trademark issues arise is in relation to domain names, which will be discussed further in the following section. In addition to trademark infringements from metatag and domain name use, the legal community has recently demonstrated that trademark use for content or product promotion purposes is also inappropriate.

The issues surrounding trademark law are complex but some scenarios have demonstrated that many of the traditional rules continue to apply online. A small Canadian software developer from Waterloo, Ontario, Pro-C Ltd., filed a lawsuit against U.S. retail giant Computer City for trademark infringement. Pro-C had registered a domain name (www.wingen.com) and owned a registered trademark in both the U.S. and Canada (WINGEN). In 1997, Computer City launched a new computer product named "Wingen." The product was offered for sale in the

TRADEMARK
A distinguishable feature such as a word, symbol, picture, logo, or design that can be used to identify the products or services of a specific individual or organization.

company's stores in the United States and through their website, www.computercity.com. No sales were actually made in Canada. The case turned on what constitutes "use" in Canada.

Since a Canadian trademark registration confers the exclusive right to use the mark in Canada in respect of the associated wares and services, if Computer City was deemed to be using the mark in Canada, then there would be infringement. At trial, the judge departed from the current state of the law as to what constitutes "use" in Canada and stated that "the determination of use in Canada requires a "holistic approach." The trial judge disregarded the language in the Trademarks Act which states that there must be use in Canada. The trial judge found Computer City liable for trademark infringement and awarded damages of approximately $1 250 000.

The case was successfully appealed. The Court of Appeal of Ontario overturned the trial decision[12] and noted that infringement in Canada is dependent upon "use" of the registered trademark as that term is defined in Trademarks Act. Particularly, the Court of Appeal held that Computer City's passive website could not constitute use in association with wares because no transfer of ownership was possible through that medium. The mere access to Canadians to a trademark on a website does not necessarily constitute use of that trademark in Canada; there has to be actual commercial activity in Canada.

The ruling indicates that trademark infringement online is as serious as through traditional channels. The jurisdiction of the case was also dealt with in this case since the Canadian court ruled that the web-based advertising was sufficient to allow a Canadian court the authority to rule.[13] (Jurisdictional issues are discussed further later in this chapter.) The Pro-C case indicates that trademark infringement is a serious matter and that all companies dealing online must take sufficient measures to ensure that they are not inappropriately using trademarks registered in any country to which they could potentially be selling.

Domain Names

The controversies over domain name use have become commonplace over the past several years. The phenomenon of cybersquatting, registering a domain name and using it in bad-faith, has caused numerous legal disputes and given rise to both legislation and dispute resolution mechanisms within North America and internationally. The vast number of registrations of the leading domains such as .com, .net, .org, and .ca in Canada has led to increased competition and controversy over domain name policies.

The legal system's early attempts to deal with domain name disputes made use of trademark law as a major portion of the decisions made. The use of trademark law to deal with domain disputes, however, has resulted in many complications, since the two concepts can be closely related but are quite distinct. Trademarks are limited in availability and not all words or marks are available to be registered—this is the key difference between trademarks and domain names. Domain names are by nature unique, can only be held by one owner, and do not need to conform to trademark legislation, as they can take any form (subject to the registrar's rules for length, characters allowed, etc.). For example, surnames such as Smith and general descriptive words such as coffee are not able to be registered as trademarks under the Canada Trademarks Act; however, an individual or organization could register the associated domain names—smith.com, smith.ca, coffee.com, coffee.ca, and so on. This distinction made it difficult for the legal system to apply trademark law in settling all domain name issues.

The complications in dealing with domain name disputes gave rise to new legislation in the United States to reduce the difficulty in settling them. The first piece of legislation to address the issue was the Trademark Dilution Act, which aimed to reduce the requirements to prove that a domain name infringed on a trademark. Prior to this act, a complainant would need to prove that the domain name was using a trademark for commercial purposes and the use was in competition with the trademark owner. This did not adequately allow trademark owners to recover domain names where the use of the domain was not in competition with the owner. For example, under these rules it would be possible to register cokeclassic.com as a domain and use the website to sell t-shirts without "infringing" on the trademark, since the company would not be in competition with Coca-Cola. Noting that this type of use could inhibit the growth of e-commerce and is contrary to the intention of trademark law, the U.S. government enacted the Trademark Dilution Act, effectively removing the requirement to show that the domain holder was in competition with the trademark owner.

The U.S. Congress later enacted a second piece of legislation to further reduce the requirements for trademark holders to prove infringement—the **Anticybersquatting Consumer Protection Act (ACPA)**. The ACPA reduces the trademark holder requirements to simply demonstrating that a domain name has been registered in bad faith and that it has been used in an attempt to make a profit.

The Canadian legal system has not made any specific amendments or enacted new legislation. The domain dispute process has been partially assisted by the establishment of dispute resolution mechanisms. The most influential domain name registrar is the **Internet Corporation for Assigned Names and Numbers (ICANN)**, which controls many of the top-level domains. ICANN is a non-profit organization that describes its own responsibilities as "Internet Protocol (IP) address space allocation, protocol identifier assignment, generic and country code domain name system management, and root server system management functions."[14] These services were originally performed under U.S. Government contract by the Internet Assigned Numbers Authority (IANA) and other entities.

The Uniform Domain Name Dispute Resolution Procedure (UDRP), established by ICANN, only applies to top-level domain names (.com, .org, .gov, .bus, etc.). It functions primarily as a written arbitration system and has in many cases provided a lower cost, quicker alternative to court proceedings in blatant cybersquatting situations. However, various aspects of the UDRP have been criticized since it was implemented. The **Canadian Internet Registration Authority (CIRA)** has also developed a dispute resolution procedure for alleged cases of cybersquatting involving .ca domain names. CIRA is a not-for-profit Canadian corporation that is responsible for operating the .ca internet country code top-level domain. As the .ca domain name dispute procedure was developed after the UDRP, CIRA attempted to address many of the perceived shortcomings with the UDRP during development of the .ca policy.

Copyright

Copyright has become one of the important issues in law with regard to digital media and the use of the internet. Copyright law is designed to protect many different things such as books, computer programs, music, website content, art, and movies. While it is often assumed that copyright protects ideas, it aims only to protect the embodiment of ideas—that is, their form and presentation. The major means by which copyright can be violated include plagiarism, piracy, bootlegging,

ANTICYBERSQUATTING CONSUMER PROTECTION ACT (ACPA)
U.S. legislation that requires a trademark holder to simply demonstrate that a domain name has been registered in bad faith and that it has been used in an attempt to make a profit.

INTERNET CORPORATION FOR ASSIGNED NAMES AND NUMBERS (ICANN)
A domain name registrar that holds control over the primary top-level domains.

ICANN
www.icann.org

CANADIAN INTERNET REGISTRATION AUTHORITY (CIRA)
A not-for-profit Canadian corporation that is responsible for operating the dot-ca internet country code top-level domain.

CIRA
www.cira.ca

and counterfeiting.[15] Each of these violations results in the inappropriate use of another's work for commercial or other purposes. The Canadian Snapshots box gives an example of copyright infringement on the internet.

The Canadian Copyright Act was first written in 1921 and changed substantially in 1988. The increased concern over copyright due to technologies such as photocopiers, fax machines, and computers led to the modifications to the act in 1988. The Copyright Act provides copyright owners with the "sole and exclusive right to reproduce, perform, or publish a work." In general, any original creation is afforded protection under the act and that protection lasts for fifty years after the death of the final author or creator. Canadian laws provide protection in over 140 countries worldwide, as well as through the application of international agreements.

The complexity of copyright law has been brought to the forefront through the Napster case. The creation of a technology that could easily allow millions of individuals to share and distribute copyrighted music files over the internet led to lawsuits that had far-reaching effects on the music industry and many others. The major defence offered in the Napster case was that the software did not result in Napster actually distributing the music files but merely helping music lovers to find each other. The opponents contended that the Napster application provided a tool that used the internet to distribute copyrighted material and, therefore, facilitated inappropriate activities online. (The Napster case is discussed in more detail on the website accompanying this text. See this text's Companion Website at **www.pearsoned.ca/trites**.) The importance of the Napster case has been to bring attention to the issues of copyright online and to encourage the legal community and governments to revisit legislation that was primarily written prior to the internet.

Napster was eventually shut down as a free file swapping service. Although the Napster case did bring attention to the issues of online copyright infringement it did not bring an end to the practice of online file swapping. New companies quickly filled the vacuum created by Napster's demise. Industry organizations have also sued the next generation of peer to peer software providers that followed Napster (Kazaa, Gnutella, etc.). In some circumstances, industry organizations such as the Recording Industry Association of America (RIAA) have even resorted to identifying and launching lawsuits against individuals allegedly downloading files in violation of copyright.

Recording Industry Association of America (RIAA)
www.riaa.com

The issues that can arise with respect to copyright online are many and can include piracy, plagiarism, linking concerns, and even website framing issues (discussed below). The piracy and plagiarism concerns are similar in many ways to the copyright issues that have existed since the creation of the printing press—protected materials being copied and misused without the owner's permission. These issues have become much more serious, however, with the evolution of the internet where material is considered free.

The concept of deep linking is one that has caused difficulty for businesses and the courts in applying existing copyright law. **Deep linking** is the creation of a link on one website to a specific part or page (not the homepage) of another website. The concern over deep linking is understandable since huge investments in web design have been made by businesses in relation to advertising, CRM, and business intelligence efforts.

DEEP LINKING
The creation of a link on one website to a specific part or page (not the homepage) of another website.

Deep linking can effectively wipe out the effectiveness of these efforts by moving users directly to a specific part of a website. Deep linking has been considered as a legal issue by various courts in different jurisdictions. Unfortunately, the results of the decisions have created uncertainty. It appeared that courts in the United States were coalescing around a position that it was legally acceptable to engage in deep linking provided that the source of the deep linked page or part

Canadian Snapshots

Rebroadcasting at iCraveTV and JumpTV

In November 1999, iCraveTV.com began retransmitting both Canadian and U.S. television signals onto the web. The Toronto-based company aimed to build a large viewing audience and build a successful online strategy. The ability to legally retransmit television signals within Canada seemed to be provided by the Copyright Act, and iCraveTV felt that its model would be successful.

The Canadian Radio-television and Telecommunications Commission (CRTC) is the regulator of broadcasting in Canada and in 1999 had specifically exempted internet-based companies from the Broadcasting Act. The exemption was designed to encourage the developing online economy and seemingly to reduce the burden on the CRTC of attempting to regulate this growing medium. This exemption combined with the Canadian Copyright Act's provision for retransmission of television signals seemed to pave the way for iCraveTV.

As one might expect, however, iCraveTV soon drew the attention of major broadcasters in Canada and in the United States, who were concerned over what they alleged was piracy and illegal activity. The Motion Picture Association of America, National Football League, and National Basketball Association filed lawsuit against iCraveTV and a Pennsylvania court granted an injunction against distribution of the U.S. content. While iCraveTV intended to utilize technology to limit its retransmission to Canadian viewers, it never successfully came back online, and by late 2001 the website was completely inaccessible.

The application of the U.S. court ruling left an opening for JumpTV Canada Inc. to try where iCraveTV had failed. In attempting to limit its signal to Canada, iCraveTV had required users to enter their postal code—however, any Canadian postal code would allow users worldwide to access the service. JumpTV claims to have developed technology that will limit the use of the service to users truly from Canada.

JumpTV has also attempted to address the issues over legally rebroadcasting signals by aiming to negotiate royalty payments with the appropriate parties. The Copyright Act requires the payment of any applicable royalties to be made to comply but the only rates established apply to cable and satellite operations. Despite JumpTV's attempts, however, the broadcasting community appears to prefer to allow JumpTV to operate without tariffs—but only for the short run, as a lengthy review process with government and the broadcasting community may begin to settle the dispute.

The Copyright Act could be amended to deal with the issues according to Industry Canada representatives, although experts argue that specific changes related to the internet could lead the legislation to become outdated quickly. The CRTC could also reverse its decision to take a hands-off approach to the issue but that may lead to extensive requirements for reviewing the activities of online businesses.

JumpTV has now changed its business model. The company now offers a selected number of channels over the internet on a subscription basis. The monthly cost is US$5.95 for dial-up access and US$9.95 for broadband access. The company no longer places geographic restrictions on its customers and accepts customers from around the world. Although the web site does not provide any explanations, it can be assumed that JumpTV has entered into revenue-sharing agreements with the TV stations that it broadcasts over the internet. As of now, JumpTV does not have any attractive channels to compete against another more successful internet venture, DirecTV. The future of internet retransmission is unclear, but these companies are trying their best to gain the legal right and make a profit at the same time.

JumpTV
www.jumptv.com

DirecTV
www.directv.com

Questions

1. Why wasn't iCraveTV's use of postal codes to limit use to Canada sufficient? Many other sites ask users to confirm they are of legal age to view material (e.g., beer advertisers). How is this different?

2. Does JumpTV's use of technological tools to determine the location of individuals raise any issues that you are concerned about?

3. Should the Canadian government be spending tax dollars evaluating these types of issues when the U.S. regulations seem to override Canadian law? Why?

SOURCES: P. Brethour and H. Scoffield, "Net Rebroadcasts to Be Targeted by Ottawa," *The Globe and Mail*, 31 May 2001; S. Bonisteel, "JumpTV Poised to Launch iCraveTV-like Service—Really," *Newsbytes* (May 1, 2001); M. Geist, "Get Ready for Reruns in Battle over Online TV," *The Globe and Mail*, 15 March 2001.

was effectively acknowledged. More recently some European courts have found that deep linking is not appropriate in any manner without proper consent. It is not clear what effect these decisions may or may not have in the United States. In considering these issues, e-businesses need to closely consider their objectives and the concerns that may be raised by others. At this time, the most prudent course of action due to the lack of legal clarity would be to obtain the consent of a site owner before establishing any deep links to another website.

A young Canadian e-business owner, Jean-Pierre Bazinet, has experienced firsthand the difficulties that can arise through the issue of copyright and deep linking. Bazinet's website, Movie-List.com, provides information about movies and links to trailers and promotional information online. In 1999 Bazinet received a request from Universal Pictures to remove all copyrighted materials from his site and later to remove all "deep links" to trailers, with the threat of legal action.[16] Having little ability to fight the case in court, Movie-List.com removed all links to Universal's trailers but left the issue in an overall state of confusion. Linking is one of the major applications of the internet; however, its use must be related back to issues of copyright concerns.

The issue of deep linking is one that may or may not continue to cause difficulties within the legal system. In considering the issues that deep linking causes, it is interesting to think of how links are established by search engines. The issue of deep linking and some out-of-court settlements seem to indicate that it may be inappropriate; however, search engines also direct individuals to specific sites below the corporate homepage of sites. This would seemingly be a similar concern since many search engines create their own database of sites without the permission of the content owners, due to the use of spiders and other web-crawling tools.

Copyright issues have also been raised with respect to databases, a vital component of many e-businesses. The concern over databases is in determining whether they are original or not—since databases determined not to be original are not protected by copyright. For example, a Canadian court ruled that the Yellow Pages' telephone listings were not protected by Canadian copyright laws since it did not meet the criteria of originality required for protection.[17] Organizations such as the World Intellectual Property Organization (WIPO) and others have called for extending the scope of protection for databases internationally, since they are the lifeblood of many organizations despite the "originality" aspect. The cost to develop and gather the data can be substantial and often the benefits obtained from the data are only realized after extensive data analysis. The issues around database protection continue to develop as e-commerce grows and the legal community and court systems address the concerns that arise.

The issue of website framing is another that has resulted in lawsuits. **Website framing** is the use of HTML and browser technology to split a page into segments, which is useful for facilitating ease of use and building impressive websites. The issue that can arise with regard to copyright and website framing occurs when one site links the material or web pages of another organization into its own frame. For example, figure 13.2 illustrates how a page might be framed with material from another company that could result in copyright issues.

The website framing issue arose in a case between Imax Corporation and Showmax Inc. of Montreal that was decided in early 2000. The issues in this case involved both offline copyright and trademark concerns as well as online issues related to framing and linking. In its arguments, IMAX stated:

> The defendant's internet website uses linking and framing technology such that viewers of the Showmax website see the IMAX mark juxtaposed with the

WEBSITE FRAMING
The use of HTML and browser technology to split a page into segments, which is useful for facilitating ease of use and building impressive websites.

Figure 13.2   Illustration of Web Framing

The display of information in a website frame can lead to legal issues—designers need to be fully aware of copyright concerns in this regard.

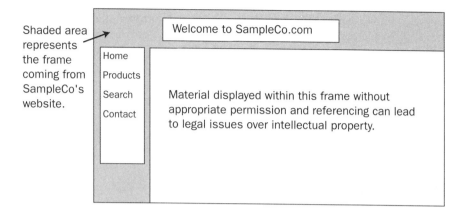

SHOWMAX mark in a manner likely to foster the mistaken belief that the two companies are related.

The use of framing was resulting in confusion for consumers that the two companies may be related and, therefore, had some validity for the court over the issue of trademark. In addition, the reproduction of materials created by IMAX on the Showmax site resulted in a reasonable argument that Showmax was infringing on the copyright materials of IMAX under the Copyright Act. The court ruled in favour of IMAX, stating that although no measurable profits or costs could be determined, the use of IMAX materials by Showmax was inappropriate.

Website designers must take the website framing issue into consideration as the increasing concerns over copyright issues can result in costly legal battles and negative publicity. In designing any framed sites in particular, it is preferred that any materials not owned by the organization be opened within a new browser window so that users are clearly aware that the material is from another location. If the material is to be viewed within a frame, it may be best to seek permission from the copyright owner to avoid concerns. The framing of copyrighted or trademark materials may not cause difficulties if it is evident to users that the material comes from another source; however, caution should be taken in judging what "evident to users" might mean, since a court may have the final decision.

Since the invention of the printing press, the legal system has attempted to deal with issues of copyright infringement. The internet may have reduced the difficulty with which copyright is violated but it has not simplified the methods for dealing with the problem. The increased efforts to deal with copyright issues in many countries and the recognition that international standards are increasingly necessary will help in the ongoing development of workable copyright solutions.

Patents

Patents are documents issued by the government that grant an inventor or patent owner the right to make and use an invention for 20 years after the patent is filed.[18] The issue of patents has recently become a concern for e-commerce and e-business because "processes" are covered as inventions that may be protected by patents. They are referred to as business method patents. Business method patents have been recognized in the United States but not in Canada, although many

PATENTS
Documents issued by the government that grant an inventor or patent owner the right to make and use an invention for 20 years after the patent is filed.

business method patent applications are pending in the hope that they will be. One of the most recognized examples of a business method patent is Amazon.com's 1-Click process of its online purchasing system that allows users to easily make purchases by speeding up the checkout process. This process was patented by Amazon in 1999, and in late 1999 the company filed suit against Barnes and Noble for infringing upon its patent through the use of "Express Lane" technology. Amazon claimed that Express Lane was copying its patented process and therefore was illegal use. Both parties claimed success at various points of the legal dispute, with Amazon winning an initial injunction and Barnes and Noble successfully overturning it on appeal. The parties eventually settled the lawsuit just before it went to trial without disclosing the terms of settlement. Ongoing issues such as the 1-Click patent process are very important to businesses that seek to maintain a competitive advantage in the online world.

Jurisdiction

The issue of jurisdiction arises on numerous occasions on the internet—the global medium of communication and e-commerce. Many of the areas of law already discussed in this chapter can be of concern such as copyright, trademark, privacy, and electronic contracts. WIPO categorizes the major complexities of jurisdiction into three main issues:

- the jurisdiction within which to adjudicate a dispute at a particular location, known as the forum
- the appropriate law applicable to the dispute (also known as choice of law)
- the recognition and enforcement of judgements within foreign jurisdictions[19]

The complications that arise due to these issues have been seen on numerous occasions in the courts within Canada, the United States, and throughout the world.

The jurisdictional issues call into question many business practices as well as actions of individuals online. For example, individuals who create personal websites could be at odds with issues of obscenity, hate speech, or slander worldwide if appropriate jurisdictional issues are not in place and enforced. The United States has much stronger protection of free speech than many countries, which complicates many matters. Their constitution prevents the courts from pursuing many issues that other countries would consider inappropriate. In addition to individual websites, businesses must be concerned with jurisdictional issues that can question the practices carried out online.

Perhaps the best-known issue with regard to free speech was the case involving Yahoo! France and the sale of Nazi memorabilia within its auctions. In late 2000, a French court ordered the company to block access within France to Nazi materials. (See the E-Business in Global Perspective box for a more detailed discussion of this case.) In early 2001, the company eliminated the sale of all such memorabilia worldwide but also elected to pursue legal action in the U.S court system to overrule the French courts. In late 2001 Yahoo! was successful in obtaining a court order in the United States stipulating that the French court had no jurisdiction over U.S.-based servers and that Yahoo! had no legal obligation to remove the Nazi memorabilia from its U.S. website. This case demonstrates the difficult balance to be made over the internet, as various international laws, customs, and business practices result in disputes. It also highlights an area in which the development of international agreements may be beneficial to both businesses and governments.

E-Business in Global Perspective

Jurisdiction at Yahoo!

The decision of a French judge in November 2000 has made it a possibility that you may not find *The Diary of Anne Frank* on a Yahoo! auction. The decision required Yahoo! to block access to all illegal memorabilia (in particular Nazi materials) from any French web surfers. The effect of the decision, however, resulted in Yahoo! removing all such materials from its auction site in order to comply, since it cannot guarantee that technological tools will block the materials to all users in France. The blocking could even restrict items with keywords deemed inappropriate (e.g., Nazi) from showing up, so the story of Anne Frank could be excluded from some searches.

The concern that Yahoo! appropriately raised was that its French subsidiary was complying in full with the rules and laws in France. However, the French court ruled that the presence of the materials on U.S. servers that could not appropriately be blocked from the country was illegal. The First Amendment in the United States gives citizens a right to free speech that would not limit the distribution of materials such as those ruled upon in this case.

The French ruling may not even be enforceable over Yahoo!, but the company decided to comply and restricted the trade of such materials from its website to avoid concern over paying fines of over US$10 000 per day for failure to comply. The company did not, however, require its subsidiary Geocities to restrict comments and discussion online, since that website is dedicated to user communities where individual members may discuss any topic. After having complied with what company owners thought was an unreasonable request, a further surprise developed—that Yahoo! CEO, Tim Koogle, was accused of "justifying war crimes and crimes against humanity" for not ensuring that 100 percent of Nazi materials were removed from all of its websites and subsidiaries.

The French decision aimed to ensure that listings of Nazi-related merchandise would not show up on the Yahoo! website. The decision in this case calls into question a number of concerns over national versus international rights. According to free-speech advocates, whether the materials in this case are controversial is not the case—the issue is that a foreign country is dictating that its own laws apply to the World Wide Web. Further moves in this direction could lead to geographic boundaries being erected in the online world—something that would significantly change the internet as we know it.

Yahoo!
www.yahoo.com

Geocities
http://geocities.yahoo.com

Questions

1. Do you feel that the French court should have had any right to rule on material on a U.S. web server?
2. How should the internet balance free speech and hate material regulation?
3. Would this issue differ if the products sold were illegal items in the U.S., such as drugs that were not illegal in the selling country?

SOURCES: R. Stross, "Pardon My French—If It's a World Wide Web, Why Is France Censoring Yahoo!?" *U.S. News & World Report*, 12 February 2001; "Business: Vive la liberté!" *The Economist*, November 25, 2000.

In attempting to deal with the issues over jurisdiction, the courts in the United States and Canada have applied a standard that has become known as the passive versus active test. The **passive versus active test** attempts to place the website of an online business along a continuum based upon the interactivity of the website to determine if operations within a jurisdiction were planned. The test may determine, for instance, that a Canadian firm's website that provides information about its products and manufacturing process is "passive" and, therefore, would not give a U.S. court the right to govern the issue. A website that resulted in online sales within an area and gathered personal information to complete the

PASSIVE VERSUS ACTIVE TEST
A standard that attempts to place the website of an online business along a continuum based upon the interactivity of the website to determine if operations within a jurisdiction were planned.

transaction, however, would be ruled to be "active," and courts within the reach of the website (globally) could attempt to claim jurisdiction. The grey area in between active and passive has been the subject of much debate and many cases that have been considered in court have used considerably different approaches in making a decision.[20]

The difficulties with the passive versus active test are many and have led to calls by some to create improved mechanisms for jurisdictional decision-making. Most notably, internet law expert Michael Geist of the University of Ottawa argues that the constant change of technology means that the "passive versus active test has not aged well."[21] Giving consideration to the changes in websites from 1995 to present the level of "active" has changed dramatically—requiring courts to constantly reconsider the issue without reliance on many outdated precedents. This has resulted in many cases in the courts overriding the passive–active test. The trial court decision in the Pro-C case indicated that the Computer City website was passive, but Computer City was still ruled to be operating within Canada due to using its online advertising as an integral part of its advertising campaign.[22] However, the trial decision was overturned, indicating that the courts are somewhat reluctant to abandon traditional trademark concepts. The court of appeal stated that mere access by Canadians to a trademark on a website does not necessarily constitute use of that trademark in Canada, and stressed that there has to be actual commercial activity in Canada.

The uncertainty over the application of law and jurisdiction will become a major threat to electronic commerce if it is not handled in the near future. Some countries such as the United States have even created legislation that claims to provide rights to govern internationally. Notably, the Children's On-line Privacy Protection Act is written to apply to both U.S. websites as well as any website in the world where a firm is targeting children from the United States. Many other cases have resulted in countries claiming jurisdiction over issues in foreign states, with little concern for the passive versus active test as well. The Alberta Securities Commission took legal action against the World Stock Exchange (of Antigua/Cayman Islands), an online exchange, in a Canadian court after it was ruled that the impact of the website substantially impacted Alberta.

The issues over jurisdiction continue to complicate e-commerce transactions but some steps may assist businesses in addressing jurisdiction. For example, many companies now include "choice of laws" clauses within their contracts to allow trading partners to agree in writing to the legal jurisdiction. This practice is common among B2B partners but should be used carefully when dealing with B2C customers. Simply including the forum for jurisdiction in an e-contract is subject to the same constraints that apply to other e-contract issues (discussed below). In the case of *Mendoza v. AOL*, an American court ruled that AOL's claim to dismiss a case brought against the company in a state outside of Virginia, where the agreement indicated, was overruled. The judge found that "it would be unfair and unreasonable because the clause in question was not negotiated at arm's length, was contained in a standard form contract, and was not readily identifiable by the plaintiff due to the small text and location of the clause at the conclusion of the agreement."[23]

Individuals must also ensure that they are aware of the legal issues they may encounter by dealing with companies in certain countries or making agreements to adhere to another area's laws. Signing an agreement that the choice of laws is in Texas, for instance, may require an individual to incur travel costs and excessive legal costs to address legal issues. Addressing these types of concerns for both businesses and individuals is of extreme importance to the future growth of online business. For now, the passive versus active test is still common, but as additional cases are reviewed the jurisdictional issues are likely to evolve to a more complex analysis.

E-Contracts

To conduct business effectively, it is necessary for contracts to be completed in an appropriate manner. The completion of contracts has evolved extensively from the original "handshake" approach to "pen and paper" and now "digital" or "e-contracts." The issue for e-commerce with respect to contracting is the need for recognition of electronic contracts to ensure enforceability equal to that of more traditional contracting approaches. The governments of many countries, including Canada, have responded to the need for recognition of electronic contracts and created legislation. For example, in Canada PIPEDA gives legitimacy to e-contracts as described below:

> The purpose of this Part [of the Act] is to provide for the use of electronic alternatives in the manner provided . . . where federal laws contemplate the use of paper to record or communicate information or transactions.[24]

Many of the provinces have also enacted legislation to address these issues at the provincial level as well. The recognition of e-contracts through legislation allows the court system to more appropriately deal with electronic contracts than was previously possible.

The United Nations Commission on International Trade Law (UNCITRAL) developed the Model Law on Electronic Commerce in 1996 to address issues such as e-contracting. The UNCITRAL Model Law attempts to guide governments in creating legislation that will stimulate international trade and lead to a harmonization of legal systems. The e-contract issue concerns such factors as the form of communication, acknowledgement of receipt, and acknowledgement of acceptance.[25] Similar to using paper-based contracts, it is necessary for e-contracts to be recognized as fluid mechanisms that can be received but unsigned at stages of the negotiations. Efforts of international organizations such as the United Nations have assisted in stimulating many countries to address these issues.

United Nations Commission on International Trade Law (UNCITRAL)
www.uncitral.org

The creation of e-commerce legislation has led to litigation over contract issues throughout the world. As a leader in e-commerce and as a litigious country, the United States has addressed many of the concerns over contracting in its court systems. According to Michael Geist, two issues arising from U.S. court rulings are key to properly dealing with e-contracts:

1. *Form of assent.* It is necessary for users to indicate by some active means that they agree to the terms and conditions found within the contract. This issue calls into question many of the standard-form contracts that we see every day and in the online world is increasingly difficult to prove.

2. *Reasonableness of contract terms.* The court systems are as likely to rule that a contract is invalid in the online world as they are in the offline world if the terms are not reasonable. The *Mendoza v. AOL* case mentioned earlier was an example where the court ruled that expecting a customer to come to a specific state to deal with a complaint was unreasonable.[26]

The concerns over issues of the form of assent have led to the development of more online jargon—clickwrap agreements. **Clickwrap agreements** are the

CLICKWRAP AGREEMENTS
The online equivalent of the standard agreements included within the shrink-wrap of software bought in physical locations.

online equivalent of the standard agreements included within the shrink-wrap of software bought in physical locations. Increasingly, e-tailers are requiring users to scroll through the terms of contracts and click on "I Agree" or some similar button to ensure that the form of assent criteria is being met. In *Ticketmaster v. Tickets.com*, a U.S. court concluded that the terms in the contract could not be enforced since users were not required to click "I Agree" to acknowledge reading the terms.[27] This issue requires website designers to clearly provide the terms of a contract and acknowledgement by the user through an active mechanism such as a button or link.

Taxation

Internet taxation is another area of e-commerce and e-business that is complex and has caused considerable difficulty for the legal system and legislators. The issues encompass both income taxation and sales taxes, the two major forms of taxation. The complexity of taxation in the bricks-and-mortar world is more than enough for lawyers, accountants, and legislators to deal with—adding the internet to the mix has added numerous issues that need to be addressed.

The issue of jurisdiction as discussed earlier also causes problems for taxation in the global economy. One of the major issues focuses on where a business is located for tax purposes—known as **permanent establishment** in Canada or **physical presence** in the United States. The permanent establishment of an online company can be very difficult to determine since it could be the location of the vendor's head office, the location of the website's ISP, the physical location of the server, or some other location such as the branch closest to the customer. This difficulty in establishing jurisdiction results in extreme difficulties in determining the appropriateness of collecting sales taxes and can also add complications to the subject of income taxation.

The Canadian sales tax system has a number of mechanisms in place to encourage compliance, but the concept of self-assessment is likely to fail in the online world equally as it has in the offline world. Sales taxes are supposed to be paid in the province where the good is consumed—the complexity arises, of course, when the vendor and customer reside in different locations. Assume that a student from Winnipeg goes online to purchase a new computer system from a New Brunswick business. The transaction should result in Manitoba sales tax being applied; however, the New Brunswick business is not likely registered as a tax collector for Manitoba. The student should self-assess the sales tax but there is very little likelihood that the transaction will be investigated by Manitoba and, therefore, collection is unknown. The complexity of this transaction grows if a foreign country is added into the scenario and issues of federal taxes and customs duties arise. These jurisdictional issues will continue to cause difficulties in the Canadian and international systems until increased harmonization occurs.

The risks of tax revenue declines as identified above have led some governments to take action, but whether the actions taken are appropriate is another question. For example, British Columbia amended its legislation in March 2000 to require "persons located outside the province that in the ordinary course of business solicit persons in British Columbia for orders to purchase tangible personal property"[28] to register and collect sales tax for the province. Some analysts claim that the legislation would not be able to force out-of-province businesses to register, since the B.C. courts don't have jurisdiction, but the intention is still controversial. While this legislation may benefit the province's tax collection, it could discourage electronic commerce. If every Canadian province and territory fol-

PERMANENT ESTABLISHMENT
A term for the definition in Canadian law that determines where a business is located for tax purposes.

PHYSICAL PRESENCE
A term for the definition in U.S. law that determines where a business is located for tax purposes.

lowed suit, online businesses would need to register and periodically file 13 sales tax forms. If each of the states in the U.S. follows suit, businesses could be required to register in over 60 separate jurisdictions. Estimates of international taxation systems reach nearly 7500—any requirements to conform to this number of systems would simply fail but the number illustrates the extent of the problem.[29] Harmonization sounds like a simple solution to this problem, but encouraging international and even provincial governments to reach a consensus on appropriate taxation methods is unlikely to occur quickly.

The United States has developed legislation to impose a moratorium on internet taxation—the Internet Tax Freedom Act. This legislation does not remove online sales taxes; it simply provides that no new internet-based sales taxes be developed that could slow the growth of e-commerce. The act also created ongoing committees that will continue to review the issue of internet taxation and make recommendations to the U.S. Congress.[30] The issue of taxation will continue to develop over time, since the existing legislation in most countries is unclear on internet transactions.

The issue of the type of income is another that e-commerce has brought attention to. The digitization of products calls into question whether the sale is a product or a service. The purchase of a software package in a retail store would clearly be a product but downloading that same software from an online store is less clear—is it now a product or a service? The distinction may seem unimportant but in many jurisdictions the tax laws vary between the two and therefore it is necessary to make a choice. For items such as music, the issue over the digital delivery leads to confusion over the type of revenue earned—is it sales, license fees, or royalties? The issue of product type, like many other tax and legal issues, is one where experts need to be consulted.

The taxation issues on the internet must be addressed by legislators and the legal system. To reduce uncertainty and encourage compliance, the system needs to be understandable and, where possible, harmonized. The lack of appropriate standards may encourage non-compliance (deliberate or not) and the development of inappropriate regulations may only lead to hasty decisions and more complexity. The evolution of taxation on the internet may take several years but one thing is for sure—we will all continue to pay taxes in some form or another, but where?

Chapter Summary

The internet's global reach has created numerous legal issues for e-businesses to be aware of. In addition, the power of technology to capture and analyze data has caused concern over individuals' right to privacy. These developing issues require the attention of managers of e-businesses to ensure that appropriate actions are taken to mitigate risks and operate in a socially responsible manner.

Privacy can be compromised through the inappropriate use of personal information about an individual. The gathering of personal information in Canada has come under the scope of new legislation known as the Personal Information Protection and Electronic Documents Act. This legislation aims to protect individuals' rights to privacy and stimulate the growth of e-commerce. To comply with the act, businesses must inform users of the information they collect and the purpose—often done through a privacy policy on the company's website.

The ease of use of the internet has also resulted in ease of "theft" of copyright materials, trademarks, and patents. These concerns over intellectual property require organizations to consider their own use of others' material as well as the protection of intangible assets owned. Activities such as linking to other sites and website design have resulted in legal cases due to inappropriate use of copyright materials, requiring managers to give thought to the legal implications of various activities.

The many disputes over trademarks and domain names have led to established processes known as dispute resolution mechanisms. While trademarks are unique in many ways, they differ from domain names in that they cannot be general in nature. The unique aspect of domain names has led to court cases whereby outcomes can be unpredictable.

The taxation of online transactions is closely related to the issue of jurisdiction on the internet. Determining where a company is located is complex in the internet age and creates uncertainty over which laws apply and what taxation mechanisms should be in place. E-businesses must examine their operations and through legal and governmental consultation ensure that they are complying with the appropriate rules and regulations in order to limit their risk.

Key Terms

Anticybersquatting Consumer Protection Act *(p. 277)*

Canadian Internet Registration Authority (CIRA) *(p. 277)*

clickwrap agreements *(p. 285)*

copyright *(p. 272)*

deep linking *(p. 278)*

industrial property *(p. 272)*

intellectual property *(p. 272)*

Internet Corporation for Assigned Names and Numbers (ICANN) *(p. 277)*

passive versus active test *(p. 283)*

patents *(p. 281)*

permanent establishment *(p. 286)*

personal information *(p. 267)*

Personal Information Protection and Electronic Documents Act (PIPEDA) *(p. 267)*

physical presence *(p. 286)*

trademark *(p. 275)*

website framing *(p. 280)*

Tools for Online Learning

To help you master the material in this chapter and stay up to date with new developments in e-business, visit www.pearsoned.ca/trites. Resources include:

- **Review Questions and Exercises**

- **Problems for Discussion**

- **Recommended Readings**

- **Updates to Case Studies and Textual Material**

- **Streaming CBC Videos with Cases**

Endnotes

1. Industry Canada, http://e-com.ic.gc.ca/english/strat/index.htmlElectronic Commerce in Canada, http://e-com.ic.gc.ca/english/strat/index.html, accessed May 9, 2004.

2. Office of the Privacy Commissioner of Canada, Privacy Legislation in Canada, www.privcom.gc.ca/legislation/index_e.asp, accessed May 9, 2004.

3. Office of the Privacy Commissioner of Canada: Privacy Commissioner of Canada, "Frequently Asked Questions," www.privcom.gc.ca/faq/faq_01_e.asp#004, accessed December 6, 2004.

4. Office of the Privacy Commissioner of Canada, "Privacy Legislation in Canada," fact sheet, www.privcom.gc.ca/fs-fi/fs2001-02_e.asp, accessed May 9, 2004.

5. Michael Geist, "Lots of Legal Challenges When Dot Coms Die," *The Globe and Mail*, 30 March 2001.

6. World Intellectual Property Organization, "Primer on Electronic Commerce and Intellectual Property Issues," www.WIPO.int, available May 9, 2004.

7. "Privacy Fears Heightened," *The Globe and Mail*, 18 March 2001.

8. World Intellectual Property Organization, "Primer on Electronic Commerce and Intellectual Property Issues," www.WIPO.int, available May 9, 2004.

9. Michael Geist, "H is for Hackers: An A to Z Guide to Cyberlaw in 1999," *The Globe and Mail*, 28 December 1999.

10. Michael Geist, "B.C. Court Shores Up Protection for Anticorporate Protest Sites," *The Globe and Mail*, 15 February 2001.

11. Lesley Ellen Harris, *Canadian Copyright Law*, 3rd ed. (McGraw Hill Ryerson: Toronto, 2001).

12. *Pro-C Limited v. Computer City* [2001] 14 C.P.R. 4th.

13. M. Geist, "Trademark Confusion Creeps into Web Site Content," *The Globe and Mail*, 7 September 2000.

14. Internet Corporation for Assigned Names and Numbers (ICANN), www.icann.org/tr/english.html, accessed May 9, 2004.

15. Lesley Ellen Harris, *Canadian Copyright Law*, 3rd ed. (McGraw Hill Ryerson: Toronto, 2001).

16. C. Kaplan, "Is Linking Always Legal? The Experts Aren't Sure," *The New York Times*, 6 August 1999.

17. Lesley Ellen Harris, *Canadian Copyright Law*, 3rd ed. (McGraw Hill Ryerson: Toronto, 2001), 20.

18. Lesley Ellen Harris, *Canadian Copyright Law*, 3rd ed. (McGraw Hill Ryerson: Toronto, 2001), 3.

19. World Intellectual Property Organization, "Primer on Electronic Commerce and Intellectual Property Issues," www.WIPO.int, available May 9, 2004.

20. Ogilvy Renault, "Jurisdiction and the Internet: Are Traditional Rules Enough?" Proceedings of the Uniform Law Conference of Canada (July 1998).

21. Michael Geist "Long Arm of the Law Needs New Guidelines for the Internet," *The Globe and Mail*, 9 August 2001.

22. Michael Geist, "Trademark Confusion Creeps into Web Site Content," *The Globe and Mail*, 7 September 2000.

23. Michael Geist, "All Electronic Contracts Are Not Created Equal," *The Globe and Mail*, 25 May 2001.

24. *Personal Information Protection and Electronic Documents Act, Statutes of Canada* 2000, c. 5 s. 32.

25. UNCITRAL, "Model Law on Electronic Commerce," United Nations, 1996.

26. Michael Geist, "All Electronic Contracts Are Not Created Equal," *The Globe and Mail*, 25 May 2001.

27. Michael Geist, "All Electronic Contracts Are Not Created Equal," *The Globe and Mail*, 25 May 2001.

28. R. Lewandowski, "The Net Tax Nightmare," *CA Magazine* (March 2001): 21.

29. Harvey M. Deitel et al., *E-Business & E-Commerce for Managers* (Upper Saddle River, NJ: Prentice Hall, 2000), 326.

30. Harvey M. Deitel et al., *E-Business & E-Commerce for Managers* (Upper Saddle River, NJ: Prentice Hall, 2000), 326.

CHAPTER 14

E-Commerce and Small Business

LEARNING OBJECTIVES

When you complete this chapter you should be able to:

1. Understand how e-commerce can be an opportunity for small businesses.

2. Discuss the development of strategy for small business e-commerce.

3. Explain how a small business can establish an e-commerce presence.

4. Identify and describe some of the useful services and sources of information on the internet for small businesses.

5. Describe the barriers to e-commerce for small businesses and how they can be overcome.

Introduction

E-commerce has brought a great deal of growth and opportunity to the small business sector. The potential to reach new markets, reduce costs of operations, and compete against larger competitors brought the potential of e-commerce to the forefront of news during the late 1990s and early 2000s. At that time, high profile dot-com startups like Amazon and eBay, no longer small businesses, generated fortunes for their founders and raised expectations to unrealistic levels. However, that time was followed by several equally high profile dot-com failures, like eToys.com and Pets.com, which significantly lowered expectations and even produced many skeptics about the opportunities for the small business sector in becoming involved in e-commerce. Nevertheless, there have been thousands of successful dot-com startups in recent years, as well as thousands of cases where established businesses have expanded their operations by developing an e-commerce initiative. In this chapter we will consider the importance of e-commerce to small businesses and consider different ways in which these companies can use the internet to their advantage.

The importance of the small business sector to the economy of Canada and, in fact, to the economies of many countries throughout the world cannot be overstated. In Canada, 98 percent of all businesses have fewer than 100 employees and much of the job growth in the country can be attributed to these small enterprises.[1] The number of small businesses combined with their importance to the economy has led to much interest in developing the use of e-commerce in the small business sector. Evidence of this interest can be found, for example, in the Government of Canada's e-commerce strategy and information website developed by Industry Canada, Strategis, which includes specific information for small companies. Many regional and provincial government agencies have developed seminars and other incentives for helping small business get started in e-commerce. In addition, many technology service providers and online services have developed products and services that are designed specifically for the small business sector.

Larger organizations and many high-growth firms have shifted their focus from the B2C market to B2B and left a massive opportunity for the right individuals wishing to launch e-businesses in the B2C arena. Some pundits predict that small businesses will be able to capture a large portion of the B2C market by focusing on what they do best—providing excellent customer service to niche markets across large geographic areas.[2] See the E-Business in Global Perspective box for an example of a successful niche strategy. How promising B2C will be to small businesses remains to be determined, but the continually increasing number of internet users represents a market too large to ignore.

Opportunities for Small Business

To stimulate small business e-commerce in Canada, it is important to make small business owners aware of the many opportunities and benefits it can offer. The small business owners must also look to how other small businesses have overcome some of the challenges of matching technology and e-commerce use to the small business setting.

The opportunities for e-commerce use in small business are many and have been realized across numerous industries and geographic regions of the world. The benefits can include access to new markets, improved customer responsiveness, increased flexibility, improved profits (through cost reductions and revenue increases), increased innovation, and better-managed resources.[3] The number and

E-Business in Global Perspective

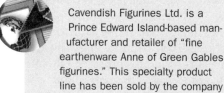

Online Retail at Cavendish Figurines Ltd.

Cavendish Figurines Ltd. is a Prince Edward Island-based manufacturer and retailer of "fine earthenware Anne of Green Gables figurines." This specialty product line has been sold by the company since its formation in 1989 and represents its primary products.

In addition to Anne of Green Gables items, the company now produces other PEI-related products including souvenirs based on the Confederation Bridge, which runs from New Brunswick to PEI and is the longest fixed land-link in the world. The company expanded its operation when the Confederation Bridge opened and now operates a manufacturing and retail facility at the Borden, PEI end of the bridge.

Cavendish Figurines was approached numerous times by website designers and e-commerce promoters to develop an online strategy, but the owners were reluctant. By 1999, changing circumstances, including an internal employee with strong computer skills and an attractive offer from an e-commerce consulting partnership, prompted the owners to pursue e-commerce.

The online presence seemed to make sense for Cavendish since many of its customers were tourists and the company's mail-order channel was quite successful. In addition, the popularity of Anne of Green Gables in Japan and certain other foreign countries made the products very suitable to niche marketing online. The key would be to develop a website that could market the high-end figurines to prospective and existing customers—perhaps transferring some customers from the more costly mail-order channel to the online site.

Following a few glitches in the development stage (one of the development partners went bankrupt), the company's website was launched a few months behind schedule. However, the site received only limited traffic and was contributing little in the way of sales. To address this issue, the site was to be optimized for search engines and continuously improved. With modifications and offline marketing efforts, the site's traffic grew and the owners are now satisfied with their success in the B2C e-commerce area.

Looking to continue growth, Cavendish Figurines would like to expand its abilities in the B2B area. The website, however, is designed primarily for B2C transactions and follows relatively closely to the mail-order catalogues in style. The company is concerned with the impact B2B e-commerce will have on the pricing and payment options used as well.

The key to growth for Cavendish may be establishing core accounts in foreign countries, such as Japan, at both the retail and wholesale levels. The company continues to develop new products and operate a manufacturing plant, retail outlets, and online retailing.

Cavendish Figurines
www.cavendishfigurines.com

Questions

1. What would some of the key issues be with regard to reaching important global markets? Visit the site and decide if you feel it is dealing with these issues.

2. What changes will be necessary for cavendishfigurines.com to establish a B2B strategy online?

3. Do you think Cavendish Figurines should have completely outsourced its online business? Why or why not?

SOURCE: InnovaQuest, "The State of Electronic Commerce in Atlantic Canada," Atlantic Canada Opportunities Agency, March 2000.

amount of benefits received in any of these categories will depend of course on factors such as the industry, products or services sold, and e-strategy chosen.

The use of the internet can be of benefit to small businesses across many functional areas. To illustrate the types of benefits that can be obtained, we will look at e-commerce and internet usage across a number of areas and provide examples where appropriate. The use of the internet can be valuable in the key areas of marketing, customer support, market intelligence, operations, sales transactions, and public relations.[4]

Marketing

The capability to market products and services to a wide audience at a reasonable cost was one of the first drivers of businesses to the internet. While some may question the value of online marketing, many examples exist of the successful use of online marketing and advertising tools. In addition to attracting new customers, small businesses have found that online advertising has provided valuable, targeted marketing campaigns that have resulted in increased business.[5] One small business operator in the tourism industry is Outside Expeditions of Charlottetown, Prince Edward Island. The owner, Bryon Howard, stated, "Yes, we have landed lots of new business as a result of our website. People have booked tours as a result. . . . Others have phoned for information, and rather than wait up to 10 days for a brochure to get to the U.S.—I can give them my website address . . . and voilà, a reservation is the result, the very same day."[6] Many businesses have had similar findings—the value of an online presence for marketing can at times outweigh other marketing efforts. From finding new customers to building a customer database, the internet offers businesses a cost-effective means of marketing in a new way. See table 14.1 for some of the uses of the internet for small business marketing efforts.

Customer Support

One of the key reasons that the internet is valuable to small businesses for customer support is the availability of the website 24/7. While many small businesses pride themselves on personal support, quite a few enquiries can often be handled without any human contact and the customer is just as happy to be served in a timely fashion. If, for example, a customer from Montreal is looking for product details at 9 a.m. their time, it is unlikely that a business in California would be open. Rather than having to wait until the afternoon, the customer can find the information themselves if the supplier has a website. This form of self-service often leads to satisfaction, since it is timely and can reduce the cost of calling long-distance to another business. The customer is now informed of all important product features (assuming a well-designed, useful website exists) and may call or place an order online.

Table 14.1   Marketing Aspects of the Internet

- Provide product or service information
- Find new customers
- Develop new export markets
- Educate customers
- Reduce marketing costs
- Enhance your image
- Build a customer/potential customer database
- Encourage requests for information
- Support traditional media campaigns
- Distribute frequently changing information
- Build brand image

One of the main tools that will reduce routine questions over the phone is a frequently asked questions (FAQ) page on the web. The FAQ page should pose questions in a manner consistent with how customers would typically ask them by phone or in person. Responses can be in basic text format or can integrate text and multimedia to give visual aids to users. The use of FAQs to reduce phone queries can benefit both the customer and the business by reducing the time and cost of dealing with these concerns individually.

Market Intelligence

The internet offers numerous tools whereby small businesses can more easily gather market intelligence. Monitoring industry information and competitors can be a time-consuming and costly task, but many internet sites allow this task to be carried out quickly and at a low cost. For example, online services such as eWatch™ offered by PR Newswire allow users to search for news by company name and even subscribe to receive e-mail notification when press releases or news items occur for selected companies. These types of services range in cost but can be invaluable to businesses in industries where timeliness and competitor monitoring are of crucial importance.

PR Newswire
www.ewatch.com

The internet also holds great potential for small businesses trying to gather data relevant to their online and offline marketing efforts. For example, the Strategis site is host to a massive volume of data from Statistics Canada and other reliable sources. It contains industry statistics, demographics, business listings, and a great deal of other information. Many others, such as the sites for the *Globe and Mail* and the *National Post*, offer the ability to search some archives for free and more distant archives for a fee. The wealth of information online (discussed in more detail later in this chapter) provides useful access to data that may assist business owners in decision-making for everyday issues and in establishing growth strategies during times of change.

Operations

The internet and e-commerce offer small businesses the opportunity to achieve efficiencies for operations in numerous ways. Some of the cost savings that can easily be achieved are through reduced long-distance telephone charges (due to e-mail), reduced postage (due to e-mail, websites, and downloads), and the time savings related to do these everyday business tasks.

The use of the internet for sharing business information with business partners can lead to greater efficiencies and improved lines of communication. For example, Trail Blazer, a family-owned business in Nova Scotia that manufactures camping, hunting, and gardening supplies, communicates almost entirely through the Canadian Tire extranet, thus saving time, phone costs, and frustrating automated message machines in the process. Canadian Tire prefers this means of communication and in many cases demands that suppliers (large and small) utilize the technology. All communication through this channel is timely and in many cases more accurate than other communication mediums.

Sales Transactions

The internet offers small businesses the tools by which they may generate potential sales leads and/or conduct online sales transactions. The growth of the B2C market has been somewhat slower than anticipated but some small businesses have been very successful in building a profitable online sales store. For example, Rogers' Chocolates of Victoria, British Columbia, decided in 1996 to make their "brochureware" site transactional to reduce the administrative time required to complete sales and create a stronger online presence. In addition to strong growth in their B2C market, Rogers found that the B2B (wholesale) market increased substantially with their new web presence (see the E-Strategy box).

The potential for online sales transactions will depend upon the industry in which the small business operates, as well as the reputation that the company is able to build. Companies that have operated previously in catalogue-sales operations, such as Rogers' Chocolates, will have an easier transition to online sales than those who have no history in the area. Customers will be familiar with the business and the company will have established logistics and distribution mechanisms in place.

Those businesses that provide services rather than products may or may not be able to provide those services with only online communication. For many products and services, the value of e-commerce is the generation of sales leads generated online. One example of generation of sales leads is Oven Head Salmon Smokers of St. George, New Brunswick, who found that its web presence actually led to enquiries from potential customers who were seeking orders beyond their existing capacity.[7] This type of lead generation is invaluable to any business seeking growth and future profitability.

Conducting online sales transactions and generating sales leads, combined with the value of online marketing, makes e-commerce a very significant tool for most small businesses. Whether the sale actually takes place over the internet is less significant than whether sales occur that would not have otherwise taken place—and much evidence exists to suggest that this does happen.

Public Relations

The internet offers small businesses the opportunity to more easily broadcast their message to media and other users in an effort to create positive PR. Many newspapers offer e-mail addresses where businesses can send press releases and other information that may be published. By preparing press releases and notifying the media, small businesses may gain exposure in local or even national newspapers that can lead to increased business or traffic to a website. The website can also include PR items that are considered of importance to the local community such as fundraising initiatives that the company is involved in, corporate donations, and community events. The potential for the internet to generate positive PR is limitless if the business is innovative in its use and may potentially lead to improved brand image and/or increased sales.

Getting Started with a Small E-Business

Developing a Small "E" Strategy

Small businesses can go into e-business in two basic ways—by starting up as a "pure play" dot-com business and by launching an e-business initiative within an established business. Either way, it is important for a small business to develop a strategy for e-commerce, implement that strategy effectively, and constantly evaluate and revise the strategy. It is also important to plan the action steps that are required to successfully implement a small e-business.

Trail Blazer, the company mentioned briefly on the previous page, decided to use its website to market its products and to provide customers with a service

E-Strategy

From Bricks to Clicks at Rogers' Chocolates

Rogers' Chocolates Ltd. opened originally as a grocery store in Victoria, British Columbia, in 1885. After a short time in operation, the entrepreneur decided that the most popular product, chocolates, should become the focus of the entire business, but the existing supplier was unable to consistently provide the product at a reasonable cost. Then Rogers soon developed their own brand of chocolates and quickly shifted the focus of the business to selling only chocolates to a local market as well as a growing number of tourists visiting the area.

Rogers realized around the turn of the last century that the tourists who had visited the store and been very impressed by the quality products represented an important market. In attempting to continue the company's growth, a mail-order marketing effort began to get the tourists who visited the shop to consider buying more products after they returned home. This represented an early form of "permission marketing," since visitors to the store were asked if they would be willing to receive catalogues and advertisements at home. Growing steadily, the mail-order business came to represent an important market to Rogers' and continues to be a strong component of today's company.

Nearly 110 years after the business had been established, Rogerschocolates.com was developed in 1995 as a marketing site with basic company information and advertising. The company decided make its website transactional in 1996, and today the website is a full e-commerce site with secure ordering capabilities, Flash-based promotional materials, visual tours, and more. Rogers' Chocolates was an early small business to progress through the major stages of website development.

The website has resulted in e-commerce sales growing rapidly from 1 percent of mail orders in 1996 to 30 percent of mail orders by 1999 and continuing to grow since then. Along with the growth in sales, Rogers has developed a high rate of repeat customers in the business-to-consumer marketplace—a significant factor in becoming profitable.

The internet's growth and the success of the B2C strategy at Rogers led the company to begin development of a B2B strategy as well. The same website is now used to allow potential retailers to contact the company. The wholesale side of Rogers's business grew from just 5 percent of sales in 1989 to over 40 percent of sales by 2004. In addition to utilizing the internet, Rogers uses EDI links with major suppliers and has embraced the capabilities of technology to enhance and improve its business.

The success at Rogers has led to excellent growth in both B2B and B2C markets, increased profile, a global expansion, and development of an important volume of repeat customers. From a mom-and-pop grocery store in 1885 to a successful e-commerce business today, Rogers' Chocolates has shown how a reasonably staged approach can lead even small businesses to capitalize on the internet. In the future the company aims to establish a secure Extranet as well as expand the functionality and services available through the existing website.

Rogers' Chocolates
www.rogerschocolates.com

Questions

1. Why was the transition to e-commerce a smooth one for Rogers' Chocolates?
2. What uses will an extranet have for rogerschocolates.com?
3. What additional services/features could be added to the website?

SOURCES: J. Andrews, "The More Things Change . . . ," *CA Magazine* (March 2000); www.rogerschocolates.com.

to find retailers rather than actually selling their products on the internet. Within each business, considerations such as these need to be thought through so as to avoid unintended consequences. One of the difficulties that is often found when dealing with small business owners, however, is that they tend not to use traditional planning and strategy-setting techniques. Therefore, it is important that consultants, government agencies, and other advisers encourage owners to think about the important issues with regard to going online. The Canadian Snapshots feature below provides another example of an internet startup and some of the issues that arise.

Canadian Snapshots

Velocity Fresh Canadian Clothing—A Pure Play Startup

In 2000, Craig Fraser and Josie Stephens graduated from university, both with BBA degrees, and set out to start their careers. They were bright and full of energy and wanted to do something special. While beginning their job hunt, they became interested in the possibility of selling some of the clothing items that Josie was creating over the internet. After spending many long nights searching for guidance on how to start a new business on the net, they developed a program of action. Through search engines and various sites devoted to helping burgeoning entrepreneurs, they found out about domain names, hosting sites, ISPs, and all they needed to know. Having little start-up money, they took a very small personal loan and used their credit cards for seed capital. They also found ways to obtain hosting and ISP services at little or no cost.

They established a website called www.canadianclothing.ca and began selling clothes with a distinct Canadian twist. As outlined on their website, the concept was to bring a new approach to Canadian clothing:

We believe that clothing is a channel for identifying your-

self and expressing your creativity. Unfortunately, there has never been an urban Canadian clothing brand that Canadians could proudly identify with. If someone wanted to show their pride they had to resort to tacky Canada Day t-shirts with "C A N A D A" blobbed across the front in oversized lettering, and butt-ugly tourist apparel adorned with beavers, Mounties, trees, boats, and miscellaneous sea creatures. Well, this is why we came about. We felt the need to design original, modern clothing that Canadians could wear without feeling like a guest in our own country. Clothing that shows we are confident, unique, and of course, proud. We hope you enjoy wearing our clothing as much as we enjoy creating it!

The company sells t-shirts, hoodies, tank tops, halters, and various accessories, like mittens and scarves.

They found their clothes sold well, and soon the fledgling busi-

ness started to grow and they had a fully functional website with an online catalogue, and an online store that received credit card payments. They found that the deposits required by the banks to set up their own credit card account were too high, so they outsourced the payment function to a provider who was paid a commission.

They soon found that they were receiving orders from various parts of the world, and their street smarts told them they would need to be careful about being paid. After one incident where a European customer didn't pay them, they began to screen their orders carefully before shipping, and in some cases, required payment in advance.

After two years, and after working many very long days for little or no reward, Josie and Craig were able to support themselves with their business and could afford a new apartment in Halifax, Nova Scotia, where they relocated themselves and their business. Now their markets have continued to expand and they are successful entrepreneurs.

Velocity Fresh Canadian Clothing
www.canadianclothing.ca

Questions

1. What would have been the main characteristics of this business that made it successful?
2. What are the pitfalls you would have expected them to encounter?
3. Where should they take this business from where it is now?

Getting Connected

The first step in becoming involved in e-commerce for those small businesses that are not already connected is to establish an internet connection. It is not absolutely necessary for a business to have a connection if all aspects of e-commerce are outsourced, but it would be unlikely that a business could understand e-commerce and take advantage of all of its potential without e-mail and web use within the firm. Numerous alternatives exist for businesses as well as consumers to connect to the internet through an internet service provider (ISP) such as dial-up, cable, ADSL (asymmetrical digital subscriber line), satellite, and other advanced connection forms. In choosing one of the alternatives from an ISP, a small business needs to consider its needs and then balance a number of tradeoffs.

Most of the ISPs, including telephone companies like Bell Telephone or cable companies such as Rogers CableSystems, offer high speed internet connections in urban areas. There are still many rural areas of the country that do not have high speed connections, but can obtain satellite connections through operators such as Bell Expressvu. Such satellite connections generally are high speed only for downloads, not uploads, which still work at telephone modem speeds. However, satellite connections are sometimes the best available if a business operator is located in a rural area. Most businesses would want high speed internet if it is available.

High speed connections through cable or telephone are most often of an "always-on" nature. This means a special modem supplied by the ISP is connected permanently to the owner's computer through which the internet can be accessed at any time without "dialing in." An "always-on" cable or ADSL connection can range from $30 per month and up, depending on the type of service and speed selected. If a business cannot afford to have its phone line frequently tied up or prefers not to purchase an additional line for internet purposes, a permanent, high speed connection is most likely the better choice.

The evaluation of ISPs should begin with a review of the performance and availability factors of the local service providers, including services offered, speed of access, historical reliability, security system performance, and other areas of concern. For some businesses it will be important to select a provider that can supply access outside of the local area without significant complexity or additional cost. For example, a business owner who travels frequently from Calgary to other locations across Canada may wish to select an ISP that has free dial-up connections that can be used with a notebook computer across the country. As with other business expenses, a careful analysis of the available options and a review of the available providers will be helpful in choosing the best alternative for the firm.

Many ISPs exist and the range of services can vary widely. The ISP used to gain access to the internet does not have to be the one used to host the business website. Most ISPs offer a variety of services, including website hosting, but it is wise to research the various hosting sites available, their cost and reliability before making a decision. It may be preferable and less costly to bundle services with one service provider, but this is not always the case. Many Canadian telecommunications companies often bundle their internet and phone packages as well, which can provide a discount for services. An overall review of the needs of the business as the strategy is implemented will be worthwhile. The selection of a service provider is not necessarily a long-term decision and ISPs can often be switched with one month's notice. However, while it is fairly easy to switch the ISP providing internet access, it is not so easy to switch the hosting provider, as it will then be necessary to transfer the website to the new host's server, which may lead to difficulties in the functionality of the site. Most companies must be careful to avoid possible service interruptions and a switch in web hosting can lead to costly outages and downtime.

Domains and Domain Name Registration

Before actually having the website hosted, a business must select and register a domain name. The process of domain name registration is described in chapter 3, and some of the marketing considerations are set out in chapter 11.

The selection of a domain name is extremely important, as this is the name that the company will be known by on the internet, and the name customers and potential customers must use to access the business' website. Ideally it should be one that evokes the name of the business and is easy to remember and to enter into a web browser. Most hosting sites will help with domain name selection and registration.

Getting Hosted

The move online will involve establishing both a website location and a website design. These activities can be performed either internally or may be outsourced depending on the capabilities and goals of the firm. The hosting of an internet site internally requires technologies that many small businesses do not have or wish to invest in; however, many small technology firms do host their own sites due to their expertise in the area. To host a website, the company would require a fast, stable, and permanent internet connection so that users can visit the site at all times. The company would also require high-performance hardware, specific software applications (e.g., web server software), and other technologies such as routers and firewalls. This requirement brings with it a number of concerns such as security risks, system performance, and internal expertise, all of which can be costly issues. Since professional web hosting packages for businesses are now available for less than $20 per month, most small businesses find outsourcing to be the best approach.

Atlantic Canada Home
www.atlanticcanadahome.com

The development of an internet presence will require close communication between the small business and the provider and, similar to other services, service levels can vary significantly. Some providers will develop and host the website, whereas others will offer discounted hosting-only solutions. Atlantic Canada Home (ACH), a diversified provider of products and services worldwide, is a small business based in Charlottetown, Prince Edward Island. The company was founded in 1997 and began to establish a website through outsourcing shortly after being formed. Unfortunately, ACH was completely dissatisfied with the progress and outcome of the website under development and decided to shift the entire contract to another service provider. The new service provider completed the site successfully, and ACH has maintained its relationship with the firm, which continues to host and maintain the site. This example is one that commonly occurs and frequently results in wasted time, frustration, and excess costs.

In identifying a service provider it is critical that owners ask for detailed information on how the project will progress as well as evaluating the types of services provided. The dissatisfaction that occurs in many outsourcing arrangements is due to a misunderstanding between the firms involved—spending more time up front can reduce the likelihood of poor outcomes.

Building the E-Commerce Presence

The implementation of an e-strategy will require the small business to consider numerous issues. Since small businesses are less likely than larger corporations to

Figure 14.1 Building the E-Commerce Presence

The process of developing an e-commerce presence can be broken down into a continuous process of design and improvements.

have their own information technology departments, chances are that a great deal of the work involved in building an e-commerce presence will be outsourced. In addition, small businesses must often continue to service and capitalize on existing markets while attempting to utilize e-commerce opportunities without additional staffing. The result of the unique aspects of small businesses entering into e-commerce is that a staged approach (see figure 14.1) is often adopted, where firms develop a basic website and then later enhance the site with additional features and capabilities. This growth mimics the stages of website evolution discussed in chapter 11.

Online Services for Small Business

The internet offers a wealth of information that can be useful to small business owners. Much of the information available online is free or low in cost. Information available online can be used to evaluate the competition, gain a better understanding of the industry, research tax and other issues, and monitor governmental programs and services.

As with the use of any external sources, it is important that online information is evaluated as to the validity of the source, its timeliness, and its accuracy. The wealth of information can be overwhelming and the process of sifting through it can be very time-consuming. For this reason it is important that web users become familiar with search techniques and develop an understanding of which sources are most relevant to the business. The sources of available information vary widely and can include government, professional firms, media, industry organizations, and many others. See the New Business Models box for an example of a business model built around information and services for small business.

The various governments and governmental organizations in Canada provide a number of useful websites for small businesses. The Strategis site mentioned earlier and in chapter 11 is the federal government resource that includes a wealth of information on numerous topics, including a section called "ebiz.enable" that is targeted to e-business B2B users. The ebiz.enable portal provides users with case studies, statistics, and the ability to ask an expert about issues related to e-business. Several other sections of the Strategis site provide information relevant to e-commerce and small business and include useful guides, information, and data related to such topics as retailing on the internet, e-commerce in service industries, and e-marketing.

New Business Models

Catering to Small Business at Microsoft's Small Business Center

The Small Business Center website is a Microsoft initiative that aims to be an information portal for small businesses and to serve as a sales platform for Microsoft products and services. The site provides articles and columns with a great deal of information for small businesses, such as how to get online, how to market on the web, and how to improve customer service. Other topics include information on preparing business plans, financing business investments, human resources, insurance, and travel. In many of these articles, empha-

sis is placed on Microsoft products and services.

In addition to providing information, the Small Business Center offers an online marketplace where small businesses can purchase goods or list their products for sale on Microsoft-affiliate sites such as MSN. The positive aspect for small businesses about the Small Business Center is that the site is dedicated to showing small businesses how they can use the internet and, of course, Microsoft technology, to allow them to compete against their larger competitors.

The Small Business Center site represents a component of Microsoft's new.Net strategy and promotes the use of "rented" software applications as the company attempts to gain a share of the important application service provider (ASP) market. The Small Business Center offers solutions that assist small businesses with website management, e-commerce, accounting, as well as ERP and CRM. The informational aspect of the Small Business Center aims to inform and educate small business owners and employees while also promoting Microsoft products and services.

Microsoft Small Business Center
www.microsoft.com/smallbusiness

Questions

1. Is a site like Microsoft's Small Business Center truly a valuable service to small businesses or just a marketing effort in disguise? Why?
2. What major benefits do ASPs like the Small Business Center have for small businesses?

SOURCE: www.microsoft.com/smallbusiness.

Another very powerful part of the Strategis site is the "Business Information by Sector" section. This section can provide useful links and information about very specific categories. For example, a crafts business can select the "Giftware" and "Crafts" sections of the Strategis site and be able to find useful contacts by province or region that may assist the company. By simply clicking on the Industry Profiles link on that page, the user can then find a wealth of data on a specific category of giftware such as the Jewellery and Precious Metals industry information. The information contained on Strategis is reliable and detailed and therefore can be beneficial for numerous businesses.

A common theme on the internet is the provision of free information, and many professional service firms have excellent websites for small business owners. For example, accounting firm Grant Thornton LLP has a website that includes a complete section dedicated to owner-managers, with news and advice on a broad range of issues. Some of the "Management issues papers" address important issues that are relevant to small business owners. Many of the major accounting and law firms also provide a large amount of information at no cost that can be of significant value to small businesses.

The media are another major source of information on the internet—including the websites of television and print media as well as online-only media outlets. Some

Grant Thornton LLP
www.grantthornton.ca

newspaper sites such as the *Globe and Mail Online* provide free access to Canadian news content, and television media (for example, CNN Money) allow users to access up-to-date financial news at no cost. Other online media (such as CNET or Wired News) are also great resources for technology and e-business news.

Operating a Small E-Business

Application Service Providers

The explosive growth of internet-based products and services has included the development of application service providers (ASPs) with solutions aimed particularly at small businesses. These ASPs offer services such as accounting systems, website tools, payroll applications, and many others. The benefits of utilizing an ASP include reduced need for internal expertise, software upgrades, and administration.

One notable ASP that has targeted the small business sector is Netsuite, which provides an integrated suite of products that handle accounting/finance, customer relationship management, employee management, and your web presence (see figure 14.2). The Netsuite ASP costs small businesses approximately US$100 per month, depending upon the modules it uses, and provides a system that is extremely powerful, fully web-integrated, and relatively hassle-free. The integration with the web allows small organizations to provide customers with the option to review their account online, pay bills, and submit orders—a service that can be very valuable. In addition, the integration allows a custom web store to be designed using information from the accounting system and to control inventory, pricing, and other issues.

Netsuite
www.netsuite.com

Marketing and Selling

The marketing efforts required by small businesses can capitalize on many of the tools available on the internet. Chapter 11 identified and described many of the marketing and online advertising approaches that can be valuable to small and large businesses. The difficulties small businesses may encounter will include search engine optimization, developing a community, and reaching new markets. The promise of global markets through e-commerce is not untrue, but is commonly misunderstood—since the "build it and they will come" approach doesn't work on the internet, where billions of websites exist. Whereas large organizations may have employees and automated tools monitoring such issues as search engine placement, many small businesses will need to outsource their website redesign or have fewer resources available. Developing an understanding of how major search engines work will help the company draw traffic to its site.

The approaches to marketing will include the use of traditional media and advertising efforts. Many small businesses now include their website address on business cards, packaging, and on brochures that customers may see. The internet allows small businesses to be innovative in their approach to developing existing customer relationships as well as in attracting new customers.

Trading Exchanges and Online Marketplaces

As already discussed in chapter 8, internet-based trading exchanges and marketplaces are an important area where small businesses can market and sell their products or services. Trading exchanges represent a growing market that allows B2B commerce to take place efficiently and effectively online.

Figure 14.2 Illustration of a Small Business ASP

NetSuite business tools allow small businesses to maintain a powerful set of financial records and develop sophisticated e-commerce capabilities with reasonable costs and relative ease.

Canadian trading exchange MERX, for example, specializes in public sector contracts from across Canada. The site, which requires a paid membership, lists daily opportunities from the provincial and federal governments as well as MASH (municipal, academic, school, and hospital) sectors from across Canada. According to MERX, over 80 percent of its customers are small and medium enterprises with less than 50 employees. Another interesting feature of the site is the "document request list" where subscribers can find out what other companies have ordered documents about a particular business opportunity. The potential is obvious: competitors and partnership opportunities can be easily identified.

Trading exchanges are an important medium that small businesses can use to have their products listed along with those of small and large competitors. The key to using trading exchanges for small businesses lies in identifying a strategy for implementation that fits the overall business objectives.

Small businesses that offer numerous products may look to trading exchanges as a means of selling excess products or may use it as a day-to-day sales channel. The key to success is to choose a strategy that the business can support and implement well—with a focus on customer service and profitability. The use of trading exchanges can also be of benefit to service-based businesses as a marketing channel and can result in important sales leads being generated.

Upon devising a strategy for the use of a trading exchange, a company must first determine which exchanges (and how many) they should utilize and then register and become familiar with how they work. The exchanges need to be monitored on an ongoing basis, similar to any other sales channel, to determine what is working and what is not.

Receiving Payment—Credit Card Processing

Accepting credit cards online has come a long way since the early days of the internet. Initially, only the largest online stores were able to process credit card transactions. Today, even very small e-businesses can quickly set up credit card processing for their websites through a variety of banks and merchant account providers. Canadian banks were quite hesitant in the beginning to provide small businesses doing business over the internet with **merchant accounts**, that is, accounts that were able to accept credit card transactions (e.g., Visa and MasterCard). Due to the new nature of e-commerce, many of the banks required small businesses to establish holding accounts of $5000 to $25 000 to ensure that fraudulent transactions would not be defaulted to the bank itself. In addition, some merchant account providers established **holdbacks** of specified amounts, such as 10 percent, that would be held in the holding account for up to six months on a rolling basis to reduce the risk of bad debts and fraudulent credit card use. Another major issue at the early stages of e-commerce, which to some degree exists even today, was the high **discount rate** charged by some merchant account providers. The discount rate is the amount that the merchant account provider takes as a percentage of sales conducted through credit cards. Normally, it would be less than 4 percent. Early online entrepreneurs, however, were sometimes faced with fees of up to 15 percent due to the high perceived risk. As a result, small businesses faced a major reduction in cash flow and were deterred from becoming involved in e-commerce.

Customized services have developed that cater to small business payment processing over the past several years. One example of such a service is InternetSecure Inc., a leading Canadian payment service provider, which established itself as an important alternative for small businesses during the period when it was very difficult to obtain an online merchant account. InternetSecure allows its customers to join the service by paying an enrolment fee, starting at approximately $300, and guarantees them merchant account status without dealing with banks or other service providers. The company looks after all payment processing and offers various methods of approving transactions such as integrated, online approval. Users of the InternetSecure service can choose from a number of packages that offer Canadian and/or U.S. currency support. The discount fee charged by InternetSecure is comparable to those of other merchant account providers. Numerous other payment service providers, who simplify the process of accepting payments compared to traditional bank/merchant account providers, have developed services similar to those offered by InternetSecure.

The banks' response to the pressure from small businesses and other lobby groups has since led to major improvements in merchant accounts. Most of the major banks now offer merchant accounts that allow internet transactions with little or no required holding amounts, as well as additional e-business related services. For example, CIBC has partnered with Global Payments Inc. to provide small businesses, web businesses, and large businesses with the ability to accept credit cards online. In this partnership, CIBC is the merchant account provider and banking solution, while Global Payments offers the technology that allows

MERCHANT ACCOUNT An account held by a business to collect payment through credit cards.

HOLDBACK An amount that credit card companies keep in escrow to reduce the risk of bad debts and fraudulent credit card use.

DISCOUNT RATE The amount that the merchant account provider takes as a percentage of sales conducted through credit cards.

InternetSecure Inc.
www.internetsecure.com

businesses to integrate their e-commerce solution with a secure payment processing technology. This is a common method by which businesses establish their e-commerce systems and allow a company that specializes in transaction processing to handle that end of payment processing.

The growth of e-commerce and demand for payment-processing mechanisms has given way to a wide variety of services being developed. The important features for small businesses to consider in selecting a payment-processing system are ease of integration, currency, and security. If the site is being outsourced or developed in-house, it is important that the payment mechanism can be easily integrated with the shopping cart or purchasing mechanism the website uses. Some services, such as the Canada Post Sell Online solution for small businesses, provide an easily integrated shopping cart technology. The Canada Post service is provided in partnership with Clic.net and allows web designers to simply cut and paste customized HTML codes into their website to integrate the shopping cart and payment process. Services such as this allow even novice web designers to create powerful, integrated e-commerce sites.

The ability to deal in multiple currencies can be of importance to online retailers operating in global markets. It is not necessary to deal in foreign currencies, but some Canadian businesses have found that allowing their U.S. customers to make purchases with the American dollar resulted in increased sales. For this reason it is important when establishing a merchant account to give consideration to the currencies that will be accepted and how they will be handled. Although credit card processing is only one small component of an e-commerce presence, it is one that is of critical importance and should be fully considered as an e-strategy is being developed. The time involved in establishing a merchant account can also be several weeks for many businesses and therefore this process should be commenced early.

Procurement

The purchase of goods and services online by small businesses represents another important aspect for an e-strategy. The number of firms, both large and small, that are targeting goods and services to small businesses through their own websites as well as through trading exchanges, affiliate sites, and other means, has grown substantially as the internet has evolved. This growth has resulted in fierce competition in many areas, thus leading to cost reductions and opportunities for the small business owner.

Small businesses can acquire a wide range of products and services online, from office supplies and computers to internet services like web design and hosting. The key to the use of e-procurement in small business is to evaluate the market and then negotiate prices (with local suppliers if they are preferred). For example, Staples (and many other firms) offers many office supply products online, where the small businesses can review the prices easily and then demand lower prices from an existing local supplier. Other savings, especially time savings, can also be achieved by using e-procurement to acquire goods through the internet, by creating electronic processes, and by using technological tools to speed up the entire process.

Training

The implementation of an e-commerce initiative may also require training for employees. The amount and type of training that will be required will vary by organization according to its size, the type of strategy being pursued, the level of internal expertise required, and the owner–manager's commitment. The implementation of any e-commerce activities should at least be accompanied by basic training sessions that provide employees with an understanding of how the company's own website works, what it offers, and the impact on internal processes so they can effectively deal with customers. In many circumstances it is also beneficial to offer employees general internet training as well, so they may evaluate competitors, understand the industry, and possibly make useful suggestions. The necessity for internet training is declining as internet use become more widespread but is still of benefit within many organizations.

Training efforts may also be necessitated by the adoption of e-commerce, depending upon the technologies being utilized and the level of outsourcing being used. For example, a business may decide to outsource initial website development but train employees to maintain the site and make minor modifications. In this instance an employee or a few employees may be trained in basic website design principles using an HTML editor. The key to training efforts is to ensure that employees are comfortable with and understand the technologies being employed and understand the business processes related to the e-commerce initiative.

Challenges to E-Commerce for Small Business

The small business sector in Canada has been relatively slow to adopt e-commerce and the use of the internet despite the growth of online commerce. Small businesses are often characterized by the ability to adapt to change quickly and to be innovative, which has created some confusion over their limited adoption of e-commerce. Many studies have concluded that the development of e-commerce in Canadian small businesses has been slower than that in other countries, particularly the United States, and is therefore a concern for the entire economy. The slow development of e-commerce in the small business sector can be attributed to several barriers, notably technological, financial, organizational, and operational barriers.

Technological Challenges

The technological barriers to e-commerce for small business continue to evolve as technology and the internet evolve. Initially, poor internet access combined with other factors was one of the major barriers to e-commerce. However, internet access and technology in general have declined in cost and Canada is now one of the most connected countries in the world.

The common barrier to technology within small businesses is often cited as a lack of knowledge of computers, the internet, and technology internally. Small business owners are often very pressed for time just to deal with the core aspects of the business and therefore cannot dedicate time to learning about technologies not considered of crucial importance to the business. The growth of e-commerce has, however, brought attention to the importance of the internet and sparked the interest of many small businesses.

The complexity of becoming involved in e-commerce is often overstated and misunderstood. Many small business owners interviewed in research studies have indicated that the task of becoming involved in e-commerce seemed too technical and they lacked internal expertise.[8] However, as described in this chapter and throughout this book, it is possible to become involved in e-commerce with only limited technology skills, and many skills can be learned quickly through practice. As businesses increase in size, it becomes more likely that an internal individual may have the capability to implement and manage an e-commerce strategy. Therefore, those small businesses at the upper end of the scale (with 75 to 100 employees) and medium-sized enterprises (those with 100 to 500 employees) are more likely than the smaller enterprises to be involved in e-commerce.

Financial Challenges

Small businesses and many large businesses must balance their financial investments across numerous activities, and e-commerce investments to date have often been considered a non-essential investment. As owners are learning the importance of developing an e-commerce strategy and an internet presence, the costs associated with the investment need to be considered. The costs of implementing an e-commerce strategy can vary widely and may include costs for hardware, software, web design, training, outsourcing, or internet access.

Organizational Challenges

The introduction of change into a small organization is likely to cause as much anxiety, confusion, and resistance as in large organizations. The major difference for small organizations is that if the owner is promoting the change it is much more likely to be accepted than if a manager is promoting change in a large business. If the owner is not the leader of change, however, small businesses may run into many of the difficulties experienced by large ones in implementing new technologies and making business process changes.

The keys to overcoming the organizational barrier of e-commerce implementation are leadership and communication. The owner–manager is in a strong position to positively affect change if he or she is able to clearly communicate the plan to employees. Employees must understand what implications e-commerce will have on the organization as well as their own job responsibilities. The industry, organization size, and many other factors will also influence the changes necessary to become a small "e" business.

Operational Challenges

The small business sector can often experience difficulty in dealing with the operational aspects of becoming an e-business. The impact that establishing an e-commerce strategy has on everyday operations may include global issues, fulfillment and logistics needs, hours of operation issues, and several other necessary changes. These issues should all be thought through before the decision to pursue e-commerce is being made.

The impact on everyday business operations can be tied into the organizational issues if employees are not prepared for the changes that are likely to occur. For example, the introduction of a B2C e-commerce website by a manufacturing company may require a complete change in the fulfillment and shipping area of the firm. This could lead to employee dissatisfaction and result in poor performance in the traditional market, the new market, or both. In establishing the e-strategy, small businesses must attempt to plan for all impacts of the implementation on operations.

Other potential issues could include language and cultural barriers if operations are expanding globally, as well as currency exchange issues. The types of problems will largely depend upon the operations of the firm prior to its e-commerce activities. For example, businesses with an established catalogue or 1-800 sales channel will often find the move to e-commerce simpler, since the delivery channel is already well established, customer service representatives are trained and knowledgeable, and comfort exists with selling to customers who are not present at the retail outlet. The type of industry and product or service will substantially impact the operational issues that the organization will face.

Chapter Summary

E-commerce represents a significant opportunity for small businesses. Not only does the internet allow small businesses to increase market reach, but it can also provide them with an opportunity to gather a wealth of valuable information. In addition, the use of the internet to conduct operational processes such as procurement and billing represents a great opportunity for small businesses to reduce their costs.

Developing a strategy for small business e-commerce requires planning and analysis similar to any other business decision. The small business must determine what opportunities exist, what costs need to be incurred, and what level of management's involvement will be required. The major issues that small businesses may have to address include overcoming technical weaknesses and ensuring that the costs involved are justified by expected outcomes.

Small businesses may use the internet to gather competitive intelligence and other useful data or for other purposes. For example, the number of services available to small businesses is expanding rapidly and they can "rent" applications from application service providers or take advantage of other online tools. The internet has assisted in reducing the in-house technical requirements for many small businesses by converting much software into simple point-and-click solutions.

The e-commerce strategy and presence for a small business can take numerous forms. The website can be a simple "brochureware" page or, with reasonable costs, can become a fully transactional online presence. The small business must determine which strategy is most appropriate for its industry and customer base. The level of e-commerce use by small businesses will continue to grow as the use of the internet by individuals and businesses becomes more commonplace.

Key Terms

discount rate *[p. 305]*   merchant account   *[p. 305]*
holdback   *[p. 305]*

Tools for Online Learning

To help you master the material in this chapter and stay up to date with new developments in e-business, visit **www.pearsoned.ca/trites**. Resources include:

■ Review Questions and Exercises

■ Problems for Discussion

■ Recommended Readings

■ Updates to Case Studies and Textual Material

■ Streaming CBC Videos with Cases

Endnotes

1. InnovaQuest, "The State of Electronic Commerce in Atlantic Canada," Atlantic Canada Opportunities Agency, March 2000.

2. Jim Carroll and Rick Broadhead, *Small Business Online* (Toronto: Prentice Hall, 1998).

3. J. Davis, "Mom and Pop Go Online," *InfoWorld* (May 28, 2001).

4. Jim Carroll and Rick Broadhead, *Small Business Online* (Toronto: Prentice Hall, 1998).

5. Jim Carroll and Rick Broadhead, *Small Business Online* (Toronto: Prentice Hall, 1998).

6. Sarah McCue, "Small Firms and the Internet: Force or Farce?" *International Trade Forum* 1 (1999): 27.

7. Jim Carroll and Rick Broadhead, *Small Business Online* (Toronto: Prentice Hall, 1998), 180.

8. G. Hunter, M. Diochon, D. Pugsley, and B. Wright, "Small Business Adoption of Information Technology: Unique Challenges," Proceedings of the Information Resources Management Association 2001 Conference.

Privacy and Legal Issues

When people do business with each other using eBay, they need to enter personal information into the system. One of the concerns of many customers is what happens to this information. They are concerned that it might be given out to other people without their consent. Because these concerns need to be addressed, eBay established a privacy policy which sets out the position of the organization with regard to information collected from customers during their involvement with eBay.

Privacy at eBay

To do business on eBay, users must be over eighteen years old and have a valid e-mail address. To buy or sell, users must register with their e-mail address, name, address, and phone number and accept a user agreement. To complete their registration, the user must specify a password and a method of payment. This is essentially the minimum amount of information that would be necessary to complete business transactions.

eBay tracks the URL, browser software, and the IP address of participants. To do so, it uses "session" cookies (which are cookies that expire at the end of a session) and collects information about the bidding and selling behaviour of individuals as well as feedback about them from other users. Users are free to decline cookies if they wish. In other words, eBay does not use cookies that gather information about their users when they are not online with eBay (known as spyware).

If the user establishes a credit account, additional information is gathered, including their billing address and such information as banking arrangements. A personal file on each user contains messages posted on bulletin boards and correspondence with the company. The company reserves the right to disclose information about a person to law enforcement or other government officials, if necessary or appropriate for an investigation of fraud, intellectual property infringements, or other illegal activities.

eBay provides aggregated information about user behaviour to advertisers without identifying individuals. Provision of aggregate information is usually not a concern, but the provision of individual information is, and eBay does have a policy of providing the information to others. For example, individuals are assigned a user ID so others can observe their activities. Since the user ID is the person's e-mail address, this information may also lead to unsolicited e-mail being sent to an individual. eBay also sometimes provides personal information to its subsidiaries or joint ventures, which it says have similar privacy policies. In addition, users who register on an eBay co-branded external service provider grant eBay permission to pass their e-mail address back to that service provider. These service providers can have different privacy policies that eBay has no control over and does not necessarily endorse.

When users register with eBay and then carry out transactions, eBay collects a good deal of information about them. Through the agreements that the users accept when they interact with the eBay website, eBay receives considerable latitude in selling and using that information for commercial purposes. It does this through setting the default on the agreements in the registration process to "yes." This means that when the users accept the agreements, they must specifically change the answers to "no," otherwise they are agreeing to the sale or sharing of their information. Naturally, users may not be aware of what the agreement says if they do not read it carefully in detail when they accept it, so they may be agreeing to something of which they are not aware. This includes the sale of the information to telemarketers. Numerous other websites also employ this technique.

In a survey carried out by the *New York Times* in 2000, most internet users listed privacy as their main reason for not shopping online. To make it worse, 92 percent of the users said they do not trust online companies to keep their information private, no matter what they say. This would indicate that even though many websites, including eBay, publish privacy policies, many people simply do not believe them, or do not believe they will be carried out as stated. This indicates a need for assurance, such as webtrust, on these policies. Some surveys have indicated very strongly that users place more confidence in a company's privacy statements if there is assurance provided on them by an independent party.

eBay is a licensee of TRUSTe and has a TRUSTe seal on its site, which indicates that it follows their requirements. The user agreement specifies that eBay has wide latitude in collecting and using information gathered about participants. If a person wants to be a registered eBay user, he or she must agree with this policy. In other words, users are deprived of the choice and consent over how their personal information is used for secondary purposes unrelated to the transaction being conducted, and have little control over the use and distribution of this information.

eBay's well-known feedback rating system, which is intended to assist customers in evaluating whether to do business with another party, also presents privacy concerns. eBay has no control over the feedback generated by participants, even if it is offensive, harmful, inaccurate, or deceptive. Even in such cases, a customer cannot post a reply, or defend his or her reputation except through a court order. eBay's policy is quite rigid about this. Feedback is removed only under exceptional circumstances, such as when a court order is actually obtained, or the feedback makes negative reference to eBay or police investigations, or is part of a campaign of harassment.

Participants in the eBay process also gather information about other participants. In their agreement with eBay, they agree not to use this information except for auction-related communications. But eBay has no control over the information or how it is used. And, since eBay does not control it and it is gathered by the participants, it is not at all clear even who owns the information.

Auction aggregators operate by connecting their sites to numerous other auction sites. Moreover, they use data mining tools that enable their users to search other auction sites for the best deal on a given good. At one point, eBay sued the auction aggregator, Bidder's Edge Inc., for stealing private information, based on the presumption that eBay owned the information. However, Bidder's

Edge responded in a countersuit that it was simply collecting public data as a service to its customers. In 2001, Bidder's Edge settled the lawsuit with eBay and ceased operations.

Privacy Assurance Services

TRUSTe and BBB*OnLine* were among the first to provide privacy assurance. WebTrust, which is offered by professional acccounting firms, is a competitor, although it is much more expensive to implement. On the other hand, the firms that offer this service, such as KPMG and Ernst and Young, have proven reputations and established expertise in the assurance business.

TRUSTe and BBB*OnLine* have similar requirements to each other. To be eligible, websites must comply with certain principles regarding privacy programs. The right of users to choose and consent to how their personal information is used and shared is one of these principles. Other principles involve posting a privacy policy, and disclosure about the collection and use of personal information, use of cookies, and third party use of cookies to collect data on the website.

TRUSTe monitors its licensees' compliance with their posted privacy policies and certain program requirements. Such monitoring includes periodic website reviews and online community monitoring. TRUSTe also addresses privacy complaints and enquiries and requires its licensees to cooperate with its procedures. A significant problem with TRUSTe's approach is that it only requires compliance with the stated privacy procedures of the licensee, and since the policies can vary widely from company to company, the seal can represent widely different standards of practice.

With WebTrust, this is not the case, as companies who wish to display the WebTrust seal must meet the standards set out in www.webtrust.org, which are quite rigorous. The professional accounting firm that provides the seal conducts an audit to determine whether the subject company is in compliance with the standards and then gives the seal after this examination. This is why the WebTrust seal is so much more expensive that the others. A further complication, however, is that the WebTrust seal also covers other services, such as business practices and security, so there is a potential to confuse consumers about which WebTrust seals relate to privacy and which do not.

Although eBay does not give its users a choice about how their personal information is used for secondary purposes, which violates both TRUSTe and WebTrust standards, it can still display a TRUSTe seal because it must only comply with its stated policies. It would have to change its procedures to obtain a WebTrust seal.

While technically, TRUSTe users must comply with TRUSTe policies, there is no record of TRUSTe having ever revoked a privacy seal, despite known violations by TRUSTe participants. On the other hand, the rate of compliance by TRUSTe's clients is high in disclosing their privacy policy, use of cookies, and use of third-party cookies. Moreover, they normally tend to have a high quality of stated privacy policy.

Some of the big accounting firms offer their own seal, some based on the WebTrust model. PriceWaterhouseCoopers, for example, offers a product called the BetterWeb seal. Ernst & Young, however, provides both WebTrust and its own CyberProcess Certification (CPC) seal, thus covering both a generalized seal and a proprietary one, but potentially splintering the WebTrust market. CPC allows management to choose its own assertions (like TRUSTe) and then Ernst & Young will provide a CPC seal.

Jamal, Maier, and Sunder (2002) programmed a web crawler to visit 100 high-traffic websites and record the cookies used by each site. Surveys indicated that users were worried about being tracked by cookies, particularly by third-party cookies used by online advertisers such as DoubleClick, which aggregate data from hundreds of websites to create user profiles for marketing purposes. Jamal, Maier, and Sunder found that all websites with a privacy seal from TRUSTe or BBB*OnLine* had posted their privacy policy and that it was easy to find. These sites all disclosed their use of cookies; 88 percent of them explained what cookies are and what information they collect, and 56 percent even explained how to turn off or monitor the cookies. Almost all (97 percent) of the sites that used third-party cookies disclosed their practices and 63 percent provided a link to the privacy policy of the third party or a link to opt-out of the third-party cookie. This rate of compliance is remarkably high, and significantly better than websites without a web seal.

In summary, there is a variety of trust seals available to provide people with some assurance about the privacy policies followed by the sites they use. eBay provides a TRUSTe seal, but this must be interpreted in the context of the current state of practice in the field of trust seals for privacy. WebTrust provides a standard for the policies and this is closely examined by the professional firms that provide the seals. On the other hand, the high quality of privacy policies and actual disclosure practices by TRUSTe and BBB*OnLine* clients seem to indicate a reasonable degree of protection is provided by these services. The accounting firms have a high degree of expertise in setting standards and performing assurance services; however, they tend to be more expensive than the other services.

Questions for Discussion:

1. Why does eBay need a privacy policy?
2. How well does the policy appear to protect the rights of the eBay users and meet their legitimate concerns?
3. What are the advantages and disadvantages of obtaining an assurance report on the privacy policy?
4. What improvements, if any, should be made to eBay's privacy policy?

cars4u Ltd.

History

Carriage Automotive Group Inc. has been in the automotive industry for over 30 years. They have seen the industry change many times in the past but knew that there would be many more changes ahead. As internet technologies increased, consumers were demanding more from industry retailers and some were towards online purchasing, due to its convenience. Carriage understood that with so much emphasis being placed on technology prior to the new millennium, there would be some potential for more competitive risk associated with the emergence of e-commerce. The reasoning was that businesses were investing in more sophisticated technologies. These new technologies allow car dealerships easier access to e-commerce capabilities, enabling them to compete in new ways. Carriage Automotive Group Inc. believed that manufacturers were going to help drive e-commerce in the automotive industry by being able to deal directly with the consumer through the internet, and in turn, being able to reduce costs and increase savings for the consumer.

As a result of these changes, Carriage decided that they would need to be able to offer their products and services online. They felt that it wasn't enough for a dealership to simply have a website. Consumers who were able to reach them via the internet would want the opportunity to use this medium for the whole purchasing process. Following Carriage's strategic decision to enter the e-business market, the business chose to change its name to cars4U Ltd.

When cars4U launched its website (www.cars4U.com) on September 6, 2000, it became the first online car dealership in Canada that allowed consumers the opportunity to purchase or lease a vehicle online at a competitive price. All necessary actions could be handled online, from research (prices, features, etc.) to payment and delivery arrangements. The site, although accessible worldwide, only offered online purchases to the Ontario region.

Since its launch, cars4U has had over one million hits, and it received over 200 orders within the first nine months of operation, putting it on track to exceed the annual volume of the average Canadian dealership.

SOURCE: This case was prepared by Myra Cholmondeley, April Wells, and Yves Leblond under the supervision of Professor David Pugsley for the sole purpose of providing material for classroom discussion. The authors do not intend to illustrate either effective or ineffective handling of a managerial situation.

The Process

One of the issues faced in e-commerce is developing an attractive website, one that is easily navigated by consumers. Even more importantly, if customers are serious about a purchase, they usually want to complete transactions quickly and without any inconvenience.

cars4U's website is simple as well as appealing. When searching for a car, the consumers have three options. They can either search for a specific make and model, search for a car that meets specific characteristics, or they can begin their search through a workbook. The purpose of a workbook is to allow consumers a secure area to save personal vehicle profiles, which makes it easier to compare prices and features each time they visit the site.

Once the consumer indicates the make, model, and price they are looking for, the site automatically lists and displays the vehicles currently available. To compensate for models that are currently unavailable, they have a section called "coming soon," which describes the new models that will be available at cars4U in the near future.

Once a vehicle is chosen, the customer can then customize it by simply browsing a list of options and checking those they wish to include on their vehicle. The vehicle is then priced automatically, where every component of the final price, including Canadian taxes, appears on the left side of the screen. The right side, which holds both lease and finance calculators, gives consumers the opportunity to compare the two payment options, as well as try out different terms, rates, and down payments.

cars4U offers financing through four or five financial institutions. The calculators automatically offer the most attractive terms available from this collection of lenders. This provides less hassle for the consumer, because the price customers see is the price they will get. This also avoids the negotiations that some consumers face when they buy at the usual dealer locations. After clicking the cash, the finance, or the lease button on the bottom of the pricing page, the consumer puts down a refundable $350 deposit using a credit card, which completes the loan application. There is also a real-time chat room available at this point where customers can get quick answers to any questions or concerns. cars4U then locates the vehicle and contacts the buyer for purchase verification and approval. Once the buyer gives the go-ahead, the deposit becomes non-refundable. Consumers can take delivery, either at the dealership, at their home, or at their office.

Supply Chain Management

For cars4U to be able to offer consumers the opportunity to purchase online, without any problems, they need full participation from their suppliers. To accomplish a close-knit relationship with its suppliers, cars4U has purchased several physical dealerships. These dealerships allow them to maintain good relations with the manufacturer, which is necessary in allowing them to offer consumers the best possible price.

cars4U owns Chrysler, Acura, and Honda dealerships within Ontario. They also have various other affiliate dealerships that provide them with particular makes and models not available at these dealerships. cars4U has established a close relationship with their affiliate dealers.

Currently, they allow these dealers to become a part of cars4U free of charge. At the same time, cars4U gets a percentage of the profit from each sale. This way, each dealer gets more exposure on the web, which increases both affiliate dealers and cars4U's revenues.

The Business Model

cars4U online follows a model that allows the customer to be in control, by providing comfort, convenience, and choice. cars4U Ltd. found that clients feel they are not in control in a traditional dealer environment, but are rather at the mercy of the seller. "For the first time in automotive dealing in Canada, the consumer has control over a process they never had control over before," said Barry Shafran, cars4U's CEO. Lilly Buchwitz, the very first customer of cars4U, certainly agreed. She knew she wanted a new Volkswagen. But she had neither the time, nor the inclination, to visit a dealer and haggle over price. "I don't believe anyone enjoys haggling over a car," she said. "It just really fills you with dread."

cars4U is also able to increase sales opportunities by giving consumers the chance to shop 24 hours a day, seven days a week, all year long. Over holiday seasons, Canadians take advantage of the fact that the cars4U's e-dealer never closes. In its first season, as many orders were placed with cars4U in December and January as there were in the previous three months. This growth was even more striking given that December and January are typically the slowest months of the year for automotive retailing. As well, spending on advertising in these two months was substantially reduced from previous levels.

In addition to providing customers with the opportunity to shop around the clock, cars4U has also improved the efficiency of its internal business processes. The whole process of ordering a vehicle now takes just a few minutes and delivery takes only a little longer than a week, if the specific vehicle is available in the manufacturer's inventory.

In the long term, as they continue to develop their business model, it may also allow cars4U to develop greater cost effectiveness by reducing concessions. For instance, by reducing costs, cars4U may eventually be able to afford more extensive delivery for consumers. Large numbers of orders would make neighbourhood truck delivery possible, straight from the factory to personal homes. However, their current model is to start a new distribution centre, which aims not to replace traditional car dealerships but rather to develop new sales channels online. This can be accomplished by targeting those customers who are looking for more comfort, convenience, and choice and are willing to shop online.

Strategy

cars4U Ltd. is moving from a 30-year old bricks-and-mortar company to a complete clicks-and-mortar organization. To finance for growth, the company went public on the Toronto Stock Exchange in May 2000.

The corporate strategy chosen by cars4U online was "launch and learn." To be the first online car dealership in Canada, cars4U's management chose to launch an incomplete site on September 6, 2000, one that was not totally integrated. However, this launch and learn strategy allowed cars4U to be the first online car dealer based in Canada. This decision was influenced by such competitors as Carpoint.ca (now Sympatico.MSN.ca Autos), the little brother of Carpoint owned by Microsoft (now MSN Autos), and Megawheel.com, which was also in the starting blocks for this type of e-commerce. cars4U felt that being the original automotive e-business in Canada would be a significant benefit to them. They hoped this would influence customers in perceiving them as being the most experienced leader in the industry.

cars4U Ltd.'s divisions, bricks-and-mortar and online, aim to satisfy consumers in their automotive investments through both quality products and services. cars4U realized that although both of its divisions share the same goals, they follow very different strategies to achieve these goals. Their bricks-and-mortar strategy involves expanding their physical dealership network to further satisfy consumers who are not comfortable with the e-business concept. On the other hand, cars4U's online strategy is to offer customers more comfort and efficiency by enabling them to make their choices conveniently in the comfort of their own home or office.

cars4U decided they had to maintain and continue to expand their bricks-and-mortar business. The reason for this decision was to maintain customer loyalty with those consumers who enjoy the experience of visiting and buying from new car dealerships. For instance, their Acura dealership was acquired in November 1999, only a few months before launching their e-business division.

The pricing structure online follows a different strategy than pricing in their traditional dealerships. cars4U stresses that the customer is in control because they do not have to worry about haggling and pricing when shopping online. The price they see is the price they get. As indicated by Lilly Buchwitz, their price was $700 cheaper than the lowest price quoted by any traditional dealer she visited. How does cars4U make money, offering such discounts? It's a matter of perception. This firm gives customers a fixed price, unlike traditional car dealers, where staff members "structure" sales according to how much they think they can get.

Advertising and Promotion

Another major issue facing cars4U was that of advertising and promotion. Since they have two separate business models for each of their divisions, they needed to develop a strategy that would promote their new online store while not giving a negative return to their physical dealerships. Advertising and promotion strategy was designed to centre around being Canada's first ever e-dealer. During the first quarter of 2001, cars4U invested $450 000 on advertising. Because of this investment, they experienced a $212 000 loss compared to their $68 353 net earnings during the first quarter of 2000. cars4U plans to continue advertising but feels they must develop a marketing strategy that will result in an overall profit for the cars4U's online and bricks-and-mortar divisions.

Privacy and Security

When trying to tackle the issues that are relevant to consumers, cars4U had to spend a significant amount of effort on security and privacy concerns. Due to the issues of fraud and hacking, it is in the best interest of the consumer to be sure that they shop only on secure sites. cars4U has outlined several areas where they have taken precautionary steps to help make their site more secure and trustworthy, outlined in a privacy statement posted on their website.

All financial information is kept completely confidential. Only information that is necessary in processing the customer's order will be made available to additional parties. These parties may include the alliance dealership that supplies the customer's vehicle, the credit card company, or the institution that finances or leases their new vehicle purchase.

When placing an order, cars4U requires the customer's name, e-mail address, mailing address, and phone number so that they can contact the customer regarding their order and delivery. This information ensures that the customer is located in an area that cars4U can service. Unfortunately, cars4U does not service areas outside of Ontario. After the customer has placed an order, cars4U will require the customer's driver's licence number, insurance company, and policy number.

While cars4U does indicate that they may provide aggregate statistics about their customers, sales, traffic patterns, and related site information to reputable third-party vendors, they ensure that no personally identifying or financially sensitive information will be passed on.

When a consumer places an order or accesses their account information, cars4U uses a secure server to transfer the data back to them. The secure server software is designed to provide encrypted communications on the internet.

All information a consumer sends through the internet is encrypted before it is sent to cars4U to reduce the likelihood of unauthorized access. cars4U maintains secure data networks protected by industry-standard backups, such as firewalls and password-protection systems. These software investments protect against the loss, misuse, and alteration of the information.

Conclusion

Barry Shafram, the CEO of cars4U, was quite pleased with the progress of their new online division. He knew, however, that there were many challenges ahead to gain a strong position in the market. For example, the company has been criticized for expanding its "bricks" operations as it expands online. In addition, increasing competition from U.S. sites like Carpoint, which were well financed and growing quickly, were causing some concerns over growth and market share. Barry Shafram needs some innovative ideas on how to strengthen cars4U's e-business.

Discussion Questions

1. Does the continued growth of cars4U's "bricks" presence make sense for an online company?
2. What alternatives could cars4U pursue instead of increasing its dealership network?
3. What can cars4U do to fight off competition from U.S. competitors?
4. How can the company develop an advertising strategy that builds on both the online and offline divisions?
5. cars4U would like to expand its operations. Should the company expand nationally or provincially and why? What about global or U.S. opportunities?
6. Read the cars4U website and comment on how the company has developed since its inception.

Monster Inc.

It was almost midnight on January 31, 2001, the eve of Monster.com's quarterly board meeting, and Chief Executive Officer Jeff Taylor continued to wrestle with what position he would present to the board in less than twelve hours. Monster, the flagship brand of Monster Worldwide Inc., sat at a momentous point in its six-year existence. Over the past several months, user levels had reached record highs, due in large part to the massive advertising efforts as well as numerous strategic partnerships with major online portals and expansion into new parts of the globe. Taylor had been the driving force behind these efforts to generate awareness and was now confident that he had achieved these objectives well beyond what he had expected.

Taylor had spent the past two weeks preparing two different proposals for the upcoming meeting, one of which he would present to the board. Which one, however, would be a last minute decision. Taylor saw Monster as being at a crossroads in its life. Since its inception, like most internet companies, Monster had operated at a loss, focused on its long-term growth. This successful stage led him to assert that perhaps 2001 would be the year to cut back on its expansion plans and focus on turning a profit. On the other hand, however, Taylor saw more potential for untapped markets and further advertising initiatives and considered that maybe now was not the time to put a halt to this operating strategy. He decided that he would examine all relevant evidence one more time and then arrive at a decision.

The Arrival of Online Recruiting

Monster is the flagship brand of Monster Worldwide Inc. Founded in 1967, Monster Worldwide, Inc., with more than 5000 employees in 26 countries in December of 2004, is the online recruitment leader, the world's largest recruitment advertising agency network, and one of the world's largest search and selection agencies. Monster Worldwide, Inc., headquartered in New York, is also the world's largest yellow page advertising agency and a provider of direct marketing services. The company's clients include more than 90 of the Fortune 100 and approximately 465 of the Fortune 500 companies.

SOURCE: This case was prepared by James Blackburn, Maher Markabi, and Arlene Pino under the supervision of Professor David Pugsley for the sole purpose of providing material for classroom discussion. The authors do not intend to illustrate either effective or ineffective handling of a managerial situation.

Based in Maynard, Massachusetts, Monster.com is the leading global careers website with 10.1 million unique visits per month, attracting nearly three times as many visitors per month as its chief competitor, HotJobs.com. It is a global online recruiting network, connecting worldwide companies with various interested employees.

Monster was retooled in January of 1999 as a result of a merger of The Monster Board (www.monster.com) and Online Career Center, founded in 1994 and 1993 respectively. The Monster global network consists of local content and language sites in 15 countries including the United States, United Kingdom, Australia, Canada, the Netherlands, Singapore, and France.

Yahoo! HotJobs: Monster's Direct Competitor

Yahoo! HotJobs is a leading career search site on the web. It earns revenues through monthly subscription fees from its 8000-plus business users, and the company is looking to boost the software-based services it offers to allow companies to manage the recruitment process from the desktop. HotJobs possesses global career portals in the United States, Canada, and Australia. The home page has links for 26 career channels, including entry-level jobs, positions with startups, and a new channel for job seekers fresh out of college. HotJobs expects that positive results are imminent with the implementation of a new headhunter database as well as general improvements to the site itself in late 2001. HotJobs is also quick to call attention to the fact that their clientele is not merely internet companies but also major international corporate players, including 80 of the Fortune 100.

Like many other dot-com companies, HotJobs relies on the importance of offline advertising, with Super Bowl ads constituting a major portion of their ad budget. Approximately US$2.4 million was spent for three pre-game spots and one during the Super Bowl XXXV game itself. It projected its advertising expenses to be approximately US$40 million in 2001, the same as the previous year.

Managers at HotJobs believe that they could strengthen their company's credibility and acknowledgment through strong offline advertising and growing word-of-mouth support. They also clearly understand the perpetual power of television. Like Monster, New York-based HotJobs.com targets an array of job seekers. At one point, HotJobs's outdoor and print campaign reflects a new, optimistic tagline: "Onward, upward." However, Marc Karasu, director of advertising at HotJobs.com, believes that television slots are key for developing an overall brand. "Outdoor ads work in conjunction with the television campaign," says Karasu.

HotJobs is also trying to target a great number of university and college students, as it kicked off a 75-campus campaign late in January of 2001. Under a partnership with Student Advantage, HotJobs has established a presence at big campus events, such as homecoming day.

A continuous objective of HotJobs is to improve its site by adding new and innovative services that would provide more convenience to its customers. Shopping carts and company blocking are just a couple of additional services that were included to target more customer expediency.

A driving force behind the success of online recruiting companies, like Monster and HotJobs, is their ability to offer more than the traditional offline recruiting services, such as newspapers, as well as operate with much lower expenses. This has allowed HotJobs to construct profitability forecasts with greater accuracy. Recently HotJobs announced that, in an effort to streamline operations and attain greater profits, they plan to cut approximately 15 percent of their work-force, or about 100 people.

Making a Name for Itself: Advertising Strategy

As a result of the increasing number of dot-com failures, online companies are developing a saner approach to online advertising. Leaders in online advertising continue to achieve customer loyalty and solid brand awareness by delivering superior services to their clients and customers, encouraging repeat purchases of goods and services. According to a report published in 2000 by the Internet Advertising Bureau (IAB), internet advertising is continually growing with revenues up 8.8 percent in the second quarter and this US$2.1 billion in revenue was 127.3 percent of the same quarter in 1999. For online recruiting firms, Monster clearly appears to be the market leader. In March 2001, "Monster.com maintained its strong-hold, with a reach of 5.7 percent, an average of 38.6 pages viewed per user, and a power ranking (1) of 220."[1] This ranking is five times that of its closest competitor. Monster has a 44 percent quarterly revenue growth rate and currently accounts for 12 percent of Monster Worldwide's revenue. As well, Monster is the 82nd most visited domain on the internet.

Over the past several years, the method of internet advertising has remained relatively constant. Banner ads account for 50 percent of online ads while e-mail ads capture only about 2 percent of online advertising. Online companies are beginning to realize the importance of offline advertising as well, moving to television advertising and other methods. As the most widely viewed annual event, the National Football League's Super Bowl is considered a powerful advertising tool. CBS reported that approximately 135 million people viewed the event this past January. But because airtime costs US$2 million per 30-second spot, advertisers must make sure that their marketing campaign generates a return on their investment. The most important thing for Super Bowl advertisers was to make sure that it's really your company that is talked about, and not just a catchy ad. It's easy to be caught up in the entertainment and lose sight of brand recognition. Often, there are many great ads during the Super Bowl, but people do not remember what they were the next day. The number of dot-com advertisers dropped from 17 to just 3 from Super Bowl XXXIV to Super Bowl XXXV. This year, both Monster and HotJobs spent millions on 30-second ads during the broadcast in the hopes of attracting new clients to their electronic resumes. For Monster, advertising during the Super Bowl paid off. Traffic peaked in the 24 hours following the Super Bowl, as 2.2 million job searches were conducted, up from half a million the week before. And about 40 000 job-seekers posted their resumes on Monster the week after.

Monster's advertising division has proposed an advertising budget of US$200 million in 2001 on their advertising campaign, centred on five TV spots, doubling the US$100 million spent last year. A move to spend US$200 million would contradict other dot-com's strategies to pull back from ad spending. Monster's strategic advertising plan focuses on the positive impact that work can have on your life. All of the commercials are skits that highlight work life and how it corresponds with life overall—an attempt to attract to Monster newly laid-off dot-com workers expected to be looking for jobs in the coming months. The underlying punch line is that when work is good, your life is good.

These advertising spots will also bring "Trump," the company's colourful signature monster to the forefront. Previously, he ran across the screen at the end of Monster.com spots. Now, he is going to be a signature signoff, intended to strengthen brand name. Trump was developed by United Virtualities in New York, and was dubbed "Shoshkeles," which is a new technology featuring animation or photography that works across all platforms and requires no plug-ins. Unlike static banner ads, at the top or bottom of a page, Shoshkeles remains in the viewer's sight even when he or she scrolls around the page. Yet it only stays on the page for a few seconds, an important selling point for people who may leave the site if they feel annoyed by advertising.

New advertising plans this year will be visits by the Monster "ground crew" at college football games and tailgating parties in the five key markets starting in the second quarter. Monster intends to continue its year-old relationship with AOL and the Monster Show, a 30-second direct response TV effort. Rounding out its advertising efforts this year include an e-mail push to 11 million MyMonster.com members and a direct mail to 50 000 companies in its job bank, in hopes of continuing service with Monster. As for future plans, Monster.com has signed on to sponsor the 2002 Olympic Games in Salt Lake City and the 2004 Olympics in Athens.

Monster has an effective marketing strategy through combining both online and offline advertising in order to attract clientele. They have built strong brand awareness encouraging customer loyalty by delivering quality services. As online recruiting firms continue to be on the rise, Monster has become the standard and leader in this industry.

Expanding Audiences: Monster's Alliances

The advent of mergers, strategic partnerships, and high-profile deals between web companies is a phenomenon that has taken the e-commerce arena by storm yet, at the same time, leaves much of the corporate community confused. The intangible, virtual nature of the deals inked by online enterprise executives often leaves many to wonder what it is exactly that these giants are actually exchanging and what impact the agreements will really have on their bottom lines and the competitive internet landscape altogether. These alliances materialize in a variety of forms: fixed sum arrangements, revenue-sharing agreements, "pay as you go" deals through methods such as per-click or per-sale compensation, barter arrangements where one company will trade advertising space with another, and the out-and-out acquisition of one company by another.

While many may believe that the benefits of these deals are immeasurable and thus often quantified inaccurately, this is rarely the case. "'The contracts for these deals often have built-in performance guarantees,' says Bryan Rutberg, director of the internet investment group at an investment bank that regularly advises web companies in these matters, 'And the companies have tracking mechanisms to make sure they're met.'"[2] These online collaborations have proved indispensable as they open companies to new markets that otherwise would likely not have been reached.

On December 2, 1999, Taylor inked a four-year US$100 million deal with America Online after a painstaking five years of negotiations. The agreement provided Monster with a contextual integration into AOL sites made available to over 19 million members. Taylor saw this partnership as a major breakthrough toward the assurance of long-run prosperity for Monster. Prior to this, Monster's aggressive offline marketing campaign had been the primary method of generating awareness. This arrangement would allow it to reach a new key demographic: online users who are merely a click away from accessing Monster.

Advice and services from Monster would be featured daily on the AOL properties, including the heavily trafficked main screen of the WorkPlace Channel (AOL Keyword: WorkPlace). Content from Monster also would be featured in the Channel's industry areas, where professionals in a variety of fields meet, trade, and conduct research online.

While AOL is certainly Monster's most significant partner in terms of user span, Monster has aligned itself with several other key portals that allow it to target a wider variety of audiences. Links through major portals such as iWon.com, ESPN, AT&T Worldnet, and World Pages provide the company with increased avenues for traffic and collectively constitute a major portion of its visitors.

The Ultimate Decision

While both alternatives offered their attractive implications, Taylor knew that he had to commit to one with conviction. Was Monster due for a positive bottom line in the eyes of the market? Did it have enough of an edge on the competition to stay dominant if advertising were cut back? Are there more potential partners on the internet that Monster could benefit from? Is there still a need for more offline advertising? He would conduct one more thorough analysis of all significant factors in arriving at a definitive conclusion.

Discussion Questions

1. What impact do you think the history of Monster Worldwide may have had on the development of Monster as an online competitor?
2. What benefits are there to being a "global online recruiting network"?
3. The main competitor of Monster appears to be HotJobs. If HotJobs has 80 of the Fortune 100 companies as clients, does it seem worthwhile to spend large amounts of money on television advertising campaigns? Why or why not?
4. What are the pros and cons of advertising during the Super Bowl?
5. Will further advertising initiatives ensure Monster an improved brand image and/or market share?

Endnotes

1. TMP Worldwide Inc. "Monster.com Continues to Lead the Online Careers Industry," www.corporate-ir.net/ireye/ir_site.zhtml?ticker=tmpw&script=410&layout=-6&item_id=125262, March 31, 2001.
2. Blaise Zerega, "Web Deals Are Different," www.redherring.com/index.asp?layout=story_generic&doc_id=RH190013219, March 31, 2001.

Mountain Equipment Co-op

In January, 2001, Geoff Campbell, President and Chairman of the board at Mountain Equipment Co-operative (a firm based in Vancouver, British Columbia, specializing in outdoor recreation and the sale of sporting equipment), sat at his office desk and contemplated the feasibility of establishing an online website. Over the past two years Campbell had been pleased with the performance of the organization, which had reached annual sales of $500 000,[1] but he felt that there were other markets that were not being reached. Campbell was beginning to question if a website was just what his organization needed to get global exposure.

Although his other job kept him from committing 100 percent of his time to researching this potential opportunity, he did have an entrusted committee supporting this prospective endeavour. Everyone respected Campbell and together they all wanted to see MEC grow globally as well as nationally.

Company Background

Mountain Equipment Co-op was spawned by a lack of mountaineering stores in Vancouver in the late 1960s. At that time, most mountaineers in need of gear would make pilgrimages to REI, which was based in Seattle. Although this worked for a time, problems arising with Canadian Customs produced a need for a similar facility north of the border. Therefore, in the spring of 1970 a group of six Canadians began to organize what would later be known in 1971 as the Mountain Equipment Co-operative (MEC).

In the beginning the decision was made to restrict business to the selling of high-quality equipment for mountaineering, rock climbing, ski mountaineering, touring, and hiking. The organization later expanded to include paddling and bicycling due to strong demand in these areas. The first store was created in Vancouver, and afterwards the organization expanded eastward into ten different locations. The Vancouver store also accommodated the head office.

Four years after the introduction of the Vancouver store another was opened in Calgary to represent the Prairie provinces. The Calgary store established an initial presence out of a U-Haul trailer full of gear driven out from Vancouver. Then

SOURCE: This case was prepared by Steve Benvie and Michael Halliday under the supervision of Professor Gerald Trites for the sole purpose of providing material for classroom discussion. The authors do not intend to illustrate either effective or ineffective handling of a managerial situation.

the Calgary storeroom moved to a cramped office space above a record store and then into an independent building downtown. The new Calgary store was the second store (after Vancouver) to employ environmentally friendly building features, such as a higher-efficiency heating, ventilation, and air-conditioning systems, as well as low-consumption water fixtures.

The next step in the expansion project was an extension to central Canada with the creation of a Toronto store in 1985. However, on March 31, 1998, a new location was needed to accommodate the high traffic volumes and the diverse product offerings. The new facility was 42 000 square feet and was committed to environmental sustainability. The four Rs—reduce, reuse, recycle, and reclaim—guided design and construction. This was truly a step towards building credibility among the Toronto community.

Due to high demand, a second store was needed to serve the Ontario market. Thus in 1992 the first Ottawa store was built in the shell of an old movie theatre. This store became known because of its location and immediate sales were phenomenal. Yet again, MEC quickly discovered that the same volume problems that plagued the Toronto store were an issue in Ottawa, and a larger location became crucial. (In June of 2000, the Ottawa store moved to a marvellously reconditioned building, which solved the problem with ease, and operations once again continued.)

Then in May of 1998, a team of market analysts determined that Edmonton, Alberta, would be a profitable location for their fifth store as it would help to expose their company to northern Alberta and even into the Territories. By converting a vacant Safeway store, MEC became a part of a changing shopping district in the neighbourhood of Old Glenora. The building is a good example of MEC's core value to respecting and protecting the natural environment. An attractive and functional facility provided the asthetics to draw in customers and once again the sophisticated equipment and design kept with their objective of significantly reducing the impact on the surrounding neighbourhood.

Throughout the first 30 years, MEC has changed both in size of store (from closet to aircraft hangar) and hours (Wednesday through Friday evenings to seven days a week). This has been directly correlated to the growth of the membership and the future is looking better than ever. To continue this trend, MEC opened their sixth store, in Halifax, Nova Scotia, in the summer of 2001. Other stores later opened in North Vancouver, Winnipeg, Montreal, and Quebec.

Market Analysis

The market for outdoor sporting equipment consists of several overlapping groups, primarily young adults and sporting enthusiasts. Changing demographics were causing MEC to think in terms of a broader market, particularly families, surrounding businesses, and, to a smaller extent, senior citizens.

Mr. Campbell identified five major market segments:

1. **Young adults.** This group consists of individuals aged 18 to 35. The majority of this group are single male and female sport enthusiasts who enjoy weekend excursions and other adventurous activities to get away from the city life and its related stress.
2. **Retired.** These are similar to the young adults only they are retired and enjoy weekend outings as well as vacations in a nature setting. Although retired, many of them are financially stable and enjoy spending money for premium products.

3. **Families.** They search for opportunities to escape from the city life and spend time together in natural surroundings. They purchase camping equipment such as sleeping bags, tents, and outerwear in multiples to accommodate all family members.

4. **Businesses.** These are individuals in the workplace that share the same interests but are competitive with one another and desire top-of-the-line products. For example, if someone buys MEC equipment, they convince their co-workers that it is a premium product and, in turn, it stimulates referral purchases.

5. **Gift buyers.** This group consists of parents purchasing equipment for their sons or daughters at Christmas, birthdays, graduations, etc. For that reason, this market is aggressively pursued in and around holidays.

There are also groups interested in this equipment for more specialized purposes, such as outdoor adventure groups who provide outdoor nature expeditions. Interest was shown all over Canada because of general trends toward more active lifestyles. The head office in Vancouver was receiving high volumes of letters from people who were interested in finding out more about MEC's products but, because of their location, couldn't visit one of the stores. Potential customers were being lost because they were either unaware of MEC or they didn't want to go through the hassle of giving their credit card and personal information on the phone and have to wait six to eight weeks to receive their products. Therefore, MEC was losing sales because customers were going to the competition.

Mr. Campbell and the rest of the board realized that there was a potential to reach many more Canadians. However, with their current operations they could not reach a majority of this market, so a change was necessary to accommodate the demand.

Competitive Analysis

MEC's equipment essentially served two customer functions. It could be used as gifts for family or friends, or for those who showed great interest in rafting, canoeing, rock climbing, camping, or any other outdoor events that required top-quality gear.

Competition came from all other sporting equipment stores but most of the competition was solely based on cheaper prices for lower-quality gear. The main direct competition is traditional retail chain stores that can provide similar gear that still satisfies consumer needs, but at an exceptionally low price. However, trends began to indicate that many of these customers were beginning to become unhappy with the quality and were looking for alternatives. They found that they were constantly replacing and returning their equipment because it was simply not durable enough for the terrain they were using it for. Interestingly enough, most purchasers of these cheaper products were aware of MEC's product line and did buy some of their equipment from MEC through mail-order catalogues. However, most found this to be a huge inconvenience because they did not want to wait for the product to come in the mail. In regards to the indirect competitors, a thorough analysis suggested that this portion was comprised of equipment recyclers like Play-It-Again-Sports who go one step further than the traditional outlet by offering second-hand, mediocre equipment at extreme discounted prices.

In a survey conducted by MEC to their members, the co-op asked if, by improving the accessibility of their products, members would increase their purchases at MEC. The response was that close to 85 percent preferred MEC gear to the competition and would increase their purchases of the gear if it was made more easily accessible to them.

Finances

Before determining how to solve their exposure problems, Mr. Campbell and the rest of the board decided to review their earnings for 1999 and evaluate the feasibility of expanding their operations, either online or through traditional bricks-and-mortar establishments. In examining the costs associated with opening more store locations as opposed to setting up a website, the board determined that, although opening more stores would be a good way to increase sales, the cost and time associated with opening more locations was extremely high. With a website the start-up costs were not even close to those of opening a new location, and Mr. Campbell was positive that it would be a success. He also felt that by having a website MEC customers could share their experiences with one another. The only problem with a website is that some people may not feel comfortable with giving their credit card number online, so Mr. Campbell felt they would have to address this issue carefully to ensure the confidentiality of all their customers.

Distribution

In the end, the Board decided to go with a website. Mr. Campbell and the rest of the board then had the task of implementing several other activities that would aid in the success of their new website. The first of these considerations was to determine how to expand their supply chain logistics to facilitate the extra business. Their mail-order catalogue as well as their telephone service required an extensive delivery system that transferred the product to each individual purchaser upon receipt of their payment. With the new website, it would be inevitable that customer orders would increase and necessitate a more comprehensive delivery system. Therefore, nurturing their already existing relationship with FedEx was mandatory, as success would ultimately depend on their combined efforts. To make this matter even more difficult, Mr. Campbell felt that the organization should also focus on reducing the amount of time it takes to deliver on orders.

Conclusion

MEC has made a significant commitment to their Canadian customers and developing a website would increase their quality of service and allow continued growth in their market. Although the company realized that it was capable of expanding the number of store locations, they felt that it was unnecessary and costly. Even though the corporate R&D department of MEC continued to research additional market share, the company needed to do a better job of forecasting its long-term opportunities.

As Mr. Campbell sat back in his chair, he felt confident and satisfied with the decision to implement a website because of the low investment needed to receive a high payoff. Even if the performance of the website were to fall below expectations, the initial investment would be minimal, certainly less than that required to open new stores.

Discussion Questions

1. How should the different market segments impact the website and e-commerce strategy?

2. Would start-up costs for an e-commerce strategy necessarily be lower than opening an additional bricks-and-mortar store?

3. What factors should be considered in deciding between an investment in a bricks-and-mortar store versus a website?

4. What supply chain management concerns must MEC overcome?

5. What types of integration between bricks and clicks should be made in terms of supply chain management?

Endnote

1. Based on Mountain Equipment Cooperative's 1999 Income Statement.

Sears Roebuck & Co.

In 2002, Sears was facing increased competition. Wal-Mart, Target, and other big-box retailers were steadily encroaching on Sears' traditional markets, especially in the United States, and top line figures were affected. In an attempt to counter this trend, Sears acquired Lands' End. Lands' End, a direct retailer of traditionally styled classic clothing operating through specialty catalogue sales and online sales through Landsend.com, was a welcome complement to Sears' offerings. Sears, best known for its exclusive brands that include Kenmore, Craftsman, DieHard and WeatherBeaters, and private apparel brands such as Covington, Apostrophe, and Canyon River Blues, operates full-line department stores located throughout the United States, Canada, Puerto Rico and Havana, Cuba.

History of Sears and Roebuck & Co.

One day in 1886, a Chicago jewellery company shipped some gold-filled watches to an unsuspecting jeweller in a Minnesota hamlet, thus launching young Sears into the watch business. The following year, Sears moved his business to Chicago and inserted a classified ad in the Chicago Daily News.

> WANTED: Watchmaker with references who can furnish tools. State age, experience and salary required. ADDRESS T39, Daily News.

Alvah C. Roebuck, of Indiana, answered the ad. He told Sears he knew watches and brought a sample of his work to prove it. Sears hired him. Here began the association of two young men, both still in their twenties, that was to make their names famous. During the next few years, they began selling through mail-orders, directed heavily to the booming rural markets in the west and Midwest, and in 1893, the corporate name of the firm became Sears, Roebuck and Co.

Richard Sears was the guiding genius of the new mail-order firm. He knew farmers, and understood their needs and desires. Better yet, he could write advertising copy that made farmers send in their money and orders. While the earliest catalogues featured only watches and jewellery, the new firm, by 1895, was producing a 532-page catalogue with a vast range of consumer items. The catalogue

SOURCE: This case was prepared by Susan Doirion and Shelley Sullivan under the supervision of Professor Gerald Trites for the sole purpose of providing material for classroom discussion. The authors do not intend to illustrate either effective or ineffective handling of a managerial situation.

offered shoes, women's garments and millinery, wagons, fishing tackle, stoves, furniture, china, musical instruments, saddles, firearms, buggies, bicycles, baby carriages and glassware, in addition to watches and jewellery. Under Sears' leadership, sales in 1893 topped $400 000. Two years later they exceeded $750 000.

In 1895 Julius Rosenwald bought into Sears, and in 1901 Rosenwald became treasurer as well as vice president. Five years later, needing additional capital, Sears and Rosenwald for the first time sold common and preferred stock on the open market. The company has been publicly owned and traded ever since.

Sears' business expanded fast—so fast, in fact that the company soon outgrew its rented five-story building. In 1896 Sears moved to a new six-story building and by the turn of the century, additional buildings were built or leased in various areas of Chicago. Meanwhile, construction was started on a 40-acre, $5 million mail-order plant and office building on Chicago's West Side. When opened in 1906, the mail-order plant, with more than 3 million square feet of floor space, was the largest business building in the world.

In early 1925 the first Sears store opened in Chicago and was an immediate success. Before the year was out the company opened seven more retail stores, four of them in mail-order plants. By the end of 1927 they had 27 stores in operation.

Another milestone was passed in 1932 when Sears established the store planning and display department. In 1942, the company opened its first store in Havana, Cuba, its first permanent retail outlet in a foreign land. But due to shortages created by World War II, refrigerators, stoves, washing machines, and fans—all the lines so familiar in Sears stores—soon disappeared from the new Havana store. In 1947, with war shortages disappearing, Sears opened a store in Mexico City. In subsequent years, Sears opened stores or sales offices in Central and South America and Europe, but in the early 1980s, Sears divested itself of many of its foreign retail operations.

In 1969, Sears announced plans to build a new headquarters building in downtown Chicago. The 110-story Sears Tower became the world's tallest building at 1454 feet when it was opened in 1973. The staggering amount of materials needed to construct the building included 76 000 tons of steel, 2 million cubic feet of concrete, 16 000 tinted windows, 1500 miles of electrical wiring, and 80 miles of elevator cable.

At the close of its 2000 fiscal year, Sears operated 863 mall-based retail stores, most with co-located Sears Auto Centres, and an additional 1200 retail locations including hardware, outlet, tire and battery stores, as well as independently owned stores, primarily in smaller and rural markets. The company's services operations include product installation and repair services; service contracts; selected installed home improvements, and direct response. Direct response includes direct response marketing, clubs and services memberships; and merchandise through specialty catalogues. Sears, Roebuck and Co. are also the majority owner of Sears Canada Inc., one of Canada's largest retailers. Sears Canada operates 125 full-line stores, 176 specialty stores, and 1550 independently owned catalogue agents and dealer stores.

Sears Moves Online

Sears continues to find innovative ways to service its customers. To this end, in 1996, Sears moved online with www.sears.com, offering 50 products for sale. By 1998, Sears online business reached US$3 million in sales. In the 1999 Christmas period, Sears online reached over a million dollars per week. In 1999, the name

Sears Online was adopted. Sears vice president of Online Sales, Scott Marshall, feels that Sears Online has many benefits. "Online for us means instant access to our products and services . . . the convenience of placing an order while you're shopping in our department stores . . . .Or the speed and control of placing an order on a secure website—Sears is unique in what it offers the Canadian customer online." A huge benefit of moving online is that customers can now choose from literally hundreds of thousands of styles and sizes of everything from apparel to bedding to appliances to tools—anytime, anywhere they want, 24 hours a day, delivered anywhere in Canada.

Sears Embraces Technology Beyond Website Sales

Jerry Miller, CIO at Sears, Roebuck and Co. has no doubt that "The adoption of web technology provides a company the opportunity to change its relationships with the organizations and individuals with which it does business." Miller see internet technology as the best way to connect with trading partners, customers, and associates. By using the internet for collaboration, communication, customer service, and cost efficiency, Miller believes any company is able to achieve operation efficiencies and reduced cost, which are the essential goals of any successful retail organization.

The greatest opportunity, according to Miller, lies in the collaborative abilities of web-based technology. Companies are able to move beyond traditional, paper-based, "serial processes," to a more "cyclical, dynamic approach" that takes place in real time. This is only achievable when all parties adapt and work from similar systems, thereby allowing the technology to aid in effective use of the internet. Miller heralds the Voluntary Inter-industry Commerce Standards Associations collaborative, planning, forecasting, and replenishing process (CPRF) as a key component in the collaborative effort. While this technology has been available for a number of years, moving it onto the internet has greatly extended its ability. The evolution of web-based trading exchanges has heightened interest in CPRF technology. CPRF requires companies to adapt their existing business processes to allow for successful implementation of CPRF. Successful implementation of this process then allows for standardization among companies and improved communication—all in real time. Information sharing among retailers, transportation companies, and importers on product shipment allows for immediate response on such instances as order delays and special offers, as well as allowing for enhanced day-to-day tracking of merchandise inventories.

The internet has allowed Sears to communicate more effectively with its customers. All parties are able to keep up to date on inventory shipment schedules and product development, thereby allowing for improved business understanding and better business relationships. Internet technology allows Sears to break down the perceived barriers to management. Sears associates can receive updates from the chairmen via the internet, as well as talk directly with him through regular web chats.

Customer focus is a main concern at Sears. Internet technology allows for more customer focus and responsiveness. Internet shoppers are now able to make their own decisions regarding shopping times, shopping choices, and delivery methods. A customer can now log on and shop virtually any time, choose from the entire Sears line, and then choose how they want their purchases shipped and the location the purchase will be shipped to. Besides allowing for this broad range of customer choice, web technology also allows the company to track the customers' buying habits and purchases. This new data is then useful to Sears for developing personalized marketing promotions, targeted promotions, and specific product offerings.

Controlling cost is one of the key strategies of any organization, and at Sears, web-based technology makes this goal easier to achieve. Internet access among the organization and its suppliers, partners, and customers allows for timely, accurate, and relevant information sharing. "The personalization, communication, and functionality that are the outcome enhance and reinforce relationships in ways not possible in the past," says CIO Miller.

Sears Embraces Integration Technology in Supply Chain Management

When one hand does not know what the other is doing, there is bound to be trouble. This is certainly true in the retail business. When one area of the supply chain is unaware of events in another area, problems are bound to arise. In established brick and mortar companies, these types of problems are more often the practice than the exception. Existing "legacy systems" comprised of various, independent, often incompatible systems, each do their own job, but fail to work as a whole to connect an entire organization, or group of organizations together. Many disparate systems may serve individual users, but do not allow for integration and complete supply chain management.

In an attempt to address the overall supply chain management issue, Sears introduced SeeCommerce supplier, inventory, and logistics applications which were also being piloted to Sears' larger suppliers. This overall integration of Sears and its major suppliers into a common system is expected to enable them to monitor movement of inventory across stores and warehouse and also monitor supplier performance. Mike Mansbach, SeeCommerce VP, says that companies like Sears will now be able to determine for themselves, through See Commerce tracking, if a supplier is delivering the quality goods they want, on time, and in the quantities requested. If a supplier does not meet Sears' expectations, the system will highlight this. With adequate supplier management in place in the areas of exception management, visibility, and business process alignment, companies like Sears would then be in a comfortable position to minimize inventory levels. Dave Giometti, Sears' supply chain and vendor relations VP, says the new technology provides "one enterprise view" of the supply network, "allowing Sears to reduce average inventories while maintaining high levels of service to our stores."

Other Innovations in the Marketplace

Sears continues to monitor new technology advancements in an effort to find ways of converting these new technologies into business opportunities. One such recent advancement was the introduction of the new Electronic Gift Card. The new credit card sized card offers Sears customers a practical and convenient solution to gift giving. Al Chow, national Manager, Sales Support, Sears Canada, suggests, "Customers can avoid the worry that can be associated with gift giving, wondering if the gift they bought will fit, if it's the right colour, do they already have one, or they simply have no idea what to buy." The Sears gift card, which can be purchased online as well as at any department, retail, or appliance store, can be used for shopping at any Sears location and is valid for two years.

Sears Continues Its IT Commitment

Sears is continuing its strong commitment to internet technology and IT with huge investments in IT equipment. In August, 2002, Sears struck a deal with Dell Computer Corporation as part of a company-wide effort to modernize its IT infrastructure. Sears plans to take advantage of streaming media technology to conduct videoconferencing and other operational tasks. The technology will also be used for e-recruiting and e-learning, both of which are new, innovative methods of combining IT and human resources needs. This new technology is in addition to the recent introduction of handhelds in its department stores. These handheld allow for simpler inventory and price checks. This announcement by Sears is contrary to traditional practices of retailers who often have been reluctant to spend money on IT. The IT spending by Sears is just the beginning of a new trend by retailers as they turn to IT to improve operational efficiencies and customer intimacy to gain market share from their competition. IDC, a major research firm, predicts IT spending in the retail sector will reach $39.4 billion by 2006.

Effects of Sears.com on the Business and Its Customers

Companies such as Sears have found that their online presence has actually enhanced their traditional bricks and mortar business. Originally, many companies such as Sears were hesitant to go online because of concerns about competing with their existing distributors and retailers, or even with their own brick-and-mortar stores. The reality has been, in fact, completely the opposite. Sears now finds that customers go on line and do side-by-side comparison shopping of their desired products, most often tools or appliances, and gather information on these products. They then come to the store informed about products, even with print-outs of data in hand, ready to finalize their purchase decision. This then allows a sales associate to process the customer's purchase much faster knowing the customer already knows a great deal about the product they are about to purchase. Sears' mission "to make it easy for our customers to do business with us, regardless of how they do it" is greatly facilitated by internet technology.

Sears Acquires Lands' End

The sluggish U.S. economy in the late '90s and increased competition have taken their toll on Sears, as they have on many large retailers. Accordingly, Sears was forced to find ways to cut costs, which resulted in the elimination of its cosmetics business, and to look for other methods to boost sales. To this end, Sears purchased a highly complementary retail clothing company, Lands' End. Lands' End is known as one of the largest direct marketers and also as a pioneer in the e-commerce world. Lands' End first introduced online transactions on their B2C website in 1995. By the year 2000, the site was generating US$138 million in sales. As an early adapter of both web retailing and instant messaging, the Lands' End website now surpasses its catalogue business in sales. They attribute much of their success to the introduction of real-time customer communication. Customers can simply click the "ask us" button on the website and instantly enter a real-time chat line especially designed to answer customers' questions and give helpful advice or directions on the website.

Lands' End has designed its online retail website to accommodate its two main B2B customer types. For small- to medium-sized companies, they offered a catalogue through which these companies can place orders, check inventory and prices, and also submit and view their own logo, online. For their larger corporate customers, Lands' End has developed a series of customized extranet sites, or "online Custom Stores." These stores are actually arranged within a "mall" structure and portrayed as individual stores. Online customized stores were developed for such high profile customers as Cisco and Saturn.

Will Lands' End Save Sears' Bottom Line?

The driving force behind Sears' decision to purchase Lands' End was the clothing brand itself, but their success in merging catalogue and online sales, as well as a reputation for high quality, played a role as well.

The decision to acquire the Lands' End Company was applauded in the industry as mutually beneficial. Lands' End will gain access to a huge bricks-and-mortar infrastructure, while Sears will benefit from the highly skilled product development, online channels, and direct-to-consumers sales of Lands' End. Will this acquisition truly become a win–win situation?

Discussion Questions

1. What benefits can be realized through the use of web technology in retail businesses like Sears?

2. Considering Sears' plans for internet technology, have they achieved their desired results so far?

3. In 1999 Sears launched its new online store. What effect did this move have on the company? Was the decision to move online the right one for Sears?

4. Sears acquired Lands' End, a well-known brand name label, in an effort to improve sales. How best should Sears proceed with this merger?

5. Lands' End's web sales actually surpassed its catalogue sales. How does Lands' End account for this boom?

Intel

An E-Business Case Study

Founded on the principles of innovation and continuous improvement, Intel, since its conception, has been the world's leading manufacturer of semiconductor technology. Driven by the desire to remain number one, the company has constantly focused on improving both the quality and the visibility of its products. As a result, the Intel brand is among the most recognized in the world. Consistent with these efforts, Intel launched a web-based marketing strategy in 1997. Soon after, the company began using the internet to improve its operations and is now seeking to extend its e-business capabilities significantly.

Company Overview

Intel manufactures semiconductor products for both the computer and communications industries. The company's primary product is the microprocessor, or central processing unit (CPU), a device that enables a computer to act intelligently by allowing it to perform the various data manipulations that are needed to complete a given task. Intel, however, also produces numerous other technology related products such as memory chips, motherboards, wireless and non-wireless networking devices, networking software, special purpose microchips for mobile phones, etc. These products are primarily sold to industry members who use the components to create computing and communication devices for the consumer market.

Intel's objective is to exist as the dominant supplier of these fundamental computing and communications components. To date, Intel has achieved this goal through extensive ad campaigns and by focusing on the quality of its products. As a result of its efforts, Intel has dominated the microchip market and currently enjoys an 80 percent share. However, in recent years, competition has increased and rivals such as AMD have been progressively eroding Intel's customer base. In turn, the company is now seeking new ways to differentiate from its competitors and provide a new foundation for growth.

SOURCE: This case was prepared by Jason Hicks, Melissa Petite, and Debbie Archibald under the supervision of Professor Gerald Trites for the sole purpose of providing material for classroom discussion. The authors do not intend to illustrate either effective or ineffective handling of a managerial situation.

To ensure that it continues to add value to its products, in 2001 Intel invested US$7.3 billion to expand and improve its manufacturing facilities. In addition, the company staffs over 6000 researchers and scientists, and spends billions of dollars to support its research and development activities. Intel's primary mission however, is to improve its overall operations by becoming a 100 percent e-corporation—a corporation that maximizes profits, responsiveness, and flexibility while adding value for the customer. To achieve this goal, Intel plans to work closely with its business partners to fully automate and integrate its supply chain and order management processes.

Company Background

Gordon Moore founded Intel on July 18, 1968, and just three years later, the company had managed to produce the world's first microprocessor. Since then, Intel has grown to become a globally operating, multibillion-dollar organization, and it continues to be a leader in the semiconductor industry today.

In the past, despite its successes, Intel felt that, as a component-based company, there was little they could do to improve the demand for their product. During the '70s and '80s, few people actually knew what a microprocessor was, and as a result, Intel believed that they had to rely on the computer vendors and software publishers to drive the computer market. In the beginning, as the only manufacturer of microprocessors, Intel was relatively unaffected by such a circumstance. However, as competition began to grow, the company quickly realized that to continue their success they had to make end-users aware of the organization that was behind the power of the personal computer. Their goal was to create a new pull for their products by encouraging end-users to request the Intel brand.

In 1989, Intel launched its first program aimed at marketing its products to end-users. The ads focused on emphasizing the function of the microprocessor and the power, reliability, and quality of the Intel brand. The effort was a great success. As consumers began to inquire about the processors within their computers, Intel experienced a new demand for its products. However, to fully communicate the value of the Intel name, the company felt that it had to get away from the ambiguous processor numbers, which were being used to express their performance. Terms such as 386 and 486 were not unique to the Intel line of microprocessors and the company believed that this would prevent users from becoming loyal to the Intel brand.

In 1991, the company initiated a new ad campaign aimed at increasing its brand recognition. In order to distinguish itself from the competition, Intel began using the terms Celeron, Pentium, Itanium, and Xeon to express the value of its processors. In addition, the company adopted a new slogan, "Intel Inside," to convey the importance of the microprocessor while associating it with the Intel name. The key to this strategy, however, was an incentive-based program aimed at encouraging computer vendors to adopt the Intel logo. To overcome the fact that they were a component-based company, Intel started a co-operative marketing program in which it offered to share the advertising costs of vendors that were willing to promote the Intel brand. Within one year of the program's launch, Intel estimated that 80 percent of personal computer buyers recognized the Intel brand, compared to only 24 percent the year before. By 1995, this estimate had risen to 94 percent and remains at this level today.

Continuing with this program, as the internet economy emerged, Intel began moving its business to the web. In 1997, the company expanded its "Intel Inside" campaign to include online advertising. Intel launched its own website aimed at providing end-users with both company and product information. However, as consumers began to look for more than just information, the "Intel Inside" program expanded once again. In 1998, Intel began working to automate its business-to-business operations and encouraged an e-business strategy for computer vendors.

These changes are part of Intel's continuing effort to remain the leading supplier of semiconductor products and have, ultimately, lead the company to its current initiative to become a 100 percent e-corporation.

The Website

In an effort to reach consumers from around the world, Intel hosts at least 50 different websites in various languages. Following a manufacturer e-business model, each site provides users with extensive information about the company and its products, and although the company uses its sites to sell some of its products directly to consumers, it does not intend to use them to bypass its distributors. Instead, the company offers these services to make the site more useful. Intel continues to encourage users to buy from its business partners by providing links to their websites and by offering only a limited number of products online.

In the past, to attract people to its site, Intel felt that it had to use a lot of graphics. However, after surveying its users, Intel learned that customers cared more about convenience and easy of use. As a result, to ensure that everyone would be able to use the Intel site easily, the company has minimized the graphics on the site and avoids the overuse of technologies such as flash media, which slow down the connection, especially when a modem is being used. In addition, to ensure that users can find the information they are looking for, the company has broken the site up into areas of interest such as home computing, business computing, software and hardware development, wireless and non-wireless networks, etc., which are easily accessed from the main page. In turn, most users today feel that the site is attractively designed and are satisfied with its performance.

The information offered on Intel's site is quite extensive. Users can access information about the company, its history, policies, culture, locations, etc. The site also includes an online version of the Intel museum, outlining the history of the microprocessor and Intel's fabrication processes. Financial and investor information is also made available to users. In addition, Intel posts all recent press releases and news articles, which involve the company and/or the technology industry in general. Intel also uses the site to promote employment opportunities and to list the requirements needed to fulfill a given position. The site also emphasizes Intel's commitment to the communities in which their facilities are located, by describing the contributions they've made to educational programs and the environment. In turn, the site enables Intel to provide users with a lot of information that helps draw them to the Intel brand. As a result, the site is a key component of Intel's marketing strategy.

Intel and E-Business

Intel launched its e-business strategy in 1998. At that time, most of the company's customer orders were received by phone, fax, or in person and had to be manually processed. As a result, the procedure took a long time to complete, was prone to errors, and required the involvement of many employees from the sales channel. Accordingly, Intel and its customers felt that the system needed to be improved.

In an effort to streamline its business-to-business processes and improve its customer service, Intel decided to move its business processes online. The goal was to develop a system that would allow customers to place orders efficiently and conveniently. The system had to be easy to use, flexible, efficient, and reliable, and provide ample room for growth. To achieve this goal, Intel developed a web-based order management system. The system provides users with a unique, customer-specific, real-time interface to Intel's ERP system, allowing them to place and change orders easily and efficiently. In addition, customers can use the system to check pricing and inventories, track deliveries, and contact customer support whenever it is needed. The system also provides users with an analytical tool called Supply Line Management (SLM), which enables Intel and its customers to work together to forecast sales figures, control inventories, and keep the supply chain running. The system makes use of electronic data interchange (EDI) to allow members at any point in the supply chain to exchange files and documents much more conveniently.

With easier, online access to Intel's ordering system, both Intel and its customers enjoy significantly more flexibility and operate much more efficiently. Errors have been reduced by 75 percent and customers can now operate according to their own schedules. Accordingly, 25 percent of Intel's customer orders now occur during off hours. Through the use of the EDI, confidential information can be exchanged within minutes instead of weeks, and Intel's employees can now process 40 percent more orders within the same time. Both Intel and its customers now have more time to spend on higher-value activities.

Intel's web-based order management system has been a huge success. Today, 85 percent of Intel's orders are conducted electronically, making the company one of the world's top producers of online revenues. Despite this success, the current system still requires a considerable amount of employee involvement. Customers must still manually enter their data into the order management system, data that they have already entered in their own information systems. As a result, the risk of error remains high and resources are still being wasted on non-value adding activities. Furthermore, the SLM application also requires additional data input at both sides of the system, and because of the various standards used by Intel's business partners, the EDI network is often quite difficult to manage. Moving towards its goal of becoming a "100 percent e-corporation," Intel plans to overcome these limitations by automating and integrating the information systems of all supply chain members.

Intel's Implementation Philosophy

Intel's integration efforts are centred around two main principles, using a best-of-breed approach and building on industrial standards. In becoming an e-corporation, Intel's goal is to create an e-business environment that will allow them to remain competitive, flexible, and responsive. By using a best-of-breed approach, Intel remains independent from any one vendor or technology. In addition, the company can avoid extensive customization efforts by implementing software that best meets a particular need. Furthermore, by adopting industrial standards Intel is making it easier to share information with its partners. Industrial standards such as extensible markup language (XML) are making the integration effort much less difficult by enabling different systems to speak the same language. Systems that are able to communicate directly will undoubtedly improve the efficiency of the supply chain.

Building an E-Corporation

With the success of its web-based order management system, Intel is now focusing more fully on becoming a 100 percent e-corporation. The company's goal is to move beyond simply processing orders online by creating a fully integrated order management and supply chain system. To achieve this goal, Intel must not only work to integrate its own systems and processes, it must also work to encourage its business partners to do the same. As a result, Intel is approaching the project at two levels, Enterprise Application Integration (EAI) and Business-to-Business Interaction (B2Bi).

At the EAI level, Intel is focusing on making all systems within its organization work together in a seamless and efficient manner. Currently, Intel's best-of-breed systems exchange information through a complex web of communication channels. Data is transferred from one part of the order management system to another in a step-by-step process. As a result, information flows more slowly and the entire system is difficult to manage. In an effort to streamline this process, Intel plans to integrate its systems on a single channel called an EAI bus. The bus will act as a pipeline for the systems, carrying all information to the entire order management system and its supporting applications at once.

At the B2B level, Intel is working closely with its business partners in an effort to streamline the entire supply chain. Currently, many of the systems used by Intel and its business partners are based on different standards. As a result, these systems are unable to exchange data directly without extensive interfaces. In turn, much of the interaction between Intel, its customers, and its suppliers still requires a significant amount of employee contribution. In an effort to increase the efficiency of its supply chain, Intel has adopted RosettaNet's XML-based industrial standards, which will help the integration process by ensuring that everyone is on the same page.

RosettaNet is a non-profit group that was formed by the technology industry in an effort to develop a set of common communication standards for e-business activities. The RosettaNet framework provides guidelines for XML structures, encryption techniques, authorization and authentication procedures, non-repudiation principles, and interface standards. Intel and its partners are using these guidelines to integrate their business-to-business processes and to facilitate direct communication between their back-end ERP systems.

Currently, Intel is working with eight of its business partners on a B2Bi pilot project. If the venture is successful, more business partners will become involved in the project as they come to realize the benefits of doing so. By fully integrating their internal systems and enabling them to communicate externally, both Intel and its partners stand to achieve even greater efficiencies in their e-business activities. Back-end ERP systems throughout the supply chain will be able to communicate directly, eliminating the need for human intervention. As a result, information flows will be both timely and accurate, essential components of a successful e-business strategy. The difficulty in reaching this point, however, lies within the size and complexity of the project itself.

Currently over 1000 customers in more than 60 countries, each with their own information systems, do business with Intel. In addition, Intel must also do business with many of its own suppliers. To achieve its goal of becoming a fully integrated e-corporation, Intel must work closely with all of these companies to ensure that they are on the same page. Furthermore, because the XML-based RosettaNet standards are still under development and are being implemented for the first time, it is uncertain how well the system will actually perform. Intel and its partners must choose their standards carefully and remain flexible to accommodate future changes. Finally, as systems and processes are changed and re-changed, change management is becoming a key component to the success of the project. Intel and its business partners must work to keep their employees informed and well trained to reduce user resistance.

Privacy and Security

Intel maintains that it is highly committed to the privacy and security of its customers. To protect them, Intel uses a combination of encryption techniques, IDs, and user passwords to authenticate clients and authorize them to access customer profiles and credit information. In addition, Intel does not sell personal information to third party organizations unless permission is given and will not retain personal profiles for any longer than is needed. In an effort to demonstrate its commitment to the privacy and security of its customers, the Intel site carries the privacy seals of both BBB*OnLine* and TRUSTe, which verify the company's compliance to required privacy practices.

Conclusion

Intel has made a significant commitment to its customers. By developing its web-based order management system, not only has Intel improved its business, it has improved the businesses of its partners as well. Continuing with these efforts, Intel views becoming a 100 percent e-corporation as a necessary, ongoing process to remain competitive in the fast-paced world of e-business. As consumers demand more from organizations, and as technology improves, undoubtedly all businesses will become e-businesses. By preparing for this change now, Intel is hoping to remain at least one step ahead of its competition.

Discussion Questions

1. Does an online strategy make sense for a component-based company like Intel? Why or why not?
2. What challenges must Intel overcome before becoming a 100 percent e-corporation?
3. What benefits should Intel expect to gain from becoming a 100 percent e-corporation?
4. What factors have led to Intel's success? What role has Intel's marketing strategy played?
5. What is the significance of Intel's implementation philosophy? Is it practical? Are there possible advantages or disadvantages?

Glossary

ad-hoc query The ability for users to generate any type of query or report they wish within the system.

ad views A measure of the number of times a page with a banner ad or other advertisement is viewed during a period of time.

affiliate programs Agreements between website operators whereby delivery of customers or prospective customers to another company's site results in compensation becoming due.

animated graphic interchange format (GIF) A file that consists of a series of frames that are shown in a particular sequence.

Anticybersquatting Consumer Protection Act (ACPA) U.S. legislation that requires a trademark holder to simply demonstrate that a domain name has been registered in bad faith and that it has been used in an attempt to make a profit.

asynchronous A term for activities that are not conducted in real time but involve delays.

asynchronous transfer mode (ATM) A switching technology that organizes digital data into 53-byte cell units and transmits them using digital signalling technology. A cell is processed asynchronously relative to other related cells; in other words, not necessarily in a pre-specified sequence.

authentication The property that confirms that a particular person or server is, in fact, the person or server that is identified in a transaction.

automated teller machines (ATMs) User-friendly, kiosk-based computers that enable bank customers to carry out their own banking transactions.

balanced scorecard A multi-dimensional measurement tool aimed to capture performance measures related to accounting and finance, human resources, internal processes, and customers.

banner ads Small icons containing advertising messages that, when clicked, take the user to the site of the advertiser.

biometrics Access controls that rely on physical characteristics such as signatures, fingerprints, palmprints, voice recognition and retina scans to authenticate the identity of a user before permitting access.

blog A website containing personal posts available to be read by web surfers.

brand A name, term, sign, symbol, design, or a combination of these attributes that is used to differentiate a product or service from its competitors.

brochureware phase An early stage of the internet's development where commercial enterprises primarily put existing marketing brochures in digital format.

brokerage sites Sites that bring together buyers and sellers to facilitate business transactions on the web.

business continuity plan A plan that ensures that a business can continue in operation after a disaster or other event occurs that could otherwise disable the computer systems for a lengthy period of time.

business intelligence (BI) A powerful application, or set of applications, that allows businesses to capture, analyze, interpret, and report on data across an enterprise, thus creating valuable information for the enterprise.

business model The manner in which a business organizes itself to achieve its objectives, which normally involve the generation of profits.

business process reengineering (BPR) Fundamental rethinking and radical redesign of existing business processes to add value or prepare for new technologies.

buy-side The purchasing end of the supply chain, which consists of suppliers and the processes that connect with them.

Canadian Internet Registration Authority (CIRA) A not-for-profit Canadian corporation that is responsible for operating the dot-ca internet country code top-level domain.

cash-to-cash cycle The length of time from purchasing materials until a product is manufactured.

certificate authorities (CAs) Organizations that issue digital certificates and sign them with digital signatures to establish the authenticity of the certificates.

channel conflict The situation in which various sales channels for a single organization operate in competition with each other.

check digits Controls that perform a calculation on a set of digits such as an employee ID number and then add the result of that calculation to the number.

click-stream analysis A method by which a user's path through a website can be tracked and analyzed.

click-through counts The number of times that users have clicked on a banner ad to take them to the website to which it refers.

clickwrap agreements The online equivalent of the standard agreements included within the shrink-wrap of software bought in physical locations.

client A computer that is used by a network user to gain access to and operate applications on the network.

client-server system A network configuration that evolved from networks built around central computers (servers) to provide computing power to the users on their own desktop computers (clients).

client-side OLAP Processing where the data warehouse passes the data from the server to the client machine, where the majority of the processing occurs.

collaborative commerce The application of technologies to allow trading partners to synchronize and optimize their partnerships; performed in collaboration.

collaborative systems Information systems that work between enterprises to enable them to work together on common business initiatives and ventures.

common gateway interface (CGI) A method used by a web server to pass a user's request that has come over the internet to an application program and receive data from the application program that can be sent back to the user.

computer telephony integration (CTI) A technology that allows telephone systems to integrate with computer systems to aid in customer service and data capture.

controls Preventive, detective, and corrective measures that are designed to reduce the risk of error, fraud, malicious acts, or disaster to an acceptable level.

control totals Amounts based on counts of records, monetary values, or hashes that are used to reconcile inputs and outputs and thereby control completeness and accuracy of processing.

cookies Small text files stored by a website on individual computers that allow the site to track the movements of a visitor.

copyright A category of intellectual property that includes literary and artistic works such as books, poems, films, and musical works.

core technologies Those technologies that provide the basic infrastructure for business intelligence.

cost per thousand (CPM) A standard measure of impressions. Charges are set for each thousand users who visit the site or see an advertisement.

cross-sell The process of encouraging customers to purchase complementary or additional products or services from the firm.

customer intelligence The use of CRM applications to explore the data to identify relevant customer information.

customer relationship management (CRM) The set of strategies, technologies, and processes that enable the business to continuously improve offerings to customers.

cybersquatting Registering domain names with the intention to use the name for financial gain without legal rights to their use.

data cubes Multidimensional database structures that allow quick drill-down and reformatting of data.

data mart A data repository that is dedicated to specific user groups and is often integrated into the data warehouse.

data mining The analysis of data for relationships that may not have previously been known.

data warehouse A central data repository utilized to organize, store, analyze, and report upon data for decision-making purposes.

daughter windows Another name for interstitials or pop-up windows.

deep linking The creation of a link on one website to a specific part or page (not the homepage) of another website.

digital certificates Electronic documents that contain the identity of a person or server and the related public key.

digital signature An encrypted message digest that can only be decrypted by a key that authenticates the sender's identity.

digitized word of mouth Mechanisms for recording feedback about e-commerce sites, products, and market participants and sharing such feedback with others.

disaster recovery plan A detailed plan of action that enables an information system to be recovered after a disaster has made it inoperable.

disasters Acts of nature such as floods, storms, tornados, earthquakes or fires; power failures; or other events that can lead to destruction of assets and disruption of business activities.

discount rate The amount that the merchant account provider takes as a percentage of sales conducted through credit cards.

disintermediation A change in the supply chain where the manufacturer or service provider and consumer interact directly with each other, thereby eliminating the need for an intermediary.

Dutch auction An auction that uses a descending price format, whereby the auctioneer begins with a high price and buyers can bid on specific quantities of inventory as the price falls.

dynamic pricing The use of market-based, negotiated prices for transactions.

electronic data interchange (EDI) A structured way of creating electronic "forms" that can be transmitted between trading partners to execute business transactions without the need to generate any paper.

electronic wallet A file that securely stores a user's information such as name, address, credit card number and ship-to address, for frequent use in executing e-commerce transactions.

e-marketing The utilization of internet and electronic technologies to assist in the creation, implementation, and evaluation of marketing strategy.

enabling technologies Technologies that provide the ability of the BI applications to interact and perform tasks within the core technologies, such as the data warehouse.

encryption The use of a mathematical formula (an algorithm) that is applied to electronic data to render it illegible to anyone without the decoding key.

English auction An auction in which the bidding occurs through an ascending price process when buyers gather in a common location (physical or digital) during specified periods of time.

enterprise application integration (EAI) The process of planning, implementing, and managing the ability of applications in an enterprise to share information efficiently, often involving legacy systems and ERP systems.

enterprise-wide systems Any software systems used throughout an enterprise with the intention of enabling a consistent type of functionality as well as enterprise-wide access to the same data.

e-procurement The complete business process of acquiring goods and services through electronic means, from requisition through to fulfillment and payment.

error An unintentional act or omission that leads to undesirable consequences.

Extensible Markup Language (XML) A markup language similar to HTML in that they both contain symbols to describe the contents of a page or file, but while HTML describes the content only in terms of how it is to be displayed and interacted with, XML describes the content in terms of what data is being included; a tool that is similar to HTML and is compatible, but does not rely on single pre-set tags to identify information.

extraction, transformation, and loading (ETL) The process of gathering data from a system, such as an

ERP system, which can be simplified and stored within the data warehouse.

extranets Computer networks that make use of internet technology and include users from outside the organization as well as inside.

fibre optics The transmission of information as light impulses along a glass or plastic wire or fibre.

firewall Separate, highly secure computers, along with related policies and procedures, through which access to the network from the internet is exclusively directed.

fraud An intentional act that relies on deception to misappropriate assets or obtain other benefits.

general controls Controls that are not unique to a particular application or applications.

hash A total based on a field that is not expected to change (e.g., total of all employee number fields in a file) and is therefore useful for ensuring that no unauthorized additions, changes, or deletions have occurred in a file of records containing that field.

hit Each download of any information from a website.

holdback An amount that credit card companies keep in escrow to reduce the risk of bad debts and fraudulent credit card use.

horizontal trading exchanges Trading exchanges that have a product or service focus, such as computers or office equipment, and do not target any specific industry.

hybrid OLAP Forms of OLAP that combine various other formats, such as ROLAP and MOLAP.

HyperText Markup Language (HTML) Code that must be inserted in a file for it to be displayed on the World Wide Web; the programming language used to create web pages.

HyperText Transfer Protocol (HTTP) A set of rules used in exchanging hypertext files (such as text, graphics, sound, and video) for display on the World Wide Web.

industrial property A category of intellectual property that includes patents, trademarks, and other industrial designs.

input masks Established formats for input areas in a screen that allow certain numbers of characters and/or digits to be entered.

integrated systems Information systems that are joined together in such a way that they can easily share data between them.

intellectual property A creation of the mind such as an invention, artistic work, symbol, name, image, or design used in commerce.

intelligent agent A program designed to assist users on the web to carry out tasks such as searching for information or to automate tasks such as up-selling or cross-selling products.

interactive phase A stage of the internet's development when websites began to allow two-way communication through e-mail and web forms.

internet A global network based on a common digital communication standard.

internet backbone An organized and managed communications system, often based on fibre-optic cables, that forms the central connection for a section of the internet.

internet business model The use of the internet as a tool to implement a business model.

Internet Corporation for Assigned Names and Numbers (ICANN) A domain name registrar that holds control over the primary top-level domains.

Internet Protocol (IP) A protocol that uses a set of rules to send and receive messages at the internet address level.

internet service providers (ISPs) Companies that offer internet access and related services to individuals and businesses for a fee. Connections are offered through telephone lines, cable, satellite, or wireless connections.

interstitials Web-based windows that pop up as a user enters an internet site, aiming to catch the user's attention.

intranets Computer networks within an enterprise that make use of internet technology.

intrusion detection system (IDS) A system that monitors devices and processes for security threats and can alert security personnel of the occurrence of unusual activity as it occurs.

Java A programming language that was originally invented for the purpose of enhancing webpages and is used to create animations and moveable, interactive icons.

key performance indicators (KPIs) Important measures that a company measures its performance against in relation to goals, competitors, and the industry.

legacy system An old, usually outdated application that has not yet been replaced or upgraded.

log file A file stored on a web server containing details of every action that has occurred.

log file analysis The process of analyzing information regarding the movements of users throughout a site based upon data captured in server log files.

logical access controls Controls that are included in software to permit access by authorized personnel in accordance with the privileges granted to them and to prevent access by unauthorized personnel.

logistics The process of planning, implementing, and controlling the efficient and effective flow and storage of goods, services, and related information from point of origin to point of consumption.

malicious acts An intentional act that leads to the destruction of facilities, hardware, software, or data.

market segment A group of customers who share common needs and/or characteristics the selling firm may be able to satisfy.

maverick buying The unauthorized purchase of goods by employees through non-routine and poorly controlled means, such as acquiring office supplies with petty cash.

Megabits per second (Mbps) A measure of speed for data transmission. Megabits means a million bits per second, and states the number of data bits that are transmitted per second on a particular medium. Gigabits means a billion bits. Terabits means a trillion bits.

merchant account An account held by a business to collect payment through credit cards.

message digest A unique number calculated from the content of a message that can then be added to the message and checked by recalculating the number to ensure that the message has not been tampered with.

metadata A structured definition of data; it is data about data.

metatags Identifiers within HTML code that identify the content of the website.

middleware Software installed to link different systems together to make them work together.

multidimensional OLAP (MOLAP) Applications that make use of data cubes to perform analysis on multidimensional databases.

non-repudiation A property that confirms that a particular person did indeed send a message and cannot deny that fact.

online analytical processing (OLAP) A process that provides the ability for users to perform detailed, summary, or trend analysis on data and allows for drill-down into that data.

online transaction processing (OLTP) system A program that facilitates and manages transaction-oriented applications, typically for data entry and retrieval transactions across a network.

order fulfillment A set of processes involved in delivering a product to the customer. It consists of procedures grouped into the main areas of order processing, warehousing, and shipping and transportation planning.

order processing Activities that take place during the fulfillment of an order. These include credit checks, inventory availability determination, accounting, billing, and replenishment requests.

packet switching A method of transmitting data by breaking it up into small segments or packets and sending the packets individually in a stream. The packets are not necessarily sent together, but rather are disassembled, transmitted separately, and then reassembled when they arrive at their destination.

page view Each download of an entire page of information.

passive versus active test A standard that attempts to place the website of an online business along a continuum based upon the interactivity of the website to determine if operations within a jurisdiction were planned.

patents Documents issued by the government that grant an inventor or patent owner the right to make and use an invention for 20 years after the patent is filed.

PayPal Payment system, owned by eBay, that allows money transfers over the internet in a variety of currencies.

permanent establishment A term for the definition in Canadian law that determines where a business is located for tax purposes.

personal information Information that could identify an individual and could potentially be used to discriminate against or invade an individual's privacy.

Personal Information Protection and Electronic Documents Act (PIPEDA) Canadian legislation that provides privacy protection for personal information and has come into full effect since January 1, 2004.

personalization phase A stage in the internet's development when websites began to develop one-to-one marketing techniques through the use of cookies and other tracking tools.

physical access controls Measures taken to secure the physical safety of a resource by restricting access to it.

physical presence A term for the definition in U.S. law that determines where a business is located for tax purposes.

point of presence (POP) An access point to the internet that has a unique IP address.

primary data Information that is gathered in an effort to better make a specific decision.

principle of least privilege Granting the minimum privileges required by individuals to complete the tasks they are responsible for, and no more.

private exchange A trading exchange that limits participation to specific buyers and sellers—normally related to the exchange provider's supply chain.

private key A set of data used to encrypt and decrypt data transmissions that is known to only one person.

protocol A special set of rules that the sending and receiving points in a telecommunication connection use when they communicate. Protocols exist at several levels, including hardware and software. Both end points must recognize and observe a protocol to be able to understand the contents of transmissions. Protocols are often described in an industry or international standard.

public exchanges Trading exchanges in which buyers and sellers register to join, and there are few limitations to joining.

public key A set of data used to encrypt and decrypt data transmissions that can be shared with anyone.

public key infrastructure (PKI) A system that stores and delivers keys and certificates as needed and also provides privacy, security, integrity, authentication, and non-repudiation support for various e-business applications and transactions.

pull system A supply chain in which the production of suppliers is determined by the needs of customers who request or order goods, necessitating production.

push system A supply chain model in which suppliers produce goods based upon their efficiencies and push them to customers rather than relying on demand to determine production.

radio frequency identification (RFID) Technology that uses radio waves to transfer data between a reader device and an item such as a smart card.

reintermediation Using the internet to reassemble buyers, sellers, and other partners in a traditional supply chain in new ways.

relational database A database that uses numerous tables and can relate fields or tables within the database to one another and can easily be reorganized or extended.

relational database system A logical database model that relates data in different tables within the database by sharing a common data element (or field) between them. The common data element can serve as a reference point in the tables to other data elements in a data record.

relational OLAP (ROLAP) Applications that allow multi-dimensional analysis within a relational database. The data processing may take place either at the server, intermediary, or client level.

request for proposal (RFP) The first stage in a procurement process whereby the buyer communicates its needs to potential suppliers, who will then submit tenders based on the requirements.

reverse auction A reverse auction has one buyer offering a supply contract to many sellers, who compete by bidding down the supply price for the contract; an auction that uses a descending price format, but the buyer creates the auction to receive bids from potential suppliers.

reverse logistics The internal processes for handling customer returns, either for a refund or for repair or replacement under warranty.

RFID tag Radio-frequency identification tags placed on shipping crates and pallets that contain embedded electronic product codes that can be used for tracking and identifying items at the individual crate and pallet level.

risk The probability of an event occurring that leads to undesirable consequences such as lost revenues, excessive costs, misappropriation or destruction of assets, unreliable information, erroneous decisions, unauthorized disclosure of confidential or private information, competitive disadvantage, disruption of business activity or legal or statutory sanctions.

sales force automation (SFA) The process of simplifying sales in the field and the integration of sales activity into the corporate information structure.

scalability The ability of the system to maintain a set rate of performance as the number of users or volume of usage increases.

sealed-bid auction An auction form often used for products/services where price is only one consideration to the decision. For example, construction contracts often go through a sealed-bid process, as the buyer will consider capabilities, product quality, timelines, and past experience of the contractor before awarding the contract.

secondary data Data that has not been developed specifically for the task at hand but may be useful for decision-making.

secure electronic transaction (SET) protocol A method of securing credit card transactions using encryption and authentication technology.

Secure Hypertext Transfer Protocol (S-HTTP) A security protocol for use with HTTP that provides security for transmissions of messages between clients and web servers.

Secure Sockets Layer (SSL) protocol A security protocol associated with TCP/IP that establishes a secure communications channel between web clients and servers.

sell-side The selling end of the supply chain, which consists of customers and the processes that connect with them.

server A large central computer that forms the nucleus of a network, and contains the network operating system, as well as case-specific network-based applications.

shipping and transportation planning (STP) The process of transporting the finished goods to the consumer quickly and efficiently.

site stickiness A term describing the amount of time and likelihood that users will stay on a particular website.

smart card A card, not much bigger than a credit card, that contains a computer chip that is used to store or process information.

sniffing The use of electronic devices attached to transmission lines that can detect and capture data transmissions on those lines. Newer models of sniffing devices can work on wireless transmissions as well.

source code The format in which a program is written that can be read by humans and that is then converted into a different format that the computer can recognize.

spam The name given to unsolicited e-mail sent in an attempt to gain commercial advantage.

strategy The sum of all the choices that a business makes to offer a unique value to its customers that differentiates its business model from those of its competitors.

stress testing A process of high-volume entry, processing, and output of test data designed to determine whether the system has the capacity to handle the volumes that will be required of it.

Superstitials® Internet advertisement spots that load into a user's browser while the internet connection is idle and then launch as a daughter window showing a short, TV-like advertisement.

supply chain The set of processes that encompasses purchases of raw materials or resources through to final delivery of a product or service to the end consumer.

supply chain management (SCM) The process of coordinating and optimizing the flow of all products or services, information, and finances among all players of the supply chain.

systems integration Process of bringing together various business systems having different technologies, functions, and platforms so they can conduct business processes in such a way that the user does not see that different systems are being used.

systems sizing The process of assessing the volume and processing requirements that will be placed on a new information system and thereby determining the size of system required, including hardware and software.

threats Conditions or forces that increase the risk of error, fraud, malicious acts, or disaster.

time stamping The process of adding a tag containing the time that a record is created, modified or moved.

trademark A distinguishable feature such as a word, symbol, picture, logo, or design that can be used to identify the products or services of a specific individual or organization.

trading exchange An online marketplace, usually on a website, that enables suppliers and customers to carry out their business electronically, often using auctioning techniques.

Transmission Control Protocol (TCP) A protocol that uses a set of rules to exchange messages with other internet points at the data packet level.

trustmark A graphic representation similar to a logo that is placed on websites to indicate that the entity complies with certain recommended e-commerce practices and is therefore a trustworthy business partner.

tunnelling A process under which data packets are transmitted over the internet by including an additional header that establishes its route through the internet.

uniform resource locator (URL) The address of a resource on the World Wide Web.

Universal Description, Discovery, and Integration (UDDI) initiative A collaborative effort that aims to improve the ability of businesses to carry out electronic transactions with each other.

up-sell The process of encouraging customers to purchase higher-priced products or services.

value added networks (VANs) Privately owned networks that are rented to users, along with a package of related services, to operate their EDI systems by providing an environment within which they can work and by connecting them to their customers and suppliers.

vendor-managed inventory (VMI) The process by which suppliers take over monitoring inventory levels through the use of technology and are responsible for replenishment of stock.

vertical trading exchanges Trading exchanges that have an industry or specific market focus, such as healthcare or energy products and services.

Vickrey auction An auction using an ascending price format in which the highest bidder wins the auction but must pay the price submitted by the second place bidder.

virtual private network (VPN) A secure and encrypted connection between two points across the internet.

viruses Computer programs that are inserted into computer systems on an unauthorized basis, unknown to the system owner or user, and with an intent to take some action on that computer that can be mischievous or malicious.

visit A collection of webpages a visitor views in a time period while on a website.

Voice over Internet Protocol (VoIP) The use of an internet telephony protocol that relays voice signals across the internet, whether in a computer-to-phone call or a computer-to-computer call.

warehousing All tasks involved with handling inventory. These processes include receiving orders of inventory from suppliers, picking, organizing, and packaging goods for delivery.

web browser Software with a user-friendly, graphics-capable interface that enables users to connect to and navigate websites on the internet.

web bugs (clear GIFs) Image files embedded into a web page that can track user movements without the user knowing.

web server A server attached to a network; it is dedicated to specific applications that must be run on the World Wide Web, or used by web users, or interfaced very closely with the web.

web services A mechanism for applications to communicate with each other from different systems across the Internet.

website framing The use of HTML and browser technology to split a page into segments, which is useful for facilitating ease of use and building impressive websites.

World Wide Web (WWW) The user-friendly, graphics-capable component of the internet.

Y2K A term referring to the year 2000. Y2K was a common abbreviation to categorize the computer glitches that were widely predicted to take place when the calendar turned to the year 2000.

Yankee auction An auction format similar to an English auction except that multiple items are sold by price, quantity, and earliest bid time. This form of auction can be used by businesses that are buying products where price is not the only factor to consider and quantity available is a key consideration.

Index

Note: Key terms and the pages on which they are defined are referenced in bold.